Wild Act

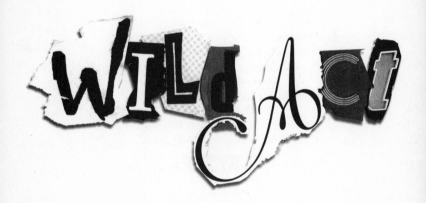

Wild Act Vol. 8
Created by Rie Takada

Translation - Ikoi Hiroe
English Adaptation - Marion Brown
Retouch and Lettering - Eva Han
Production Artist - Vicente Rivera, Jr.
Copy Editor - Peter Ahlstrom
Graphic Designer - James Lee
Cover Design - Patrick Hook

Editor - Julie Taylor
Digital Imaging Manager - Chris Buford
Pre-Press Manager - Antonio DePietro
Production Managers - Jennifer Miller and Mutsumi Miyazaki
Art Director - Matt Alford
Managing Editor - Jill Freshney
VP of Production - Ron Klamert
President and C.O.O. - John Parker
Publisher and C.E.O. - Stuart Levy

A  Manga

TOKYOPOP Inc.
5900 Wilshire Blvd. Suite 2000
Los Angeles, CA 90036

E-mail: info@TOKYOPOP.com
Come visit us online at www.TOKYOPOP.com

ISBN: 1-59182-566-0

First TOKYOPOP printing: September 2004
10 9 8 7 6 5 4 3 2 1
Printed in the USA

VOLUME 8

BY RIE TAKADA

HAMBURG // LONDON // LOS ANGELES // TOKYO

WILD ACT

DO YOU WANT TO SHARE YOUR LOVE FOR WILD ACT WITH FANS AROUND THE WORLD? WILD ACT IS TAKING SUBMISSIONS OF FAN ART, POETRY, OR ANY OTHER THOUGHTS YOU'D LIKE TO SHARE!

HOW TO SUBMIT:

1) SEND YOUR WORK VIA REGULAR MAIL (NOT E-MAIL) TO:

WILD ACT
C/O TOKYOPOP
5900 WILSHIRE BLVD.
SUITE 2000
LOS ANGELES, CA 90036

2) ALL WORK SUBMITTED SHOULD BE IN BLACK AND WHITE AND NO LARGER THAN 8.5" X 11". (AND TRY NOT TO FOLD IT TOO MANY TIMES!)

3) ANYTHING YOU SEND WILL NOT BE RETURNED. IF YOU WANT TO KEEP YOUR ORIGINAL, IT'S FINE TO SEND US A COPY.

4) PLEASE INCLUDE YOUR FULL NAME, AGE, CITY AND STATE FOR US TO PRINT WITH YOUR WORK. IF YOU'D RATHER US USE A PEN NAME, PLEASE INCLUDE THAT TOO.

5) IMPORTANT: IF YOU'RE UNDER THE AGE OF 18, YOU MUST HAVE YOUR PARENT'S PERMISSION IN ORDER FOR US TO PRINT YOUR WORK. ANY SUBMISSIONS WITHOUT A SIGNED NOTE OF PARENTAL CONSENT CANNOT BE USED.

6) FOR FULL DETAILS, PLEASE CHECK OUT HTTP://WWW.TOKYOPOP.COM/ABOUTUS/FANART.PHP

DISCLAIMER: ANYTHING YOU SEND TO US BECOMES THE PROPERTY OF TOKYOPOP INC. AND, AS WE SAID BEFORE, WILL NOT BE RETURNED TO YOU. WE WILL HAVE THE RIGHT TO PRINT, REPRODUCE, DISTRIBUTE, OR MODIFY THE ARTWORK FOR USE IN FUTURE VOLUMES OF WILD ACT OR ON THE WEB WITHOUT PAYMENT TO YOU.

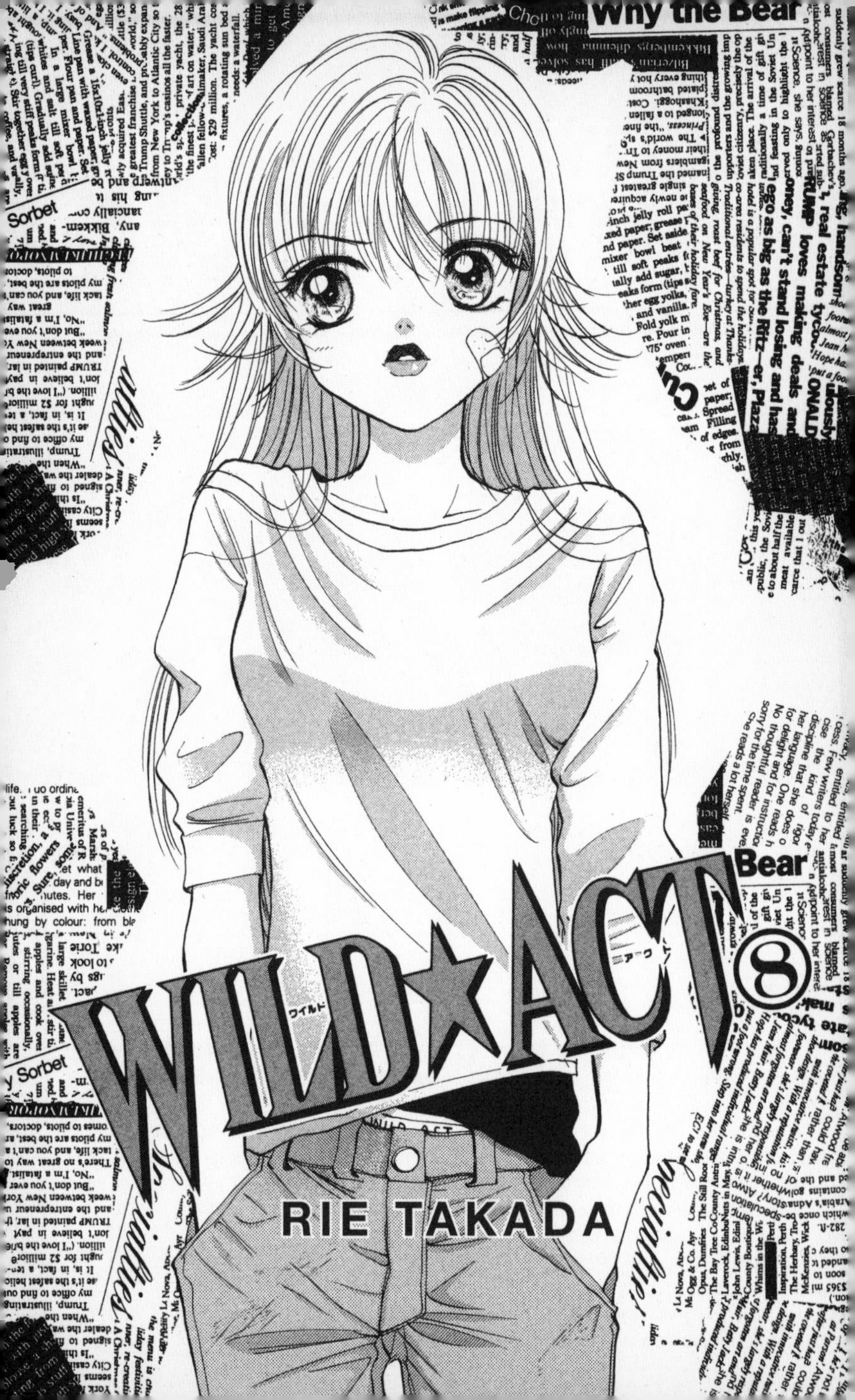
WILD★ACT
ワイルド
アクト
8
RIE TAKADA

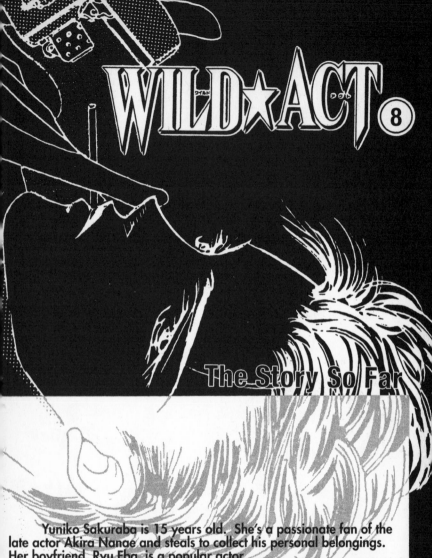

WILD★ACT 8

The Story So Far

Yuniko Sakuraba is 15 years old. She's a passionate fan of the late actor Akira Nanae and steals to collect his personal belongings. Her boyfriend, Ryu Eba, is a popular actor.

To dispel the rumor that Ryu is her brother, Yuniko decides to start stealing items from her mother's past in order to help her mother regain her memory. Suddenly Ryu receives an offer from Akira's former agent to represent him in Hollywood. Yuniko doesn't want to hold Ryu back, but she's devastated about being separated from him. Confused, she breaks up with Ryu and decides to go out with Maki instead. However, she cannot ignore her feelings and decides to go to Hollywood with Ryu. What kind of adventures await the young couple in America?

Yuniko Sakuraba

This girl is a Nanae-maniac! She's out to steal back Akira's personal possessions from the fanatical fans that ransacked his belongings after his death.

Akira Nanae

He was the first Japanese actor to succeed in Hollywood. He was killed in a tragic accident at the young age of 25.

Kamui and Cinnamon

Yuniko's pet flying squirrels. They are Yuniko's best friends and partners in crime.

Ryu Eba

He's a popular actor now, though he's only 17 years old. People call him the "New Nanae," but he hates the comparison.

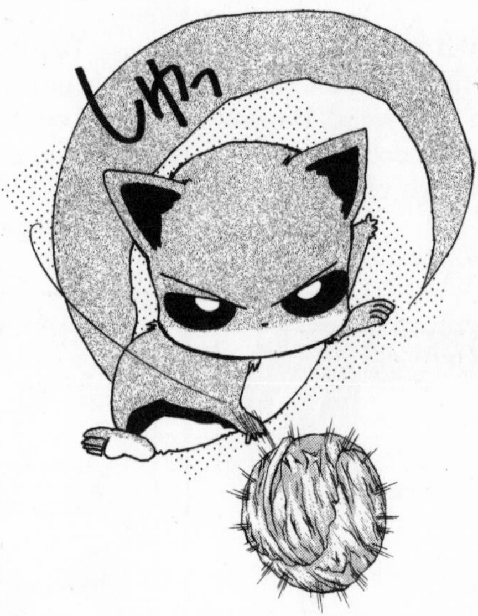
しゅっ

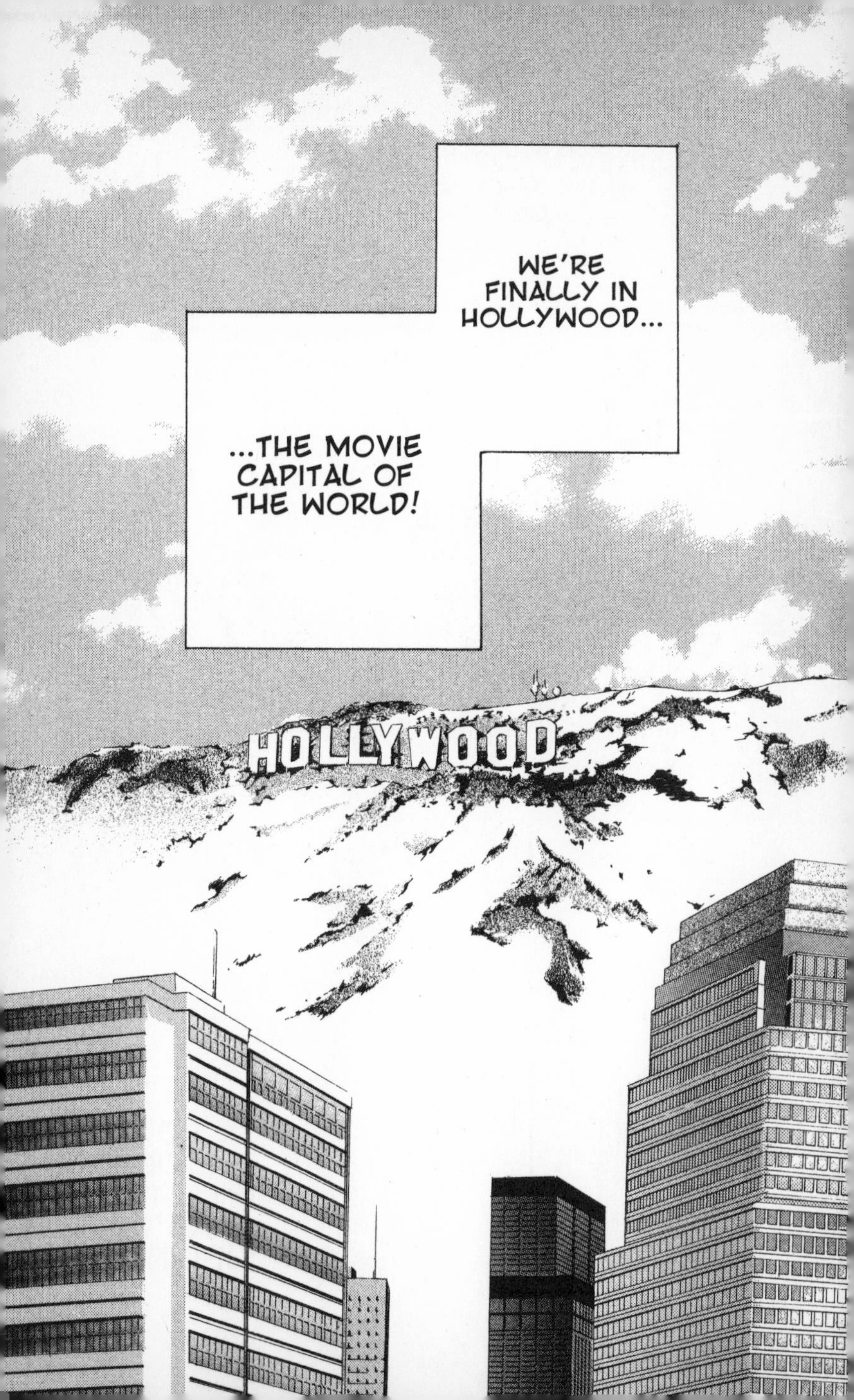
WE'RE FINALLY IN HOLLYWOOD...
...THE MOVIE CAPITAL OF THE WORLD!
HOLLYWOOD

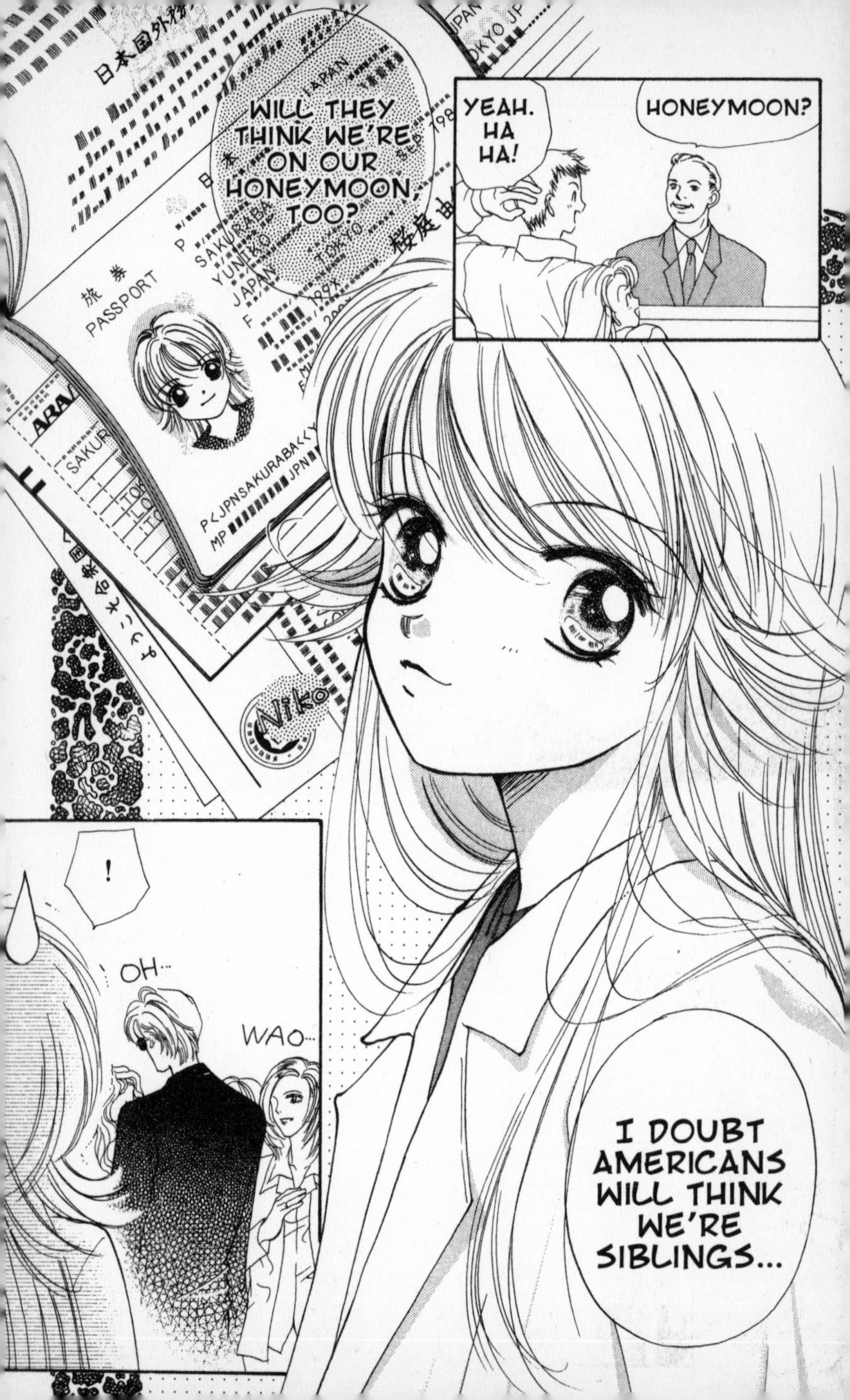
HONEYMOON?
YEAH. HA HA!
WILL THEY THINK WE'RE ON OUR HONEYMOON, TOO?
日本国外務省
旅券
PASSPORT
SAKURABA
YUNIKO
JAPAN
TOKYO
桜庭由
Niko
I DOUBT AMERICANS WILL THINK WE'RE SIBLINGS...
!
OH...
WAO...

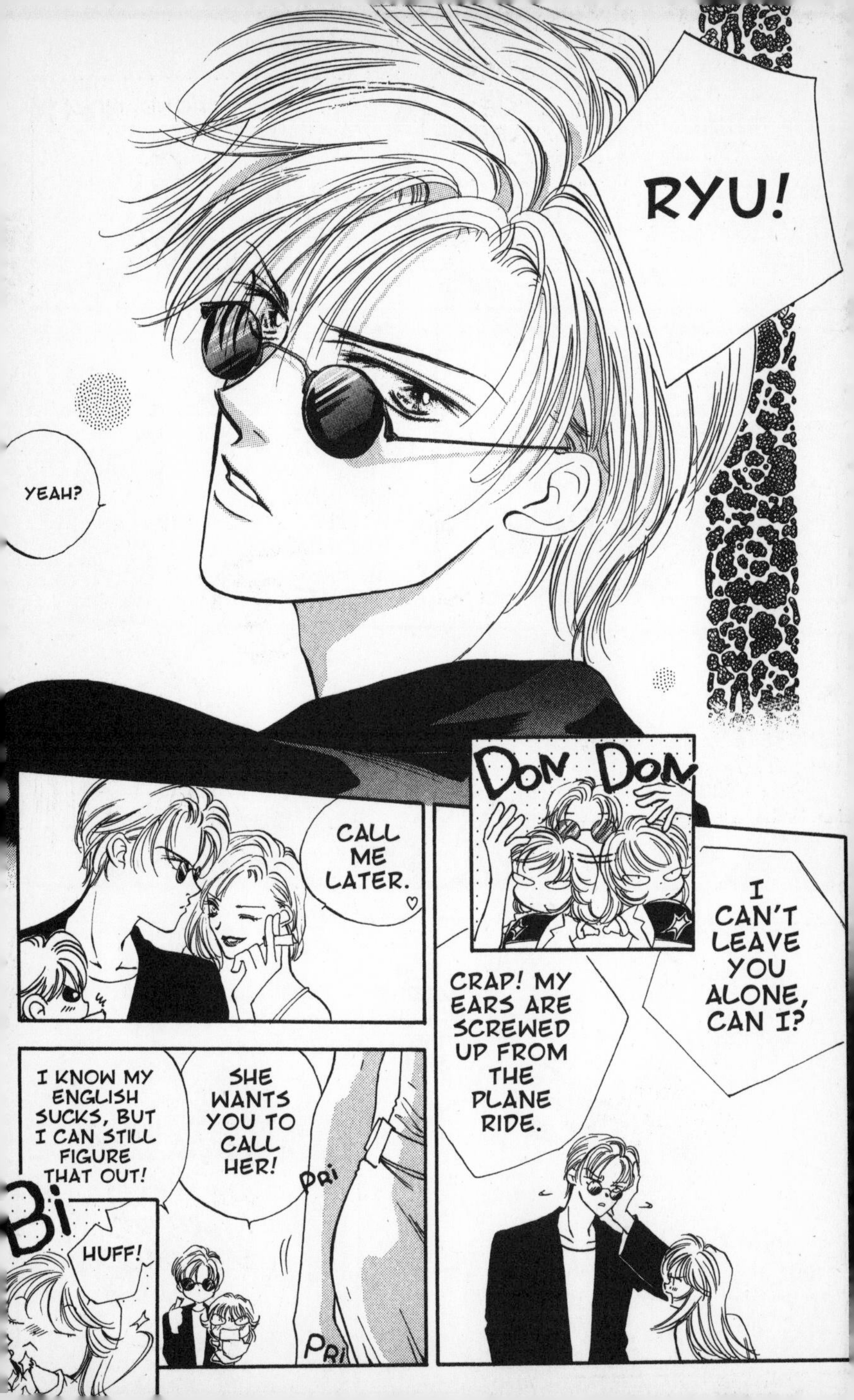
RYU!
YEAH?
DON DON
I CAN'T LEAVE YOU ALONE, CAN I?
CRAP! MY EARS ARE SCREWED UP FROM THE PLANE RIDE.
CALL ME LATER. ♡
SHE WANTS YOU TO CALL HER!
I KNOW MY ENGLISH SUCKS, BUT I CAN STILL FIGURE THAT OUT!
PRI
PRI
Bi
HUFF!

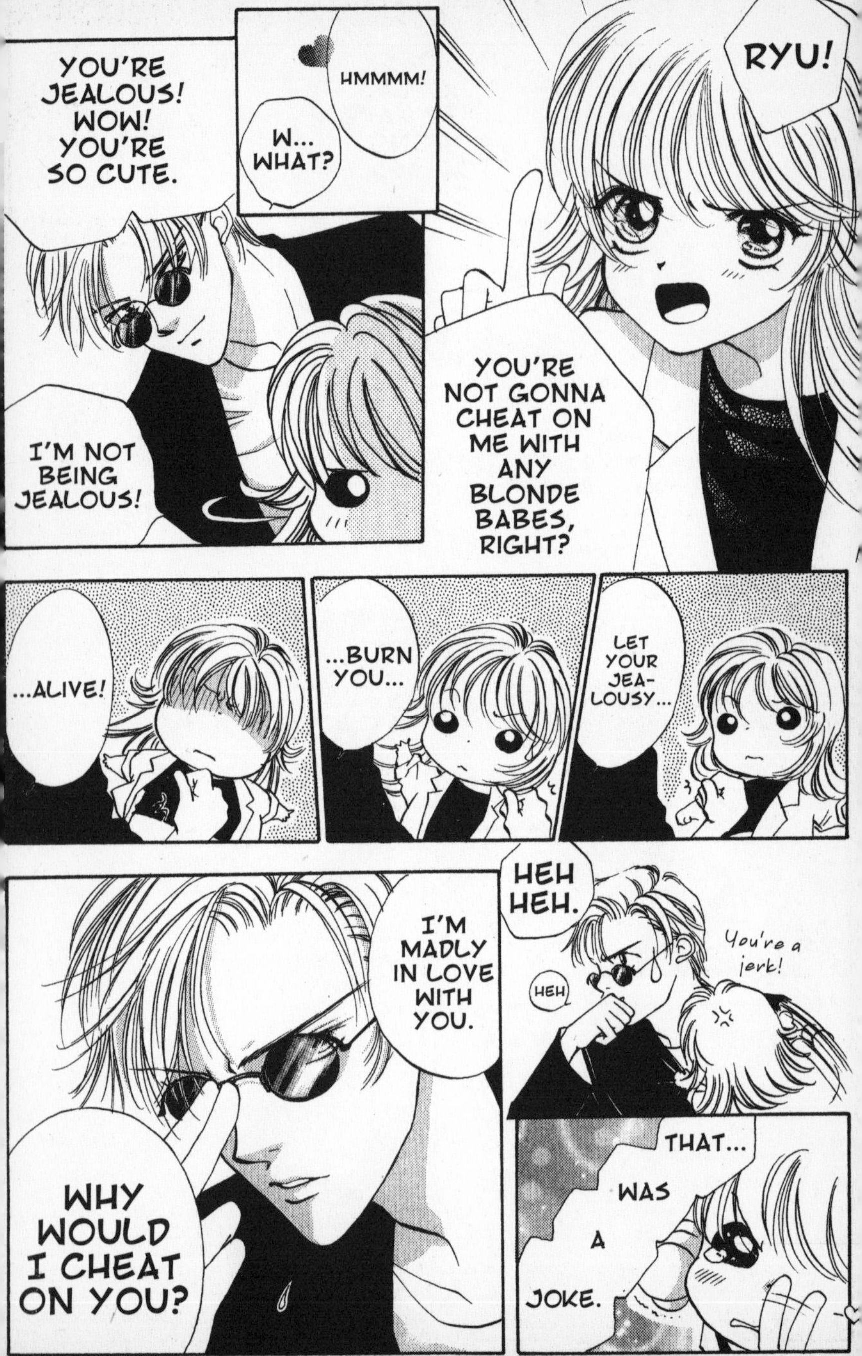
RYU!
YOU'RE NOT GONNA CHEAT ON ME WITH ANY BLONDE BABES, RIGHT?
HMMMM!
W... WHAT?
YOU'RE JEALOUS! WOW! YOU'RE SO CUTE.
I'M NOT BEING JEALOUS!
LET YOUR JEA-LOUSY...
...BURN YOU...
...ALIVE!
HEH HEH.
HEH
You're a jerk!
THAT... WAS A JOKE.
I'M MADLY IN LOVE WITH YOU.
WHY WOULD I CHEAT ON YOU?

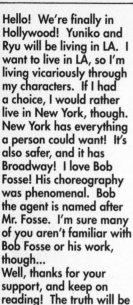

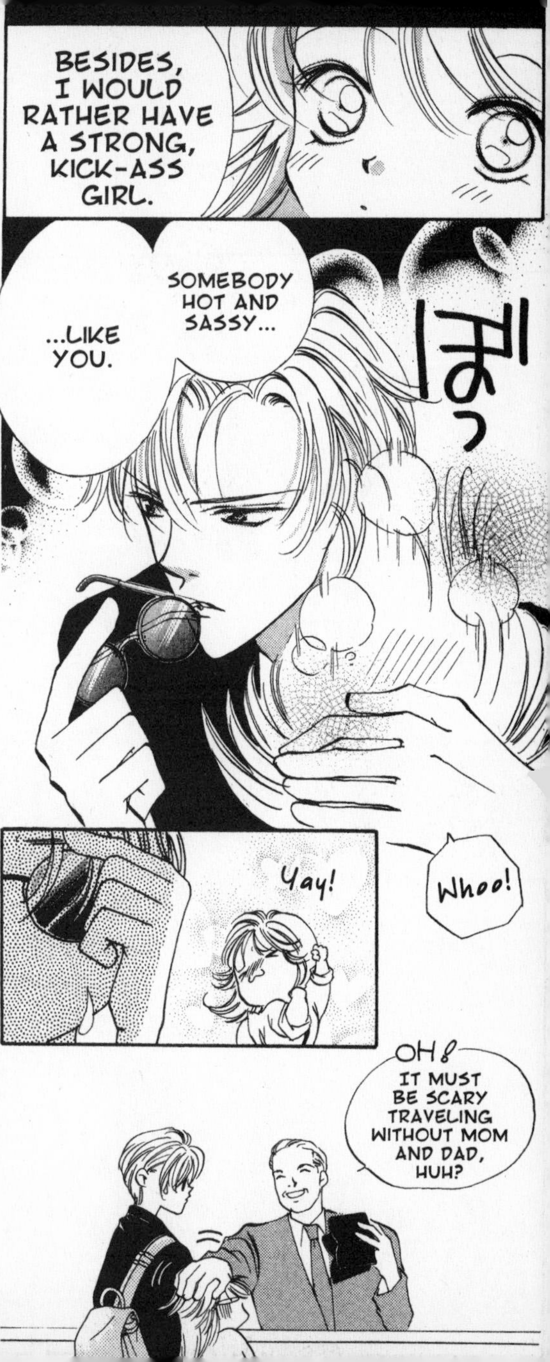
BESIDES, I WOULD RATHER HAVE A STRONG, KICK-ASS GIRL.
SOMEBODY HOT AND SASSY...
...LIKE YOU.
ぼっ
Whoo!
Yay!
OH! IT MUST BE SCARY TRAVELING WITHOUT MOM AND DAD, HUH?

Hello! We're finally in Hollywood! Yuniko and Ryu will be living in LA. I want to live in LA, so I'm living vicariously through my characters. If I had a choice, I would rather live in New York, though. New York has everything a person could want! It's also safer, and it has Broadway! I love Bob Fosse! His choreography was phenomenal. Bob the agent is named after Mr. Fosse. I'm sure many of you aren't familiar with Bob Fosse or his work, though...
Well, thanks for your support, and keep on reading! The truth will be revealed soon. I've got the flu. Sob!

Rie Takada

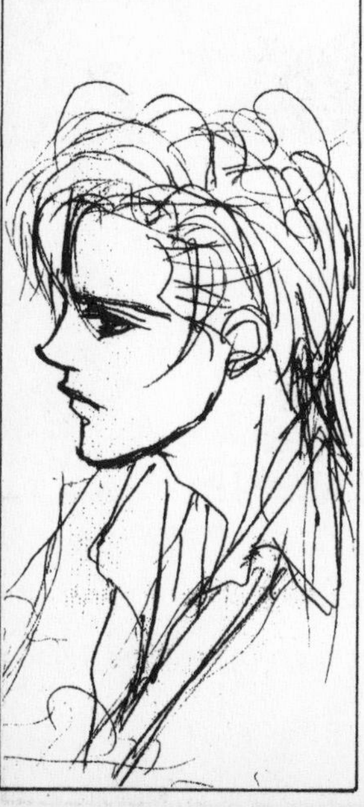

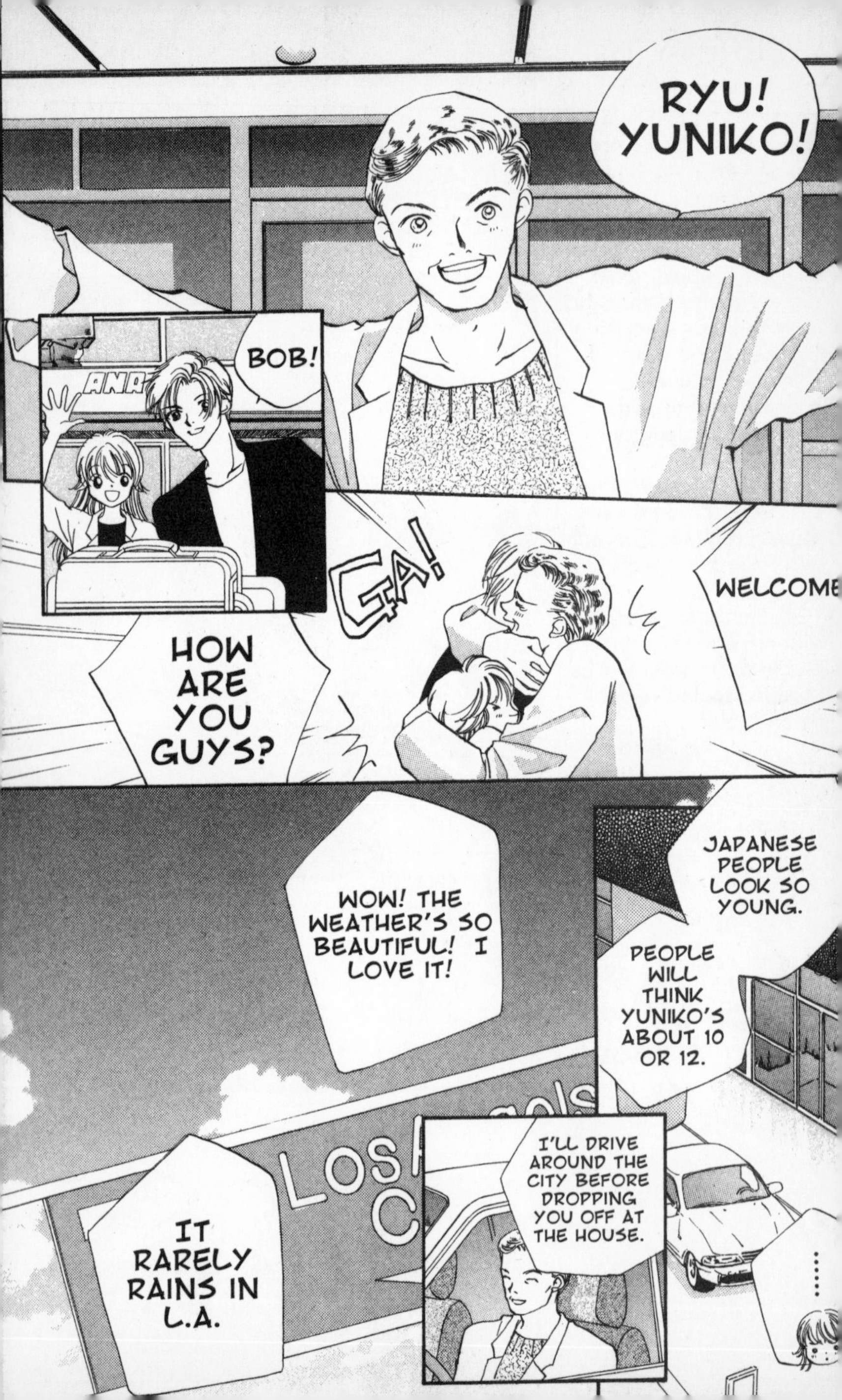
RYU! YUNIKO!
BOB!
ANA
WELCOME
GA!
HOW ARE YOU GUYS?
WOW! THE WEATHER'S SO BEAUTIFUL! I LOVE IT!
IT RARELY RAINS IN L.A.
JAPANESE PEOPLE LOOK SO YOUNG.
PEOPLE WILL THINK YUNIKO'S ABOUT 10 OR 12.
I'LL DRIVE AROUND THE CITY BEFORE DROPPING YOU OFF AT THE HOUSE.
......

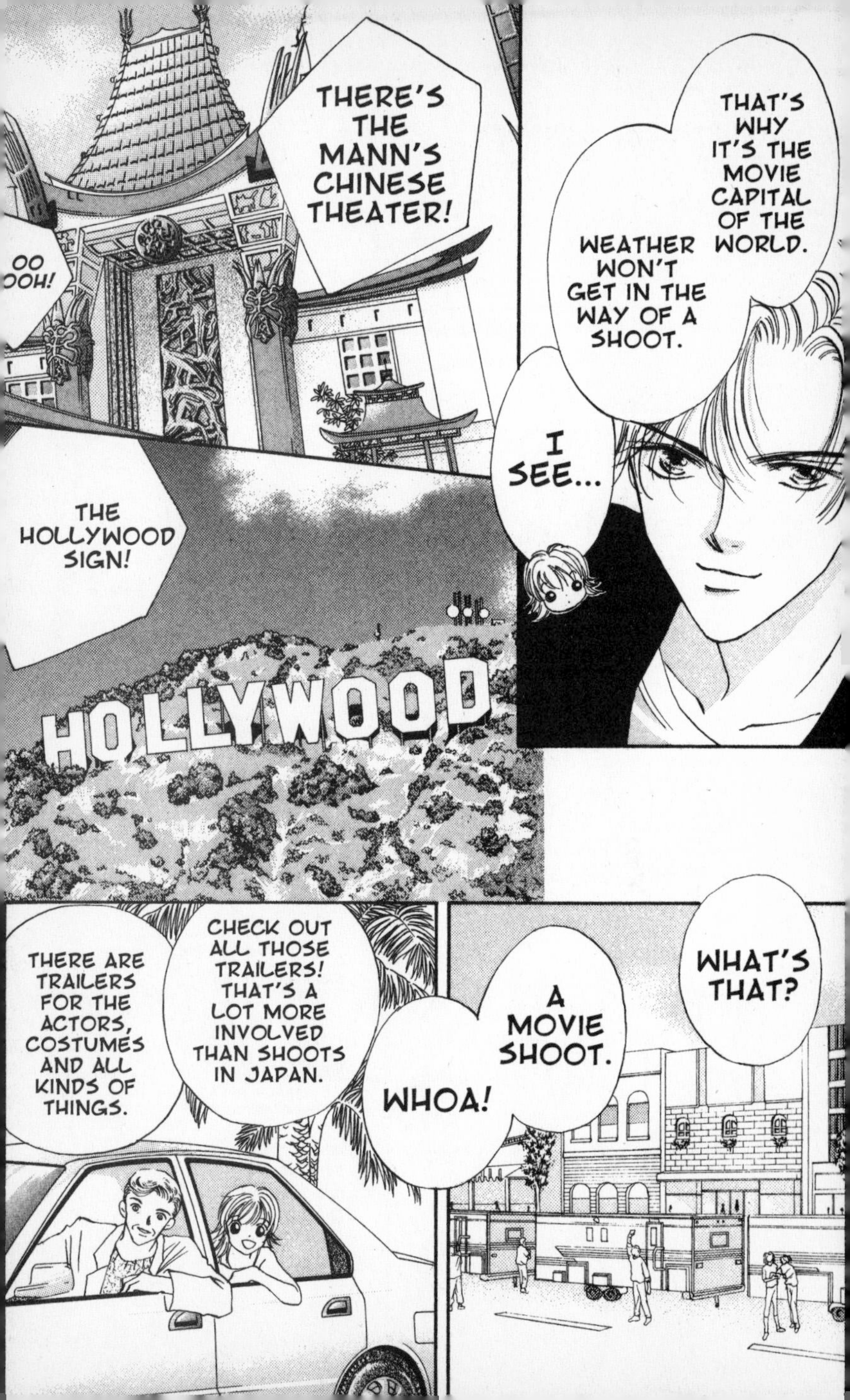
THAT'S WHY IT'S THE MOVIE CAPITAL OF THE WORLD.
WEATHER WON'T GET IN THE WAY OF A SHOOT.
I SEE...
THERE'S THE MANN'S CHINESE THEATER!
OO OOH!
THE HOLLYWOOD SIGN!
HOLLYWOOD
WHAT'S THAT?
A MOVIE SHOOT.
WHOA!
CHECK OUT ALL THOSE TRAILERS! THAT'S A LOT MORE INVOLVED THAN SHOOTS IN JAPAN.
THERE ARE TRAILERS FOR THE ACTORS, COSTUMES AND ALL KINDS OF THINGS.

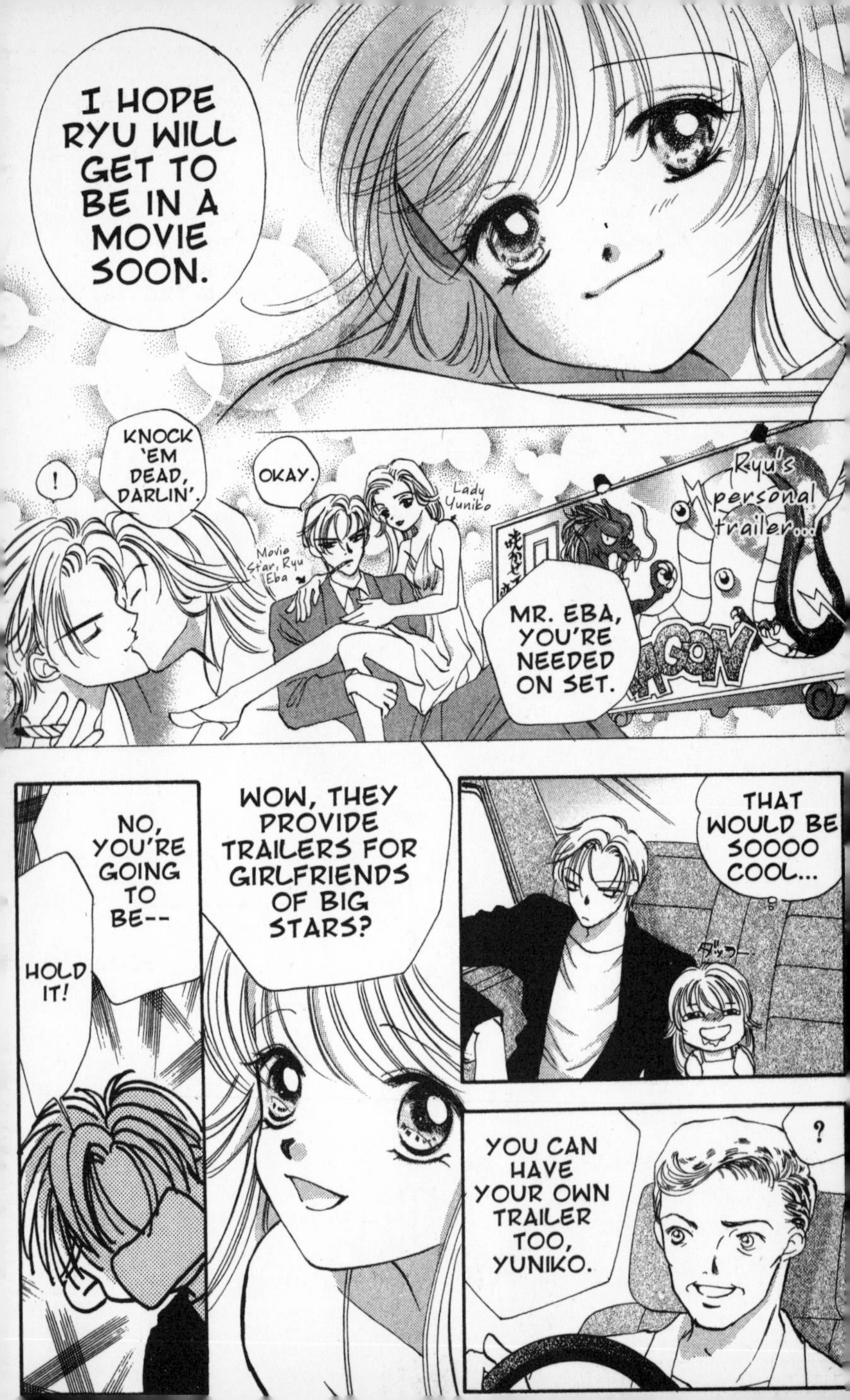
I HOPE RYU WILL GET TO BE IN A MOVIE SOON.
Ryu's personal trailer...
MR. EBA, YOU'RE NEEDED ON SET.
Lady Yuniko
OKAY.
Movie Star, Ryu Eba
KNOCK 'EM DEAD, DARLIN'.
!
THAT WOULD BE SOOOO COOL...
?
YOU CAN HAVE YOUR OWN TRAILER TOO, YUNIKO.
WOW, THEY PROVIDE TRAILERS FOR GIRLFRIENDS OF BIG STARS?
NO, YOU'RE GOING TO BE--
HOLD IT!

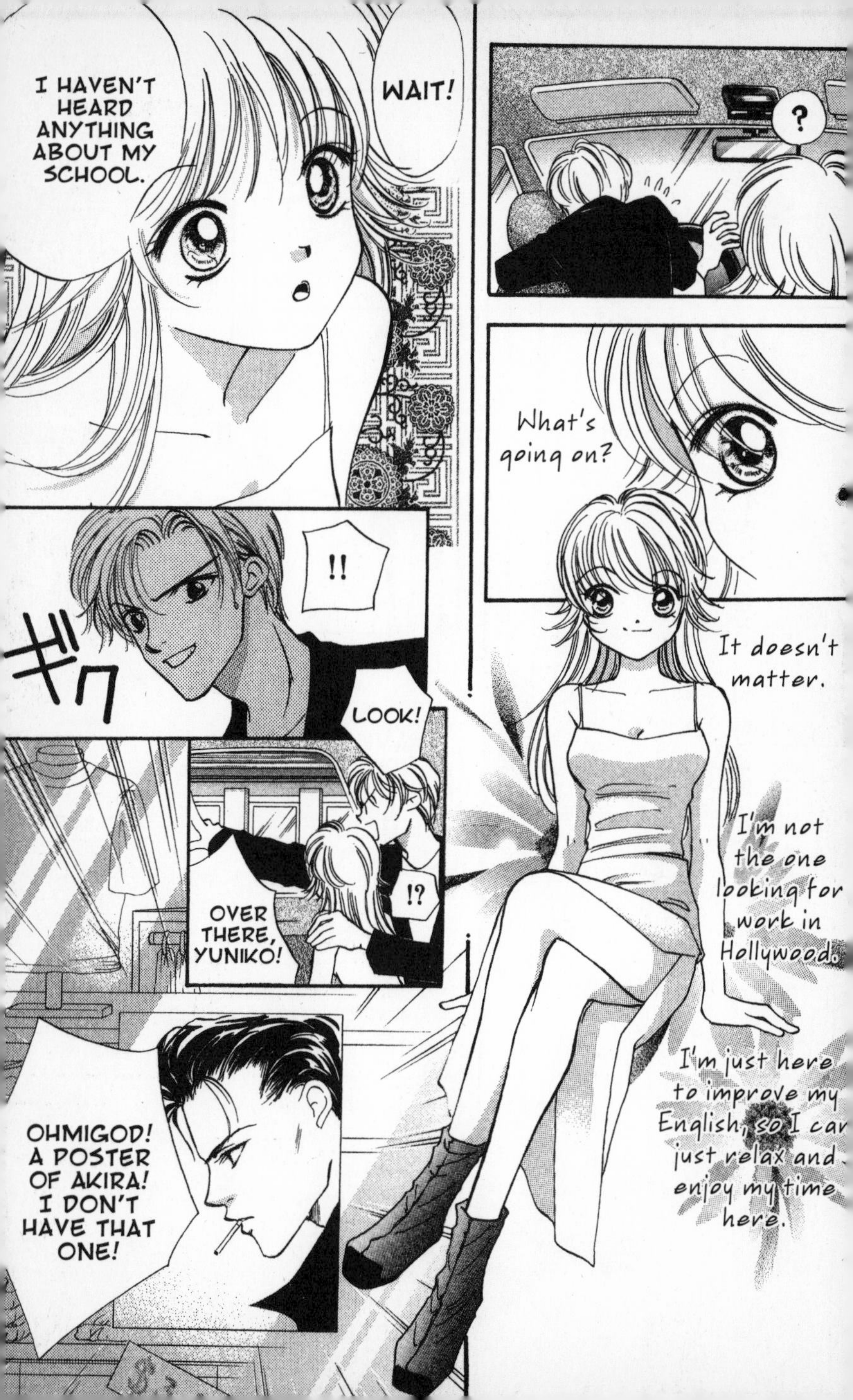
?
What's going on?
It doesn't matter.
I'm not the one looking for work in Hollywood.
I'm just here to improve my English, so I can just relax and enjoy my time here.
WAIT!
I HAVEN'T HEARD ANYTHING ABOUT MY SCHOOL.
!!
ギク
LOOK!
!?
OVER THERE, YUNIKO!
OHMIGOD! A POSTER OF AKIRA! I DON'T HAVE THAT ONE!

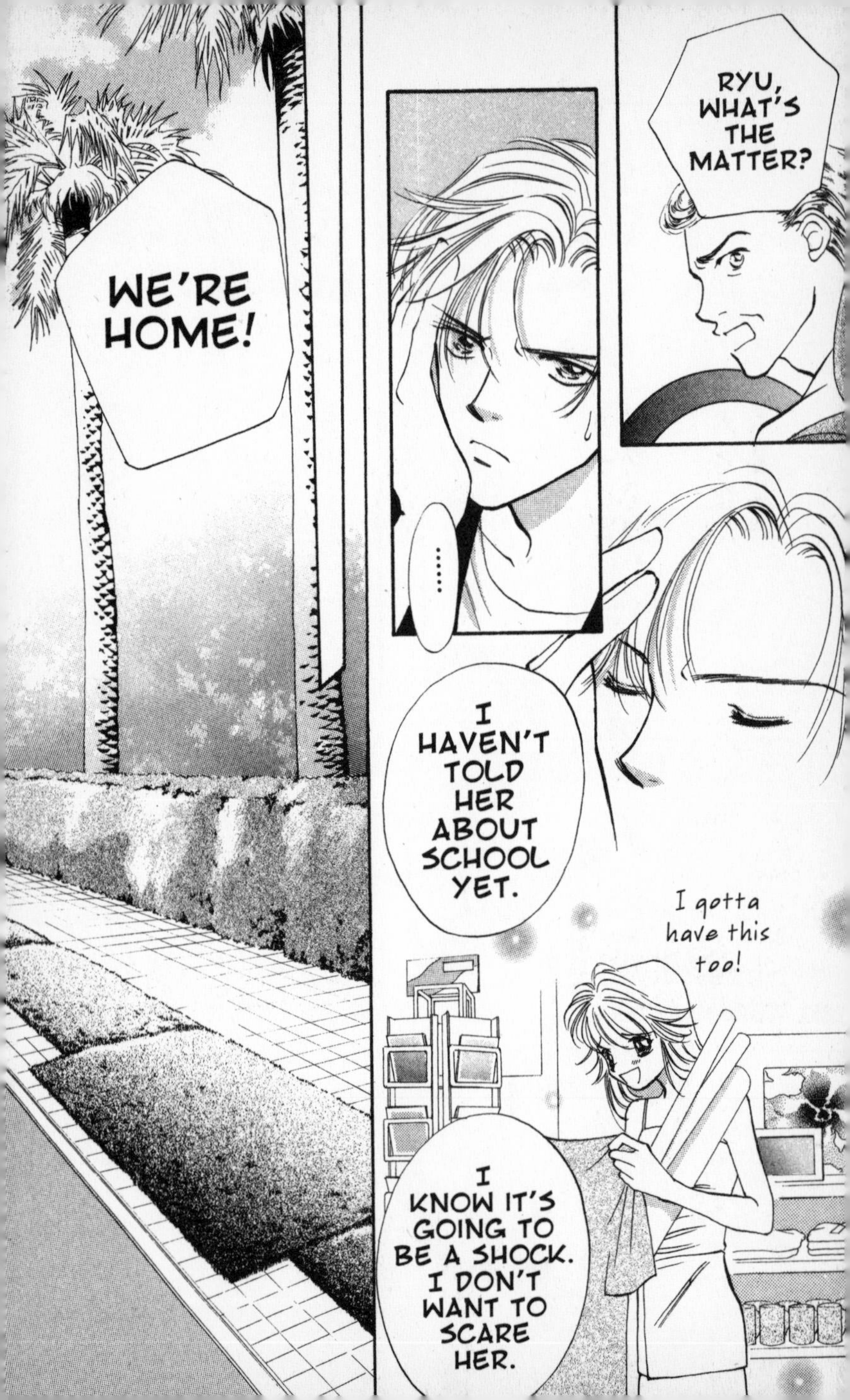
RYU, WHAT'S THE MATTER?
......
I HAVEN'T TOLD HER ABOUT SCHOOL YET.
I gotta have this too!
I KNOW IT'S GOING TO BE A SHOCK. I DON'T WANT TO SCARE HER.
WE'RE HOME!

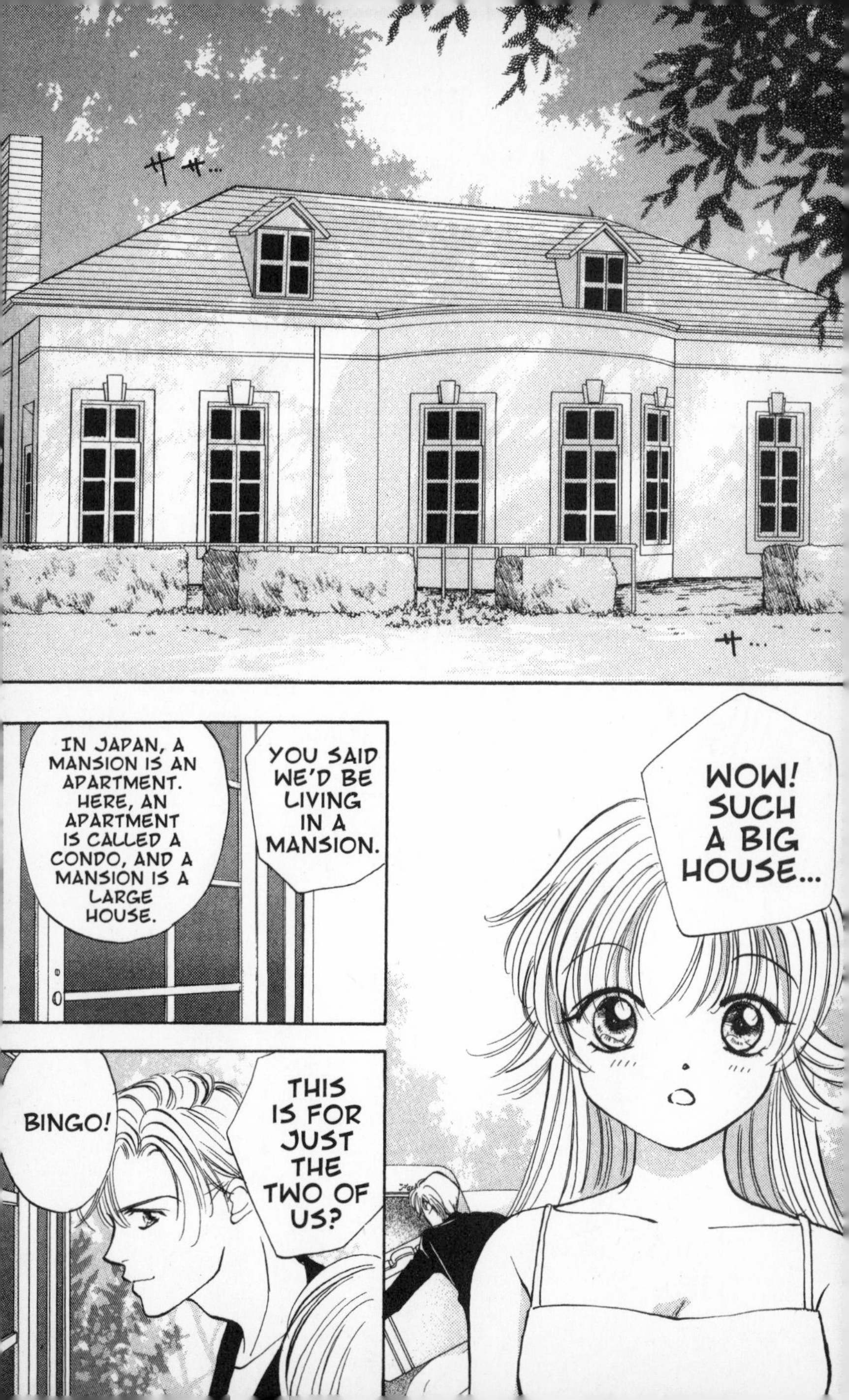
サ サ…
サ…
WOW! SUCH A BIG HOUSE...
YOU SAID WE'D BE LIVING IN A MANSION.
IN JAPAN, A MANSION IS AN APARTMENT. HERE, AN APARTMENT IS CALLED A CONDO, AND A MANSION IS A LARGE HOUSE.
THIS IS FOR JUST THE TWO OF US?
BINGO!

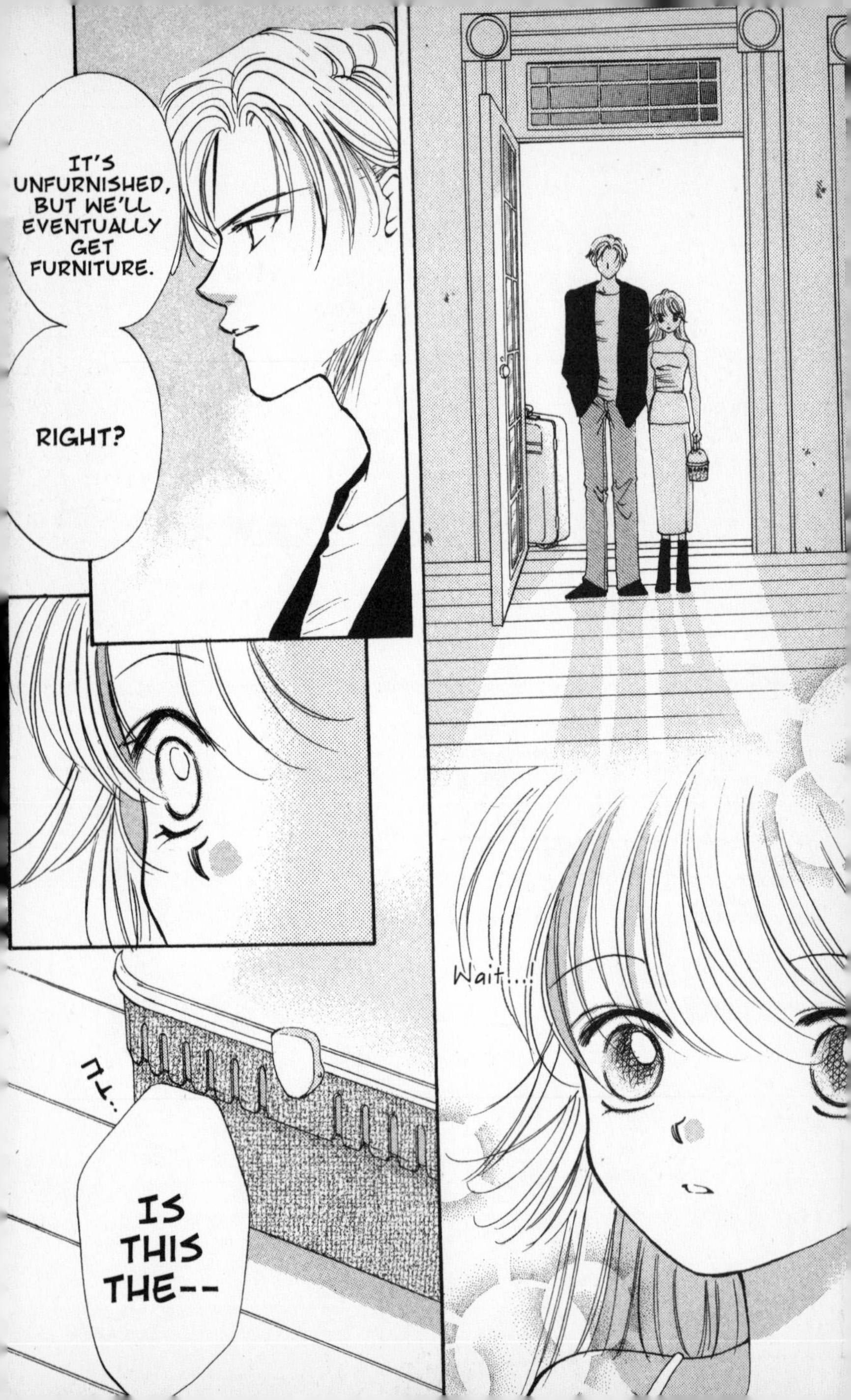
IT'S UNFURNISHED, BUT WE'LL EVENTUALLY GET FURNITURE.
RIGHT?
ハッ...
IS THIS THE--
Wait...!

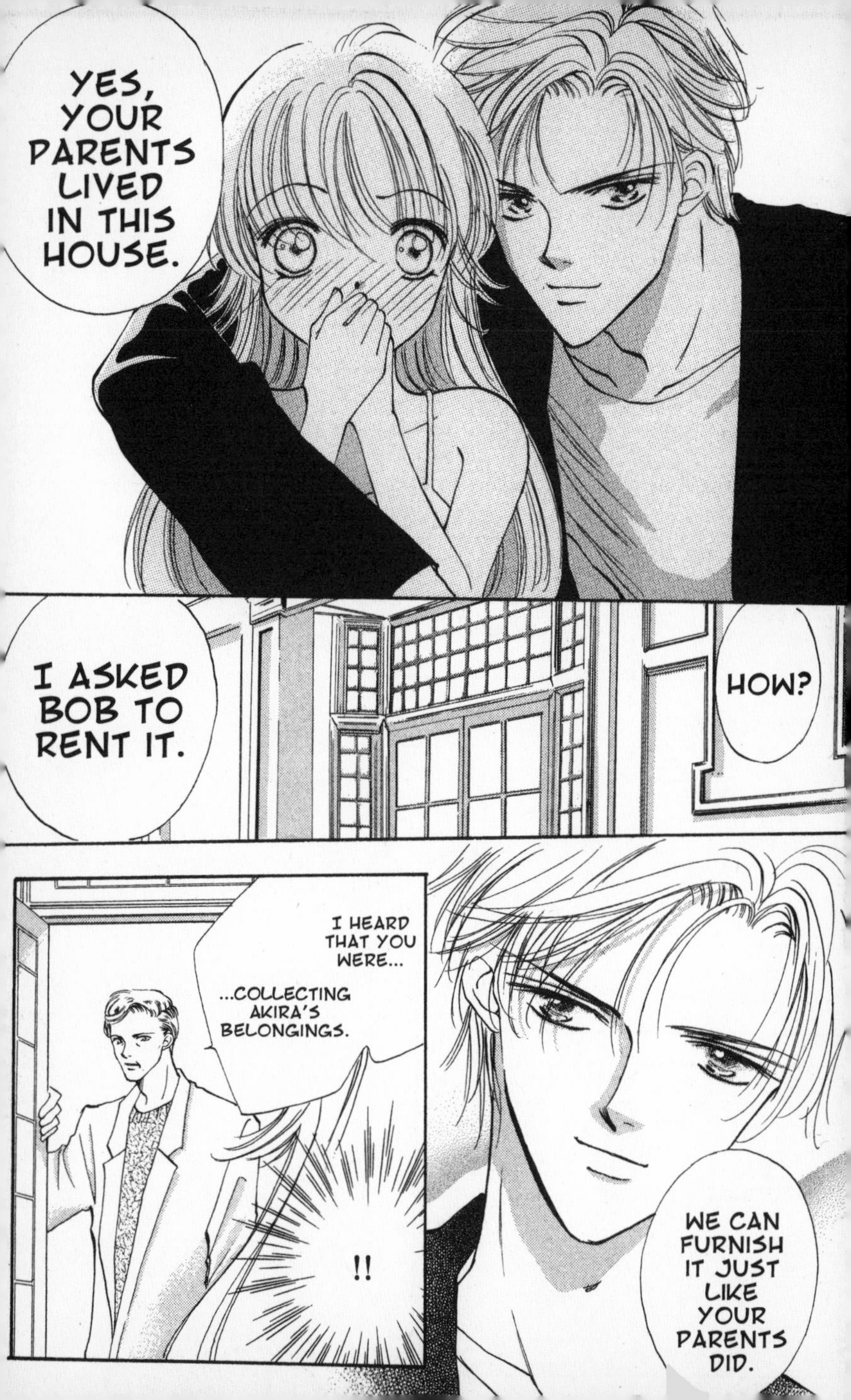
YES, YOUR PARENTS LIVED IN THIS HOUSE.
HOW?
I ASKED BOB TO RENT IT.
WE CAN FURNISH IT JUST LIKE YOUR PARENTS DID.
I HEARD THAT YOU WERE...
...COLLECTING AKIRA'S BELONGINGS.
!!

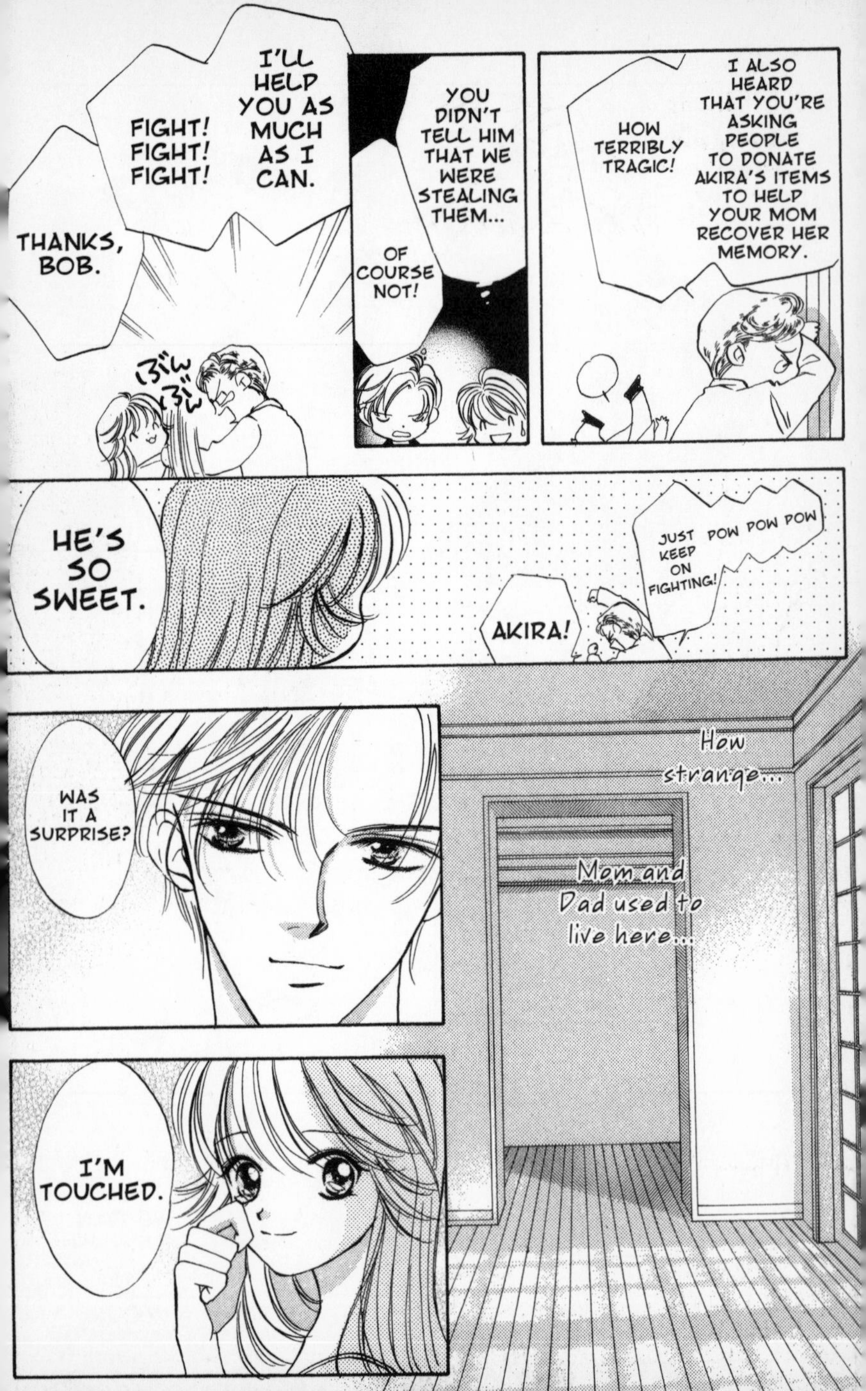
I ALSO HEARD THAT YOU'RE ASKING PEOPLE TO DONATE AKIRA'S ITEMS TO HELP YOUR MOM RECOVER HER MEMORY.
HOW TERRIBLY TRAGIC!
YOU DIDN'T TELL HIM THAT WE WERE STEALING THEM...
OF COURSE NOT!
I'LL HELP YOU AS MUCH AS I CAN.
FIGHT! FIGHT! FIGHT!
THANKS, BOB.
ぶん ぶん
POW POW POW
JUST KEEP ON FIGHTING!
AKIRA!
HE'S SO SWEET.
How strange...
Mom and Dad used to live here...
WAS IT A SURPRISE?
I'M TOUCHED.

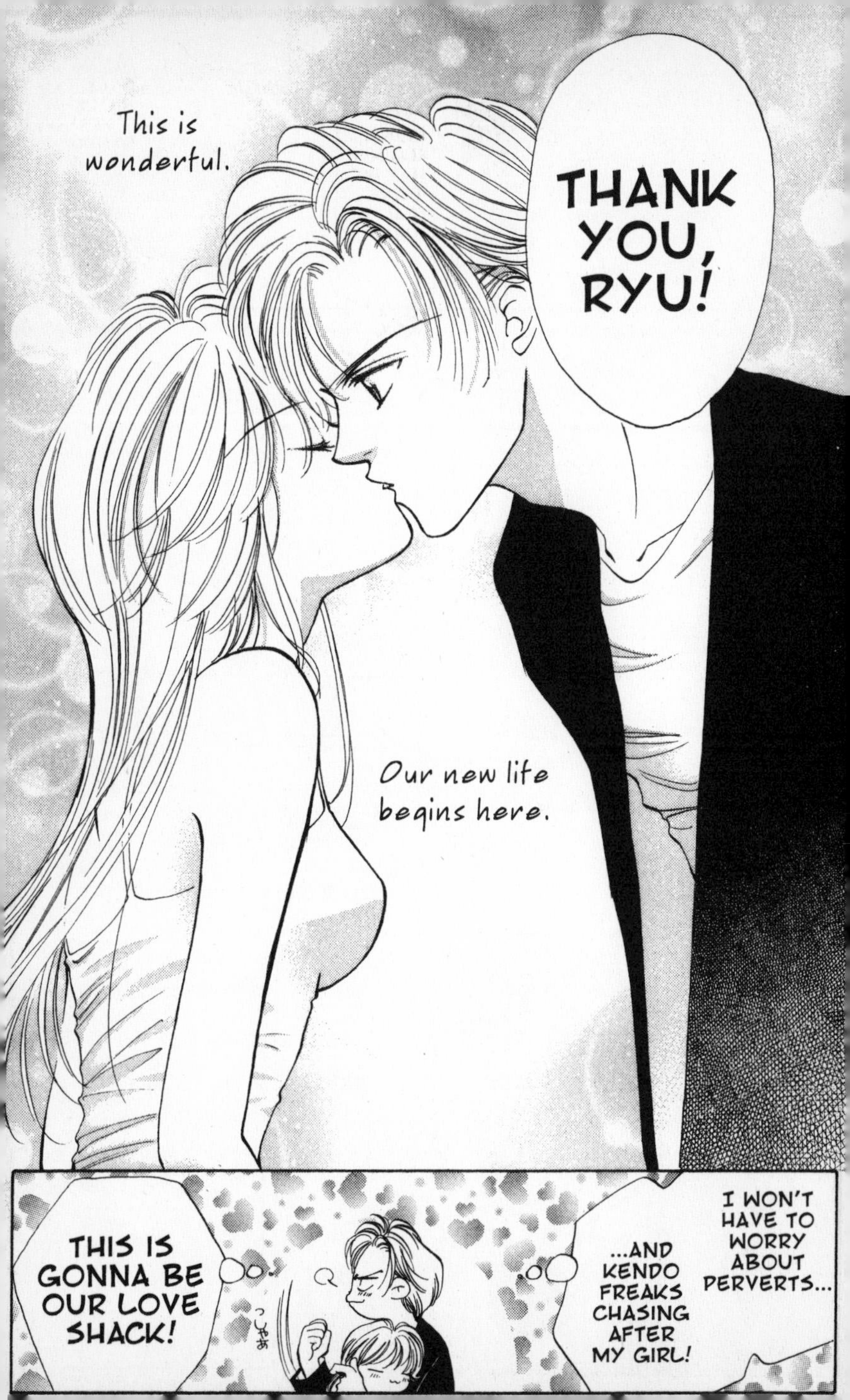
THANK YOU, RYU!
This is wonderful.
Our new life begins here.
I WON'T HAVE TO WORRY ABOUT PERVERTS...
...AND KENDO FREAKS CHASING AFTER MY GIRL!
THIS IS GONNA BE OUR LOVE SHACK!

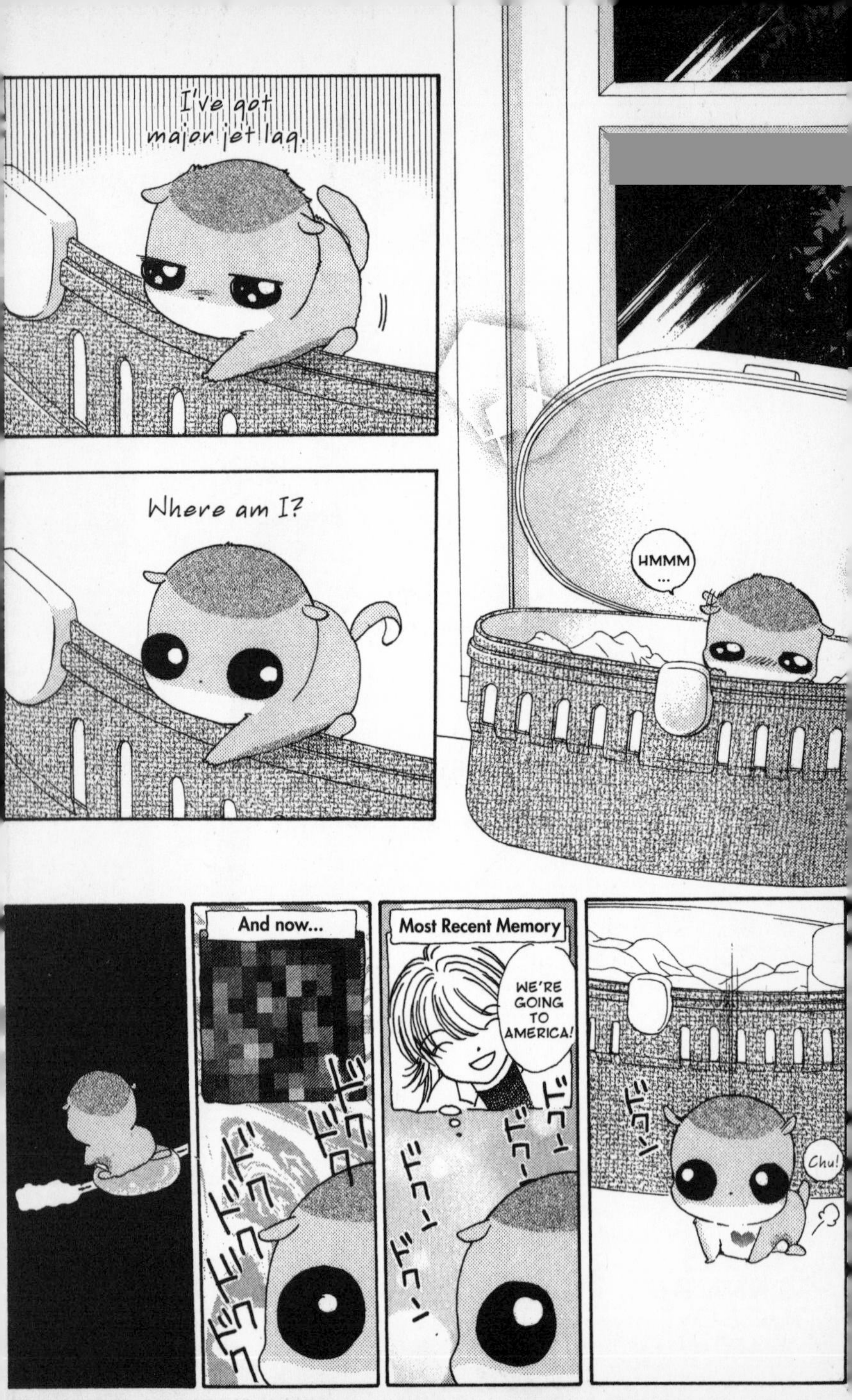
HMMM...
I've got major jet lag.
Where am I?
ドクン
Chu!
Most Recent Memory
WE'RE GOING TO AMERICA!
ドクーン
ドクーン
ドクーン
And now...
ドクドク
ドクドク
ドクドク

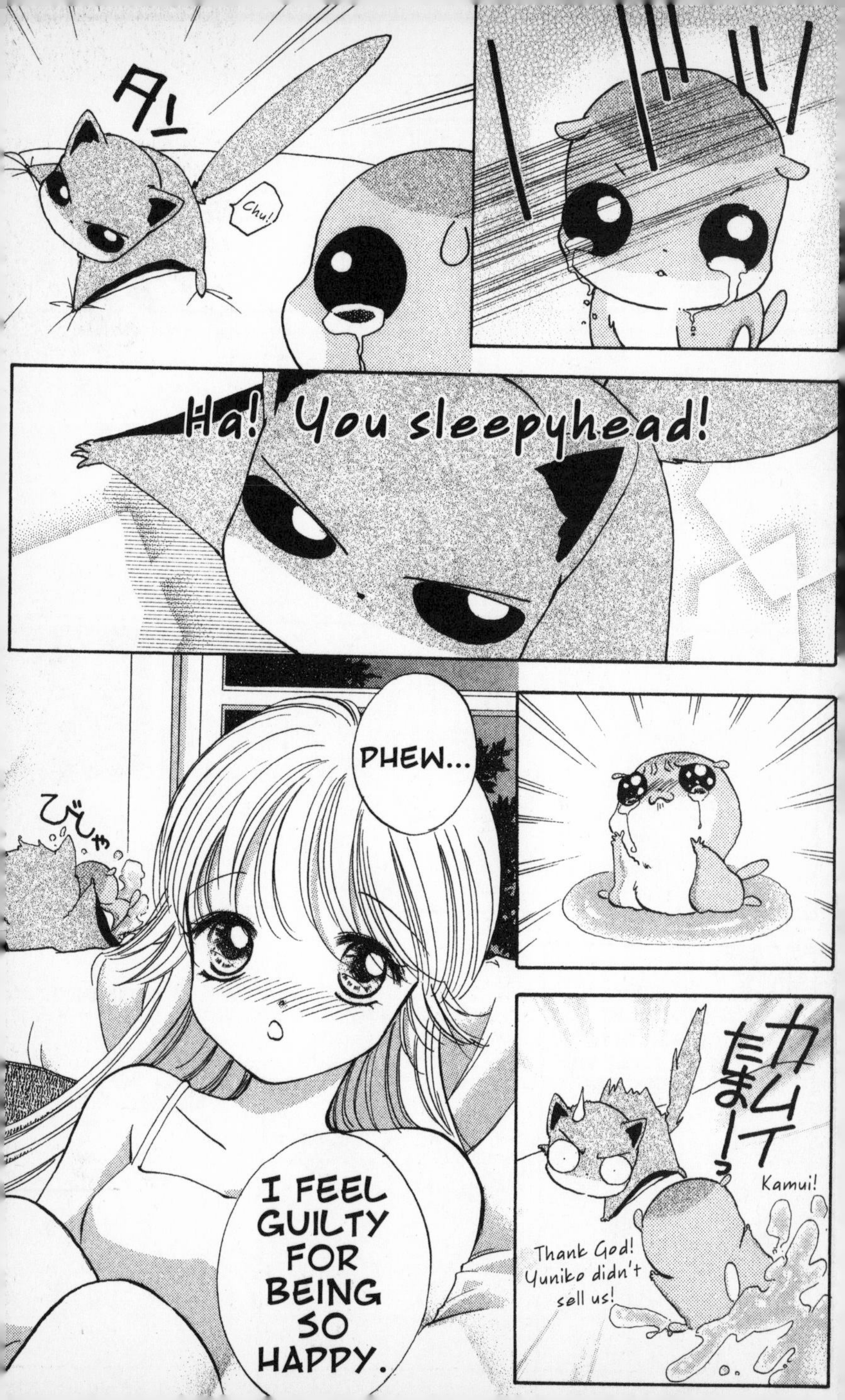
タン
Chu!
Ha! You sleepyhead!
カムイ
たまーっ
Kamui!
Thank God! Yuniko didn't sell us!
PHEW...
びしゃ
I FEEL GUILTY FOR BEING SO HAPPY.

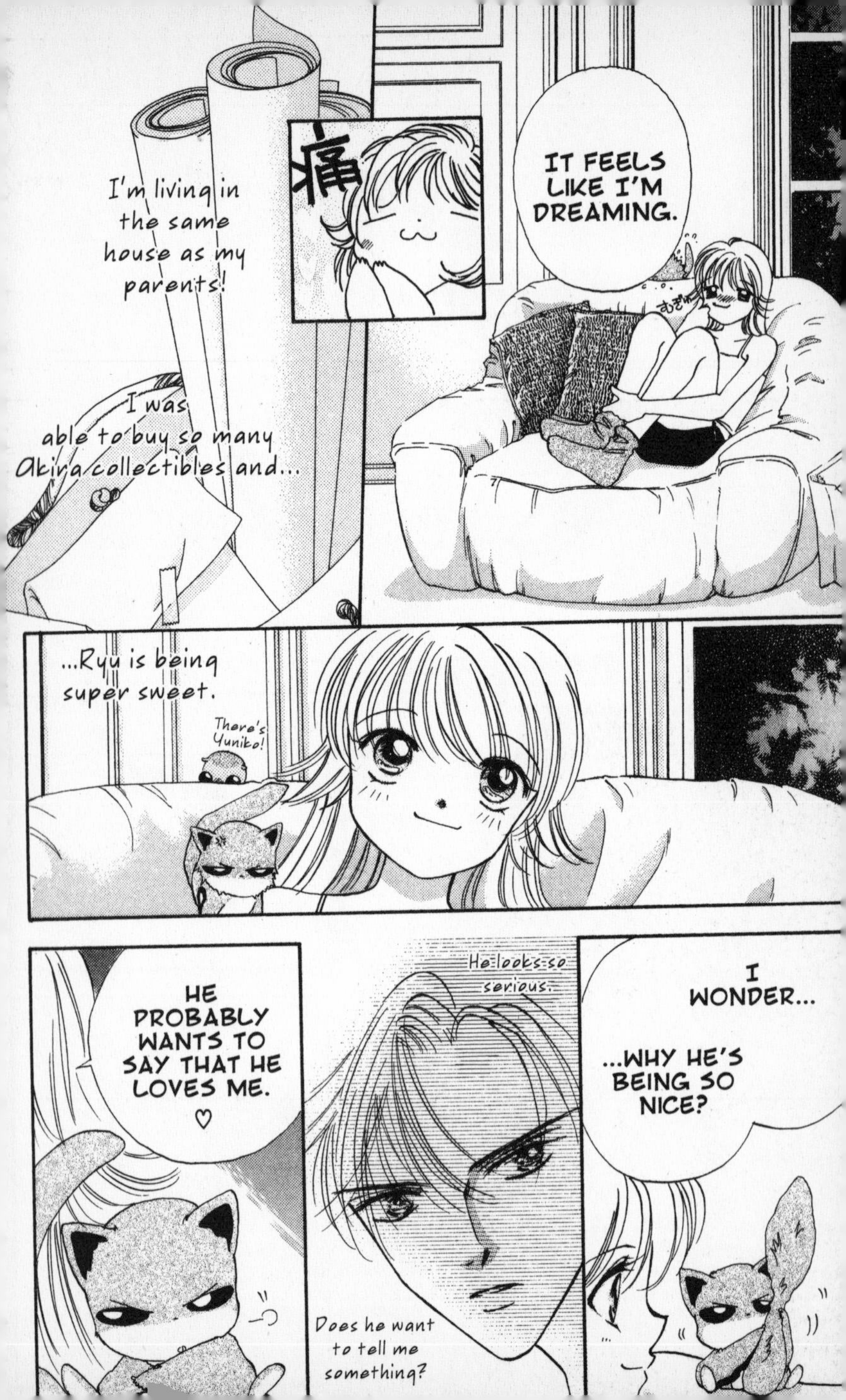
IT FEELS LIKE I'M DREAMING.
I'm living in the same house as my parents!
痛
I was able to buy so many Akira collectibles and...
...Ryu is being super sweet.
There's Yuniko!
I WONDER...
...WHY HE'S BEING SO NICE?
He looks so serious.
Does he want to tell me something?
HE PROBABLY WANTS TO SAY THAT HE LOVES ME. ♡

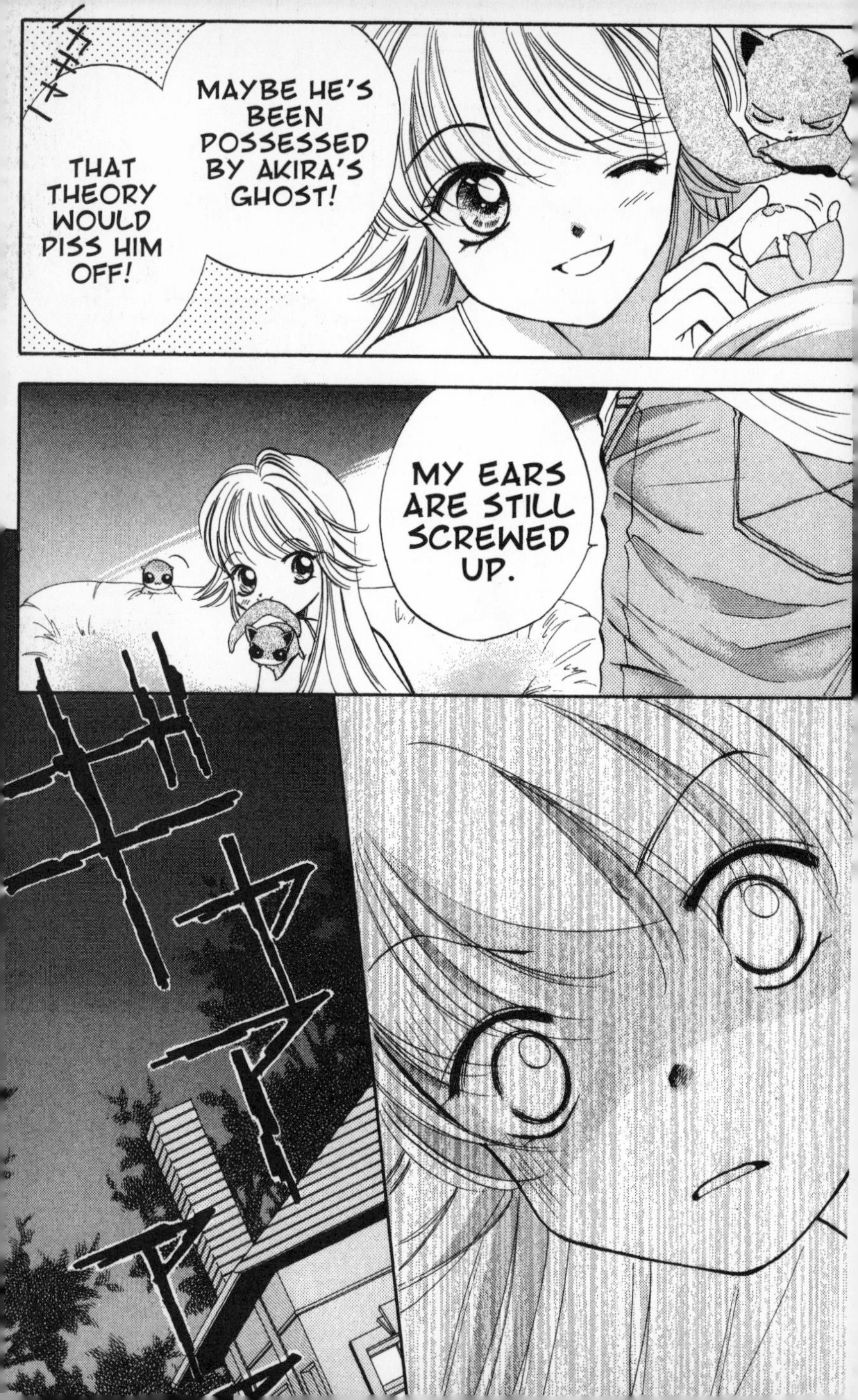
MAYBE HE'S BEEN POSSESSED BY AKIRA'S GHOST!
THAT THEORY WOULD PISS HIM OFF!
MY EARS ARE STILL SCREWED UP.
キャアア

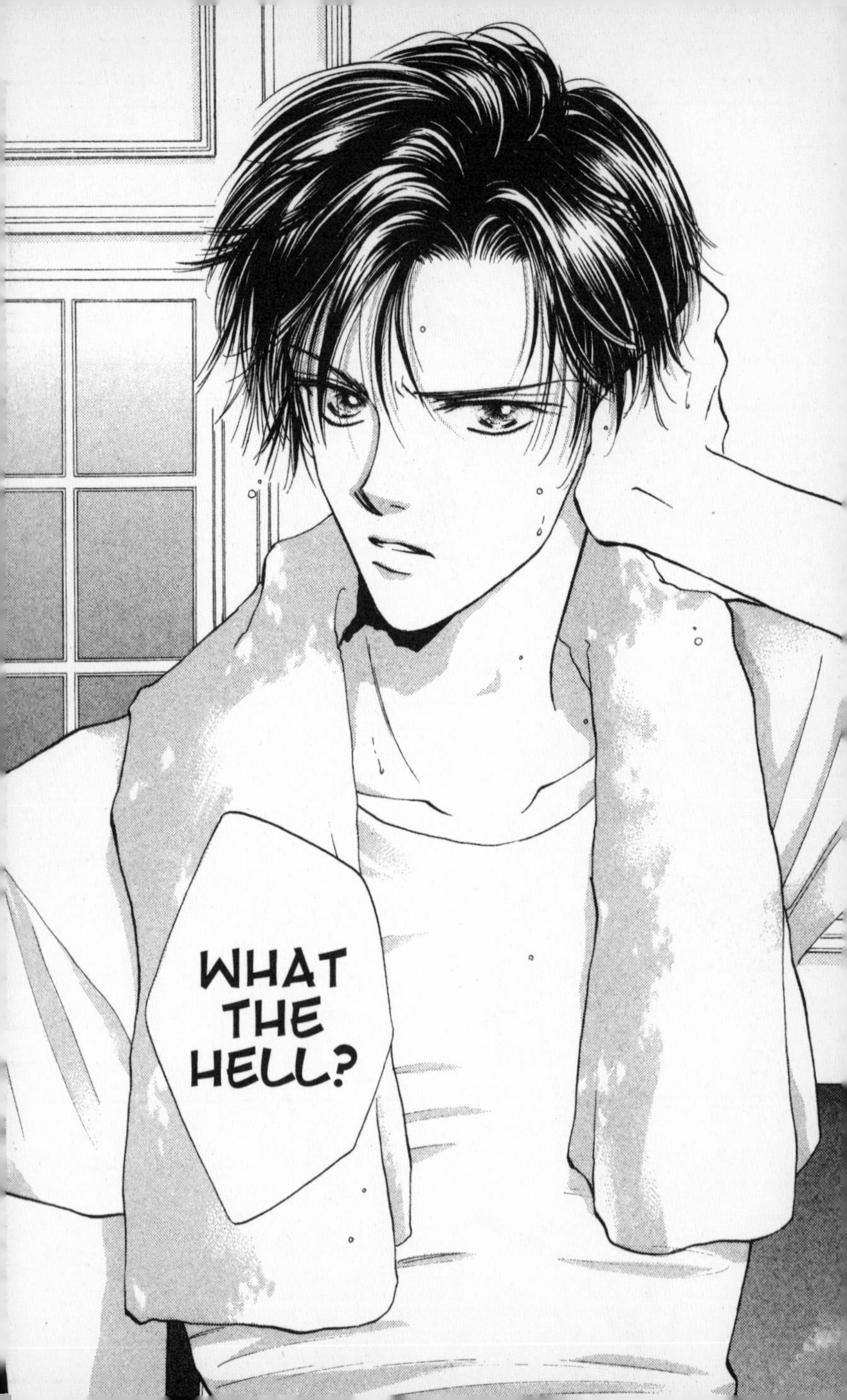
WHAT THE HELL?

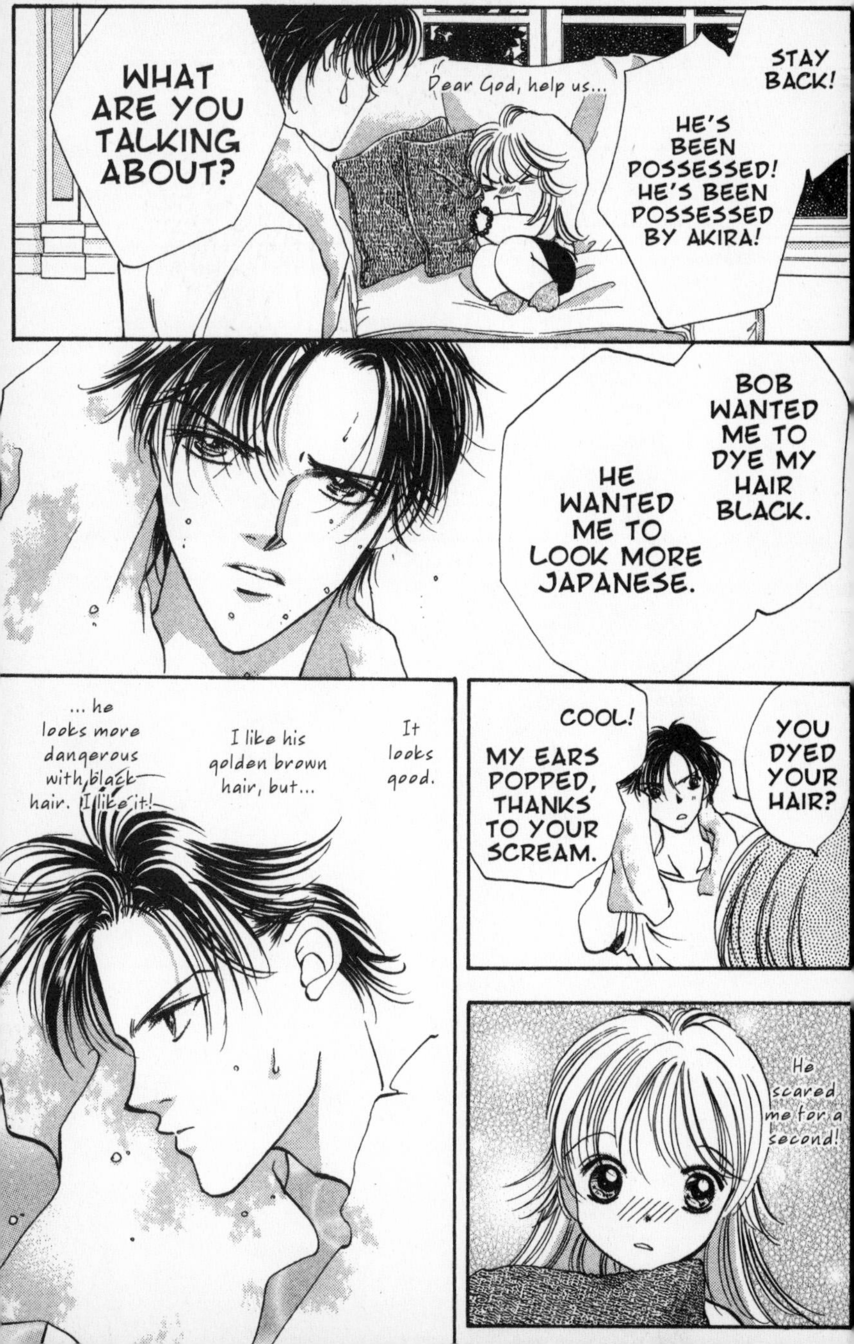
STAY BACK!
HE'S BEEN POSSESSED! HE'S BEEN POSSESSED BY AKIRA!
Dear God, help us...
WHAT ARE YOU TALKING ABOUT?
BOB WANTED ME TO DYE MY HAIR BLACK.
HE WANTED ME TO LOOK MORE JAPANESE.
YOU DYED YOUR HAIR?
COOL!
MY EARS POPPED, THANKS TO YOUR SCREAM.
He scared me for a second!
It looks good.
I like his golden brown hair, but...
... he looks more dangerous with black hair. I like it!

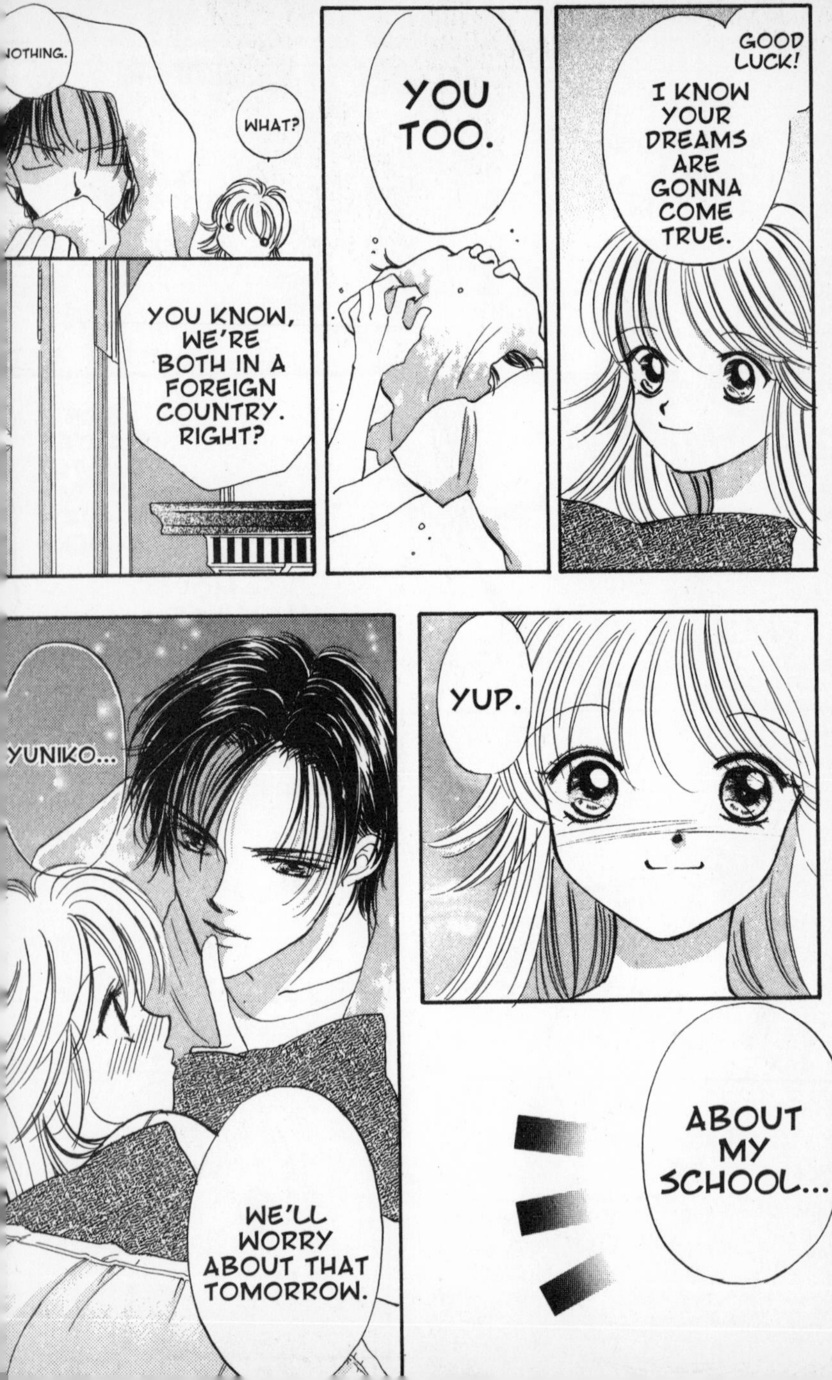
GOOD LUCK!
I KNOW YOUR DREAMS ARE GONNA COME TRUE.
YOU TOO.
WHAT?
NOTHING.
YOU KNOW, WE'RE BOTH IN A FOREIGN COUNTRY. RIGHT?
YUP.
ABOUT MY SCHOOL...
YUNIKO...
WE'LL WORRY ABOUT THAT TOMORROW.

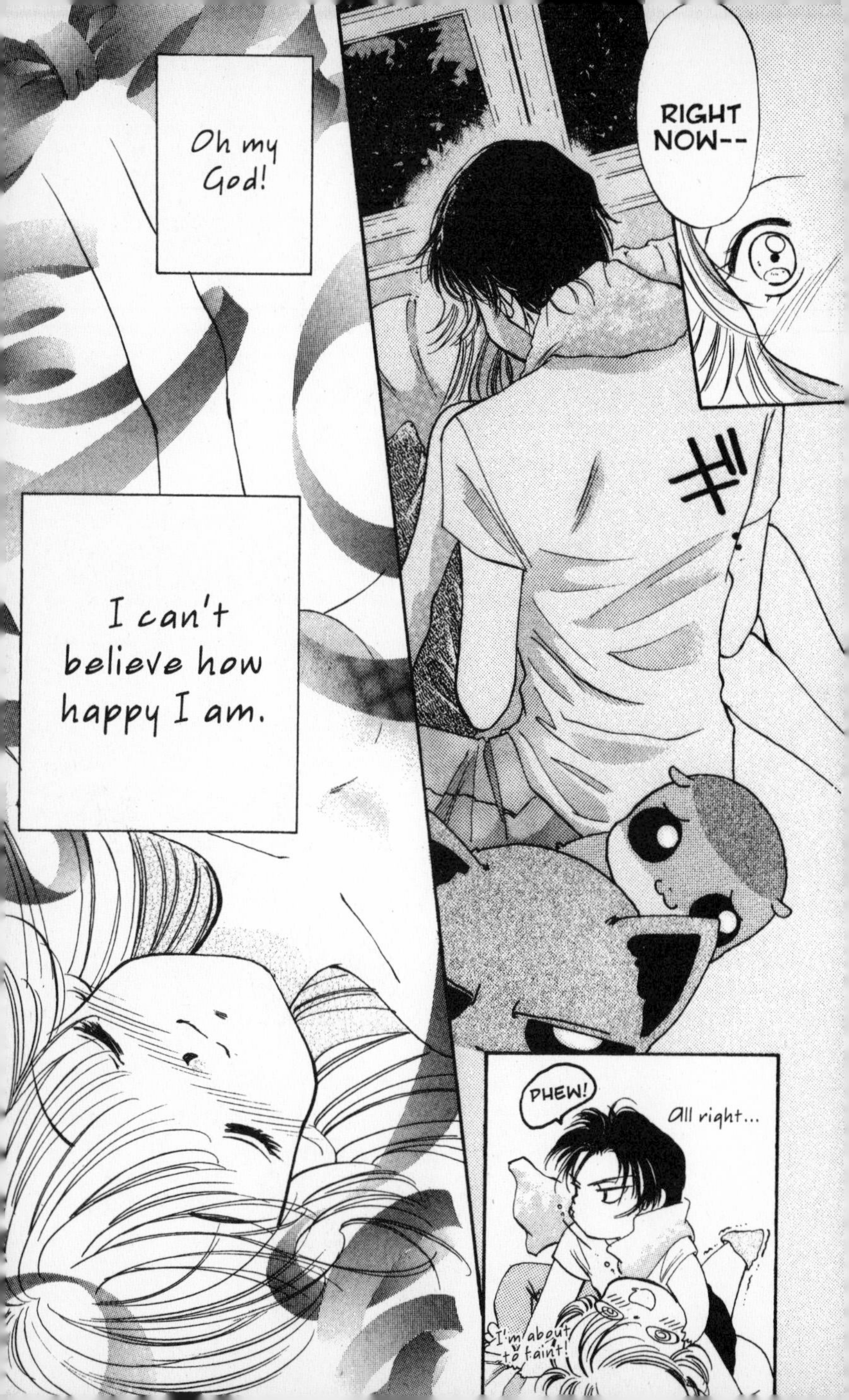
RIGHT NOW--
ギ
PHEW!
All right...
I'm about to faint!
Oh my God!
I can't believe how happy I am.

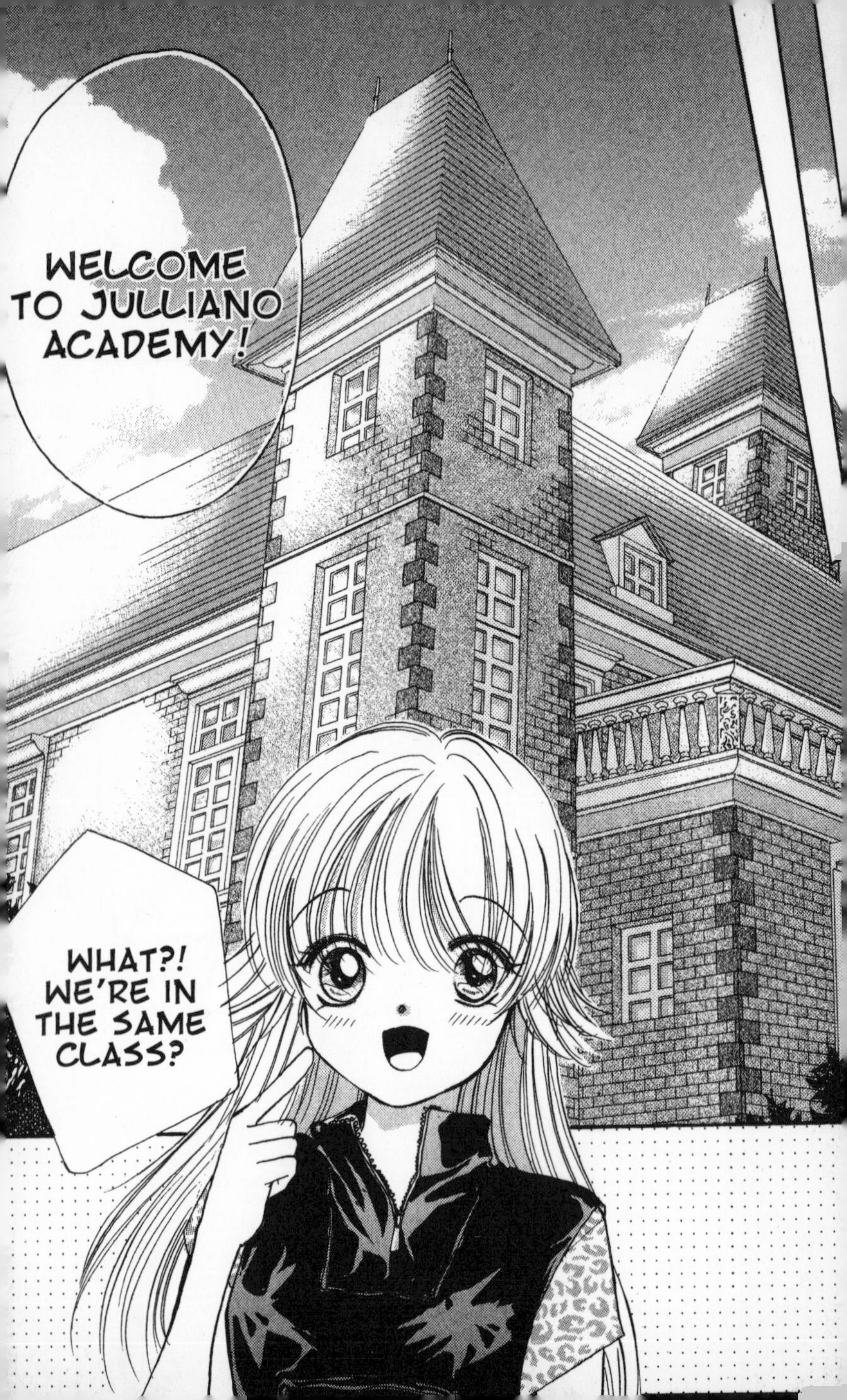
WELCOME TO JULLIANO ACADEMY!
WHAT?! WE'RE IN THE SAME CLASS?

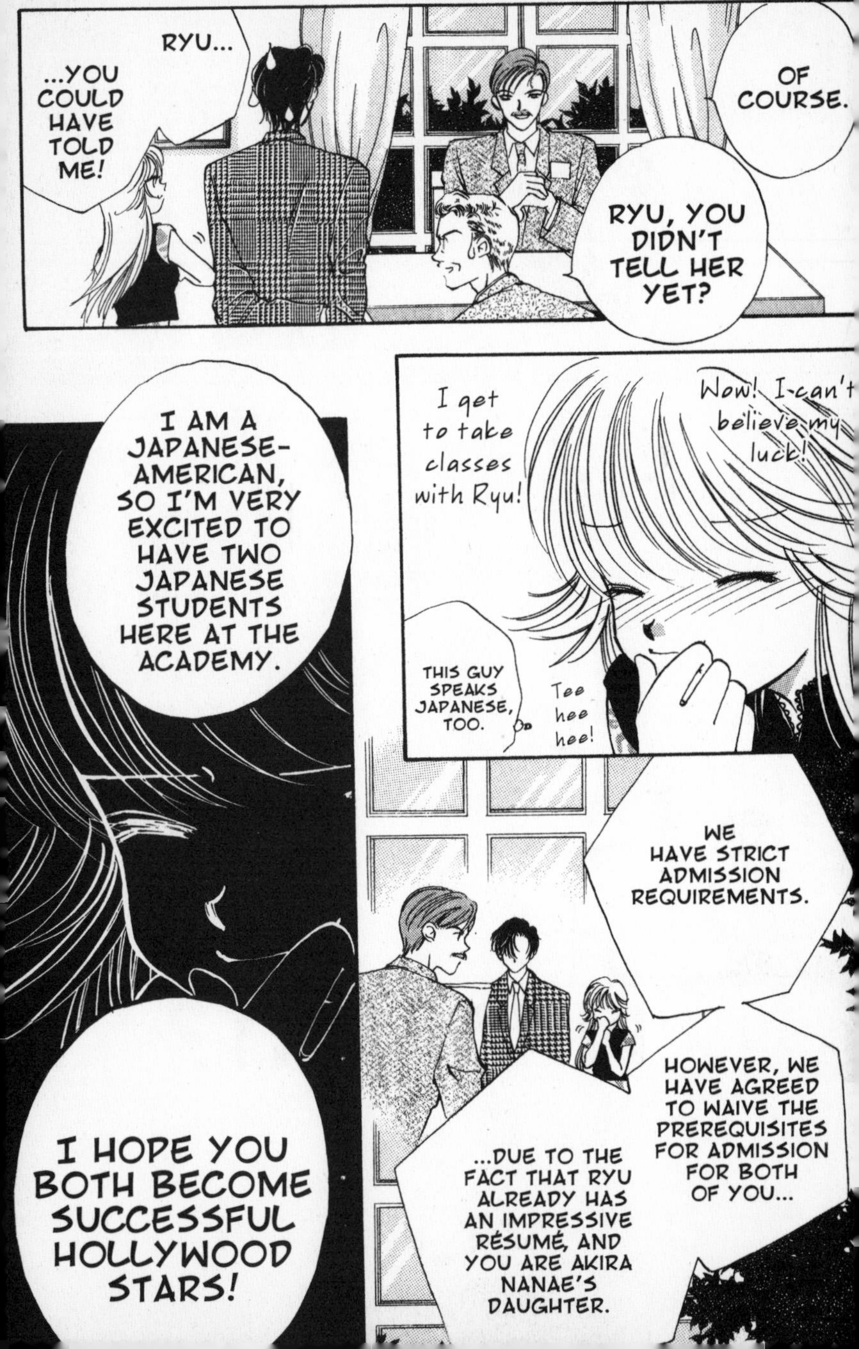
OF COURSE.
RYU, YOU DIDN'T TELL HER YET?
RYU...
...YOU COULD HAVE TOLD ME!
Wow! I can't believe my luck!
I get to take classes with Ryu!
Tee hee hee!
THIS GUY SPEAKS JAPANESE, TOO.
WE HAVE STRICT ADMISSION REQUIREMENTS.
HOWEVER, WE HAVE AGREED TO WAIVE THE PREREQUISITES FOR ADMISSION FOR BOTH OF YOU...
...DUE TO THE FACT THAT RYU ALREADY HAS AN IMPRESSIVE RÉSUMÉ, AND YOU ARE AKIRA NANAE'S DAUGHTER.
I AM A JAPANESE-AMERICAN, SO I'M VERY EXCITED TO HAVE TWO JAPANESE STUDENTS HERE AT THE ACADEMY.
I HOPE YOU BOTH BECOME SUCCESSFUL HOLLYWOOD STARS!

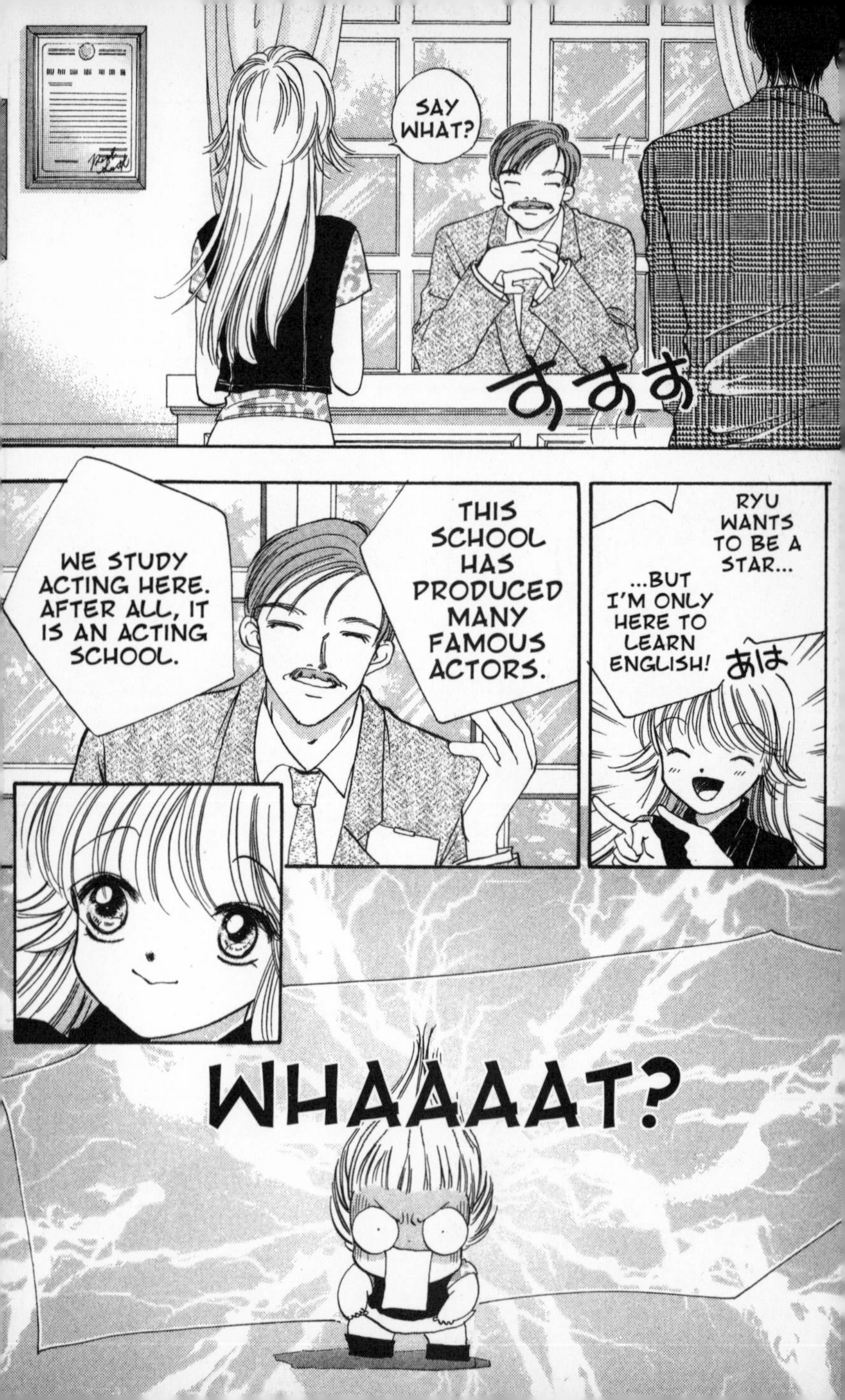
SAY WHAT?
すすす
RYU WANTS TO BE A STAR...
...BUT I'M ONLY HERE TO LEARN ENGLISH!
あは
THIS SCHOOL HAS PRODUCED MANY FAMOUS ACTORS.
WE STUDY ACTING HERE. AFTER ALL, IT IS AN ACTING SCHOOL.
WHAAAAT?

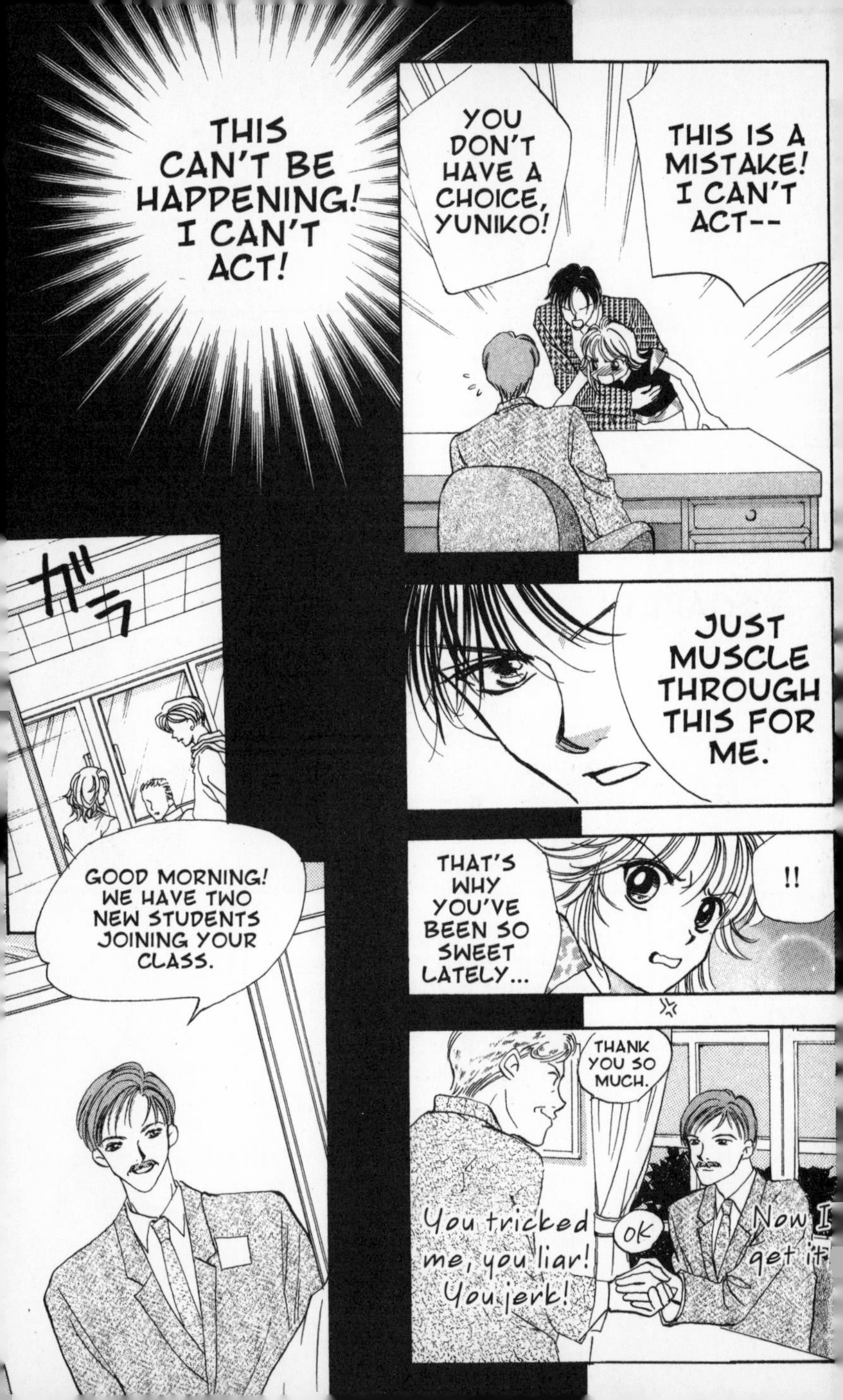
THIS IS A MISTAKE! I CAN'T ACT--
YOU DON'T HAVE A CHOICE, YUNIKO!
THIS CAN'T BE HAPPENING! I CAN'T ACT!
JUST MUSCLE THROUGH THIS FOR ME.
!!
THAT'S WHY YOU'VE BEEN SO SWEET LATELY...
THANK YOU SO MUCH.
Now I get it
OK
You tricked me, you liar! You jerk!
ガラ
GOOD MORNING! WE HAVE TWO NEW STUDENTS JOINING YOUR CLASS.

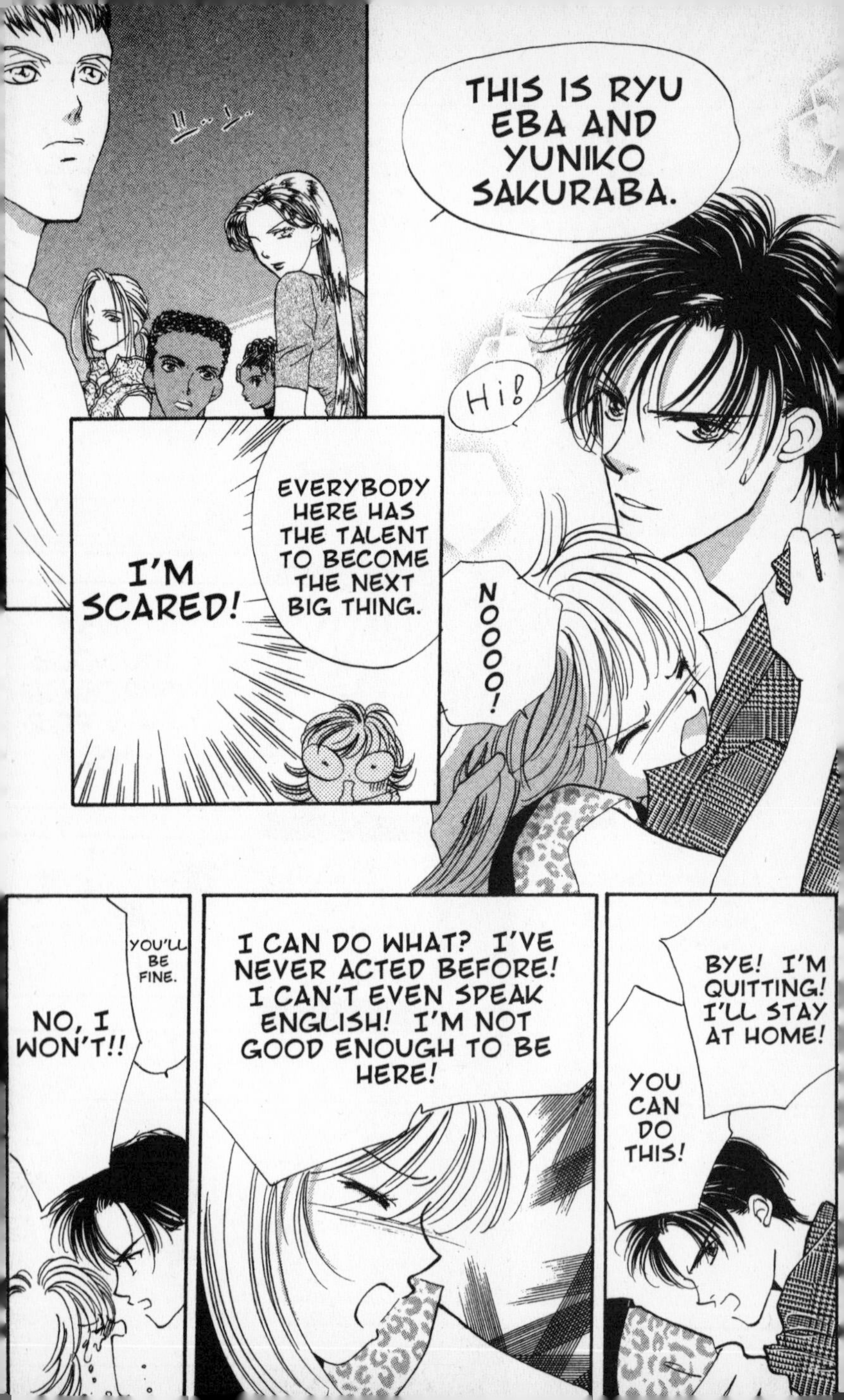
THIS IS RYU EBA AND YUNIKO SAKURABA.
Hi!
NOOOO!
EVERYBODY HERE HAS THE TALENT TO BECOME THE NEXT BIG THING.
I'M SCARED!
BYE! I'M QUITTING! I'LL STAY AT HOME!
YOU CAN DO THIS!
I CAN DO WHAT? I'VE NEVER ACTED BEFORE! I CAN'T EVEN SPEAK ENGLISH! I'M NOT GOOD ENOUGH TO BE HERE!
YOU'LL BE FINE.
NO, I WON'T!!

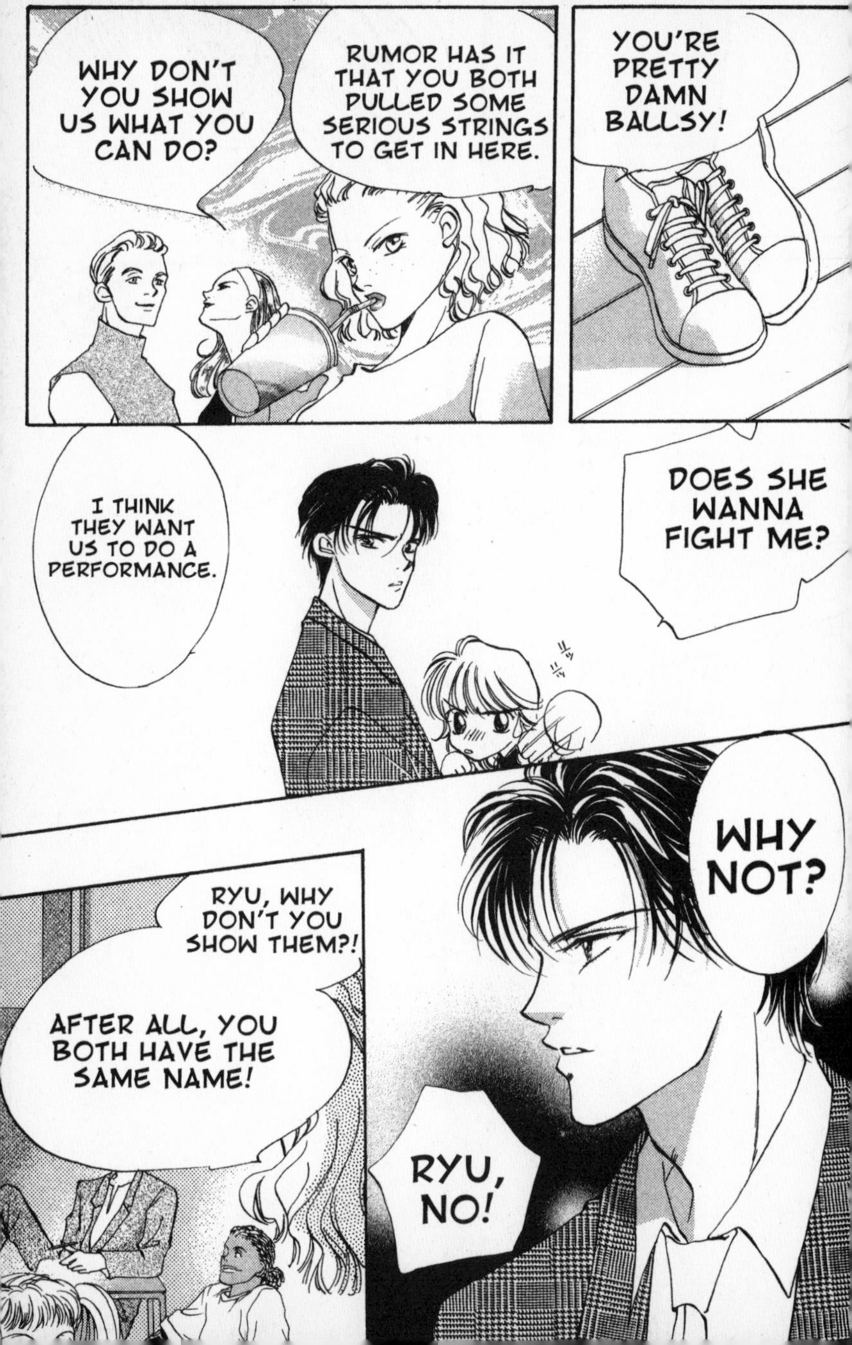
YOU'RE PRETTY DAMN BALLSY!
RUMOR HAS IT THAT YOU BOTH PULLED SOME SERIOUS STRINGS TO GET IN HERE.
WHY DON'T YOU SHOW US WHAT YOU CAN DO?
DOES SHE WANNA FIGHT ME?
I THINK THEY WANT US TO DO A PERFORMANCE.
WHY NOT?
RYU, NO!
RYU, WHY DON'T YOU SHOW THEM?!
AFTER ALL, YOU BOTH HAVE THE SAME NAME!

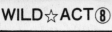

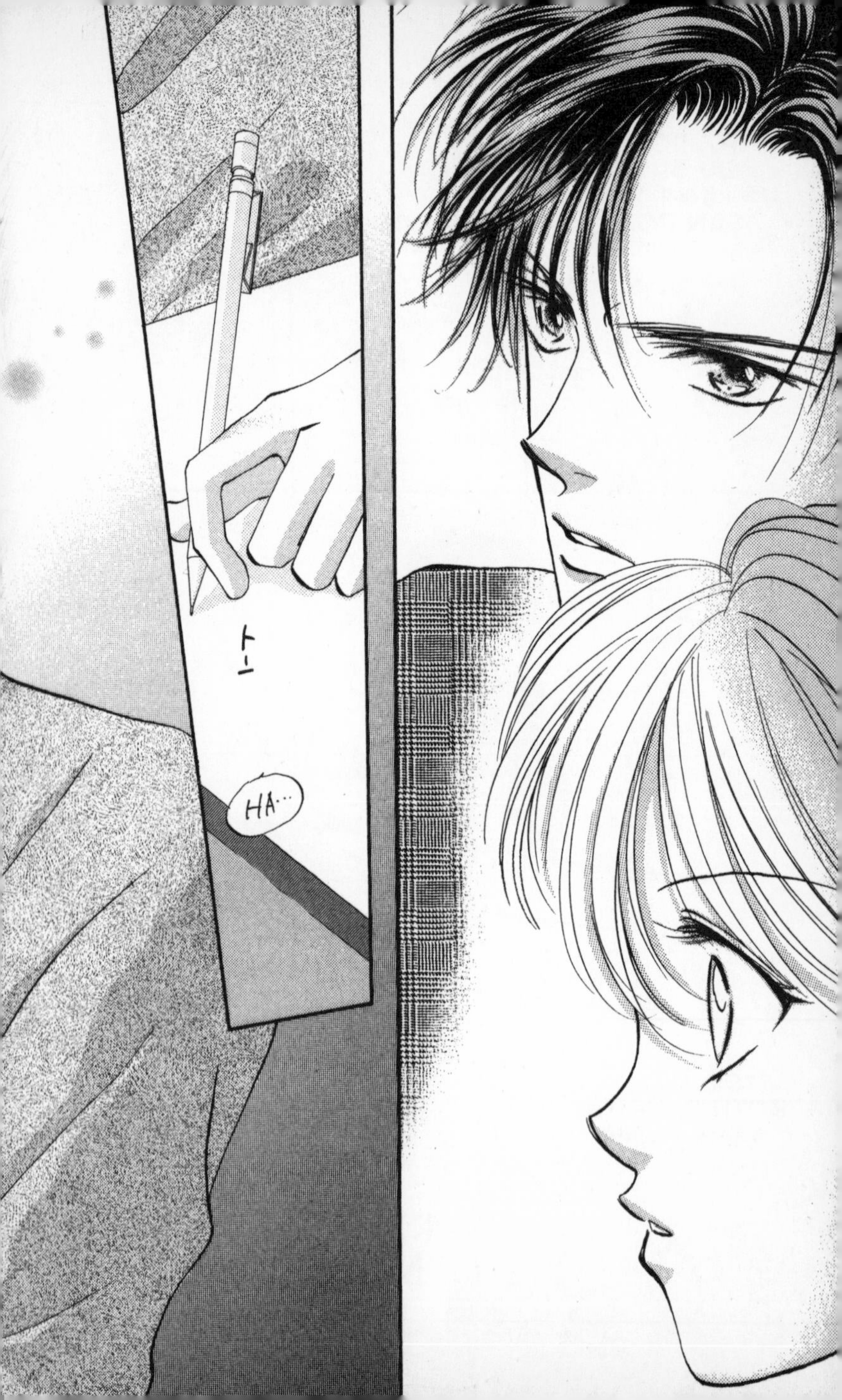
HA...

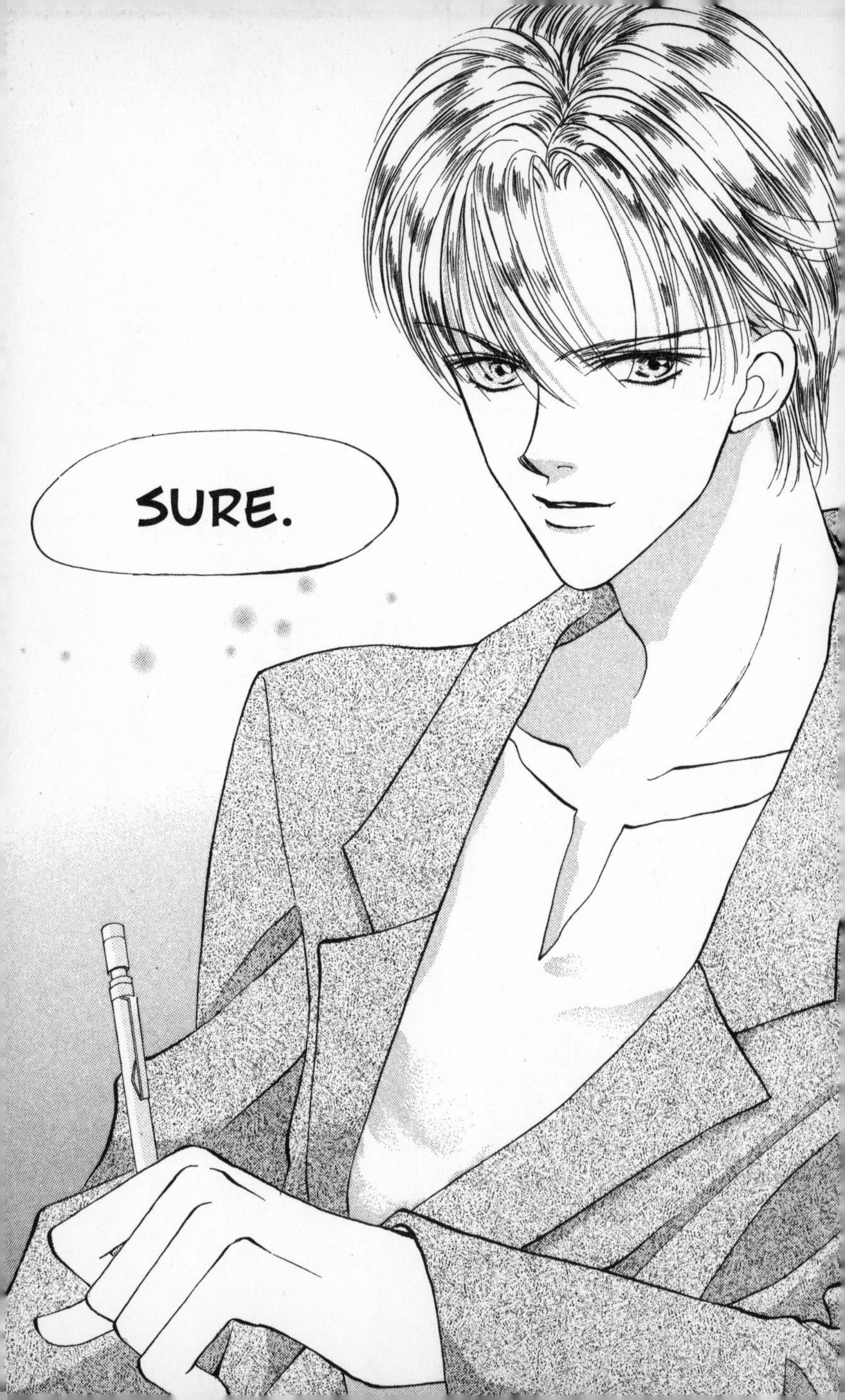
SURE.

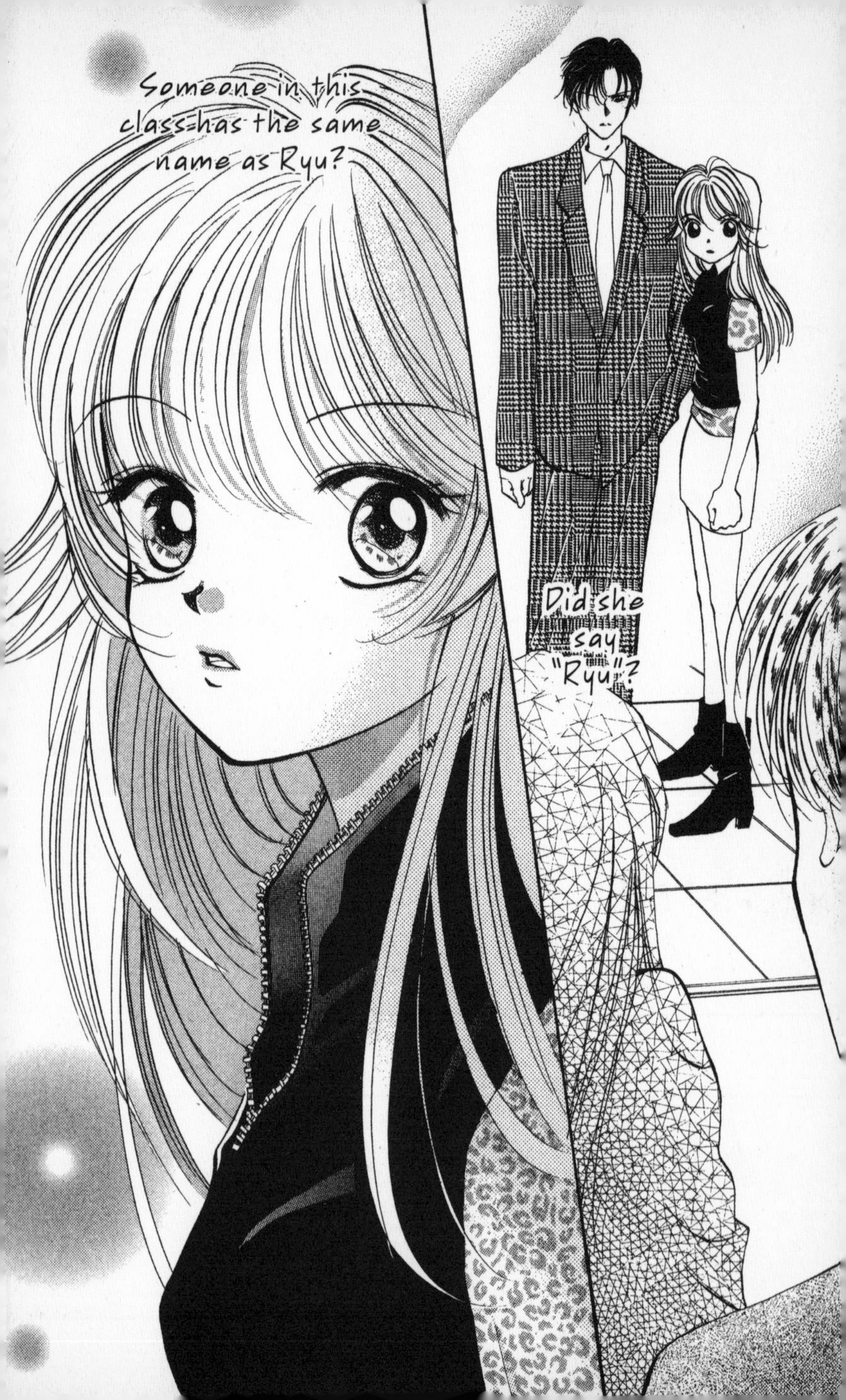
Did she say "Ryu"?
Someone in this class has the same name as Ryu?

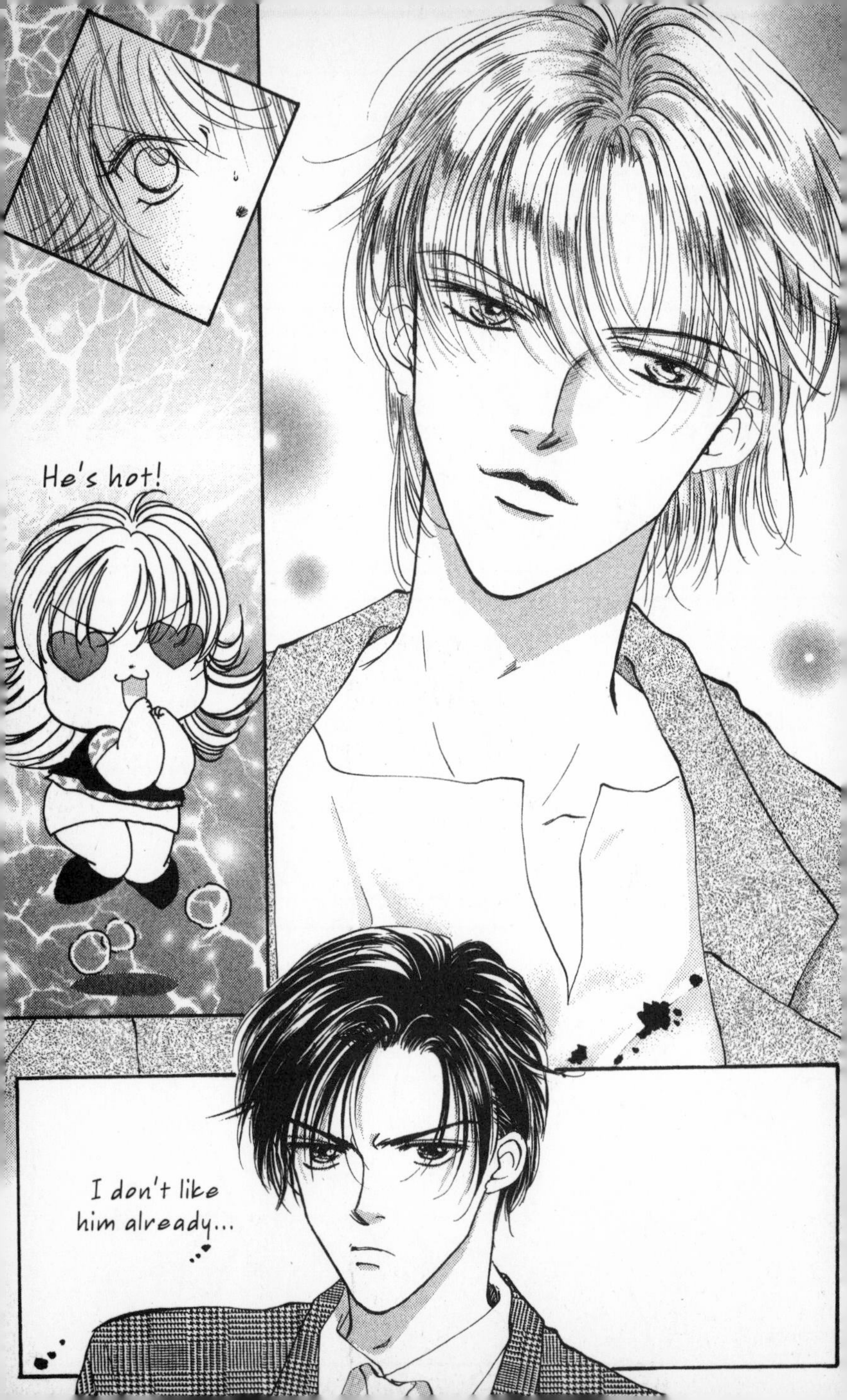
He's hot!
I don't like him already...

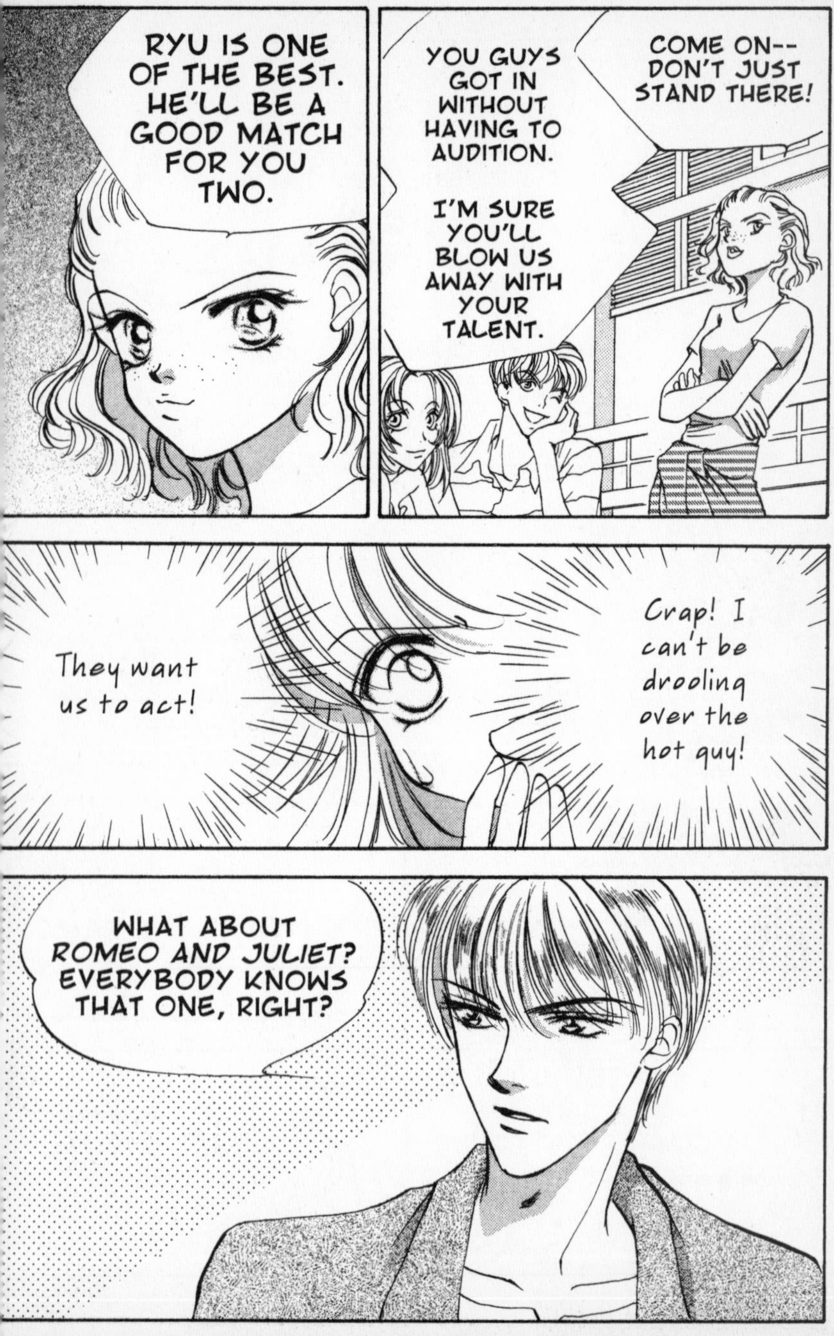
COME ON-- DON'T JUST STAND THERE!
YOU GUYS GOT IN WITHOUT HAVING TO AUDITION.
I'M SURE YOU'LL BLOW US AWAY WITH YOUR TALENT.
RYU IS ONE OF THE BEST. HE'LL BE A GOOD MATCH FOR YOU TWO.
Crap! I can't be drooling over the hot guy!
They want us to act!
WHAT ABOUT ROMEO AND JULIET? EVERYBODY KNOWS THAT ONE, RIGHT?

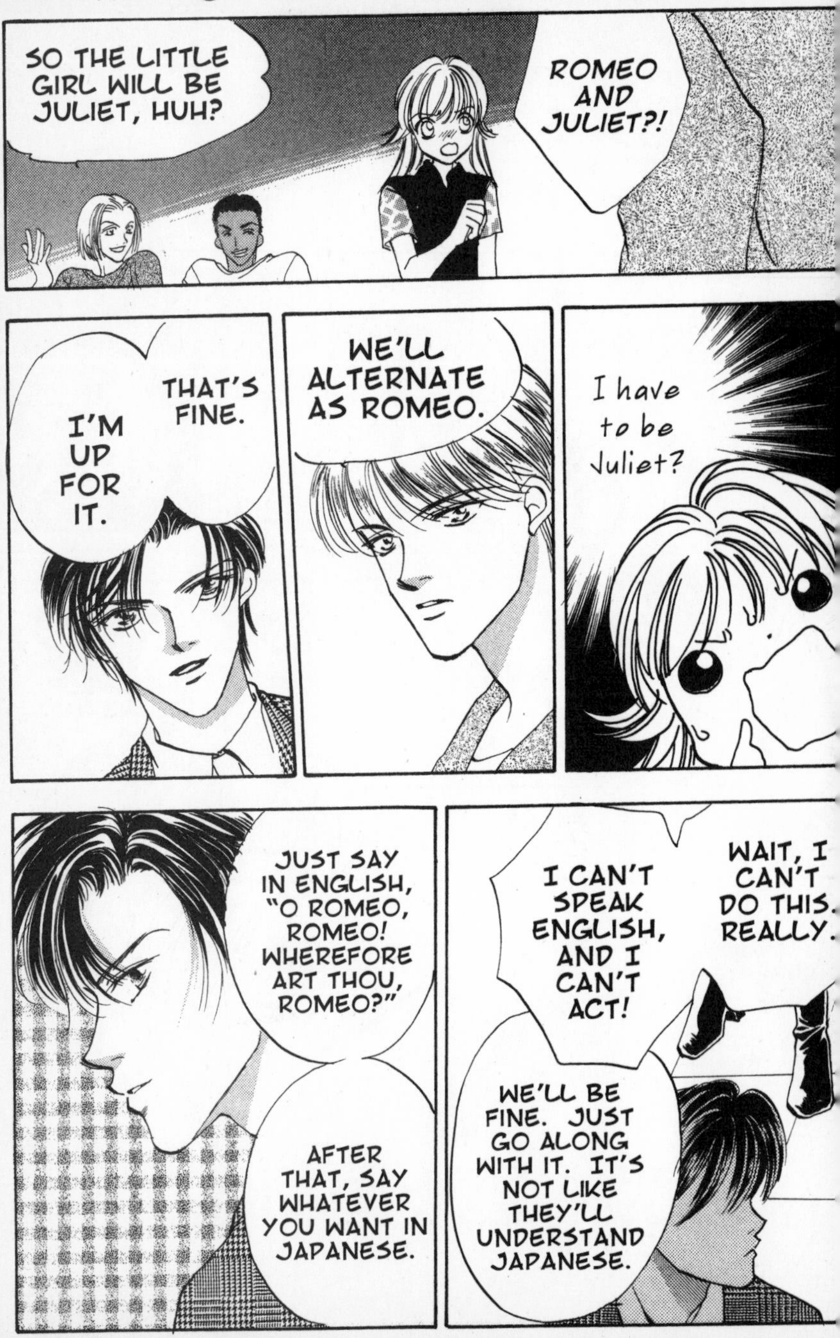
ROMEO AND JULIET?!
SO THE LITTLE GIRL WILL BE JULIET, HUH?
I have to be Juliet?
WE'LL ALTERNATE AS ROMEO.
THAT'S FINE.
I'M UP FOR IT.
WAIT, I CAN'T DO THIS. REALLY.
I CAN'T SPEAK ENGLISH, AND I CAN'T ACT!
WE'LL BE FINE. JUST GO ALONG WITH IT. IT'S NOT LIKE THEY'LL UNDERSTAND JAPANESE.
JUST SAY IN ENGLISH, "O ROMEO, ROMEO! WHEREFORE ART THOU, ROMEO?"
AFTER THAT, SAY WHATEVER YOU WANT IN JAPANESE.

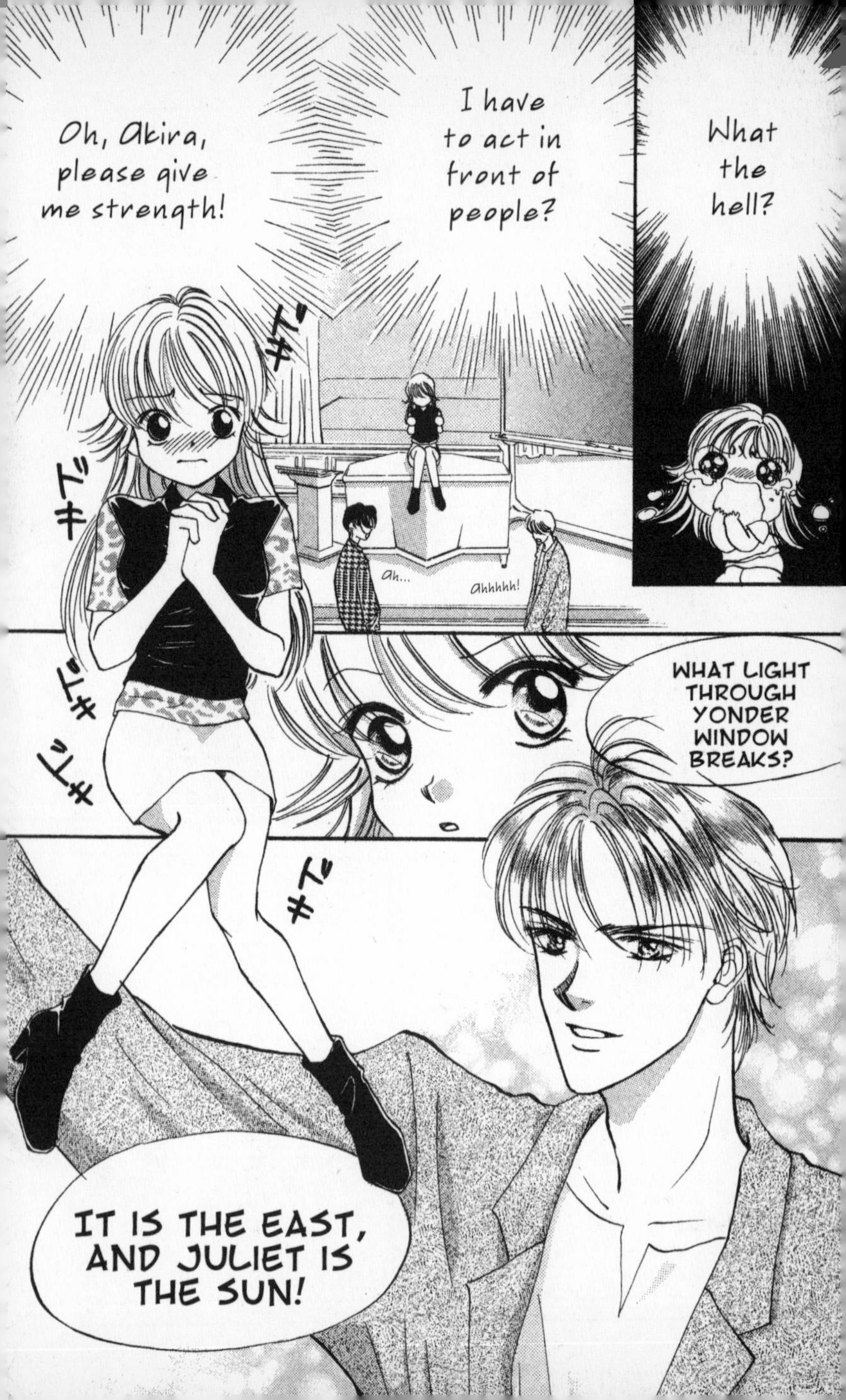
What the hell?
I have to act in front of people?
Oh, Akira, please give me strength!
ドキ
ドキ
ドキドキ
ah...
ahhhhh!
WHAT LIGHT THROUGH YONDER WINDOW BREAKS?
ドキ
IT IS THE EAST, AND JULIET IS THE SUN!

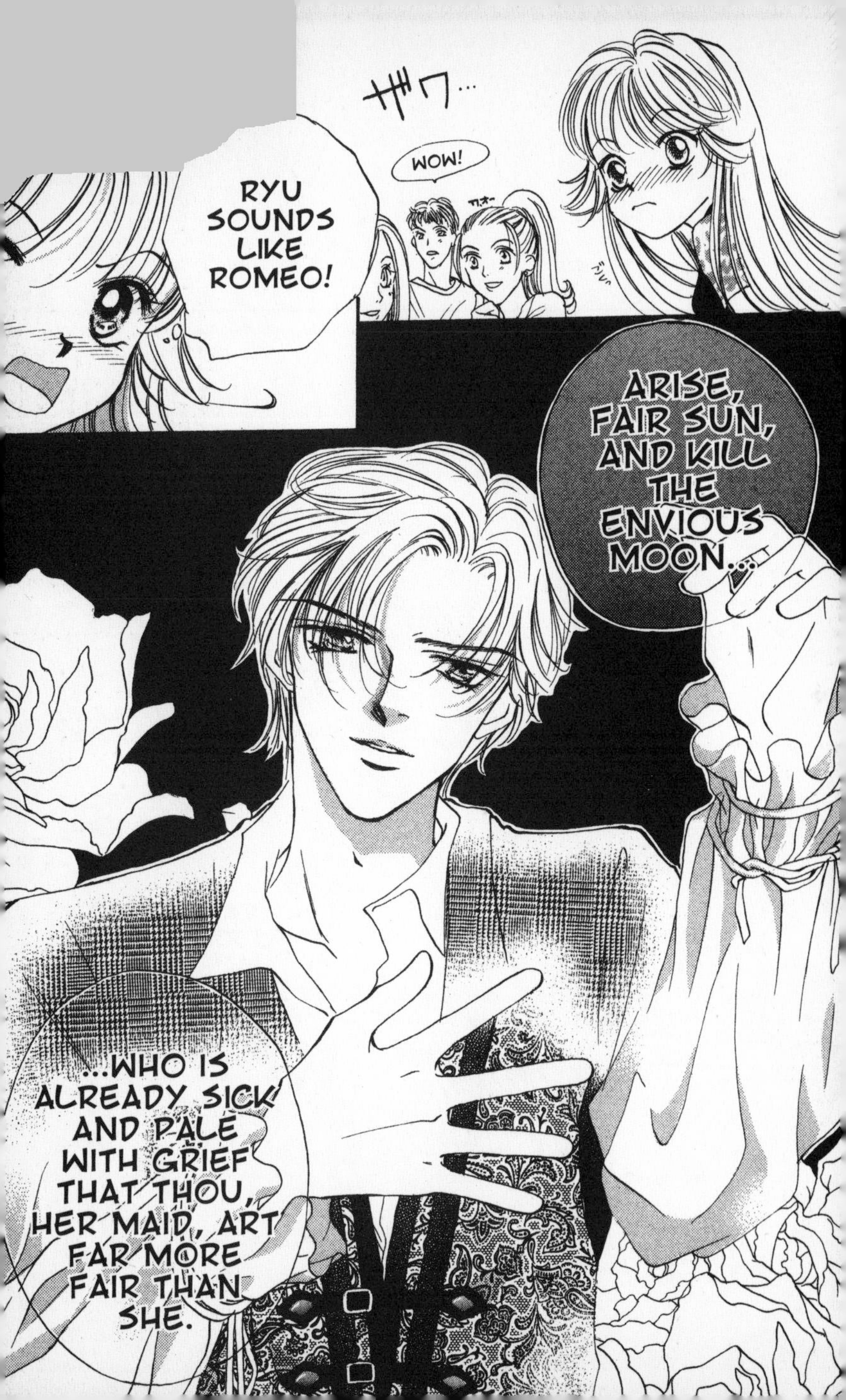
ザワ…
WOW!
RYU SOUNDS LIKE ROMEO!
ARISE, FAIR SUN, AND KILL THE ENVIOUS MOON...
...WHO IS ALREADY SICK AND PALE WITH GRIEF THAT THOU, HER MAID, ART FAR MORE FAIR THAN SHE.

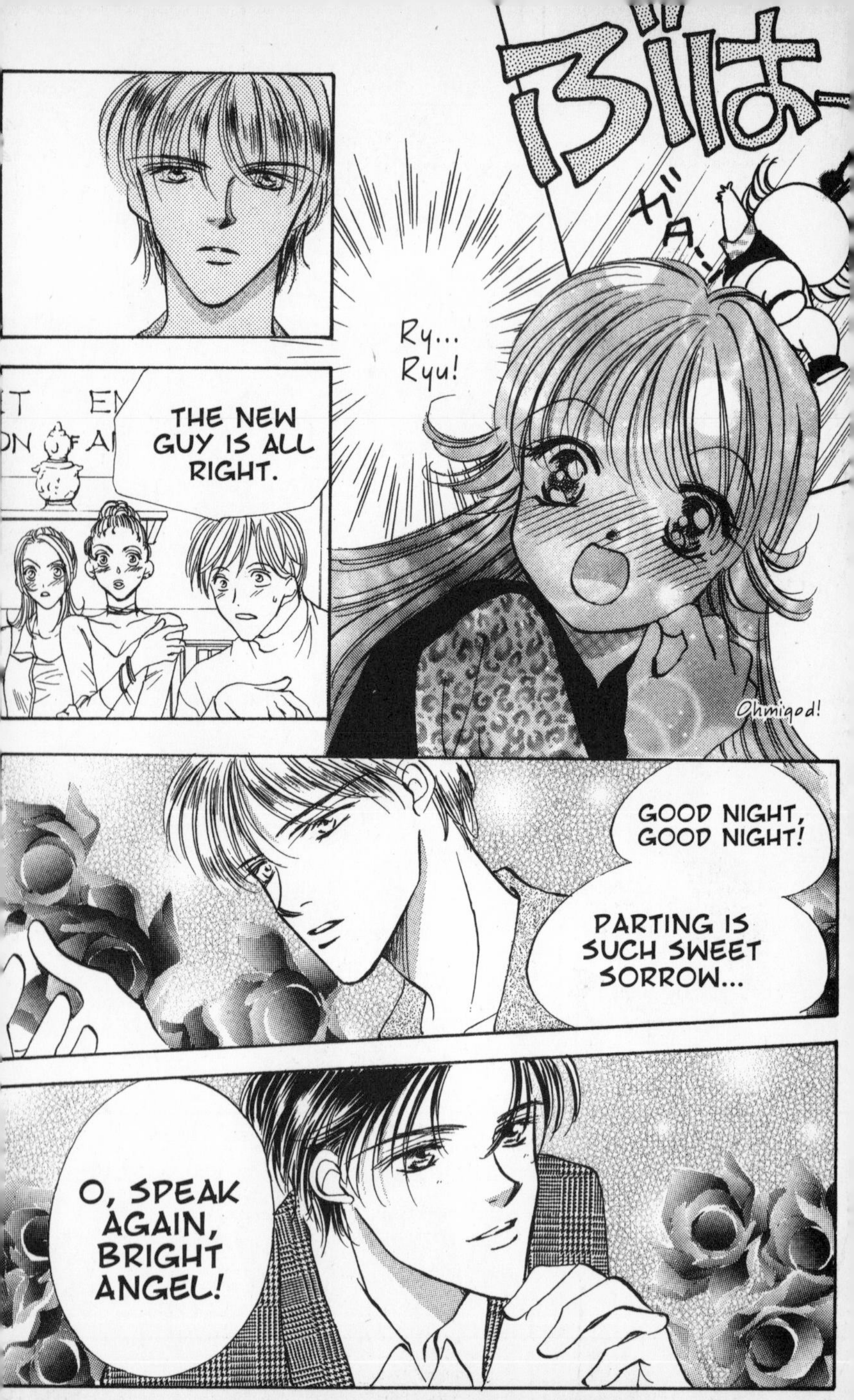
ろ゛はー
ガA...
Ry... Ryu!
Ohmigod!
THE NEW GUY IS ALL RIGHT.
GOOD NIGHT, GOOD NIGHT!
PARTING IS SUCH SWEET SORROW...
O, SPEAK AGAIN, BRIGHT ANGEL!

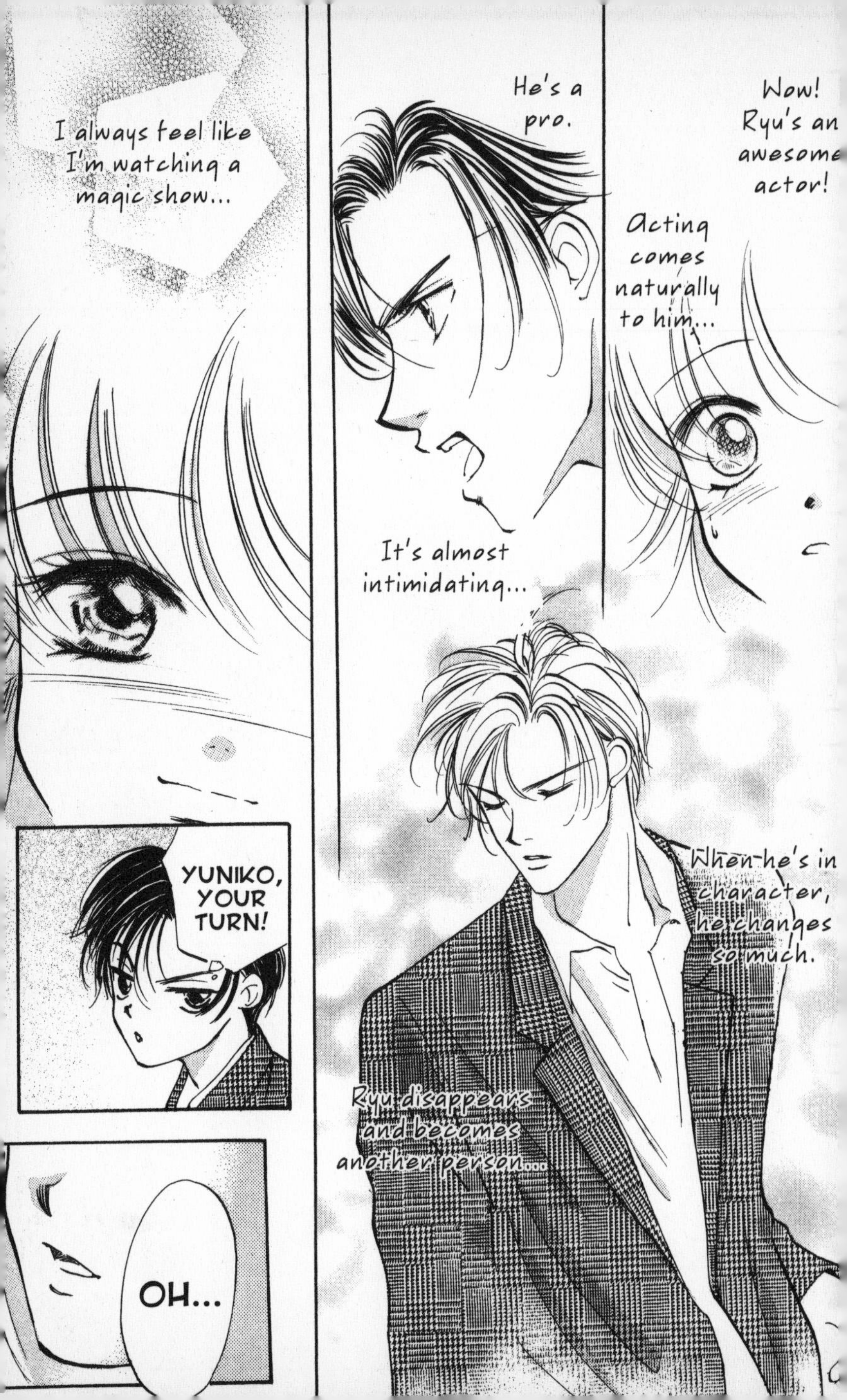
Wow! Ryu's an awesome actor!
Acting comes naturally to him...
He's a pro.
It's almost intimidating...
When he's in character, he changes so much.
Ryu disappears and becomes another person...
I always feel like I'm watching a magic show...
YUNIKO, YOUR TURN!
OH...

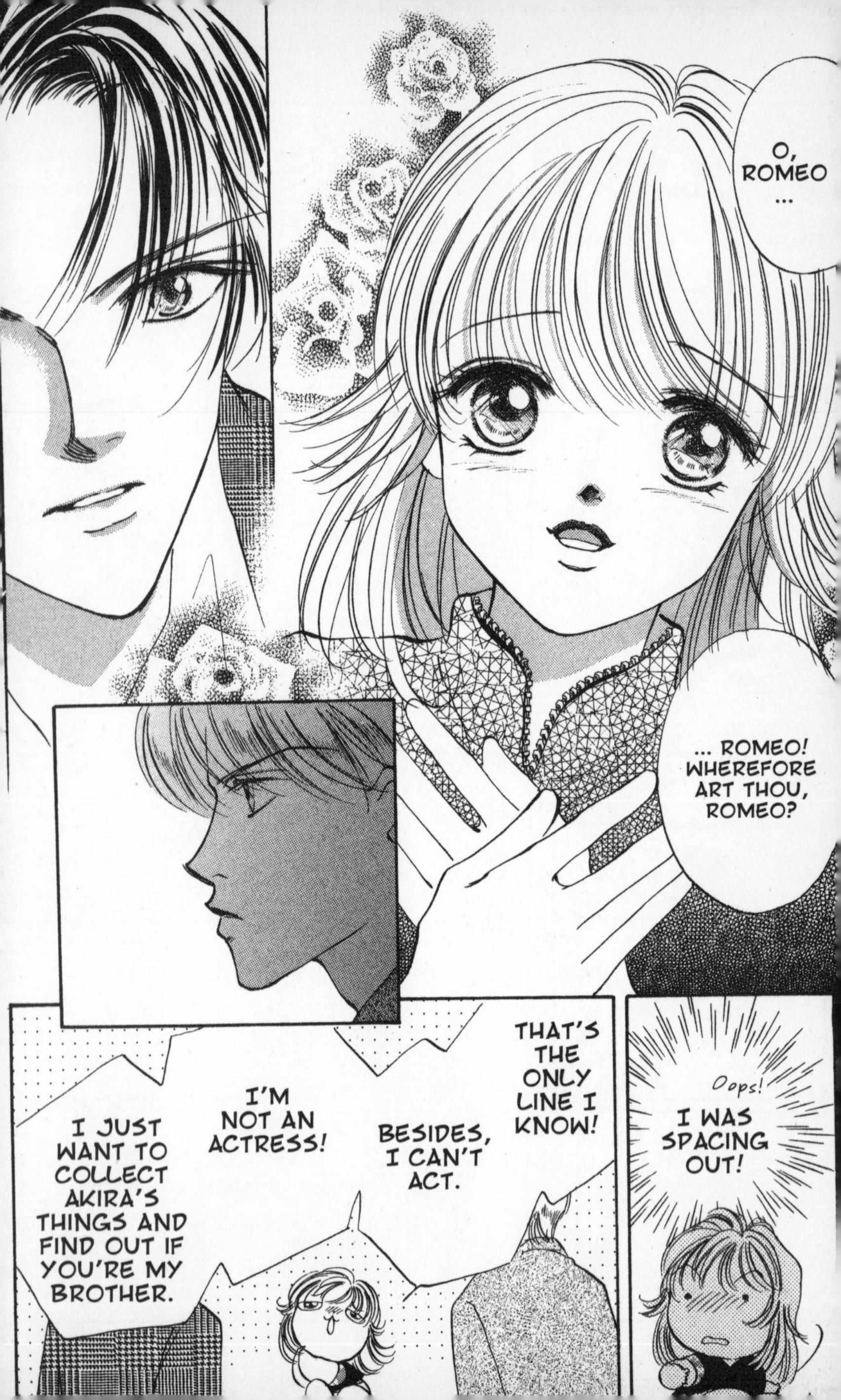
O, ROMEO ...
... ROMEO! WHEREFORE ART THOU, ROMEO?
Oops!
I WAS SPACING OUT!
THAT'S THE ONLY LINE I KNOW!
BESIDES, I CAN'T ACT.
I'M NOT AN ACTRESS!
I JUST WANT TO COLLECT AKIRA'S THINGS AND FIND OUT IF YOU'RE MY BROTHER.

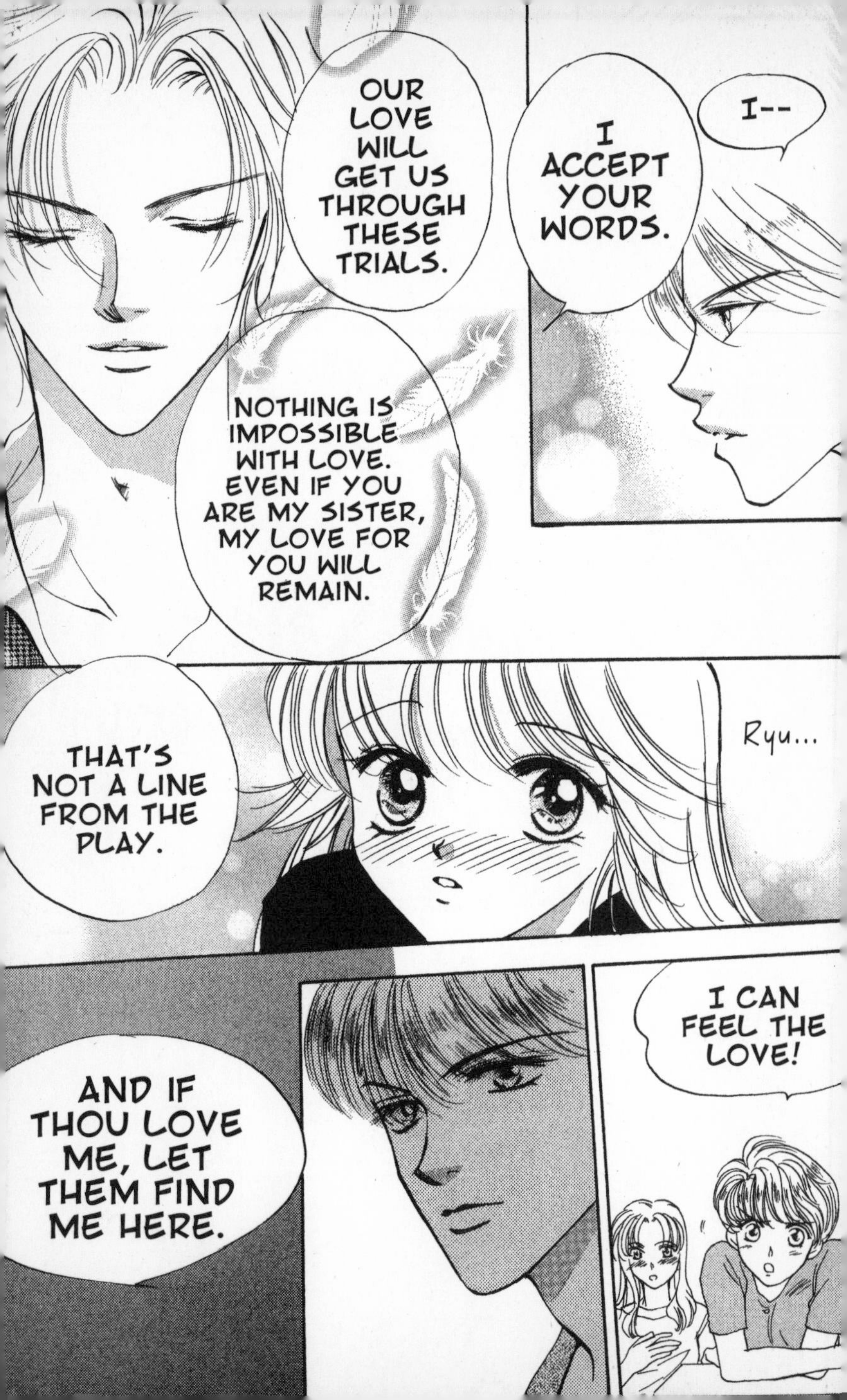
I--
I ACCEPT YOUR WORDS.
OUR LOVE WILL GET US THROUGH THESE TRIALS.
NOTHING IS IMPOSSIBLE WITH LOVE. EVEN IF YOU ARE MY SISTER, MY LOVE FOR YOU WILL REMAIN.
Ryu...
THAT'S NOT A LINE FROM THE PLAY.
I CAN FEEL THE LOVE!
AND IF THOU LOVE ME, LET THEM FIND ME HERE.

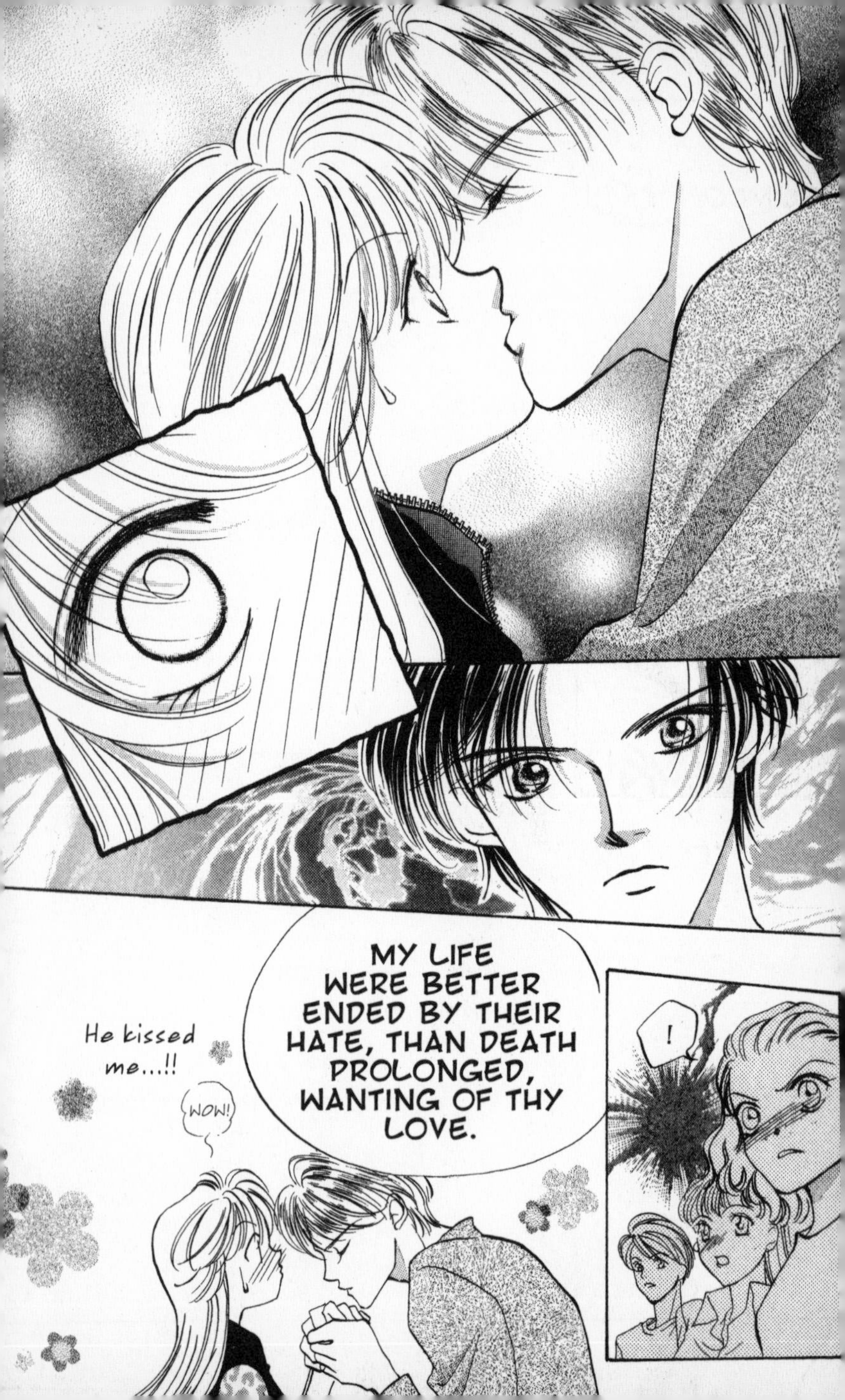
!
MY LIFE WERE BETTER ENDED BY THEIR HATE, THAN DEATH PROLONGED, WANTING OF THY LOVE.
He kissed me...!!
WOW!

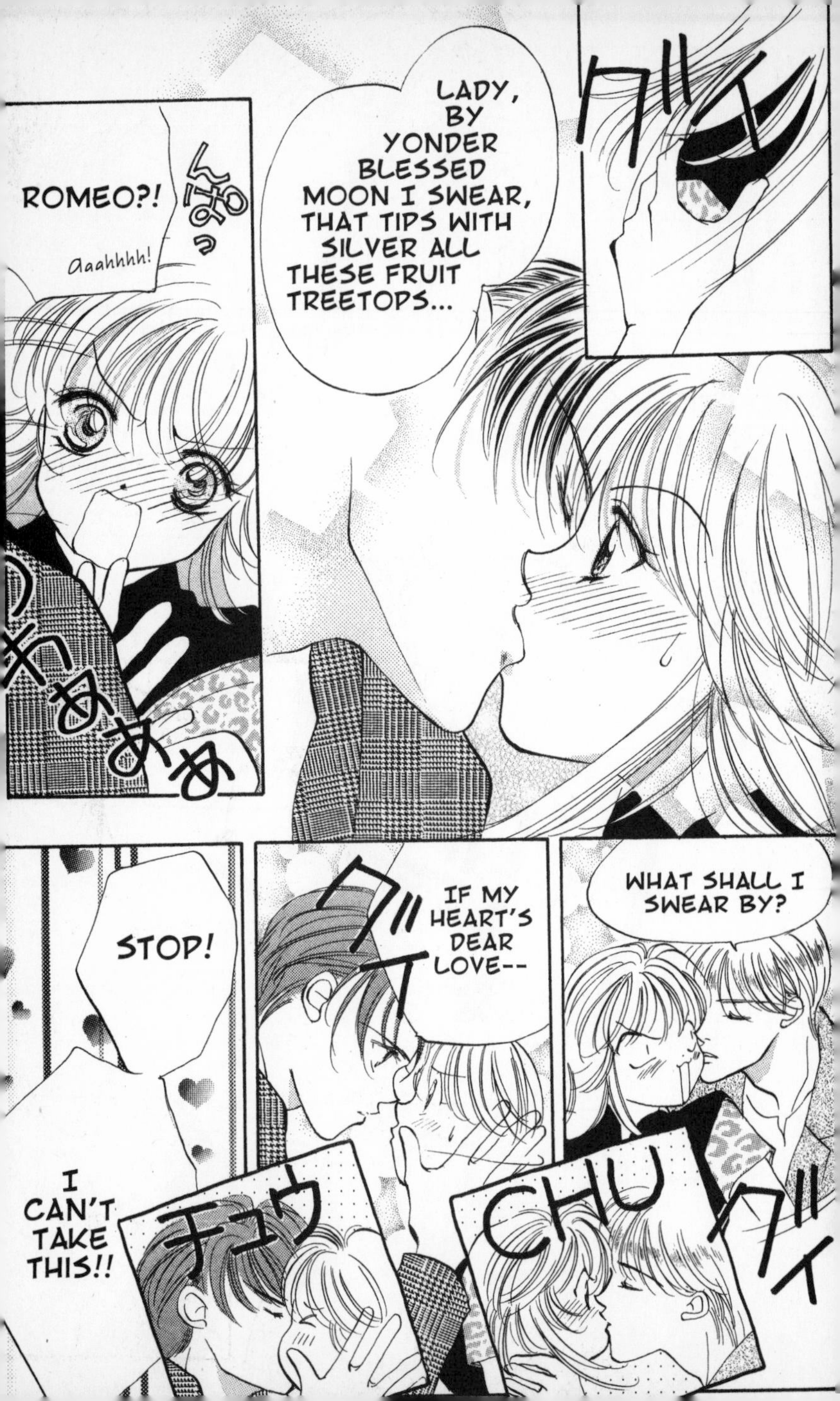

グイ
LADY, BY YONDER BLESSED MOON I SWEAR, THAT TIPS WITH SILVER ALL THESE FRUIT TREETOPS...
ROMEO?!
Aaahhhh!
WHAT SHALL I SWEAR BY?
IF MY HEART'S DEAR LOVE--
グイ
STOP!
I CAN'T TAKE THIS!!
グイ
CHU
チュウ

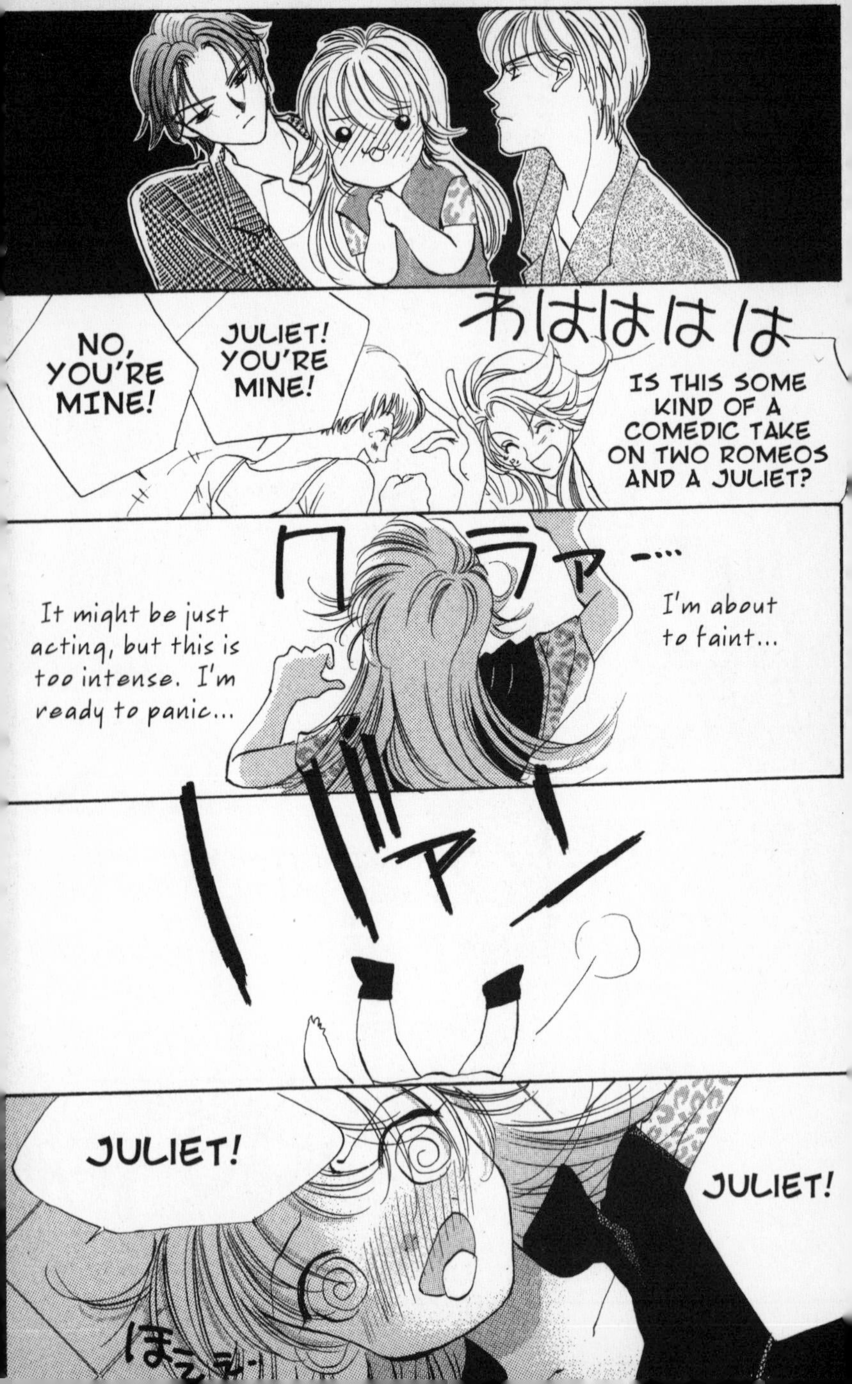
わはははは
IS THIS SOME KIND OF A COMEDIC TAKE ON TWO ROMEOS AND A JULIET?
JULIET! YOU'RE MINE!
NO, YOU'RE MINE!
ワラァー…
I'm about to faint...
It might be just acting, but this is too intense. I'm ready to panic...
バァー
JULIET!
JULIET!
ほえぇー

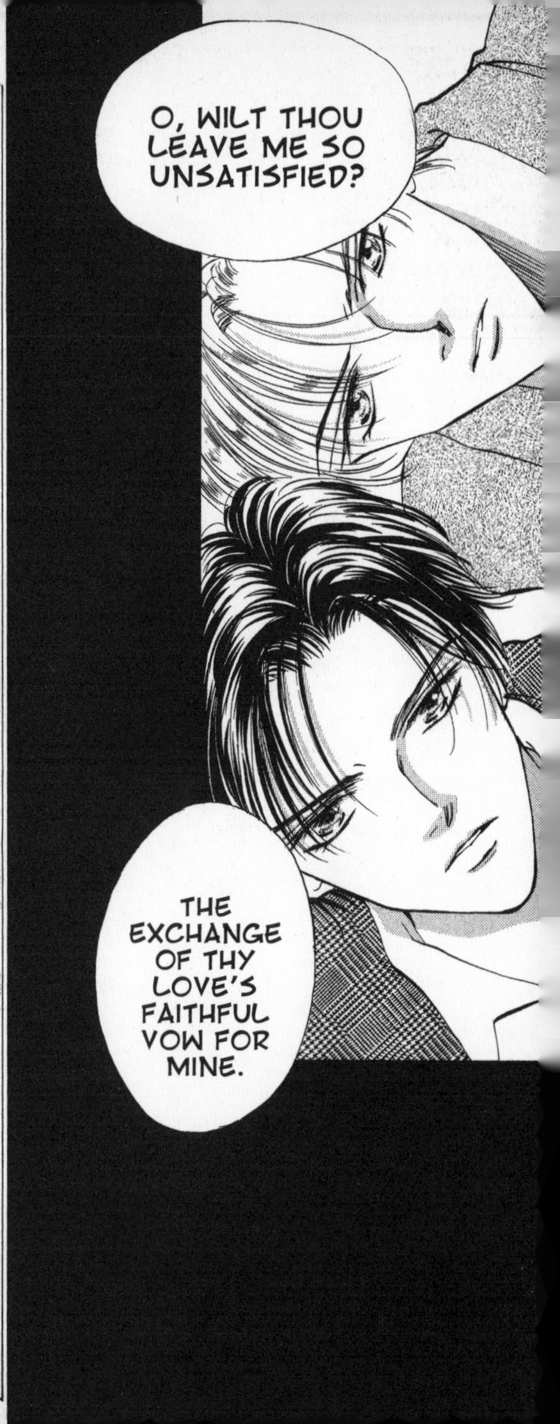
O, WILT THOU LEAVE ME SO UNSATISFIED?
THE EXCHANGE OF THY LOVE'S FAITHFUL VOW FOR MINE.

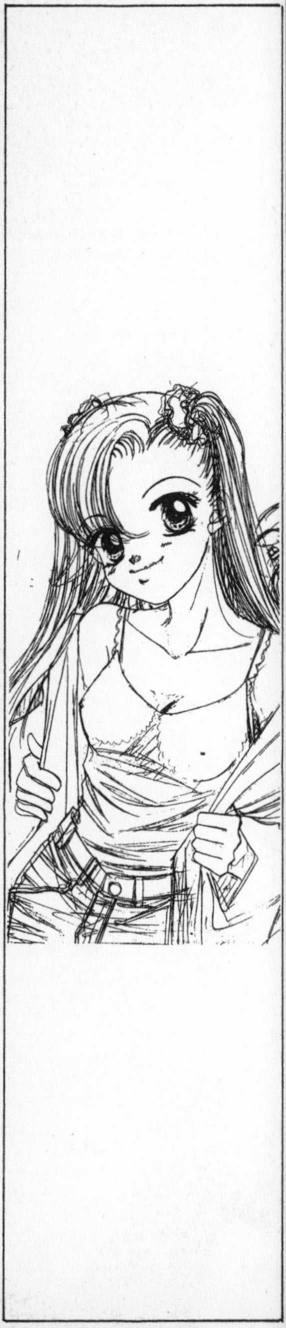

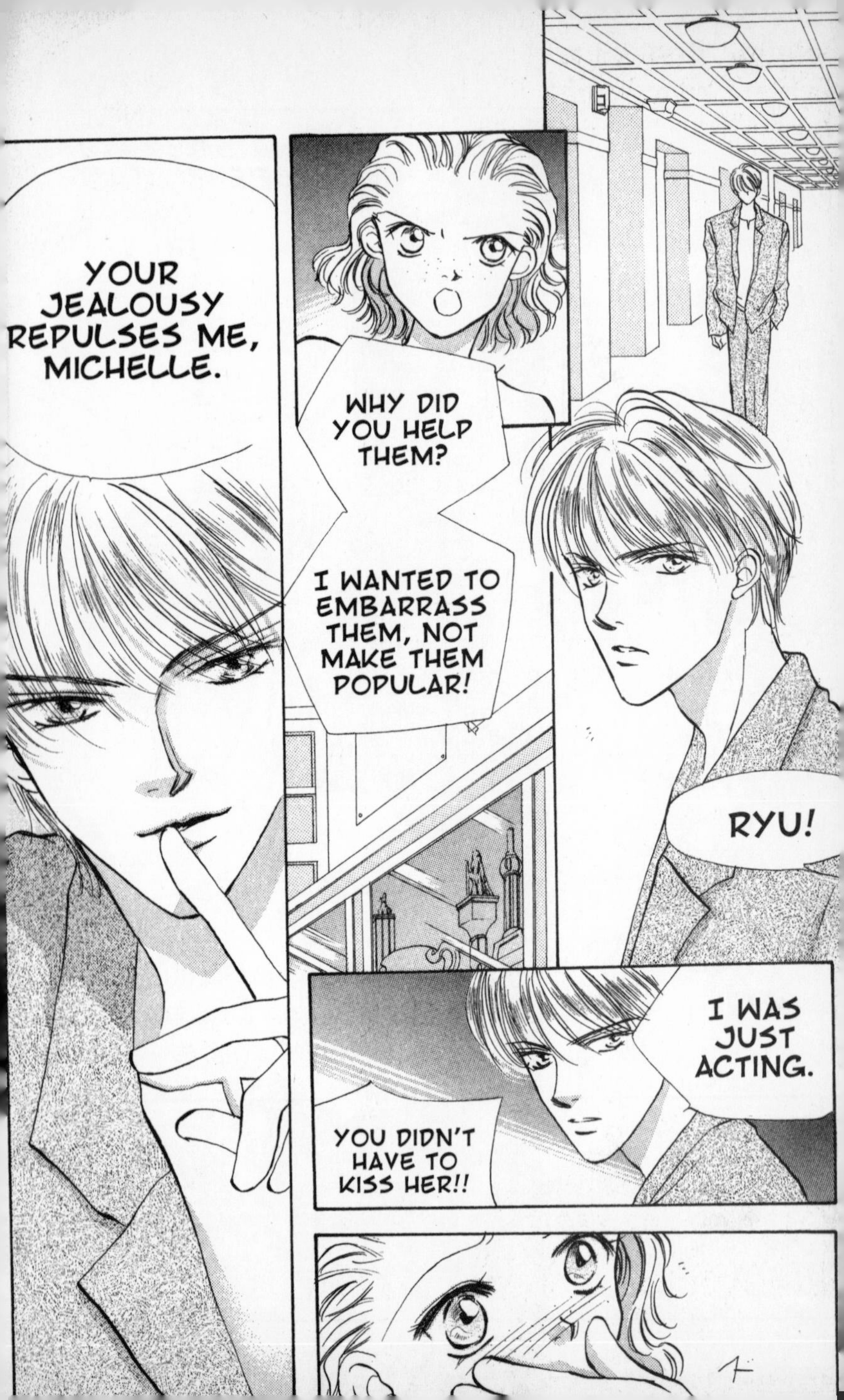
RYU!
WHY DID YOU HELP THEM?
I WANTED TO EMBARRASS THEM, NOT MAKE THEM POPULAR!
I WAS JUST ACTING.
YOU DIDN'T HAVE TO KISS HER!!
YOUR JEALOUSY REPULSES ME, MICHELLE.

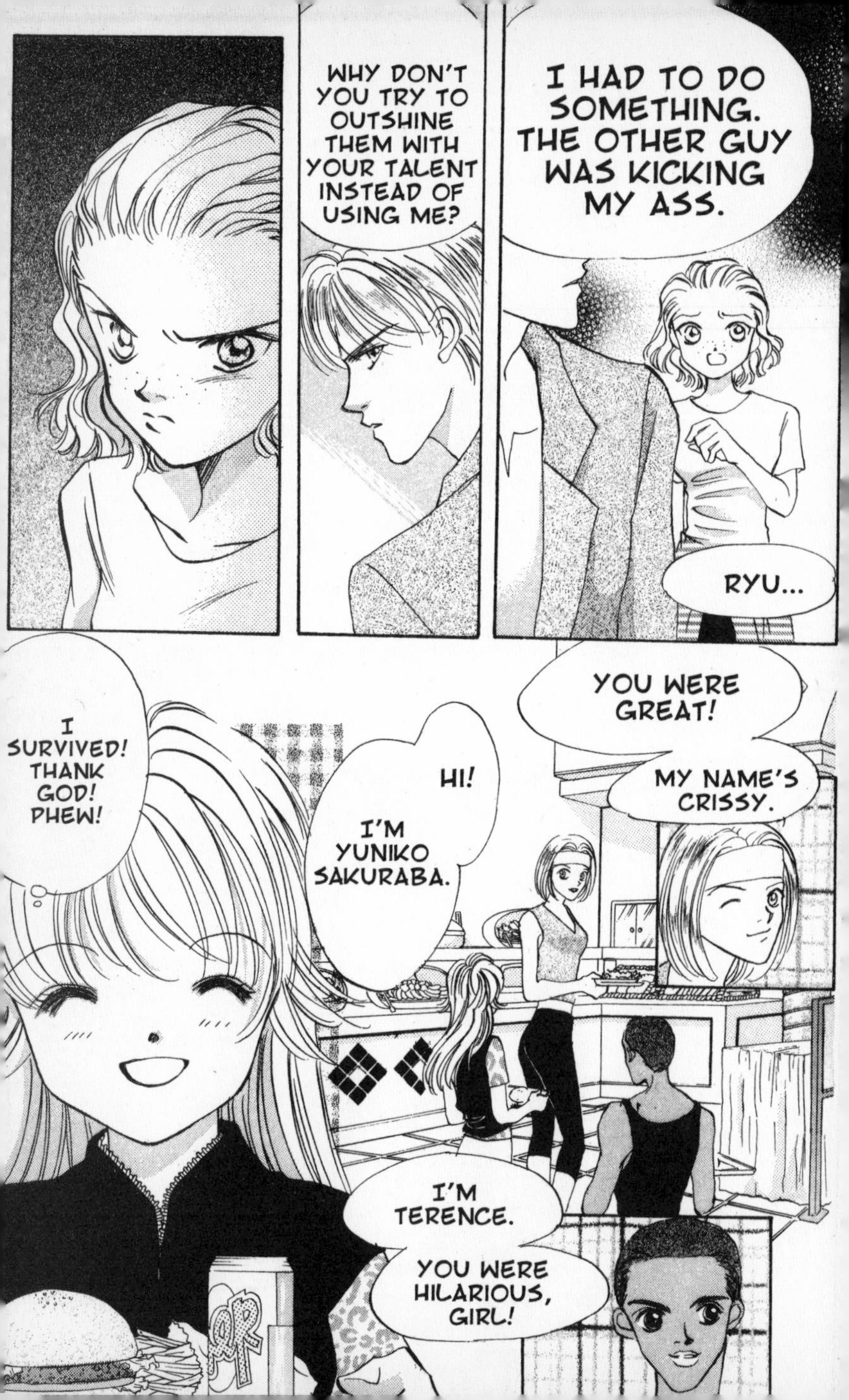
I HAD TO DO SOMETHING. THE OTHER GUY WAS KICKING MY ASS.
RYU...
WHY DON'T YOU TRY TO OUTSHINE THEM WITH YOUR TALENT INSTEAD OF USING ME?
YOU WERE GREAT!
MY NAME'S CRISSY.
HI!
I'M YUNIKO SAKURABA.
I SURVIVED! THANK GOD! PHEW!
I'M TERENCE.
YOU WERE HILARIOUS, GIRL!

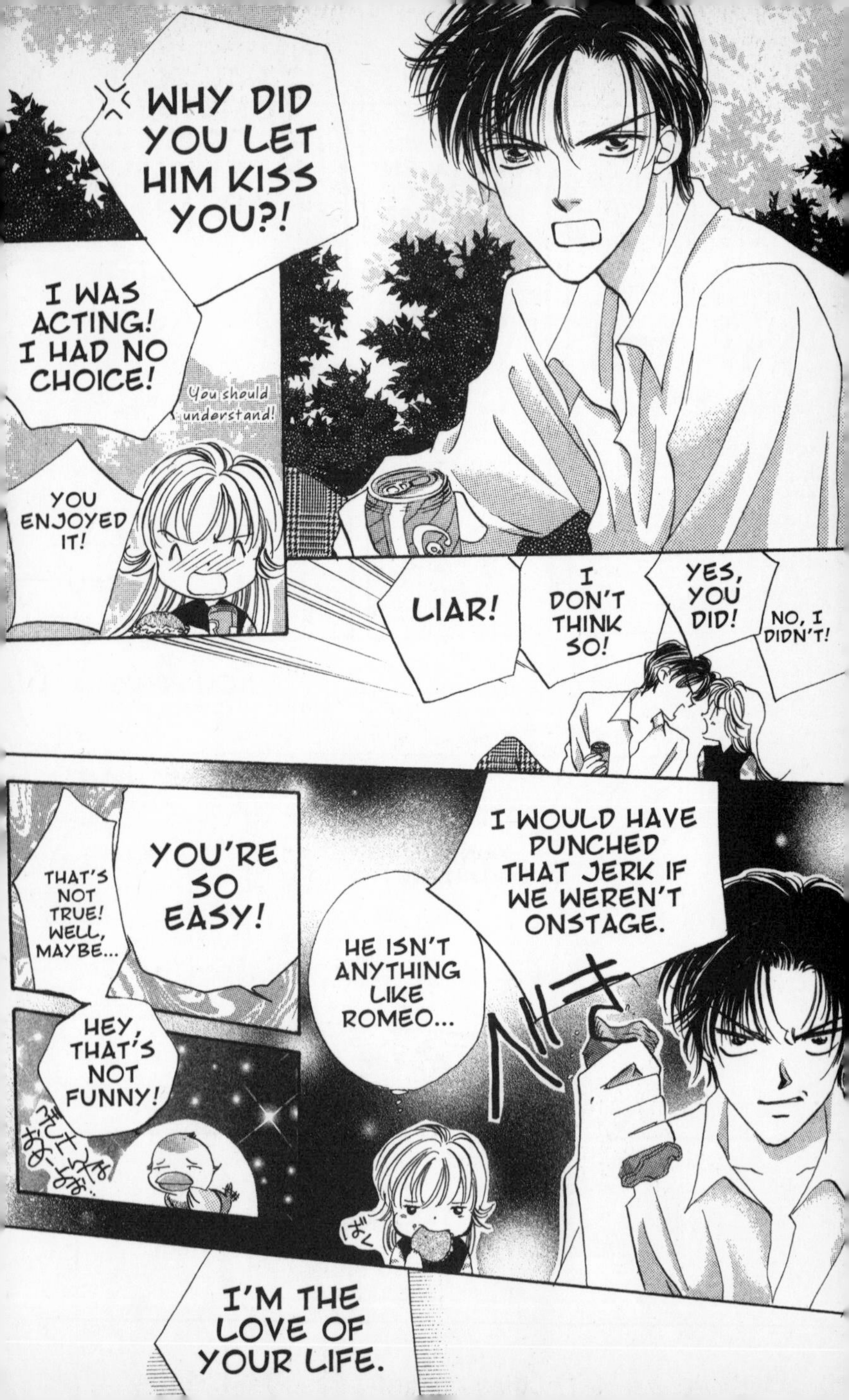
WHY DID YOU LET HIM KISS YOU?!
I WAS ACTING! I HAD NO CHOICE!
You should understand!
YOU ENJOYED IT!
NO, I DIDN'T!
YES, YOU DID!
I DON'T THINK SO!
LIAR!
I WOULD HAVE PUNCHED THAT JERK IF WE WEREN'T ONSTAGE.
HE ISN'T ANYTHING LIKE ROMEO...
YOU'RE SO EASY!
THAT'S NOT TRUE! WELL, MAYBE...
HEY, THAT'S NOT FUNNY!
I'M THE LOVE OF YOUR LIFE.

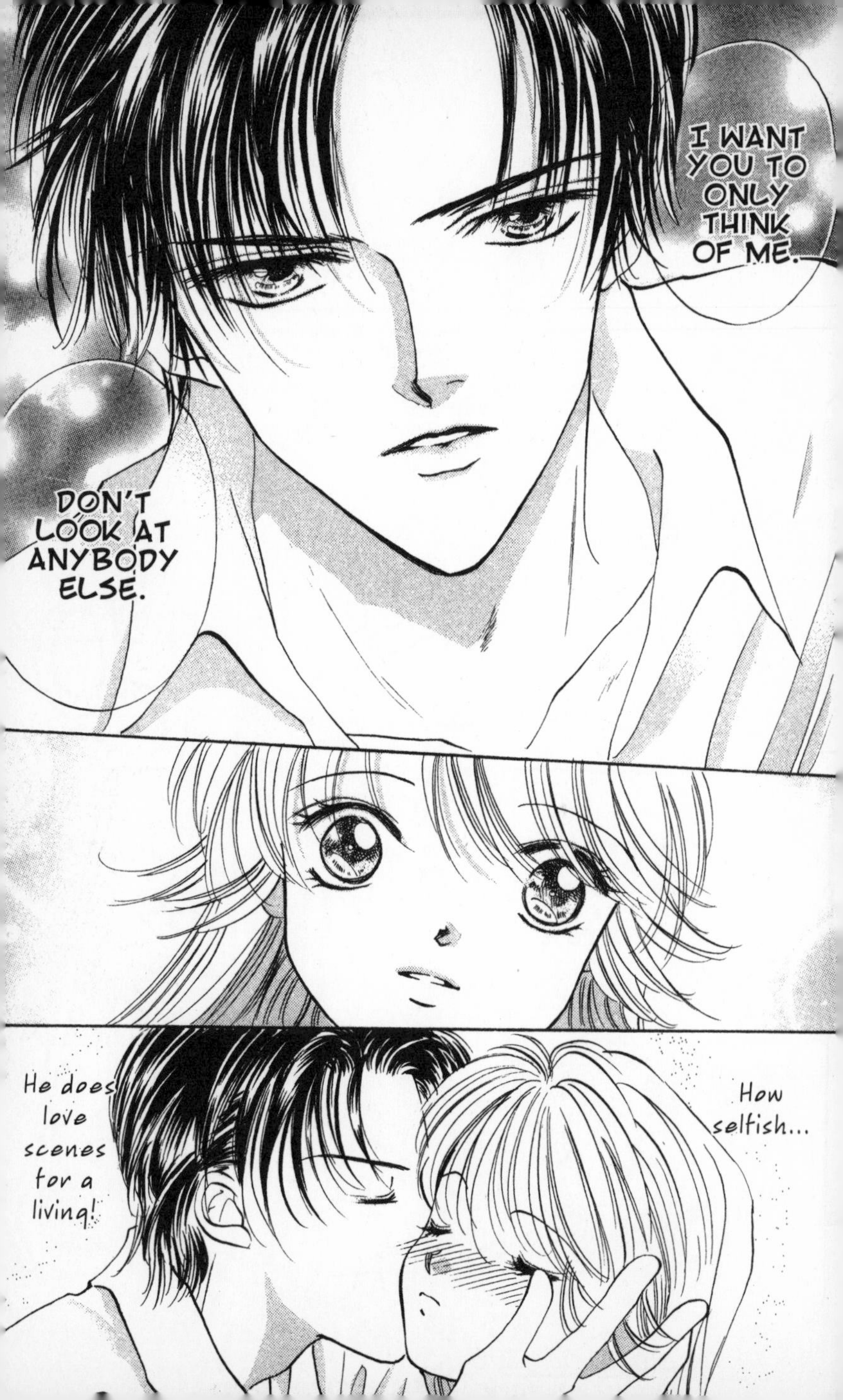
I WANT YOU TO ONLY THINK OF ME.
DON'T LOOK AT ANYBODY ELSE.
How selfish...
He does love scenes for a living!

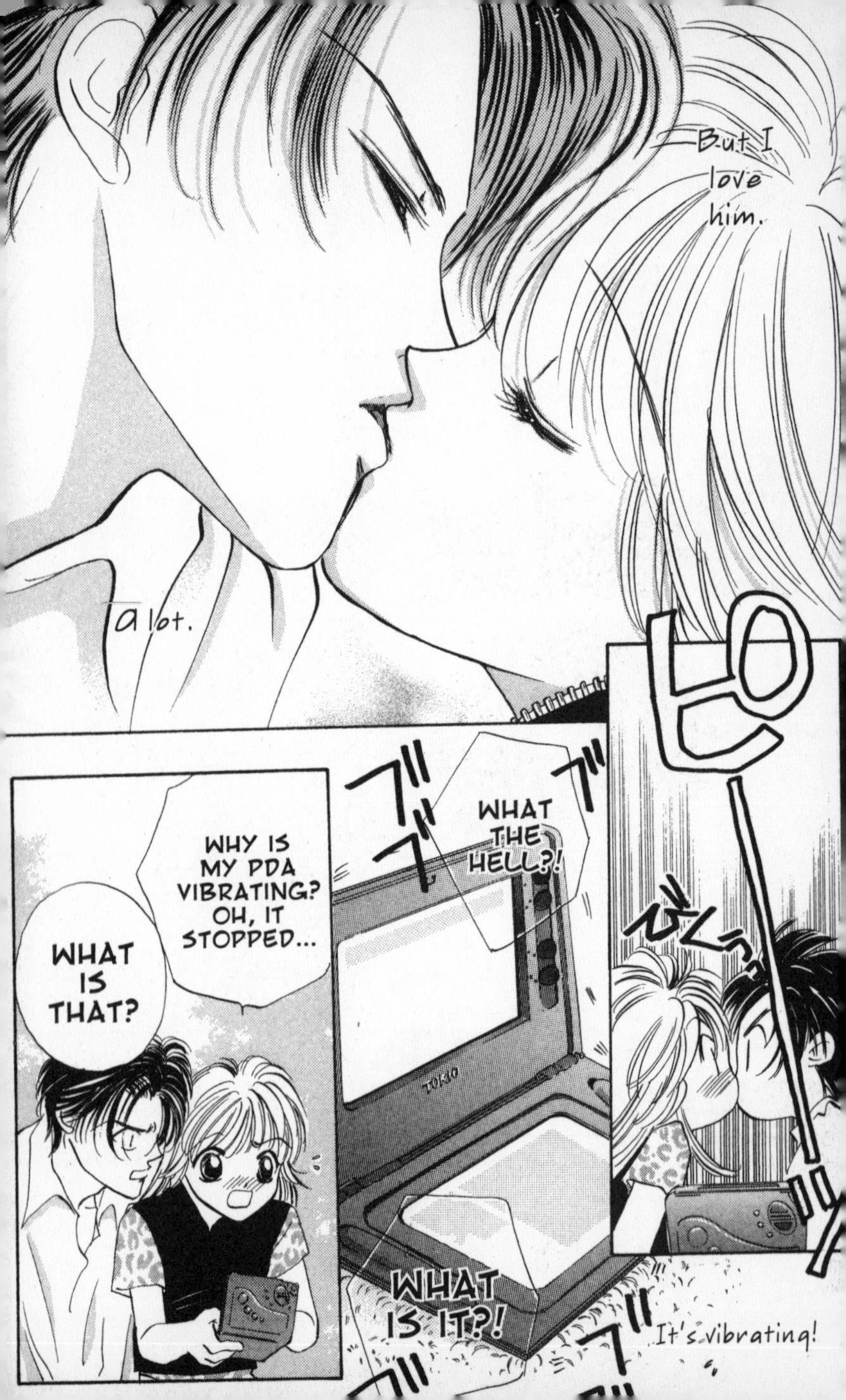

But I love him.
a lot.
It's vibrating!
WHAT THE HELL?!
WHAT IS IT?!
WHY IS MY PDA VIBRATING? OH, IT STOPPED...
WHAT IS THAT?

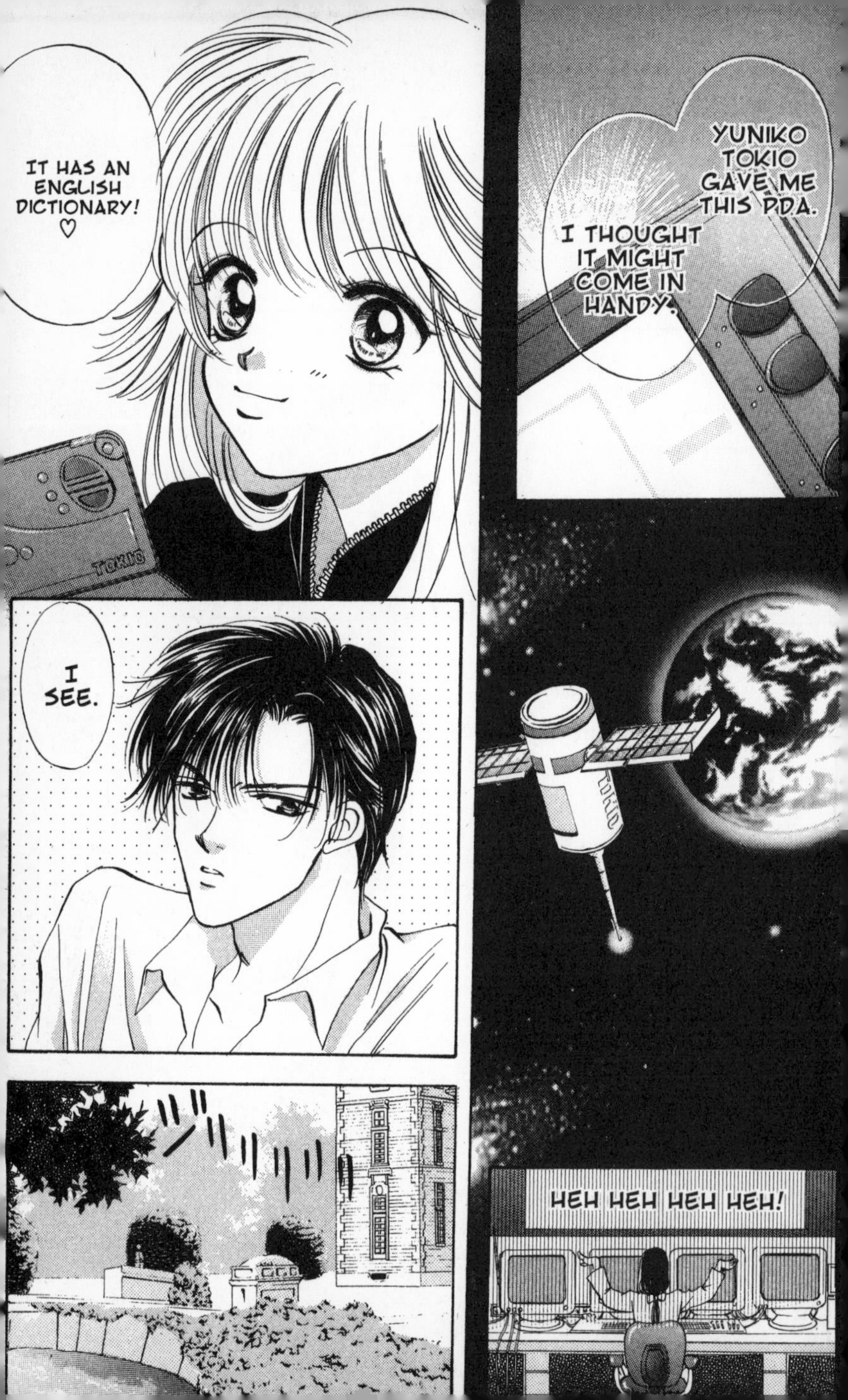
YUNIKO TOKIO GAVE ME THIS PDA.
I THOUGHT IT MIGHT COME IN HANDY.
IT HAS AN ENGLISH DICTIONARY! ♡
I SEE.
TOKIO
HEH HEH HEH HEH!

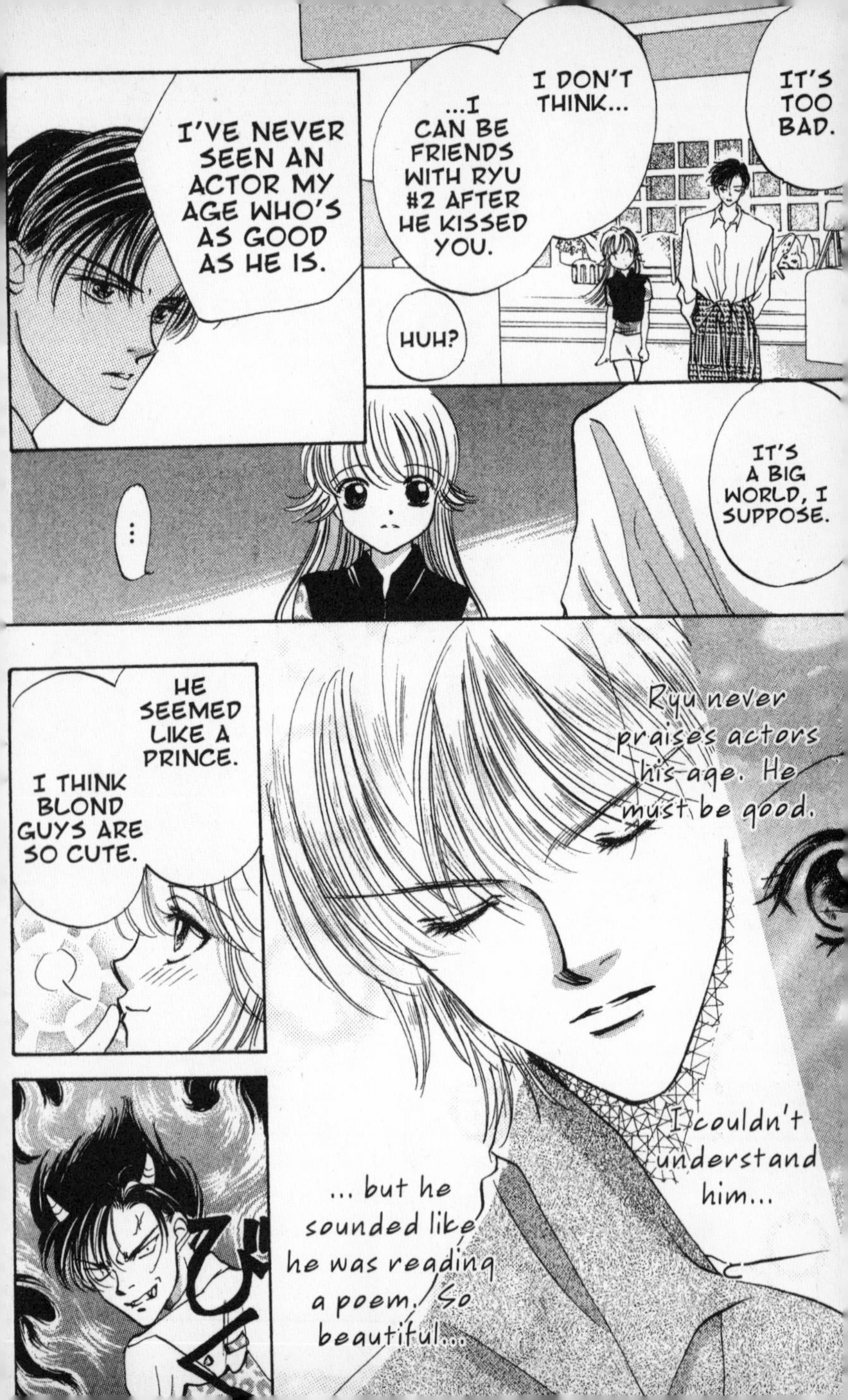
IT'S TOO BAD.
I DON'T THINK...
...I CAN BE FRIENDS WITH RYU #2 AFTER HE KISSED YOU.
HUH?
I'VE NEVER SEEN AN ACTOR MY AGE WHO'S AS GOOD AS HE IS.
IT'S A BIG WORLD, I SUPPOSE.
...
Ryu never praises actors his age. He must be good.
I couldn't understand him...
... but he sounded like he was reading a poem. So beautiful...
HE SEEMED LIKE A PRINCE.
I THINK BLOND GUYS ARE SO CUTE.

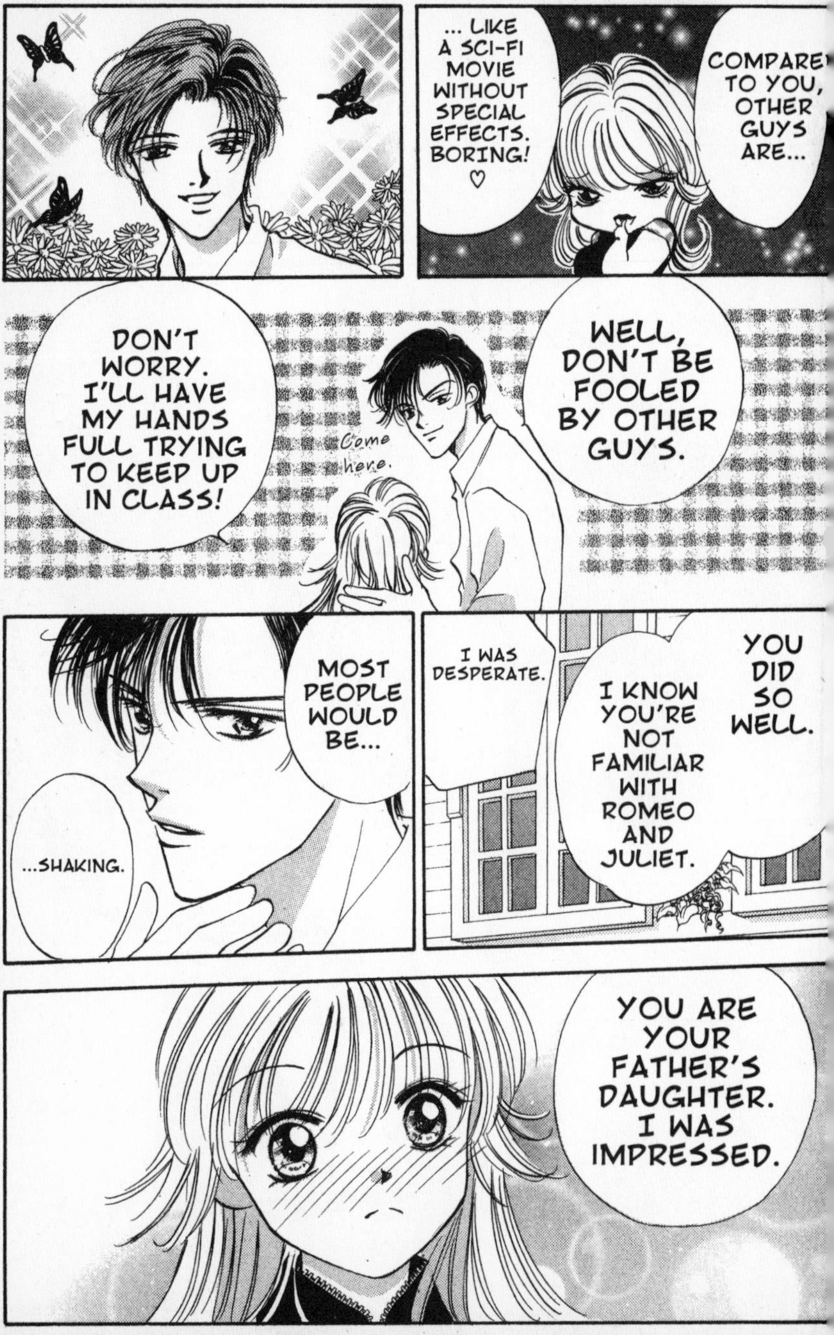
COMPARE
TO YOU, OTHER GUYS ARE...
... LIKE A SCI-FI MOVIE WITHOUT SPECIAL EFFECTS. BORING! ♡
WELL, DON'T BE FOOLED BY OTHER GUYS.
Come here.
DON'T WORRY. I'LL HAVE MY HANDS FULL TRYING TO KEEP UP IN CLASS!
YOU DID SO WELL.
I KNOW YOU'RE NOT FAMILIAR WITH ROMEO AND JULIET.
I WAS DESPERATE.
MOST PEOPLE WOULD BE...
...SHAKING.
YOU ARE YOUR FATHER'S DAUGHTER. I WAS IMPRESSED.

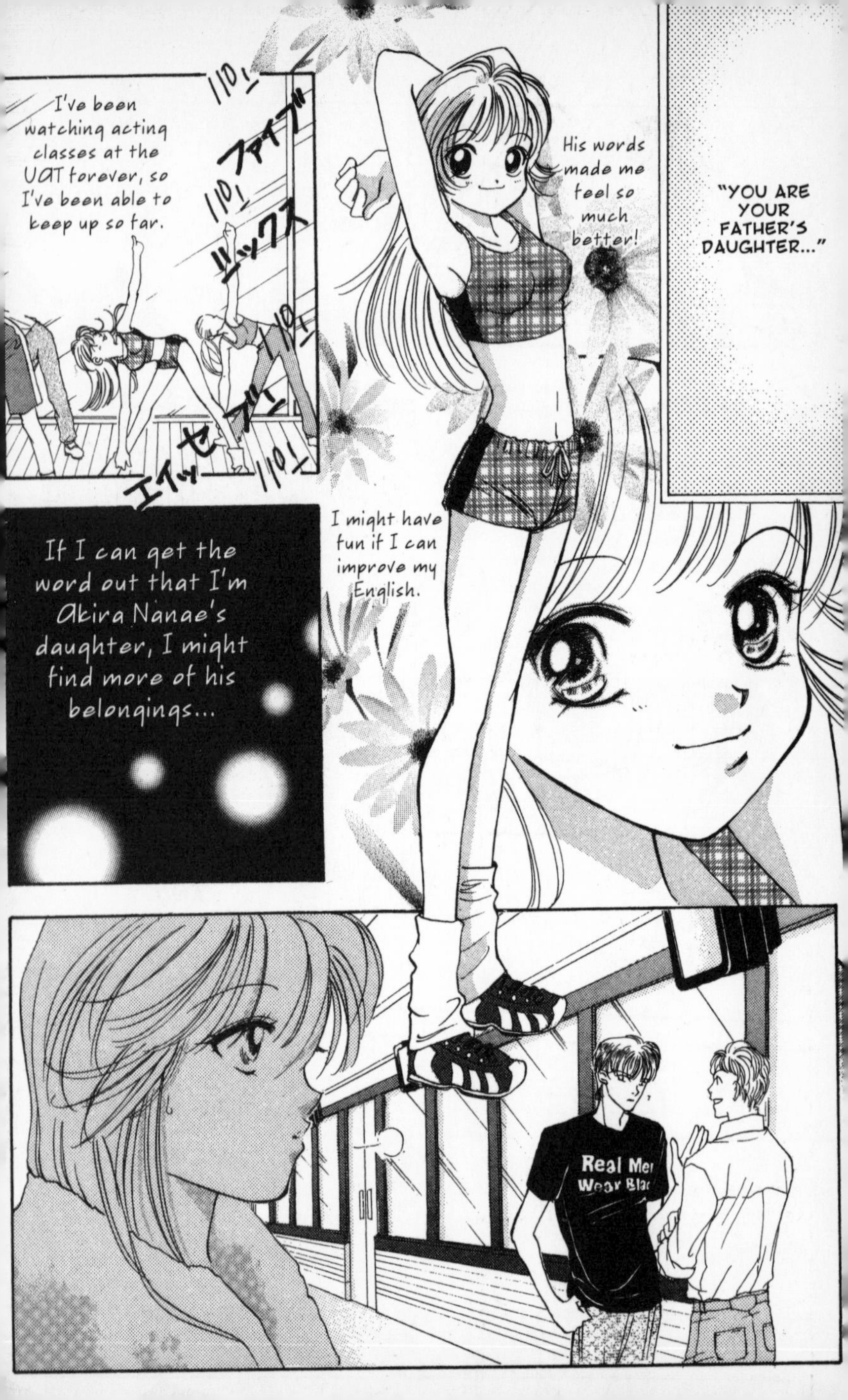

"YOU ARE YOUR FATHER'S DAUGHTER..."
His words made me feel so much better!
I've been watching acting classes at the UAT forever, so I've been able to keep up so far.
ハイッ ファイブ
ハイッ シックス
ハイッ セブン
エイッ
I might have fun if I can improve my English.
If I can get the word out that I'm Akira Nanae's daughter, I might find more of his belongings...

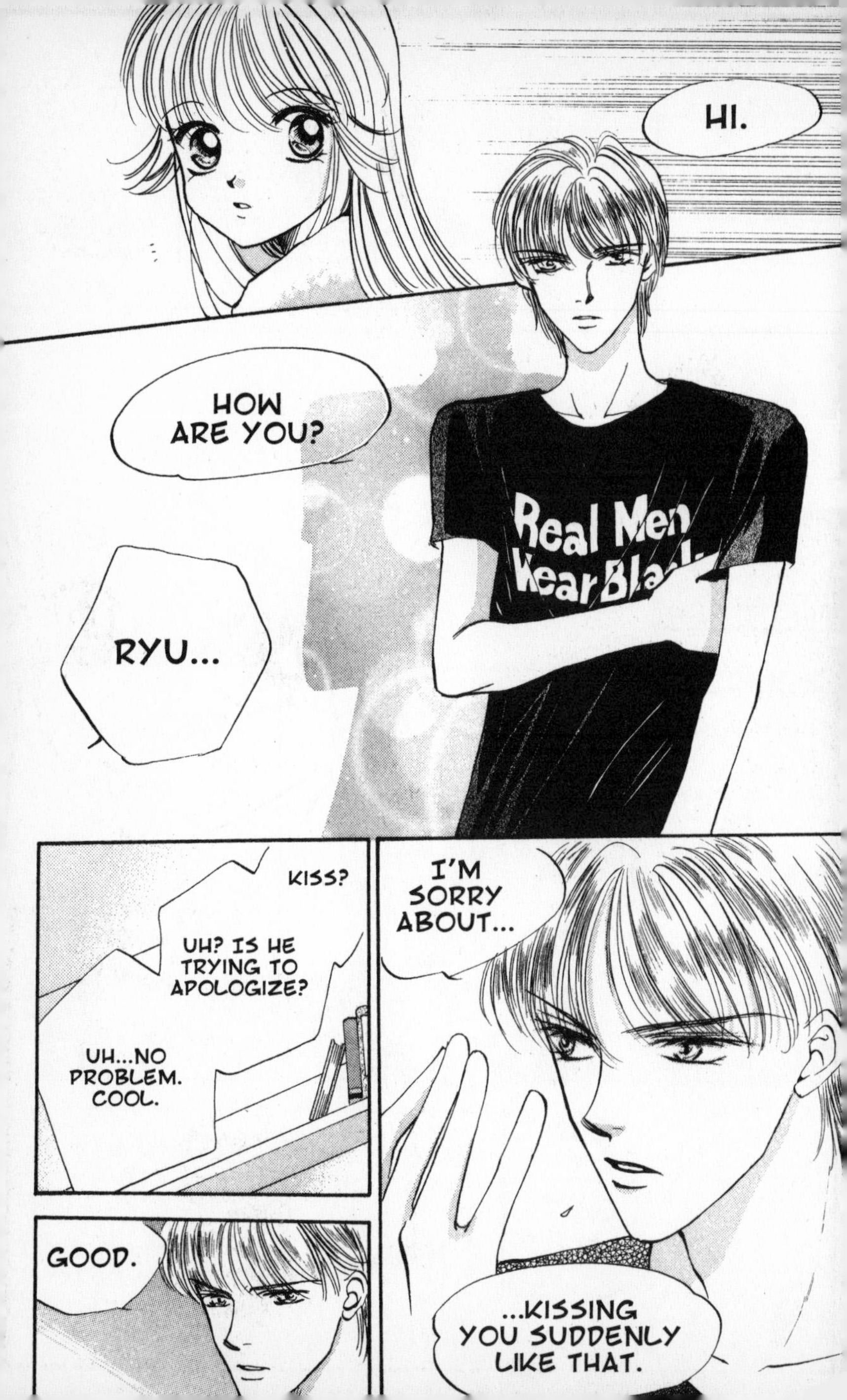
HI.
HOW ARE YOU?
RYU...
Real Men
I'M SORRY ABOUT...
...KISSING YOU SUDDENLY LIKE THAT.
KISS?
UH? IS HE TRYING TO APOLOGIZE?
UH...NO PROBLEM. COOL.
GOOD.

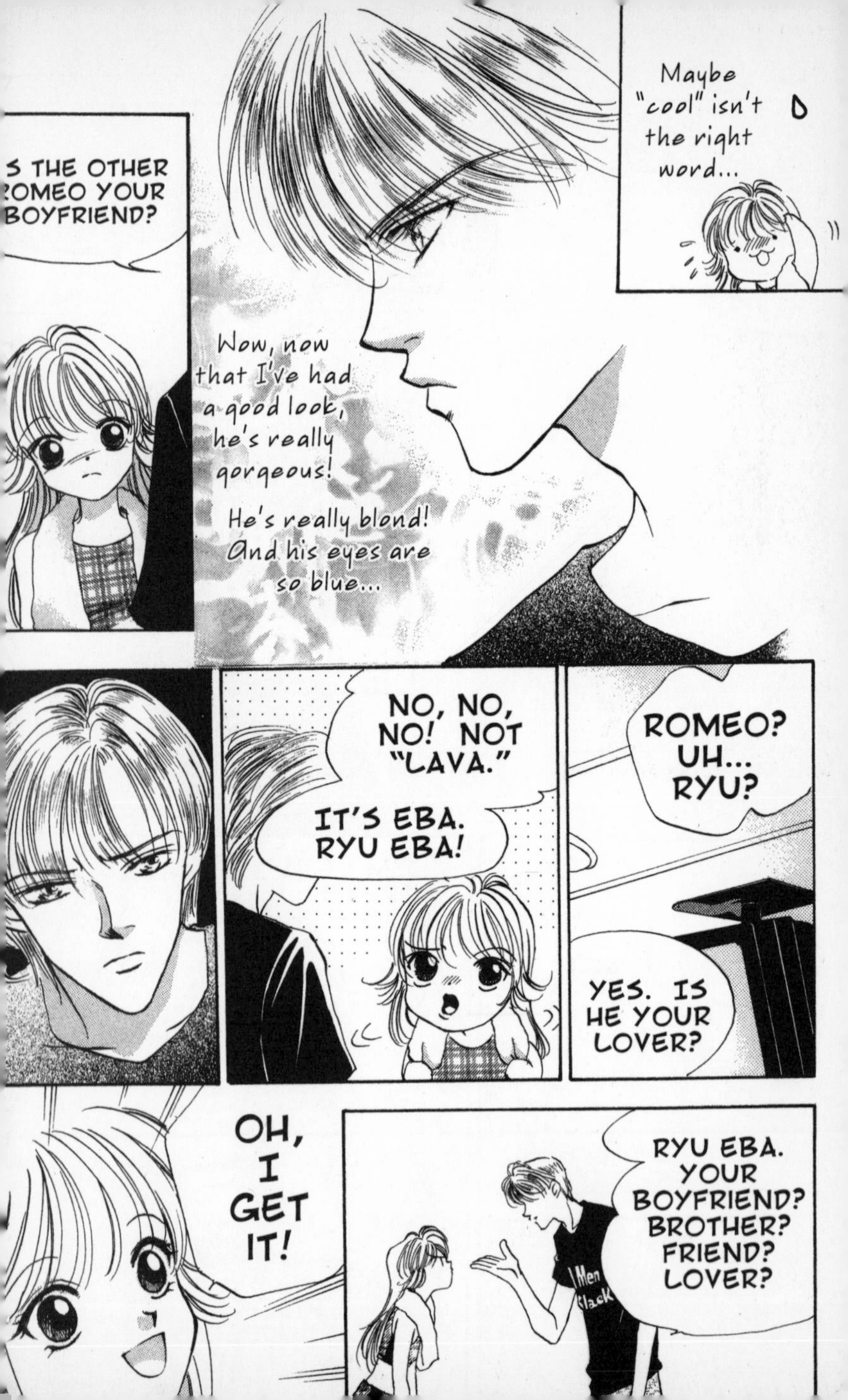
Maybe "cool" isn't the right word...
Wow, now that I've had a good look, he's really gorgeous!
He's really blond! And his eyes are so blue...
S THE OTHER
OMEO YOUR
BOYFRIEND?
ROMEO? UH... RYU?
YES. IS HE YOUR LOVER?
NO, NO, NO! NOT "LAVA."
IT'S EBA. RYU EBA!
RYU EBA. YOUR BOYFRIEND? BROTHER? FRIEND? LOVER?
OH, I GET IT!

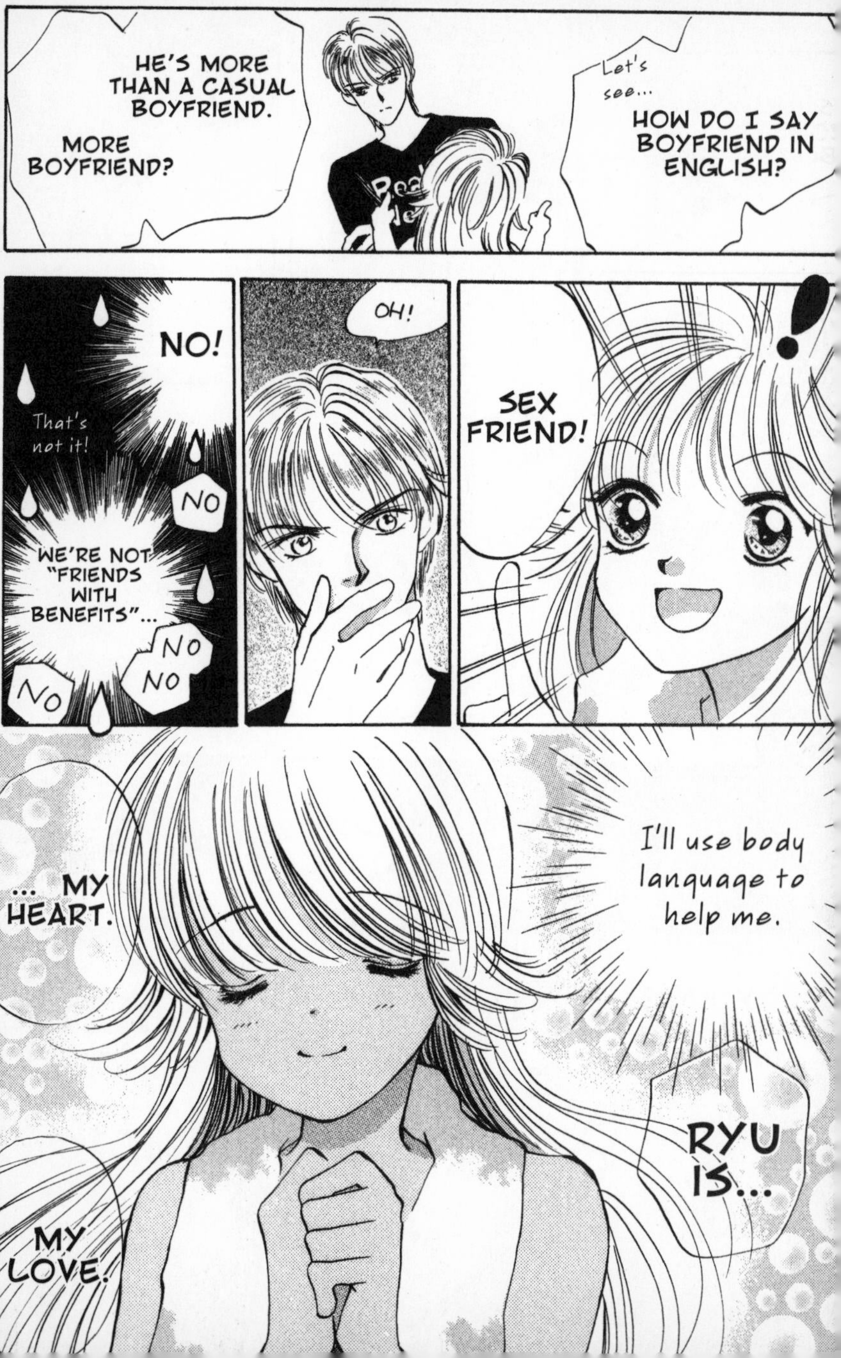
Let's see...
HOW DO I SAY BOYFRIEND IN ENGLISH?
HE'S MORE THAN A CASUAL BOYFRIEND.
MORE BOYFRIEND?
SEX FRIEND!
OH!
NO!
That's not it!
NO
WE'RE NOT "FRIENDS WITH BENEFITS"...
NO
NO
NO
I'll use body language to help me.
RYU IS...
... MY HEART.
MY LOVE.

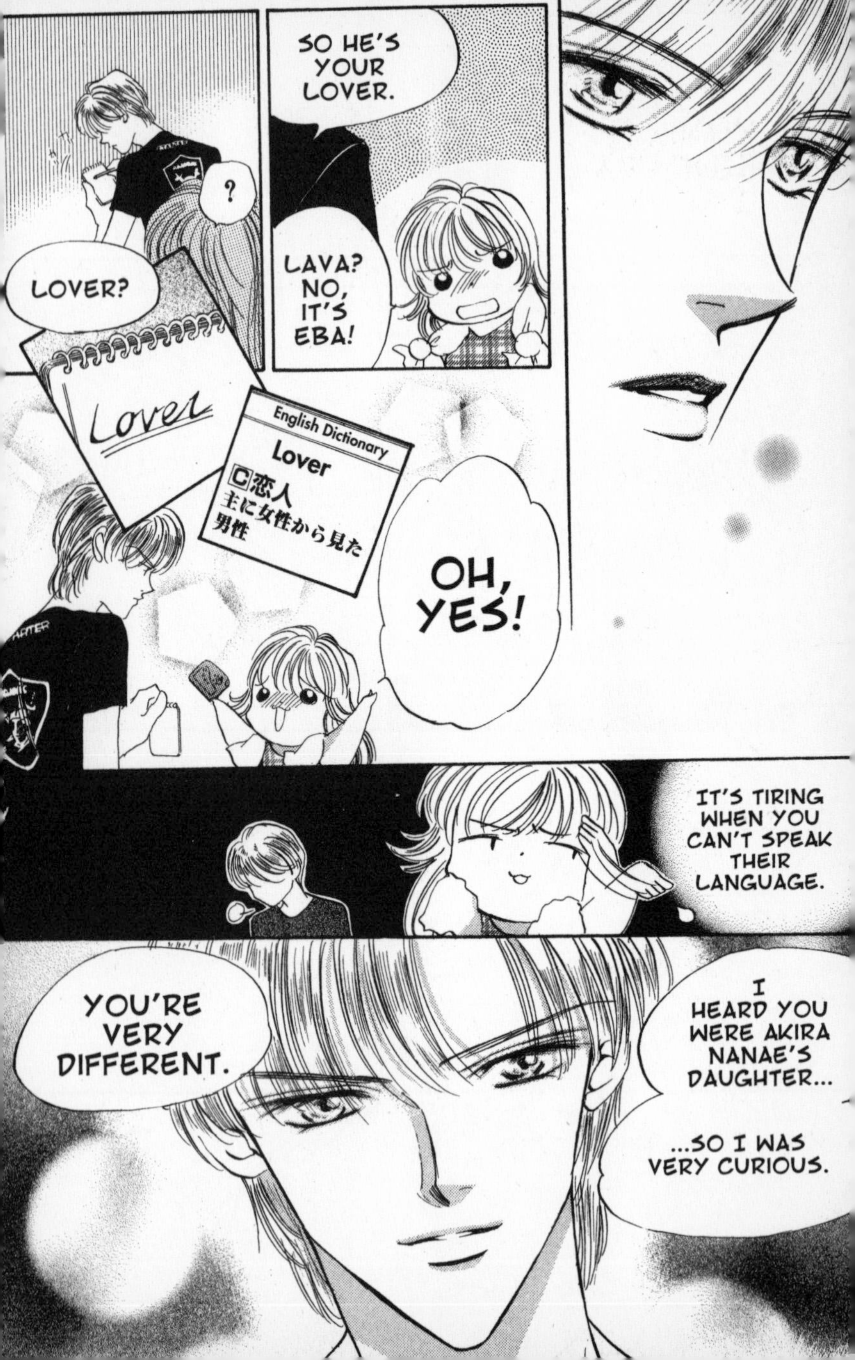
SO HE'S YOUR LOVER.
LAVA? NO, IT'S EBA!
?
LOVER?
Lover
English Dictionary
Lover
C 恋人
主に女性から見た男性
OH, YES!
IT'S TIRING WHEN YOU CAN'T SPEAK THEIR LANGUAGE.
I HEARD YOU WERE AKIRA NANAE'S DAUGHTER...
...SO I WAS VERY CURIOUS.
YOU'RE VERY DIFFERENT.

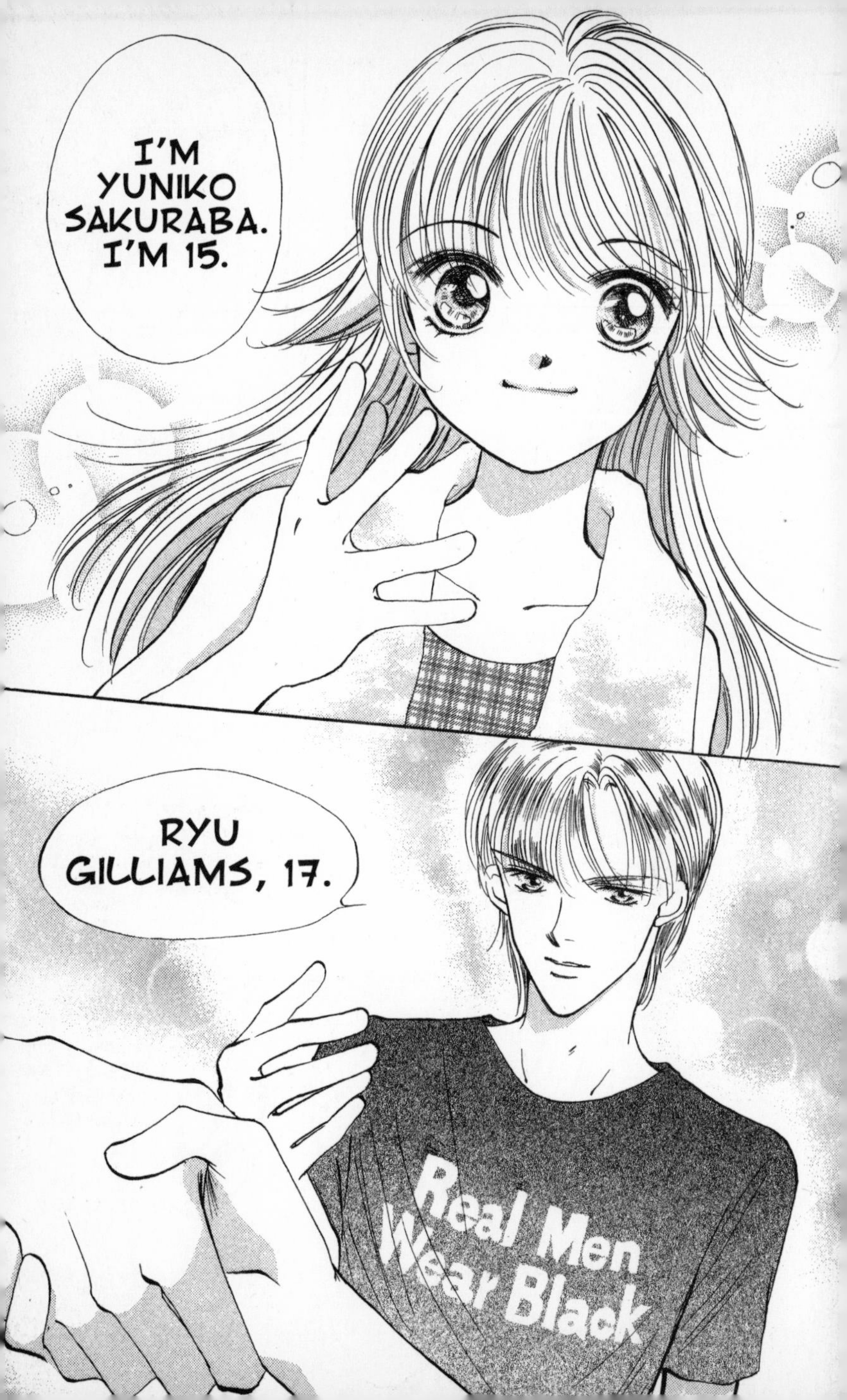
I'M YUNIKO SAKURABA. I'M 15.
RYU GILLIAMS, 17.
Real Men Wear Black

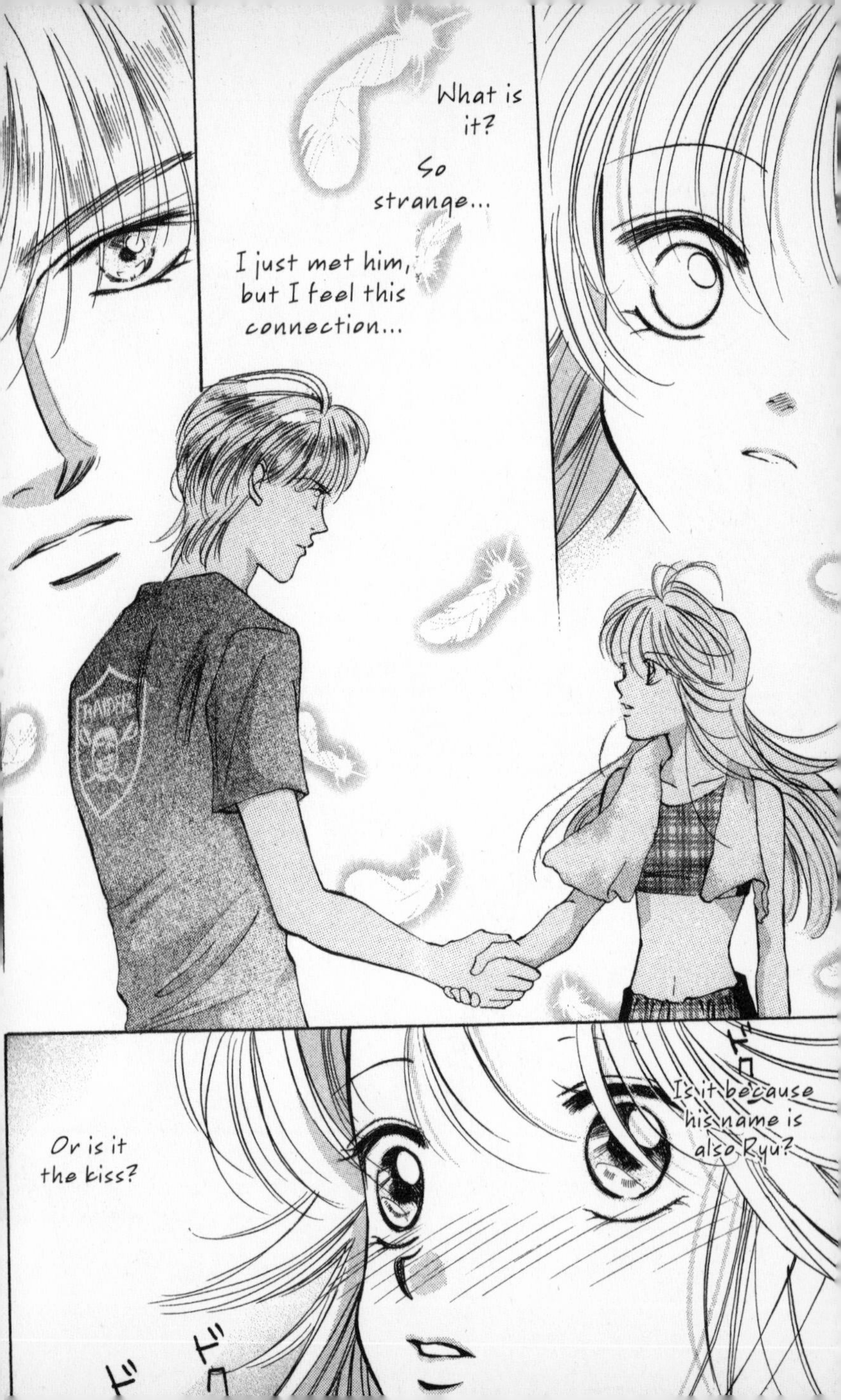
What is it?
So strange...
I just met him, but I feel this connection...
Is it because his name is also Ryu?
Or is it the kiss?

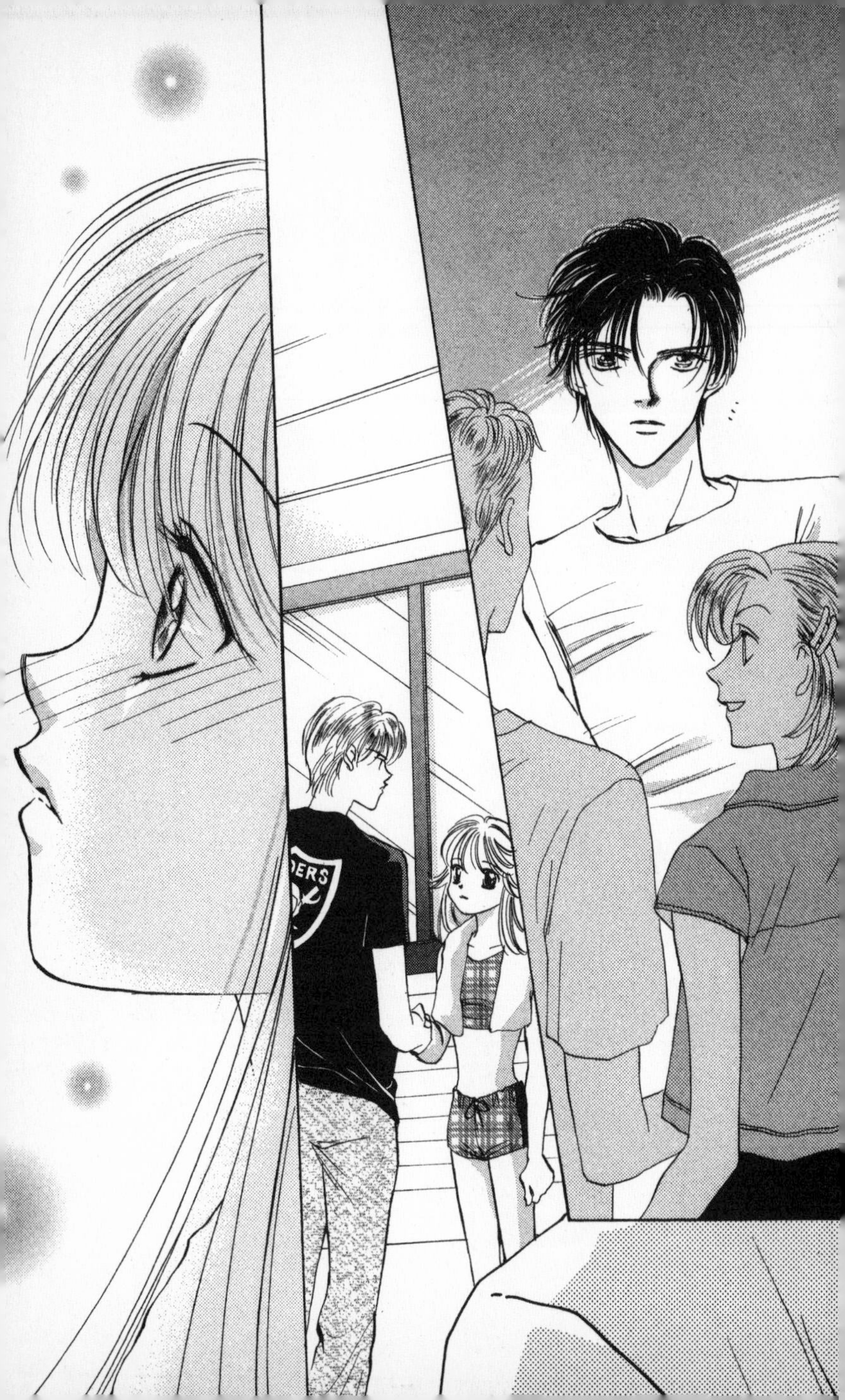
DERS

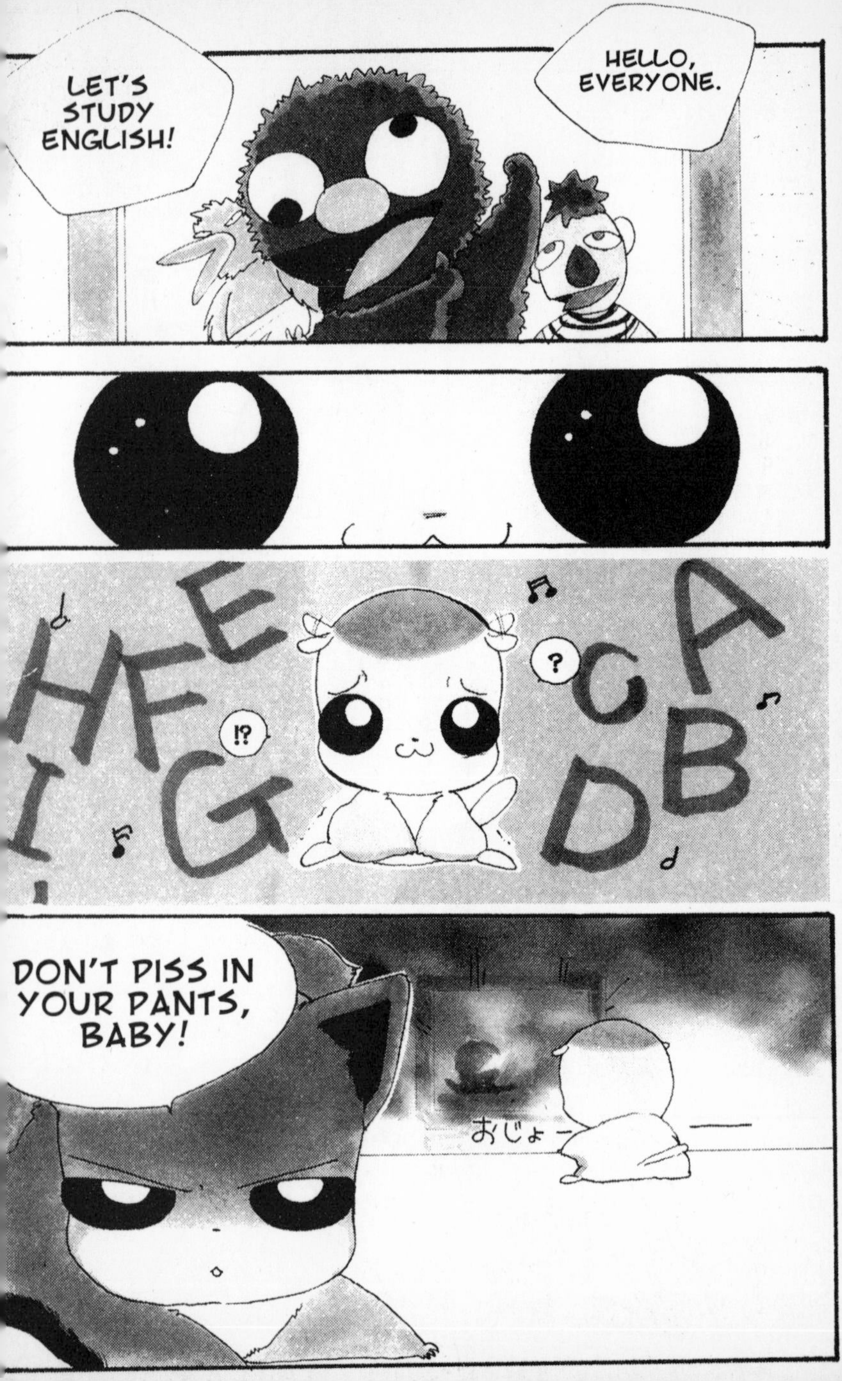
HELLO, EVERYONE.
LET'S STUDY ENGLISH!
?
!?
DON'T PISS IN YOUR PANTS, BABY!
おじょー

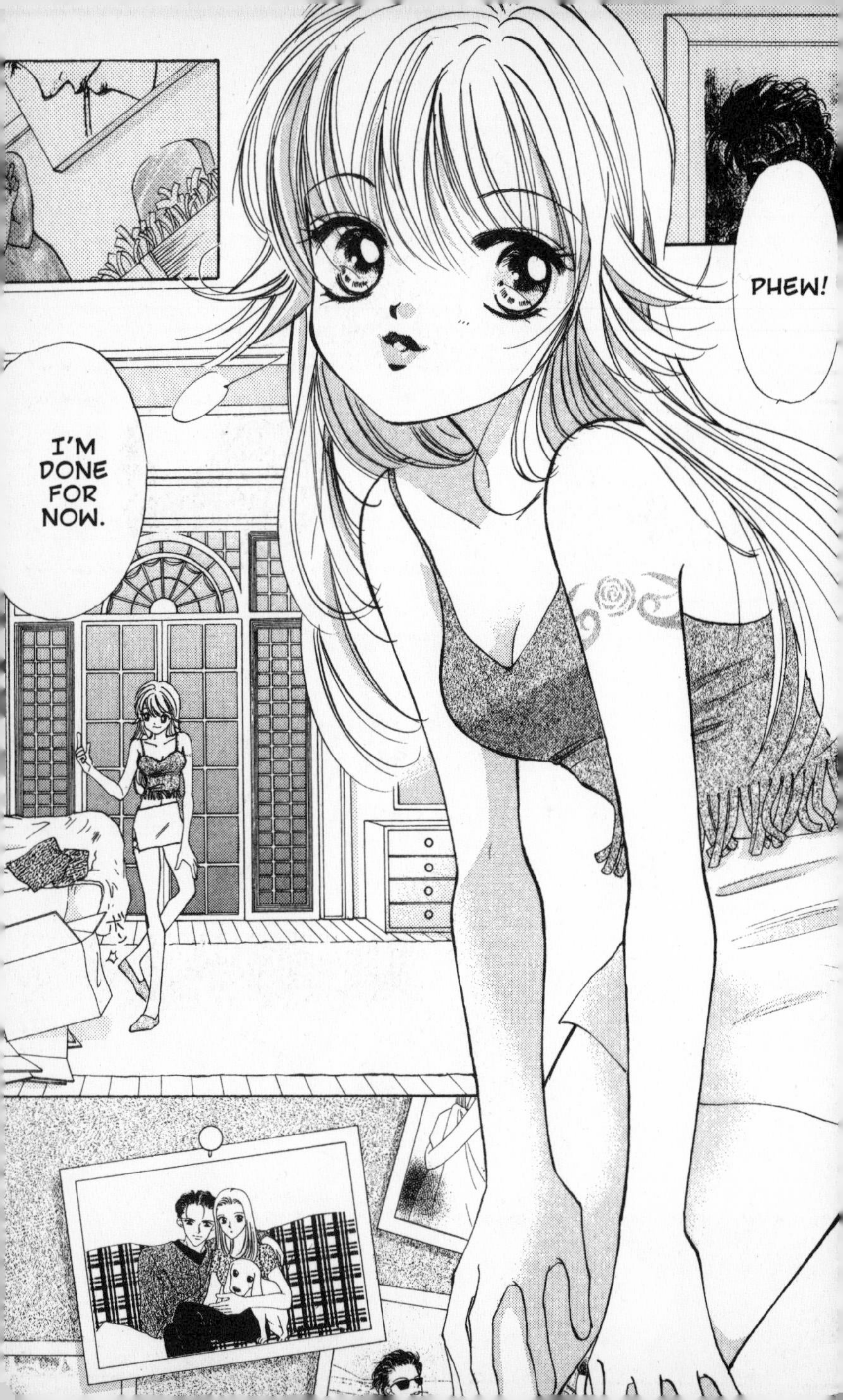
PHEW!
I'M DONE FOR NOW.

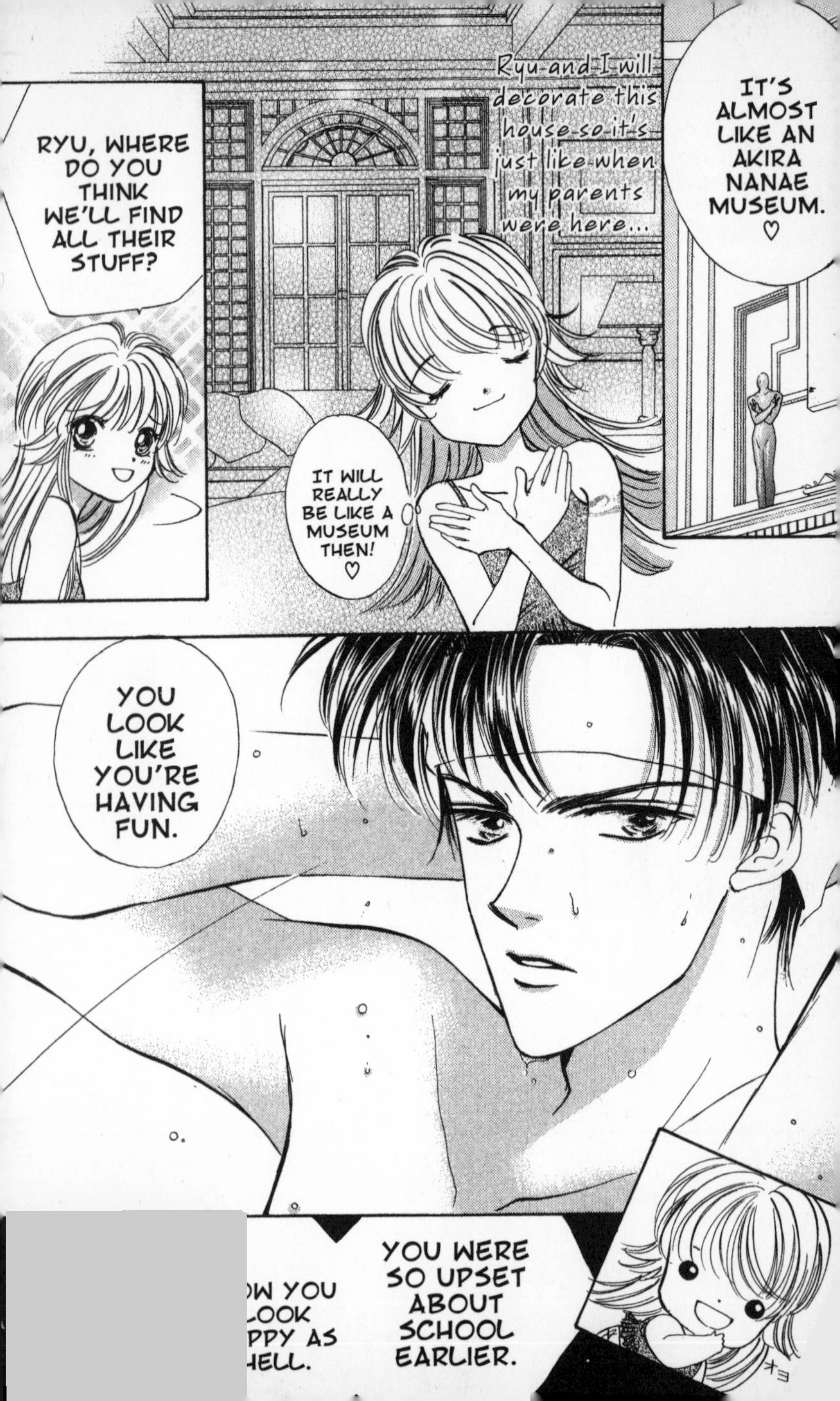
IT'S ALMOST LIKE AN AKIRA NANAE MUSEUM. ♡
Ryu and I will decorate this house so it's just like when my parents were here...
IT WILL REALLY BE LIKE A MUSEUM THEN! ♡
RYU, WHERE DO YOU THINK WE'LL FIND ALL THEIR STUFF?
YOU LOOK LIKE YOU'RE HAVING FUN.
YOU WERE SO UPSET ABOUT SCHOOL EARLIER.
OW YOU LOOK PPY AS HELL.

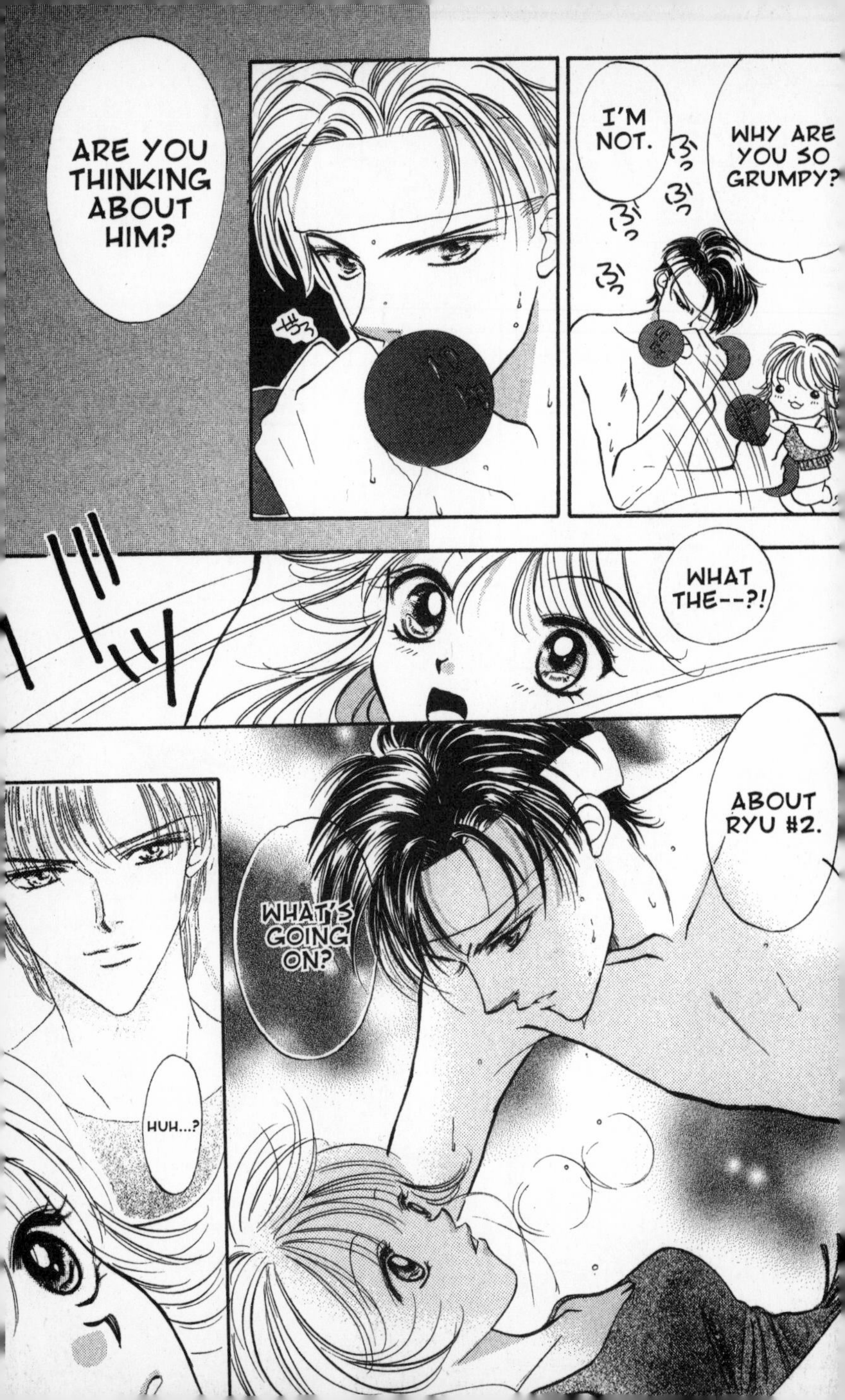
WHY ARE YOU SO GRUMPY?
I'M NOT.
ARE YOU THINKING ABOUT HIM?
WHAT THE--?!
ABOUT RYU #2.
WHAT'S GOING ON?
HUH...?

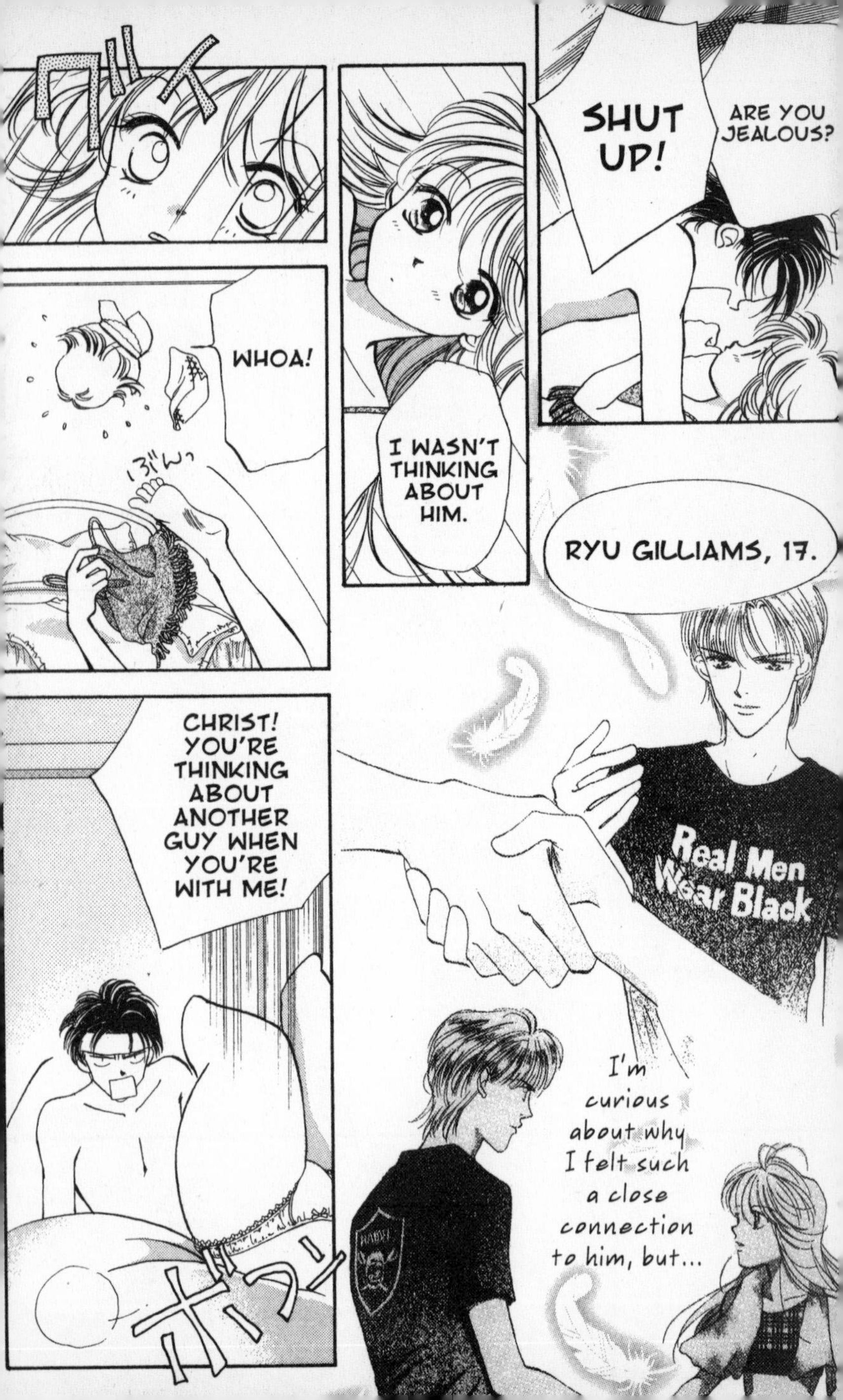

ARE YOU JEALOUS?
SHUT UP!
I WASN'T THINKING ABOUT HIM.
WHOA!
RYU GILLIAMS, 17.
Real Men Wear Black
I'm curious about why I felt such a close connection to him, but...
CHRIST! YOU'RE THINKING ABOUT ANOTHER GUY WHEN YOU'RE WITH ME!

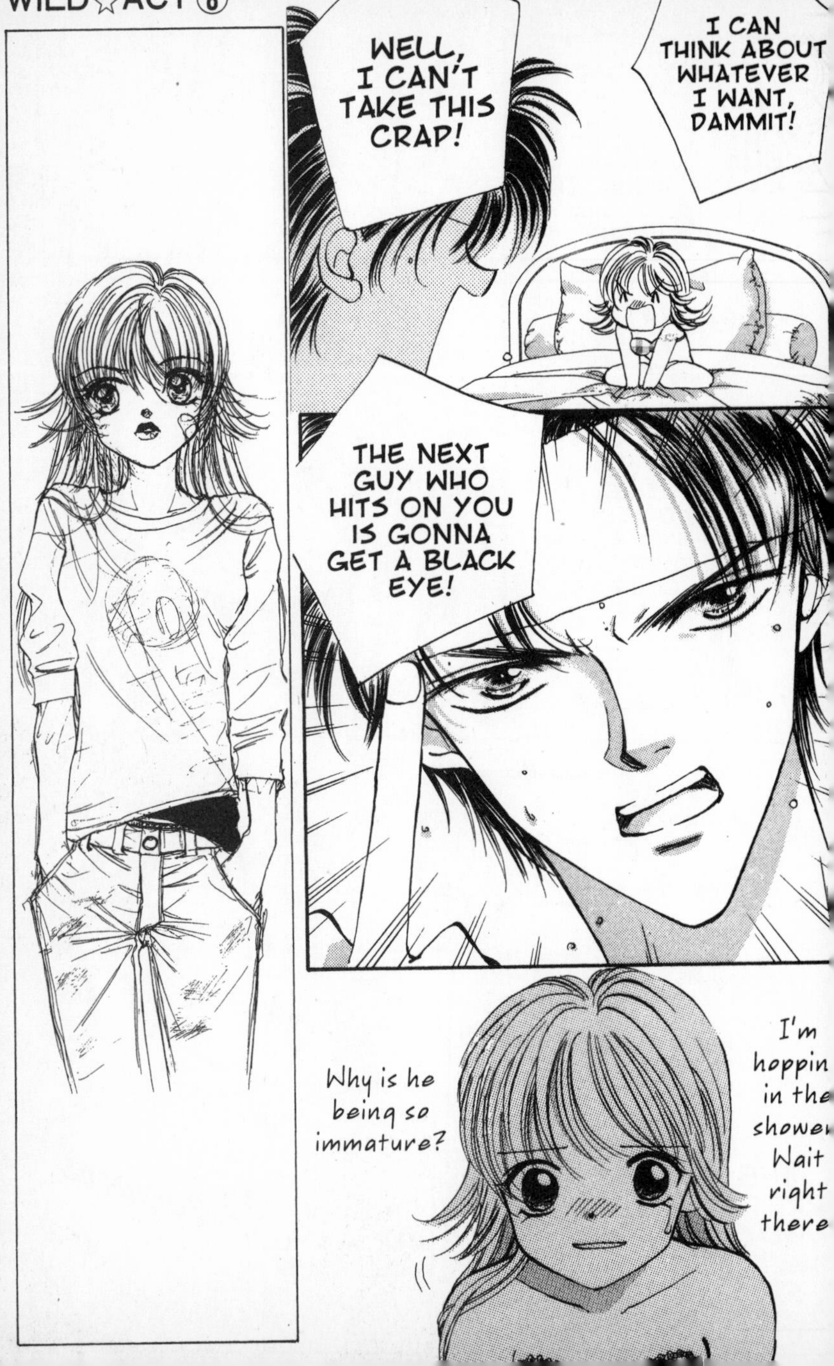
I CAN THINK ABOUT WHATEVER I WANT, DAMMIT!
WELL, I CAN'T TAKE THIS CRAP!
THE NEXT GUY WHO HITS ON YOU IS GONNA GET A BLACK EYE!
I'm hoppin in the showe Wait right there
Why is he being so immature?

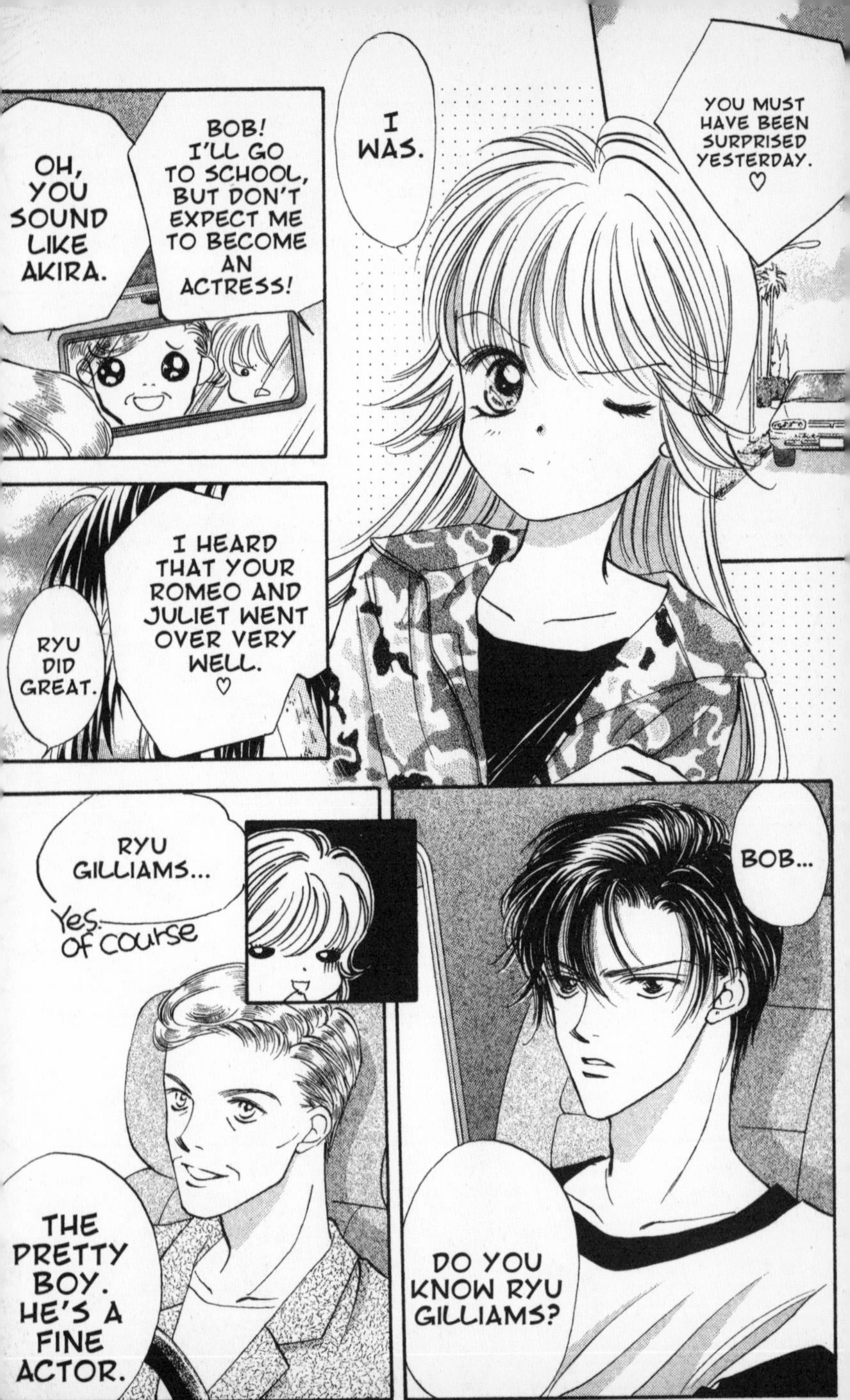
YOU MUST HAVE BEEN SURPRISED YESTERDAY. ♡
I WAS.
BOB! I'LL GO TO SCHOOL, BUT DON'T EXPECT ME TO BECOME AN ACTRESS!
OH, YOU SOUND LIKE AKIRA.
I HEARD THAT YOUR ROMEO AND JULIET WENT OVER VERY WELL. ♡
RYU DID GREAT.
BOB...
DO YOU KNOW RYU GILLIAMS?
RYU GILLIAMS...
Yes. of course
THE PRETTY BOY. HE'S A FINE ACTOR.

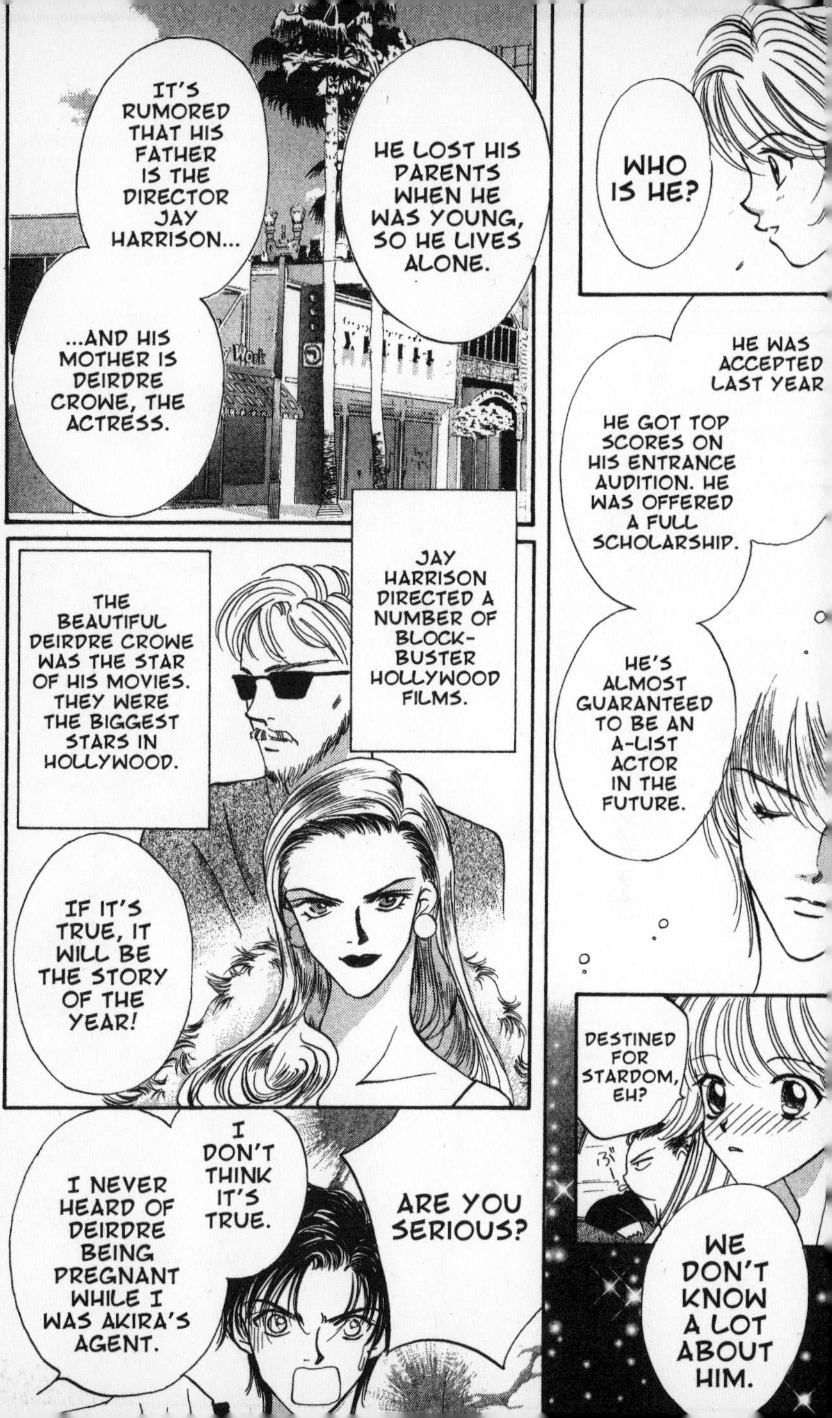
WHO IS HE?
HE WAS ACCEPTED LAST YEAR
HE GOT TOP SCORES ON HIS ENTRANCE AUDITION. HE WAS OFFERED A FULL SCHOLARSHIP.
HE'S ALMOST GUARANTEED TO BE AN A-LIST ACTOR IN THE FUTURE.
DESTINED FOR STARDOM, EH?
WE DON'T KNOW A LOT ABOUT HIM.
HE LOST HIS PARENTS WHEN HE WAS YOUNG, SO HE LIVES ALONE.
IT'S RUMORED THAT HIS FATHER IS THE DIRECTOR JAY HARRISON...
...AND HIS MOTHER IS DEIRDRE CROWE, THE ACTRESS.
JAY HARRISON DIRECTED A NUMBER OF BLOCK-BUSTER HOLLYWOOD FILMS.
THE BEAUTIFUL DEIRDRE CROWE WAS THE STAR OF HIS MOVIES. THEY WERE THE BIGGEST STARS IN HOLLYWOOD.
IF IT'S TRUE, IT WILL BE THE STORY OF THE YEAR!
ARE YOU SERIOUS?
I DON'T THINK IT'S TRUE.
I NEVER HEARD OF DEIRDRE BEING PREGNANT WHILE I WAS AKIRA'S AGENT.

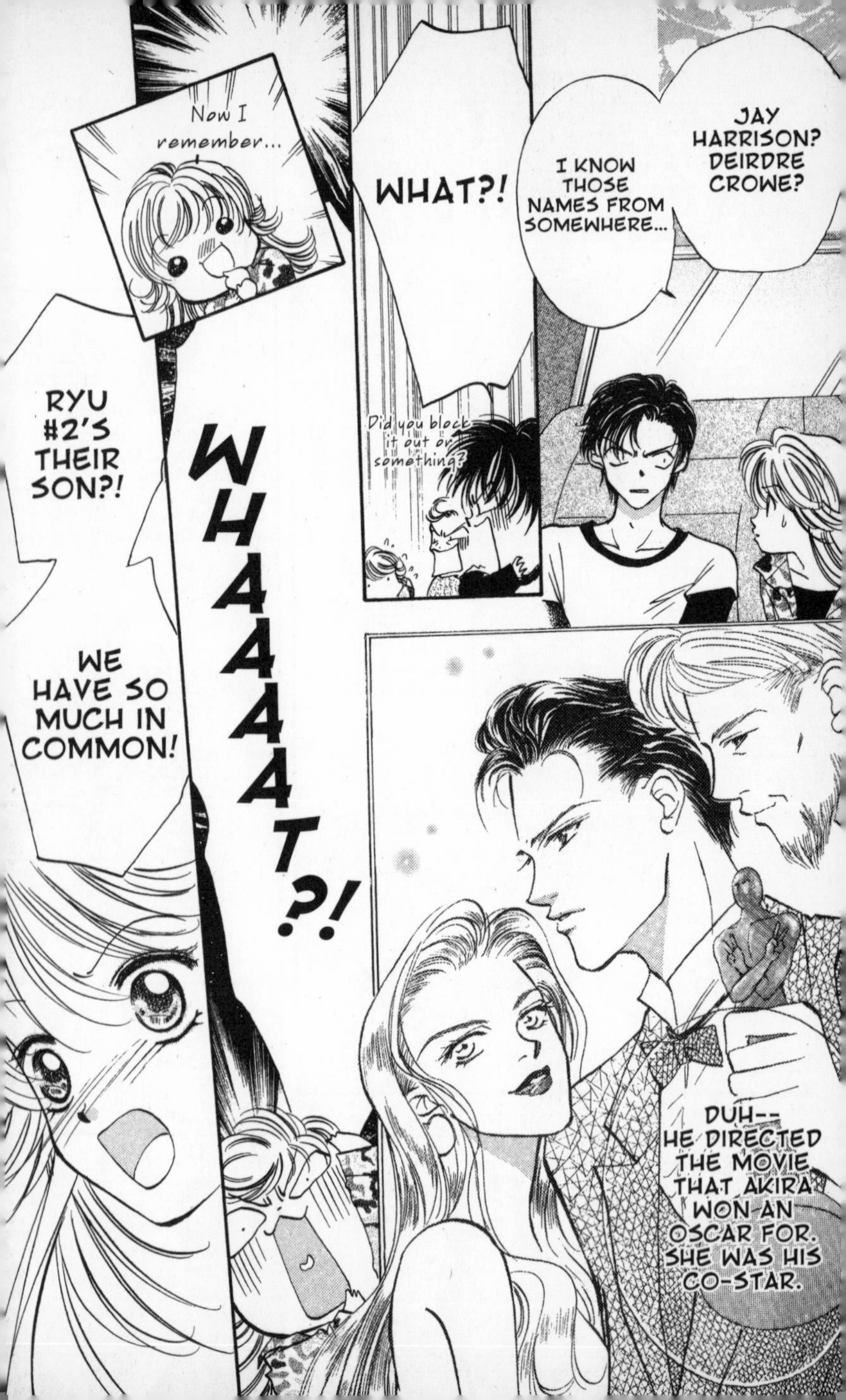
JAY HARRISON? DEIRDRE CROWE?
I KNOW THOSE NAMES FROM SOMEWHERE...
WHAT?!
Did you block it out or something?
DUH-- HE DIRECTED THE MOVIE THAT AKIRA WON AN OSCAR FOR. SHE WAS HIS CO-STAR.
Now I remember...
RYU #2'S THEIR SON?!
WE HAVE SO MUCH IN COMMON!
WHAAAAT?!

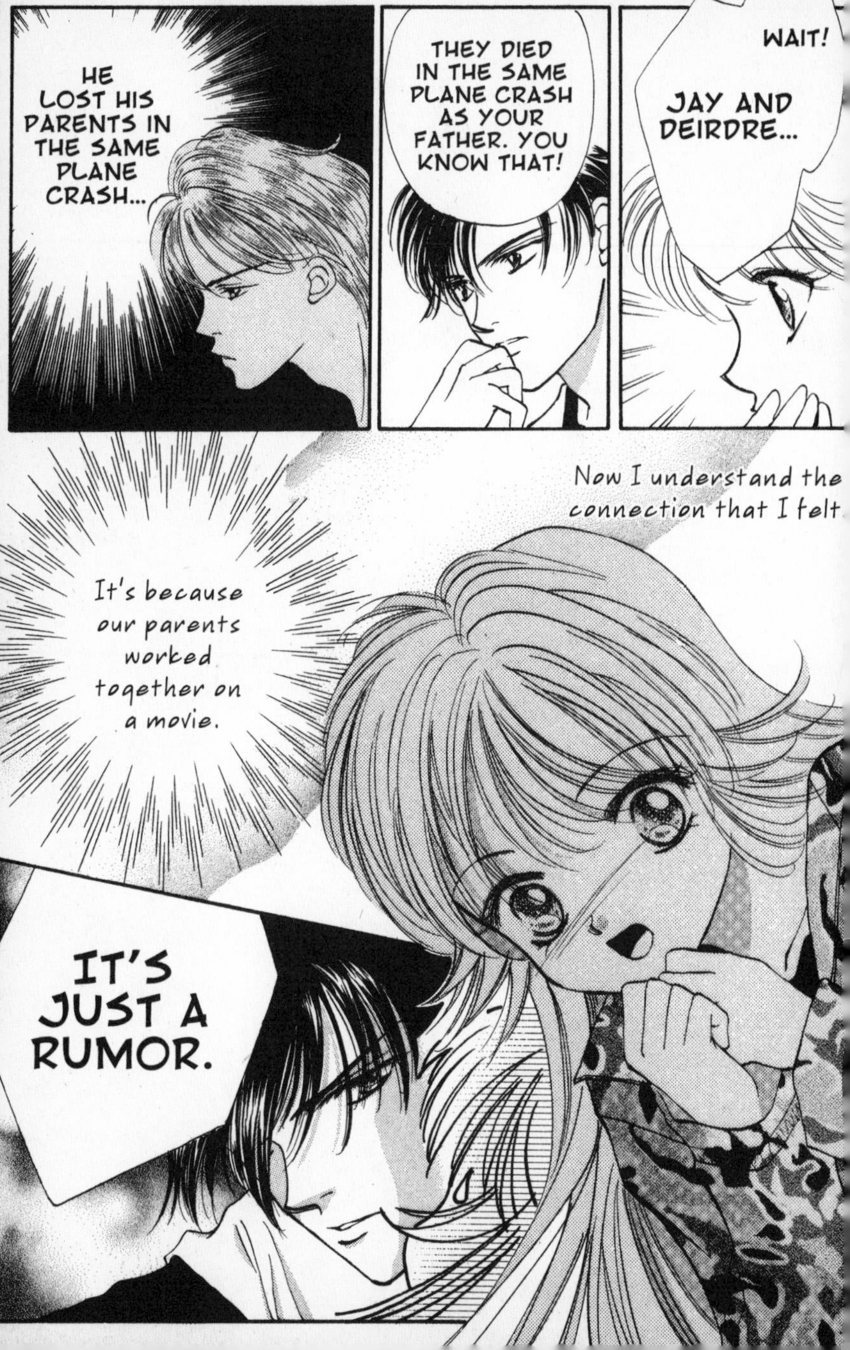
WAIT!
JAY AND DEIRDRE...
THEY DIED IN THE SAME PLANE CRASH AS YOUR FATHER. YOU KNOW THAT!
HE LOST HIS PARENTS IN THE SAME PLANE CRASH...
Now I understand the connection that I felt
It's because our parents worked together on a movie.
IT'S JUST A RUMOR.

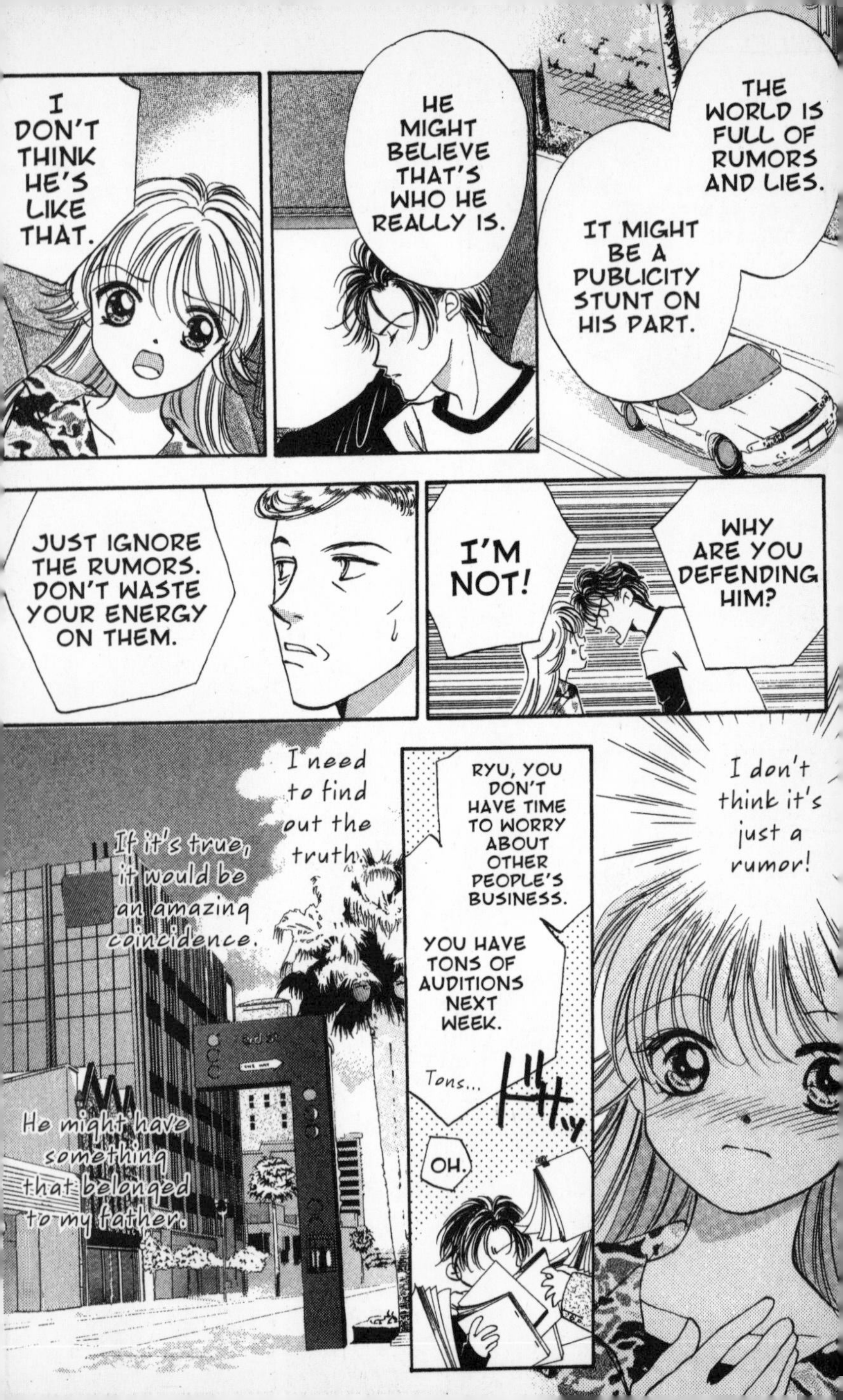
THE WORLD IS FULL OF RUMORS AND LIES.
IT MIGHT BE A PUBLICITY STUNT ON HIS PART.
HE MIGHT BELIEVE THAT'S WHO HE REALLY IS.
I DON'T THINK HE'S LIKE THAT.
WHY ARE YOU DEFENDING HIM?
I'M NOT!
JUST IGNORE THE RUMORS. DON'T WASTE YOUR ENERGY ON THEM.
I don't think it's just a rumor!
RYU, YOU DON'T HAVE TIME TO WORRY ABOUT OTHER PEOPLE'S BUSINESS.
YOU HAVE TONS OF AUDITIONS NEXT WEEK.
Tons...
OH.
I need to find out the truth.
If it's true, it would be an amazing coincidence.
He might have something that belonged to my father.

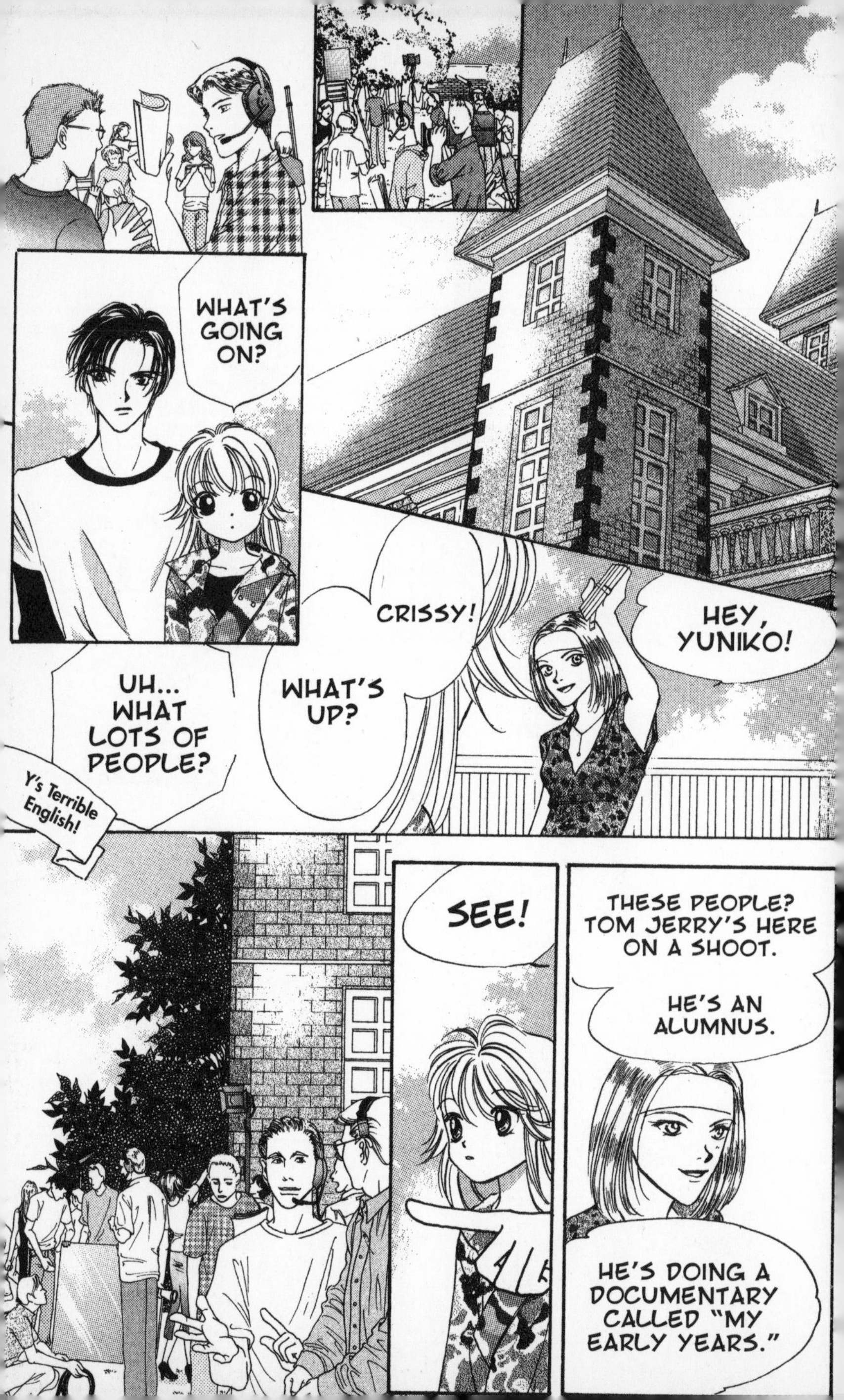
WHAT'S GOING ON?
HEY, YUNIKO!
CRISSY!
WHAT'S UP?
UH... WHAT LOTS OF PEOPLE?
Y's Terrible English!
THESE PEOPLE? TOM JERRY'S HERE ON A SHOOT.
HE'S AN ALUMNUS.
HE'S DOING A DOCUMENTARY CALLED "MY EARLY YEARS."
SEE!

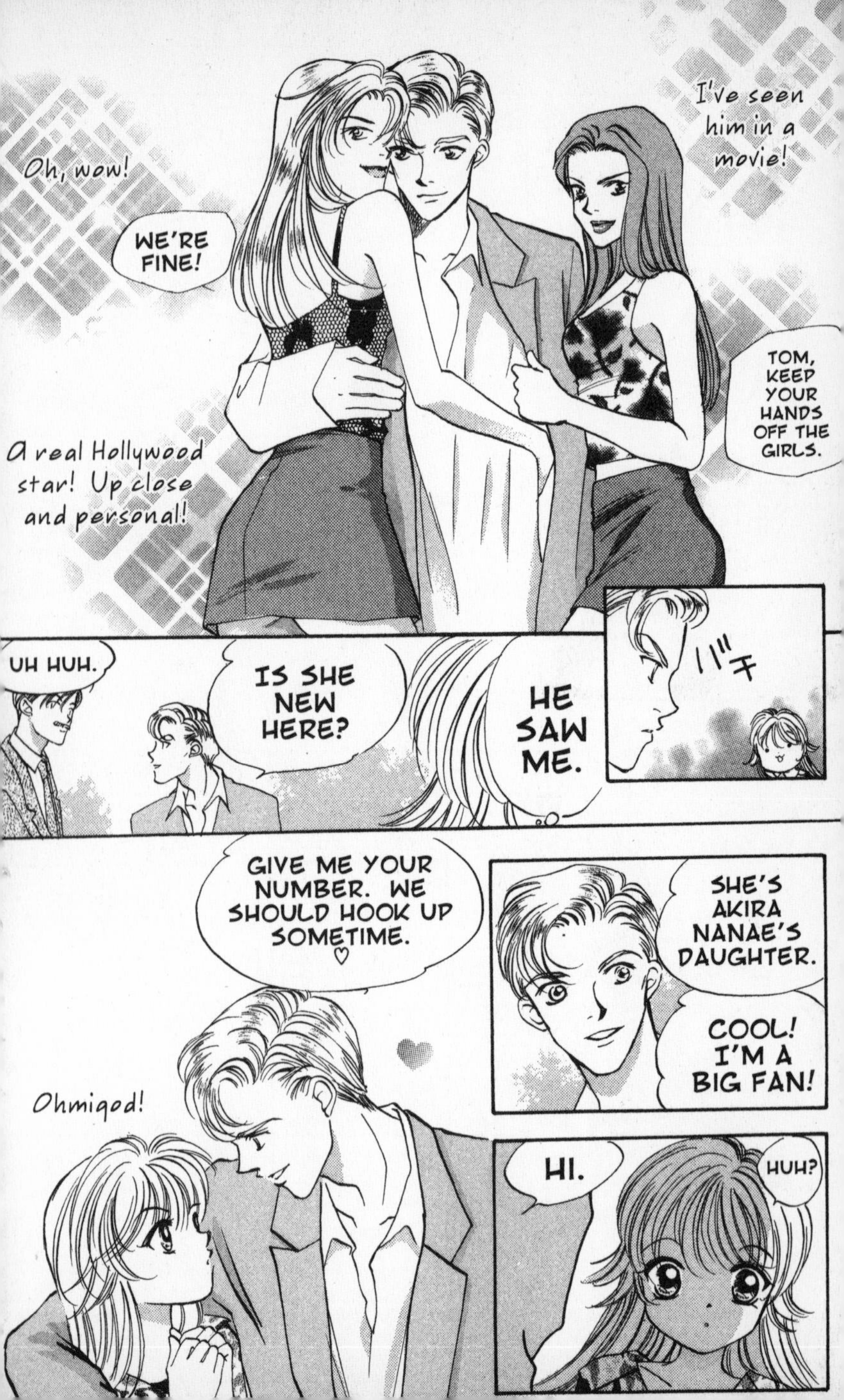
I've seen him in a movie!
Oh, wow!
WE'RE FINE!
TOM, KEEP YOUR HANDS OFF THE GIRLS.
A real Hollywood star! Up close and personal!
バチ
HE SAW ME.
IS SHE NEW HERE?
UH HUH.
SHE'S AKIRA NANAE'S DAUGHTER.
COOL! I'M A BIG FAN!
HUH?
HI.
GIVE ME YOUR NUMBER. WE SHOULD HOOK UP SOMETIME. ♡
Ohmigod!

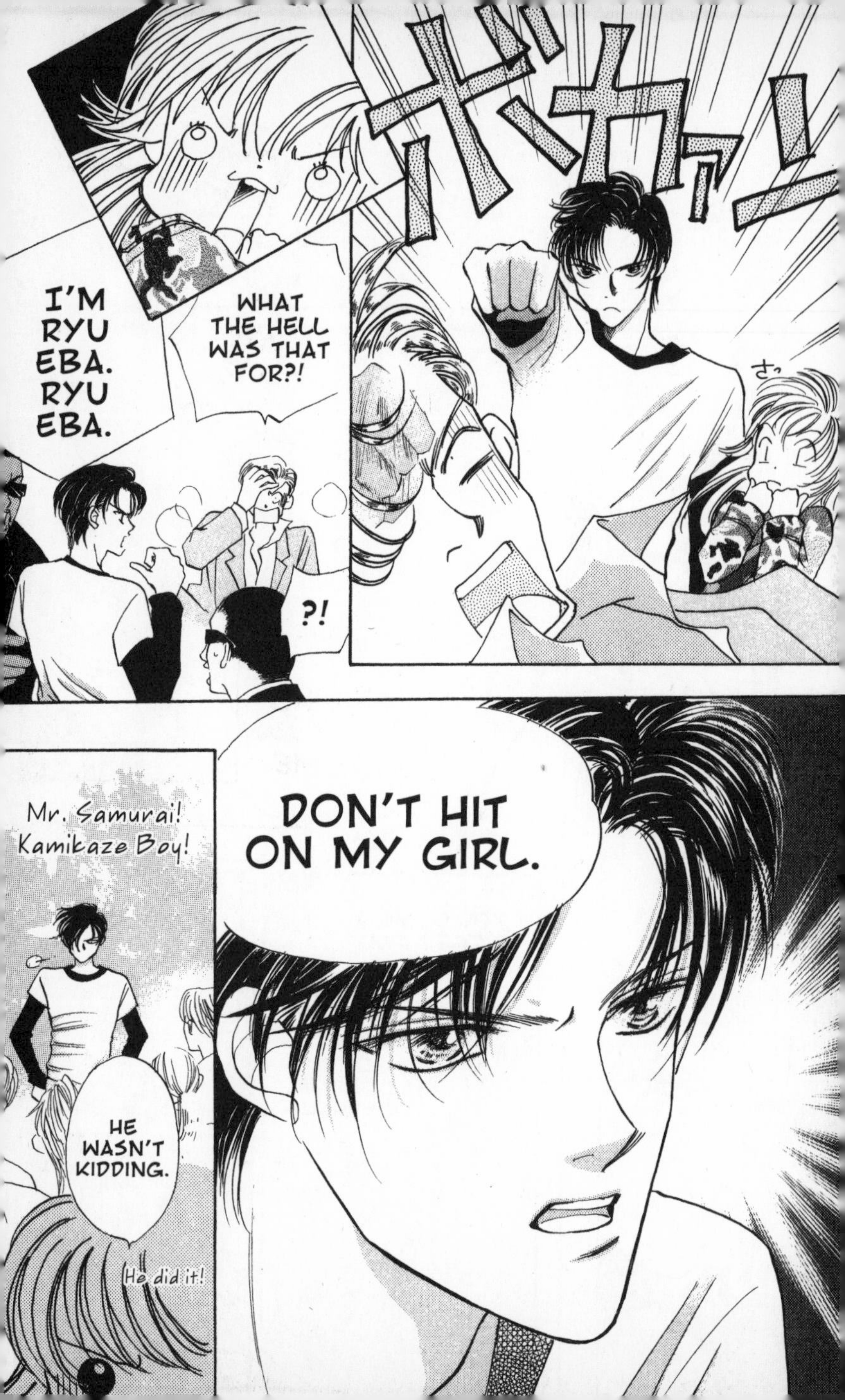
ボカァン
さっ
WHAT THE HELL WAS THAT FOR?!
I'M RYU EBA. RYU EBA.
?!
DON'T HIT ON MY GIRL.
Mr. Samurai! Kamikaze Boy!
HE WASN'T KIDDING.
He did it!

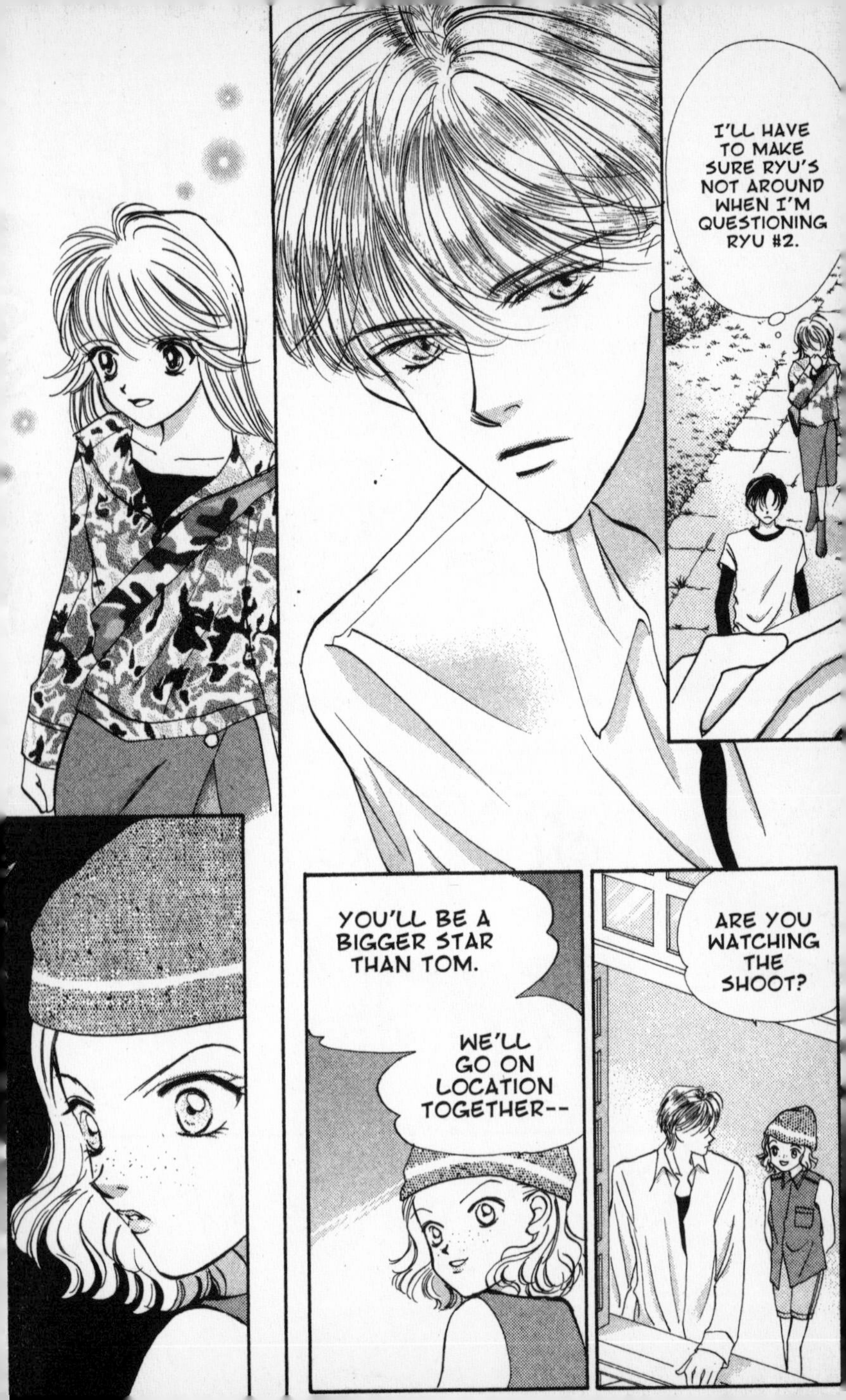
I'LL HAVE TO MAKE SURE RYU'S NOT AROUND WHEN I'M QUESTIONING RYU #2.
ARE YOU WATCHING THE SHOOT?
YOU'LL BE A BIGGER STAR THAN TOM.
WE'LL GO ON LOCATION TOGETHER--

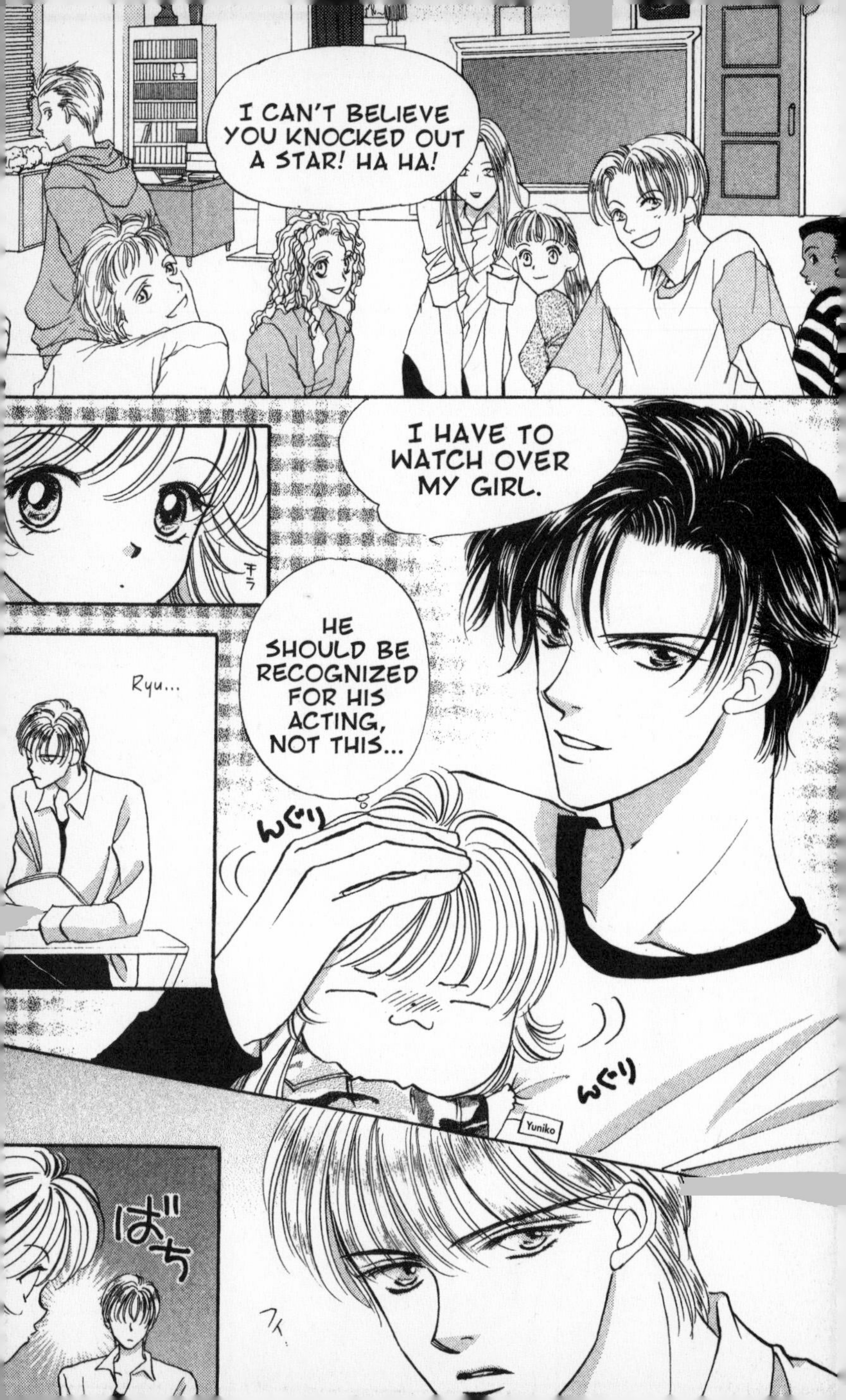

I CAN'T BELIEVE YOU KNOCKED OUT A STAR! HA HA!
I HAVE TO WATCH OVER MY GIRL.
HE SHOULD BE RECOGNIZED FOR HIS ACTING, NOT THIS...
Yuniko
キラ
Ryu...
ぱち

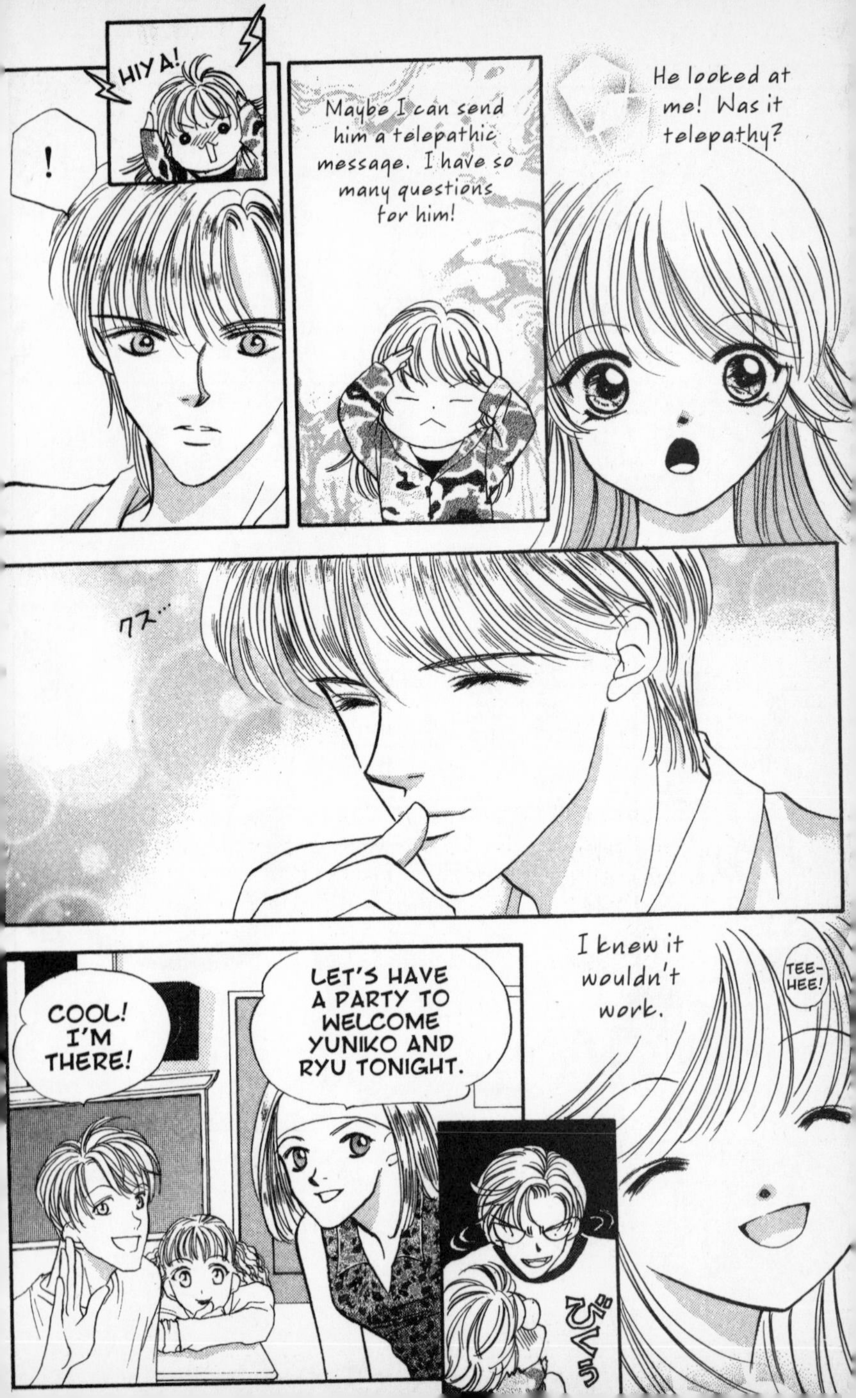
He looked at me! Was it telepathy?
Maybe I can send him a telepathic message. I have so many questions for him!
HIYA!
!
クス…
I knew it wouldn't work.
TEE-HEE!
LET'S HAVE A PARTY TO WELCOME YUNIKO AND RYU TONIGHT.
COOL! I'M THERE!
ぴくっ

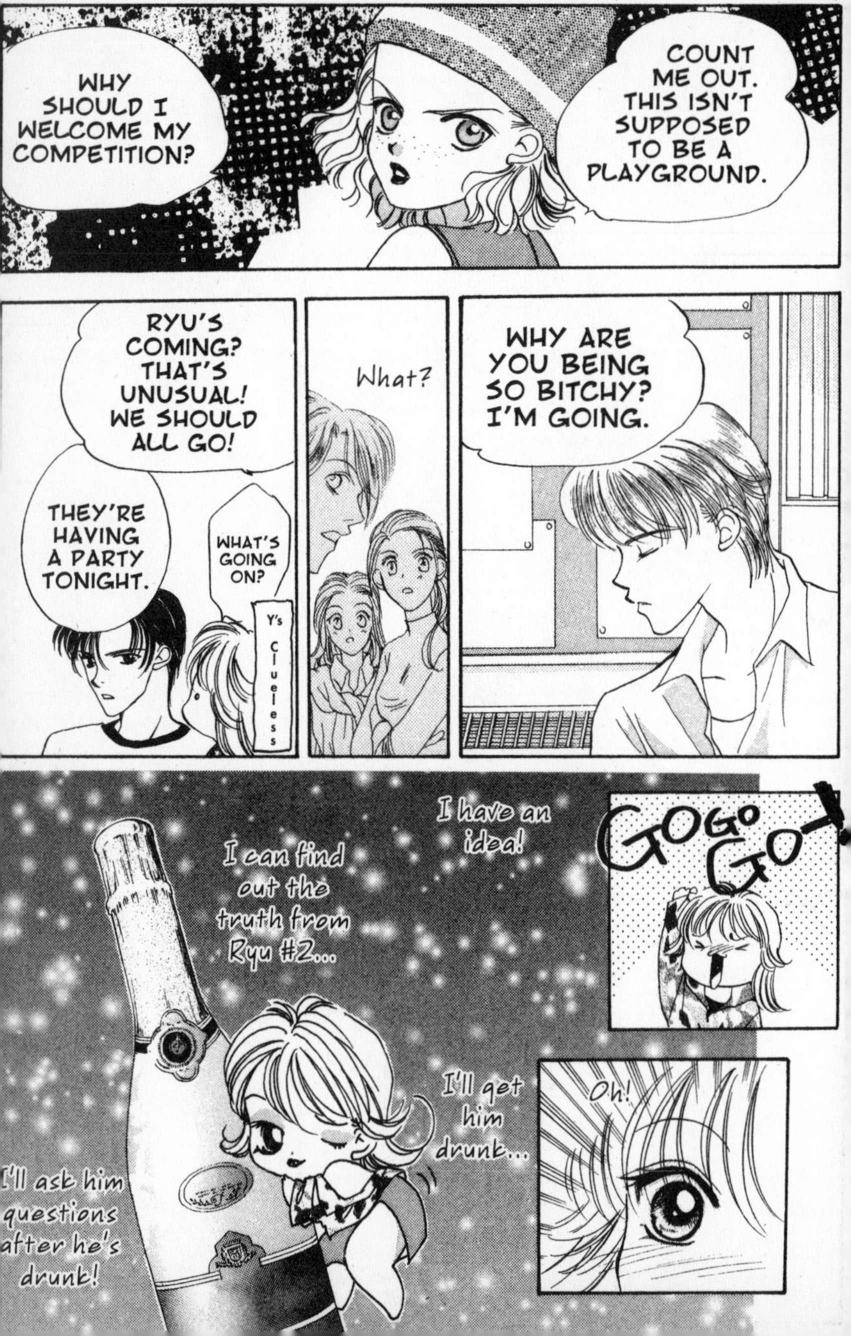
COUNT ME OUT. THIS ISN'T SUPPOSED TO BE A PLAYGROUND.
WHY SHOULD I WELCOME MY COMPETITION?
WHY ARE YOU BEING SO BITCHY? I'M GOING.
What?
RYU'S COMING? THAT'S UNUSUAL! WE SHOULD ALL GO!
WHAT'S GOING ON?
THEY'RE HAVING A PARTY TONIGHT.
Y's Clueless
GOGO GO—!
Oh!
I have an idea!
I can find out the truth from Ryu #2...
I'll get him drunk...
I'll ask him questions after he's drunk!

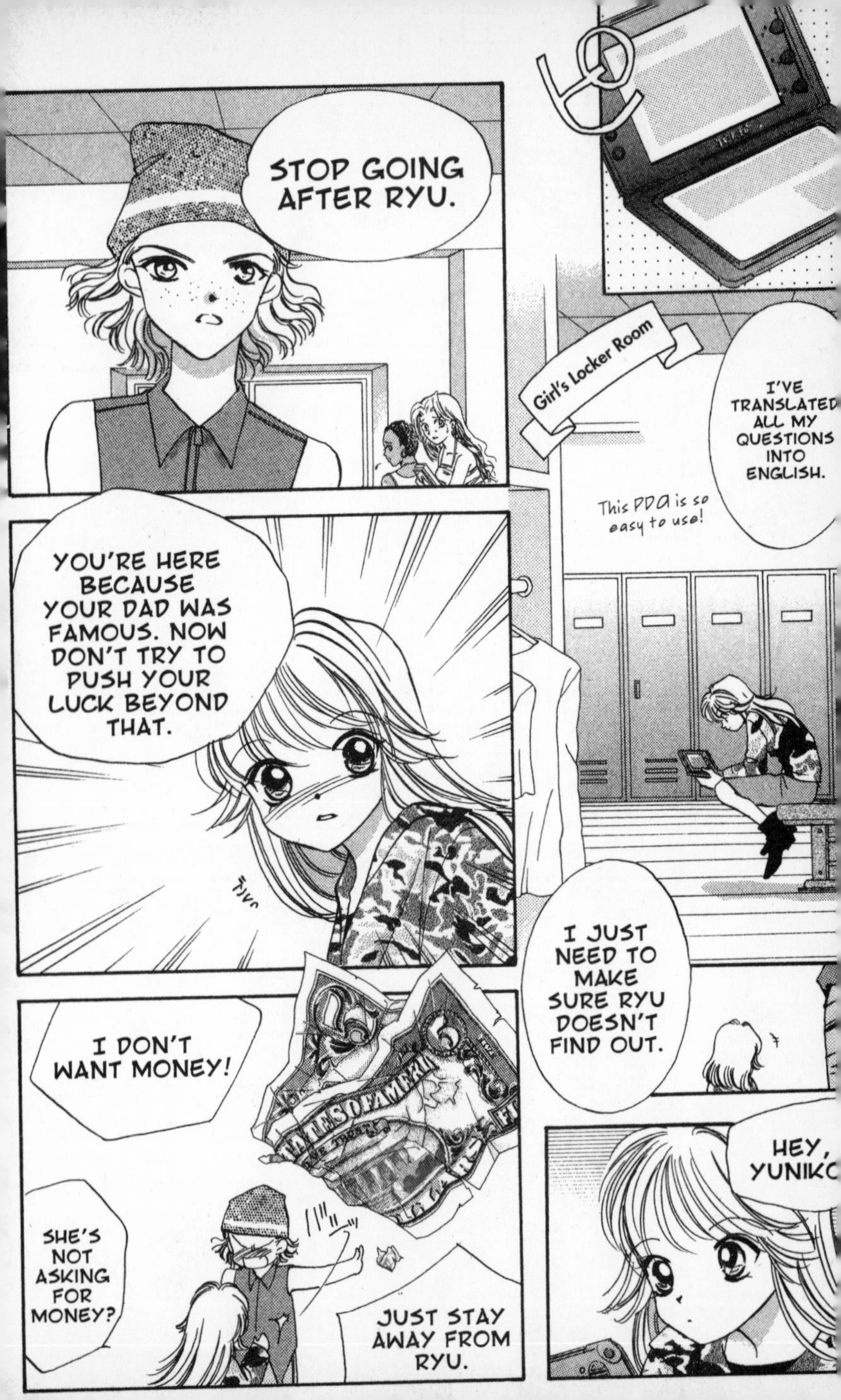
Girl's Locker Room
I'VE TRANSLATED ALL MY QUESTIONS INTO ENGLISH.
This PDA is so easy to use!
I JUST NEED TO MAKE SURE RYU DOESN'T FIND OUT.
HEY, YUNIKO
STOP GOING AFTER RYU.
YOU'RE HERE BECAUSE YOUR DAD WAS FAMOUS. NOW DON'T TRY TO PUSH YOUR LUCK BEYOND THAT.
I DON'T WANT MONEY!
JUST STAY AWAY FROM RYU.
SHE'S NOT ASKING FOR MONEY?

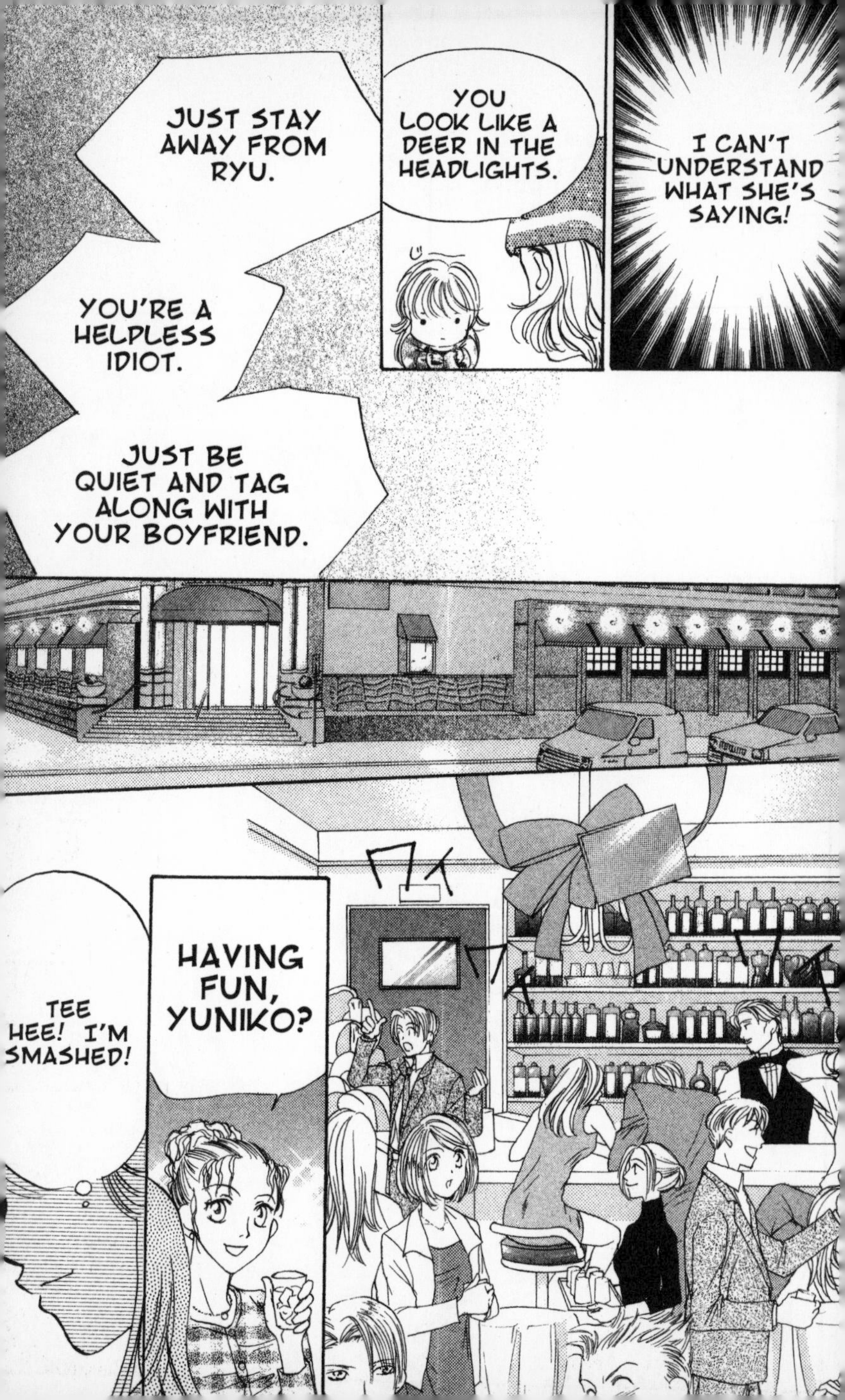
I CAN'T UNDERSTAND WHAT SHE'S SAYING!
YOU LOOK LIKE A DEER IN THE HEADLIGHTS.
JUST STAY AWAY FROM RYU.
YOU'RE A HELPLESS IDIOT.
JUST BE QUIET AND TAG ALONG WITH YOUR BOYFRIEND.
ワイ
ワイ
HAVING FUN, YUNIKO?
TEE HEE! I'M SMASHED!

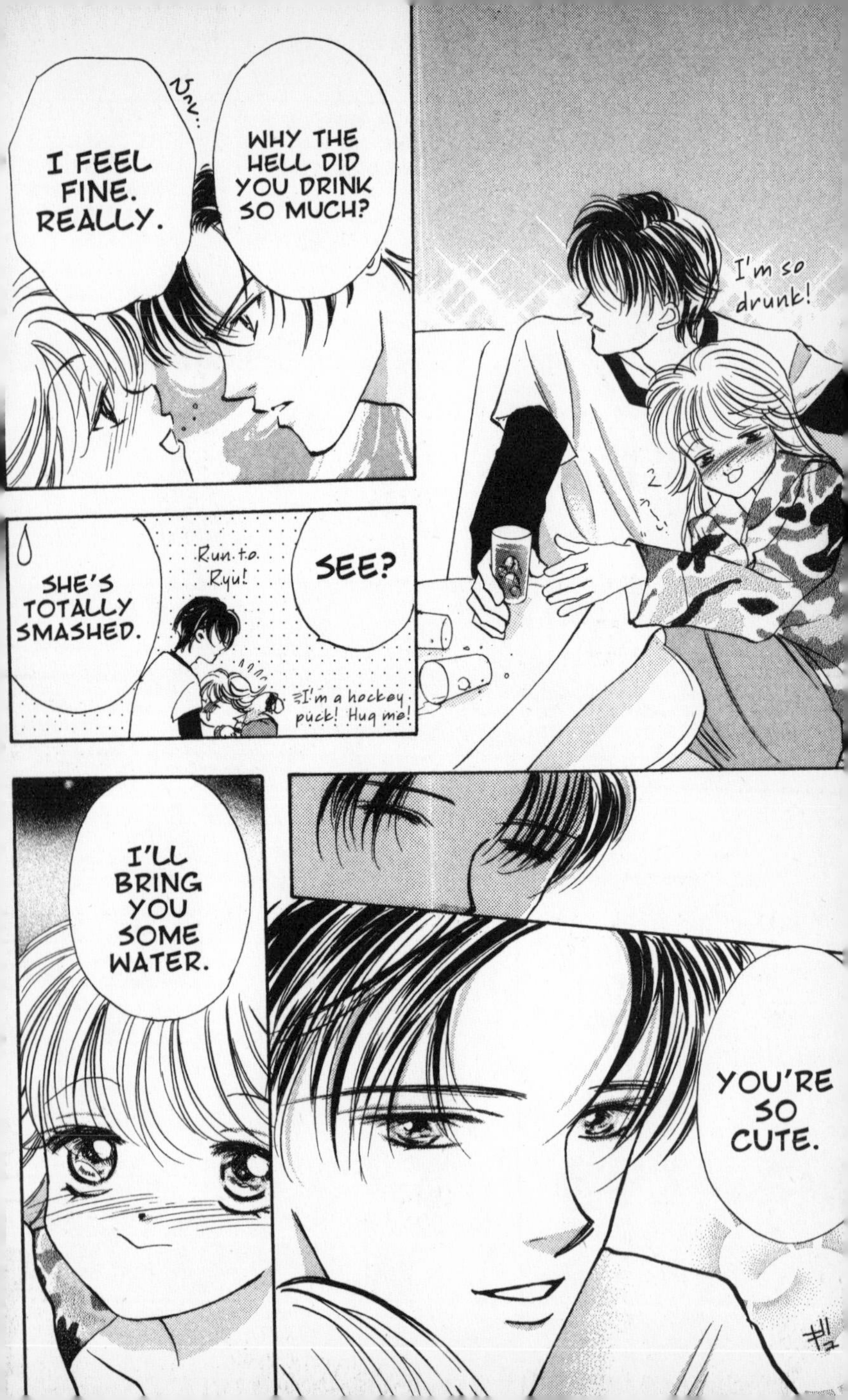
I'm so drunk!
WHY THE HELL DID YOU DRINK SO MUCH?
I FEEL FINE. REALLY.
SEE?
Run to Ryu!
SHE'S TOTALLY SMASHED.
I'm a hockey puck! Hug me!
YOU'RE SO CUTE.
I'LL BRING YOU SOME WATER.

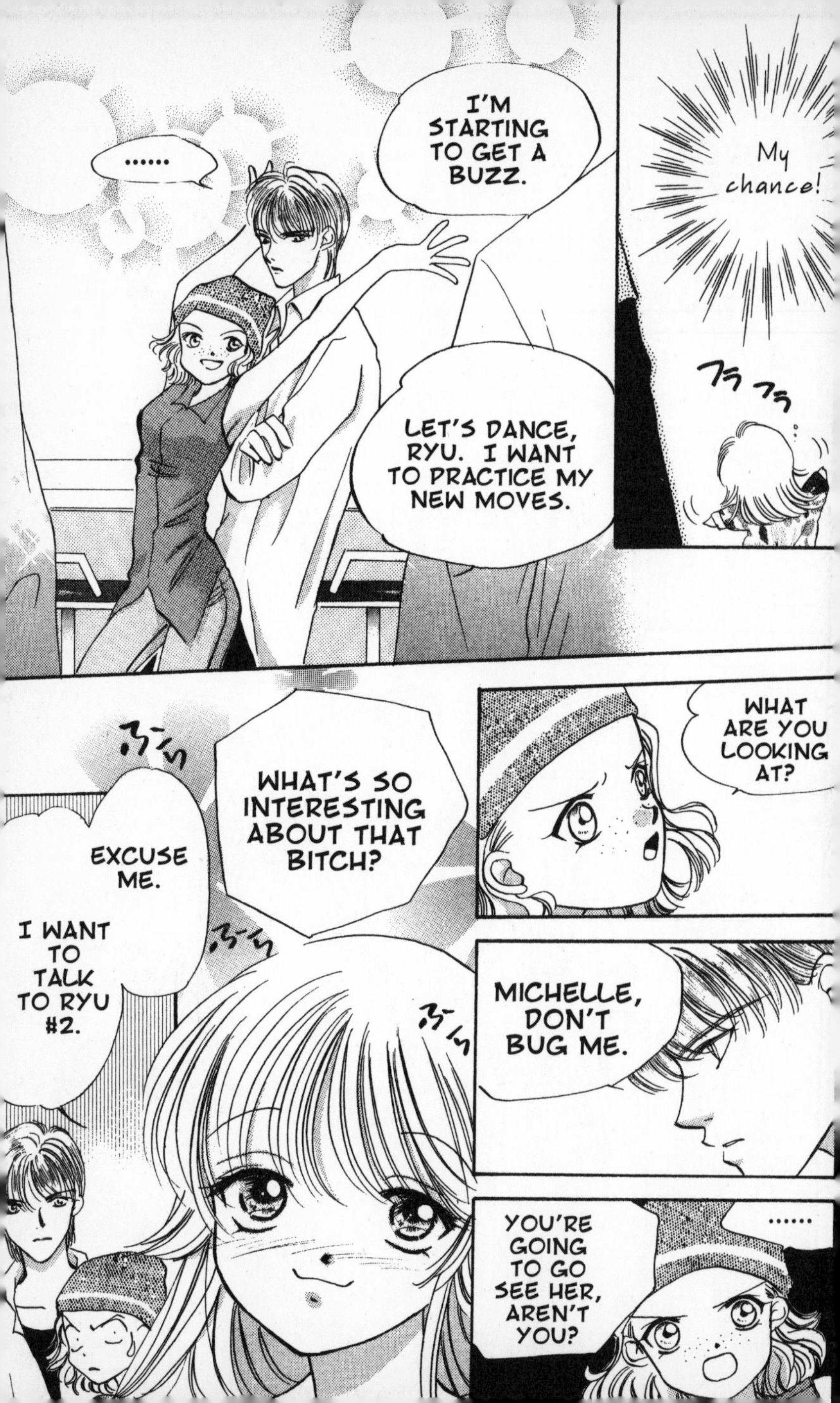
My chance!
フラ フラ
I'M STARTING TO GET A BUZZ.
......
LET'S DANCE, RYU. I WANT TO PRACTICE MY NEW MOVES.
WHAT ARE YOU LOOKING AT?
MICHELLE, DON'T BUG ME.
YOU'RE GOING TO GO SEE HER, AREN'T YOU?
......
WHAT'S SO INTERESTING ABOUT THAT BITCH?
EXCUSE ME.
I WANT TO TALK TO RYU #2.

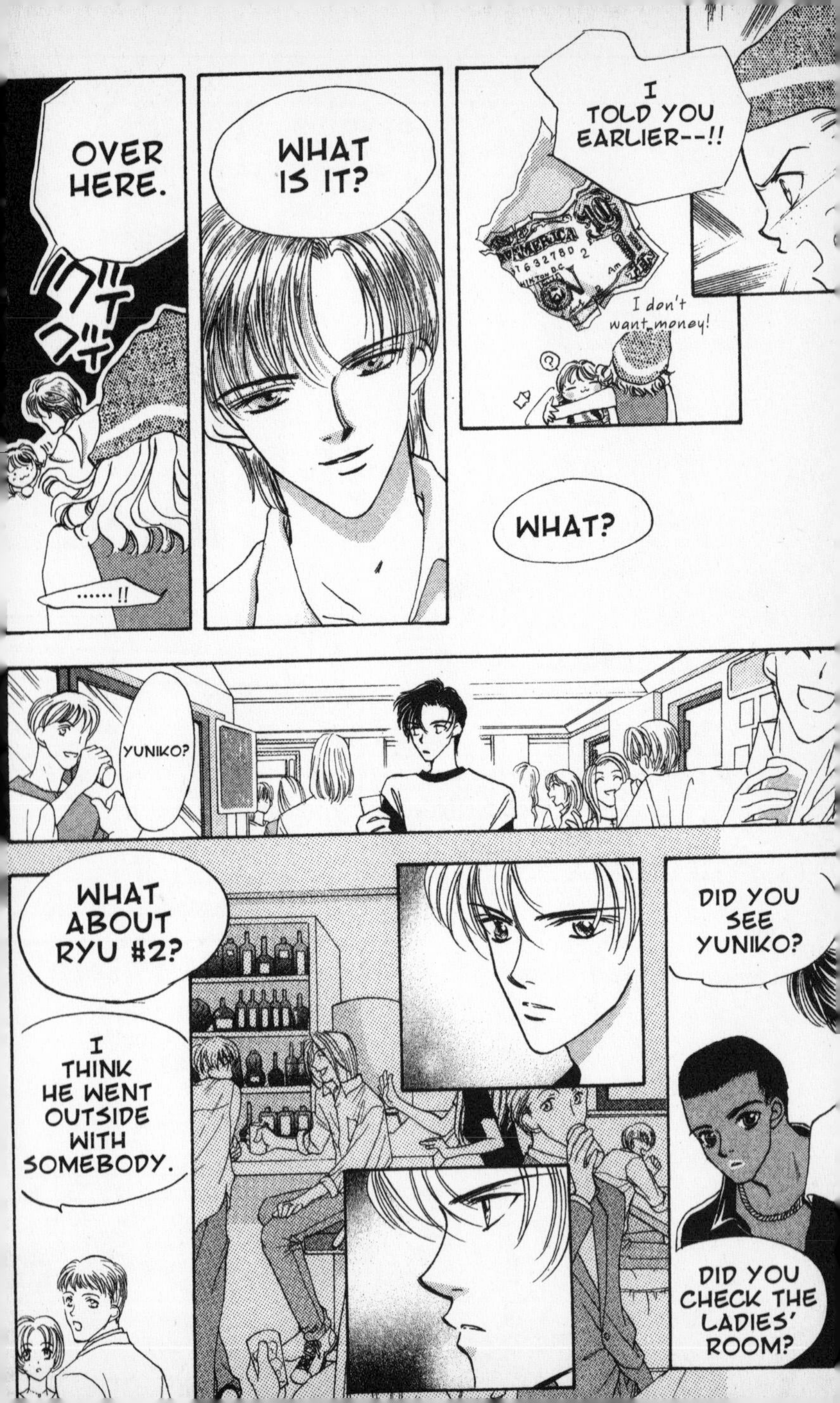
I TOLD YOU EARLIER--!!
I don't want money!
WHAT?
WHAT IS IT?
OVER HERE.
グイグイ
......!!
YUNIKO?
DID YOU SEE YUNIKO?
DID YOU CHECK THE LADIES' ROOM?
WHAT ABOUT RYU #2?
I THINK HE WENT OUTSIDE WITH SOMEBODY.

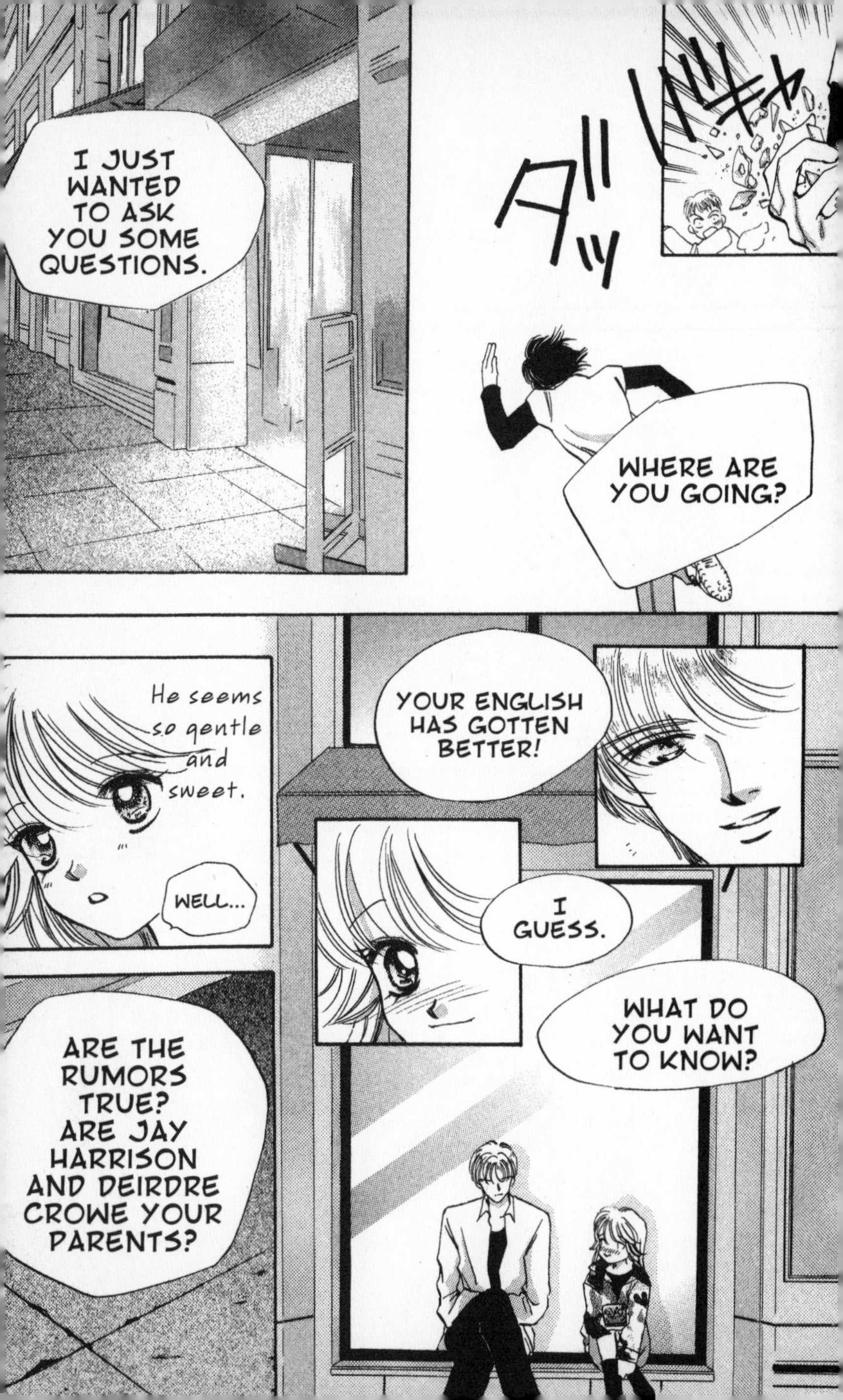
ダッ
WHERE ARE YOU GOING?
I JUST WANTED TO ASK YOU SOME QUESTIONS.
YOUR ENGLISH HAS GOTTEN BETTER!
He seems so gentle and sweet.
WELL...
I GUESS.
WHAT DO YOU WANT TO KNOW?
ARE THE RUMORS TRUE? ARE JAY HARRISON AND DEIRDRE CROWE YOUR PARENTS?

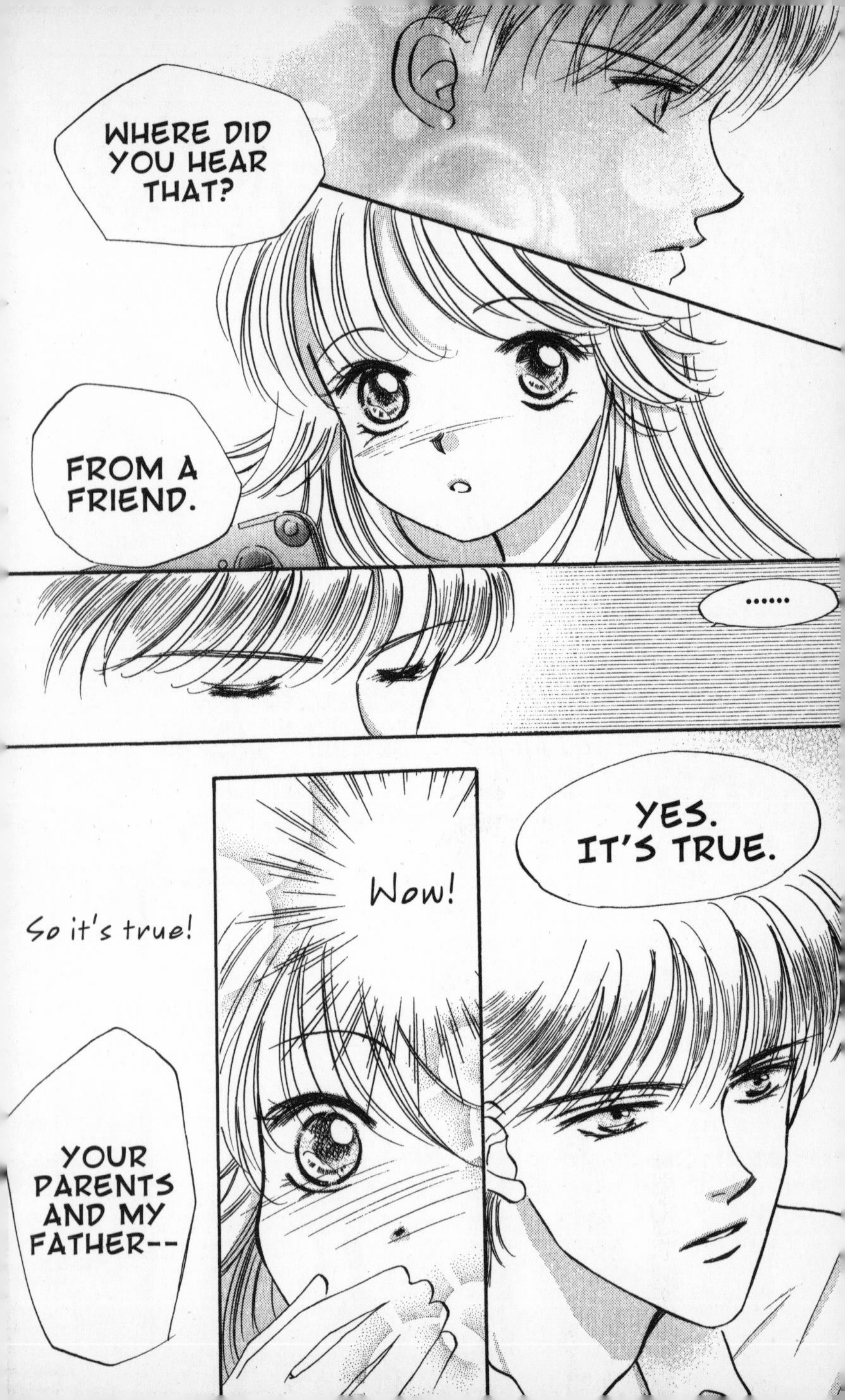
WHERE DID YOU HEAR THAT?
FROM A FRIEND.
......
YES. IT'S TRUE.
Wow!
So it's true!
YOUR PARENTS AND MY FATHER--

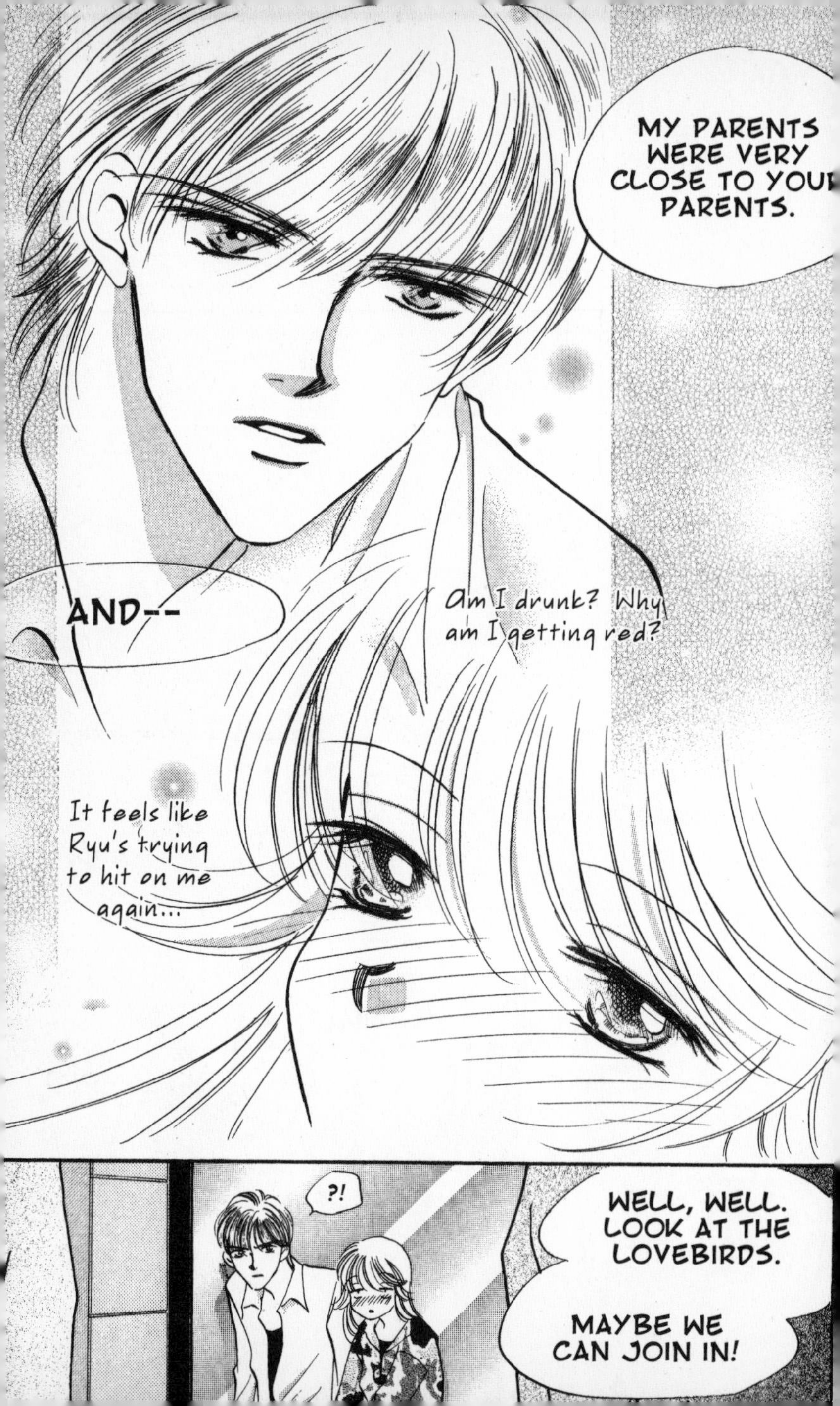
MY PARENTS WERE VERY CLOSE TO YOUR PARENTS.
AND--
Am I drunk? Why am I getting red?
It feels like Ryu's trying to hit on me again...
WELL, WELL. LOOK AT THE LOVEBIRDS.
MAYBE WE CAN JOIN IN!
?!

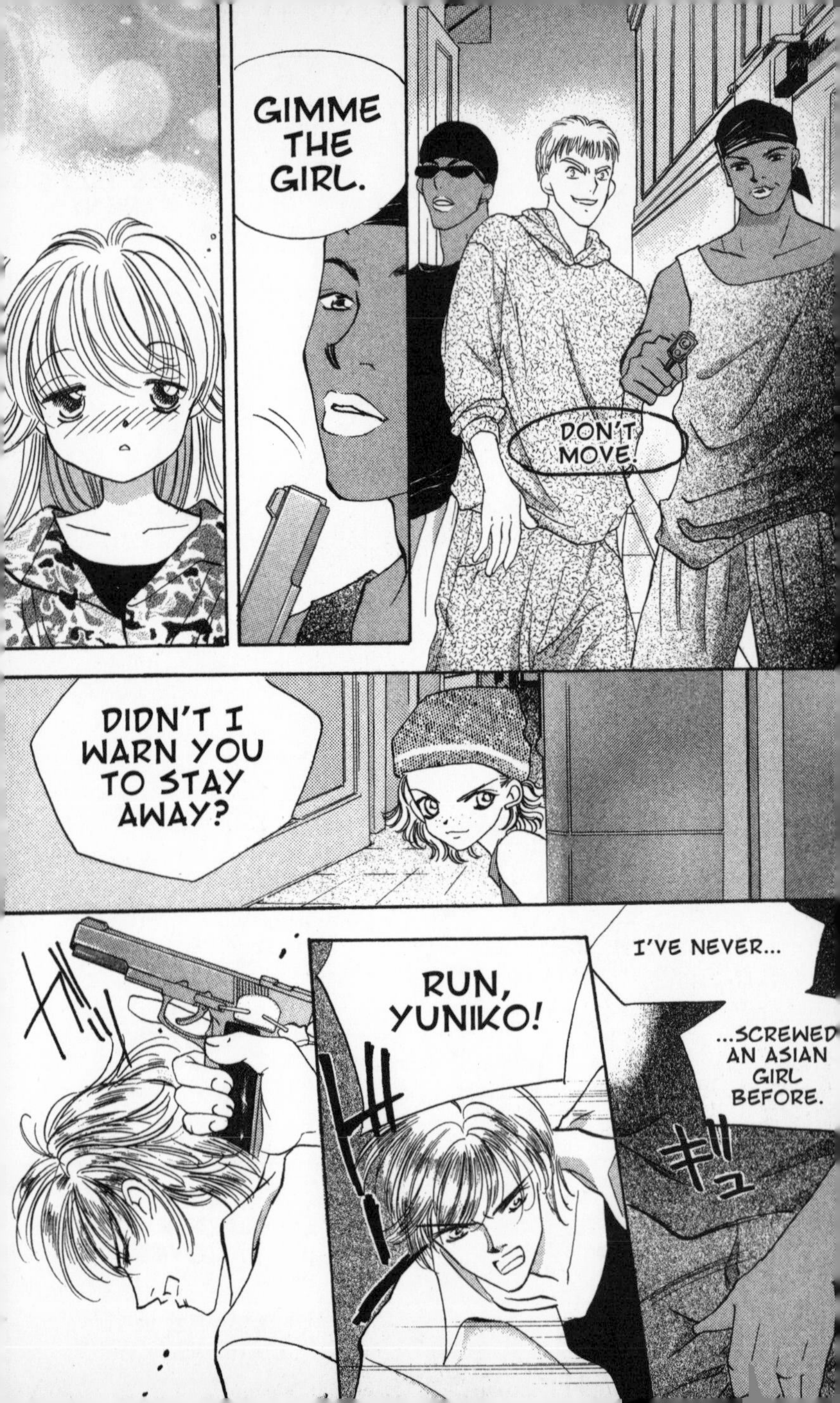
DON'T MOVE.
GIMME THE GIRL.
DIDN'T I WARN YOU TO STAY AWAY?
I'VE NEVER...
...SCREWED AN ASIAN GIRL BEFORE.
ギュ
RUN, YUNIKO!

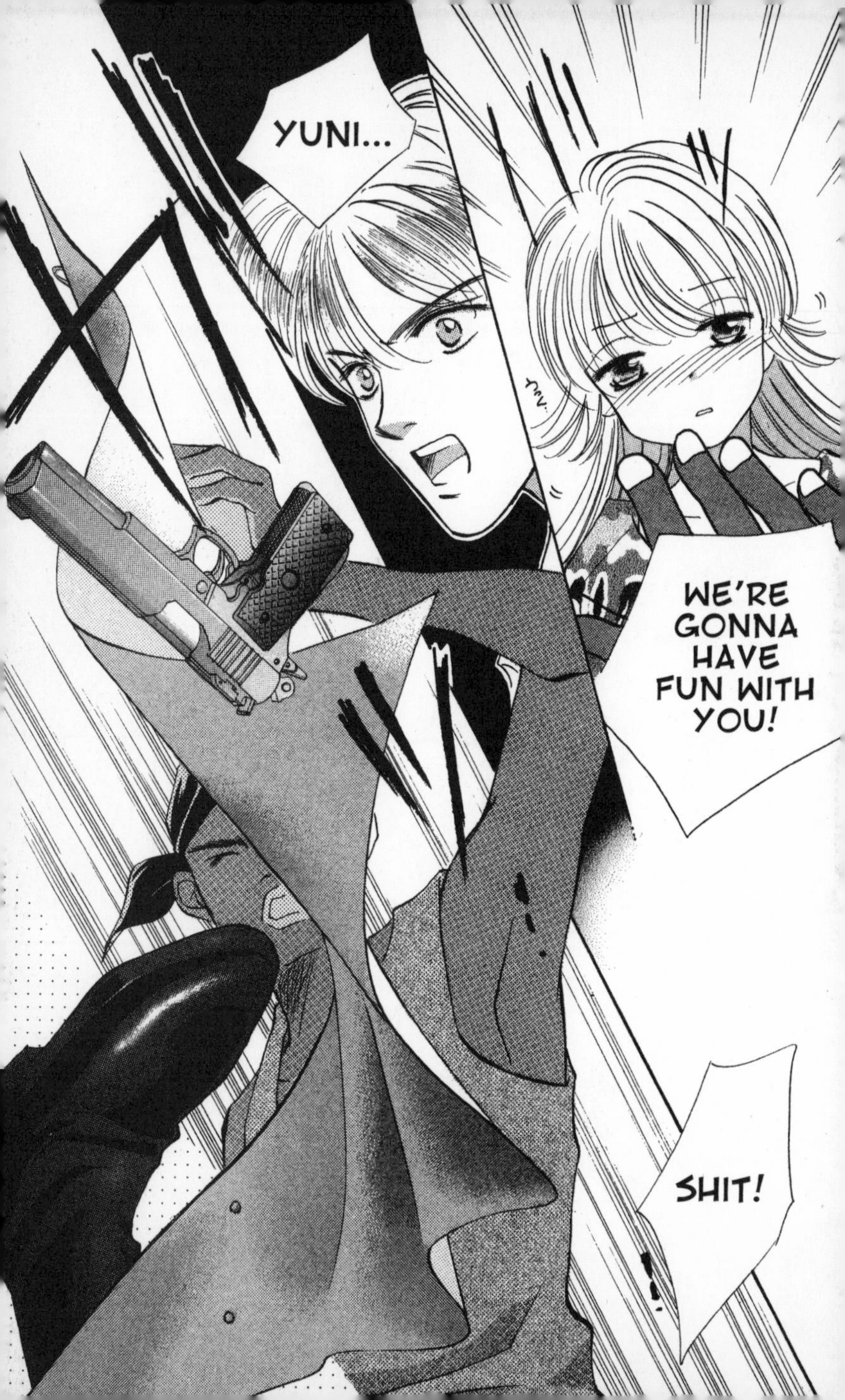
YUNI...
WE'RE GONNA HAVE FUN WITH YOU!
SHIT!

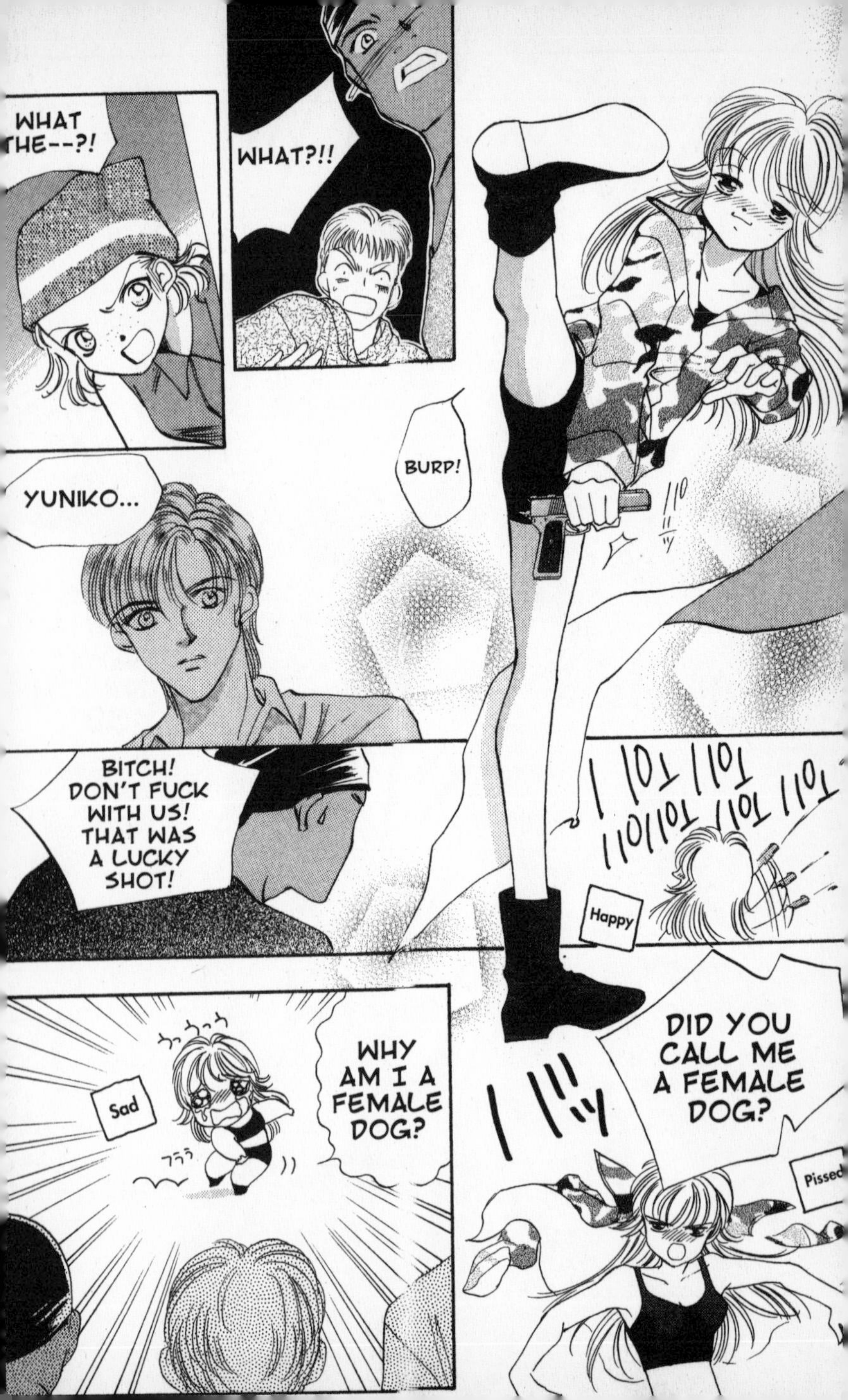
BURP!
WHAT?!!
WHAT THE--?!
YUNIKO...
Happy
BITCH! DON'T FUCK WITH US! THAT WAS A LUCKY SHOT!
DID YOU CALL ME A FEMALE DOG?
Pissed
WHY AM I A FEMALE DOG?
Sad

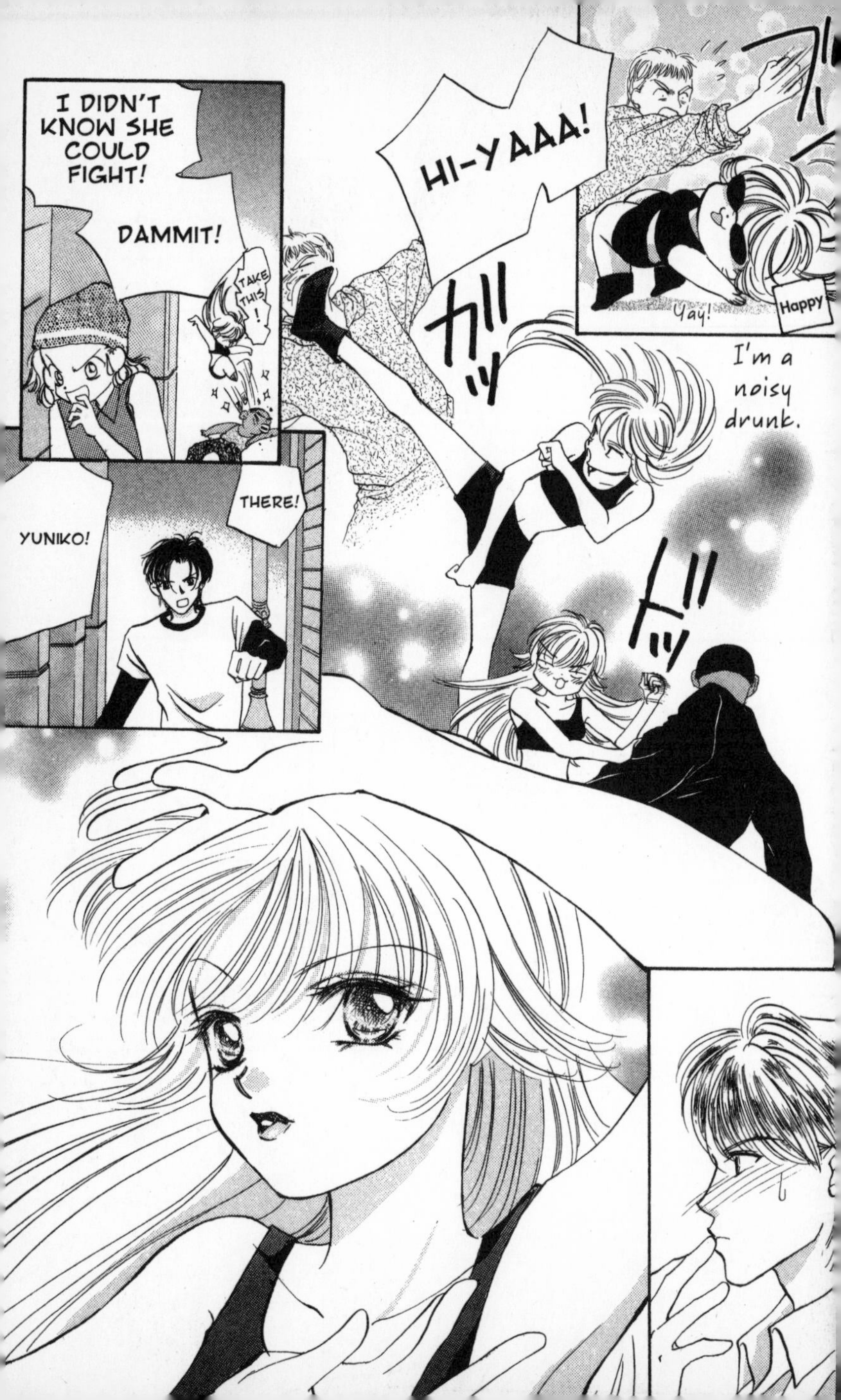

Happy
Yay!
HI-YAAA!
ガッ
I'm a noisy drunk.
ドッ
I DIDN'T KNOW SHE COULD FIGHT!
DAMMIT!
TAKE THIS!
THERE!
YUNIKO!

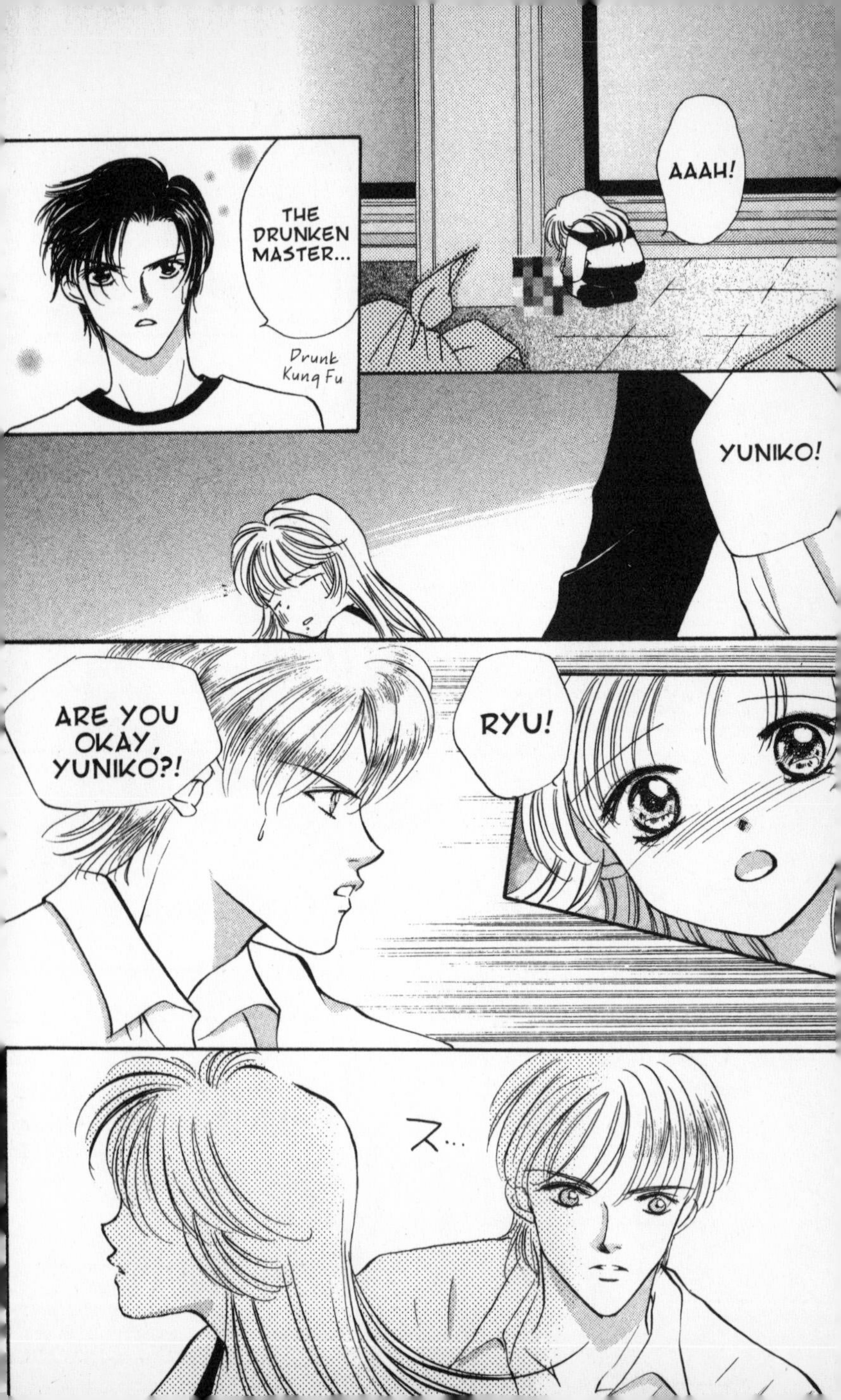
AAAH!
THE DRUNKEN MASTER...
Drunk Kung Fu
YUNIKO!
RYU!
ARE YOU OKAY, YUNIKO?!
ス...

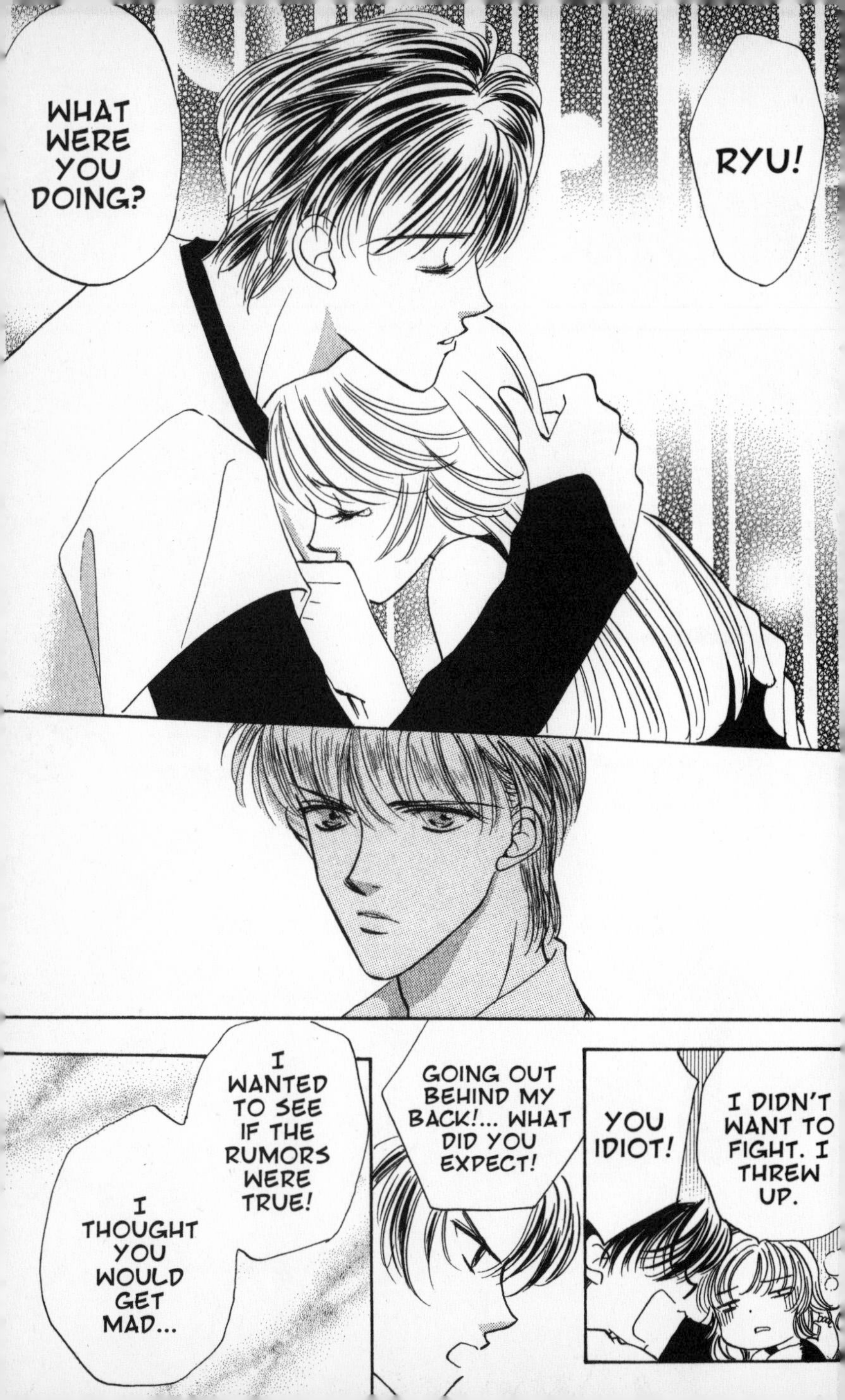
RYU!
WHAT WERE YOU DOING?
I DIDN'T WANT TO FIGHT. I THREW UP.
YOU IDIOT!
GOING OUT BEHIND MY BACK!... WHAT DID YOU EXPECT!
I WANTED TO SEE IF THE RUMORS WERE TRUE!
I THOUGHT YOU WOULD GET MAD...

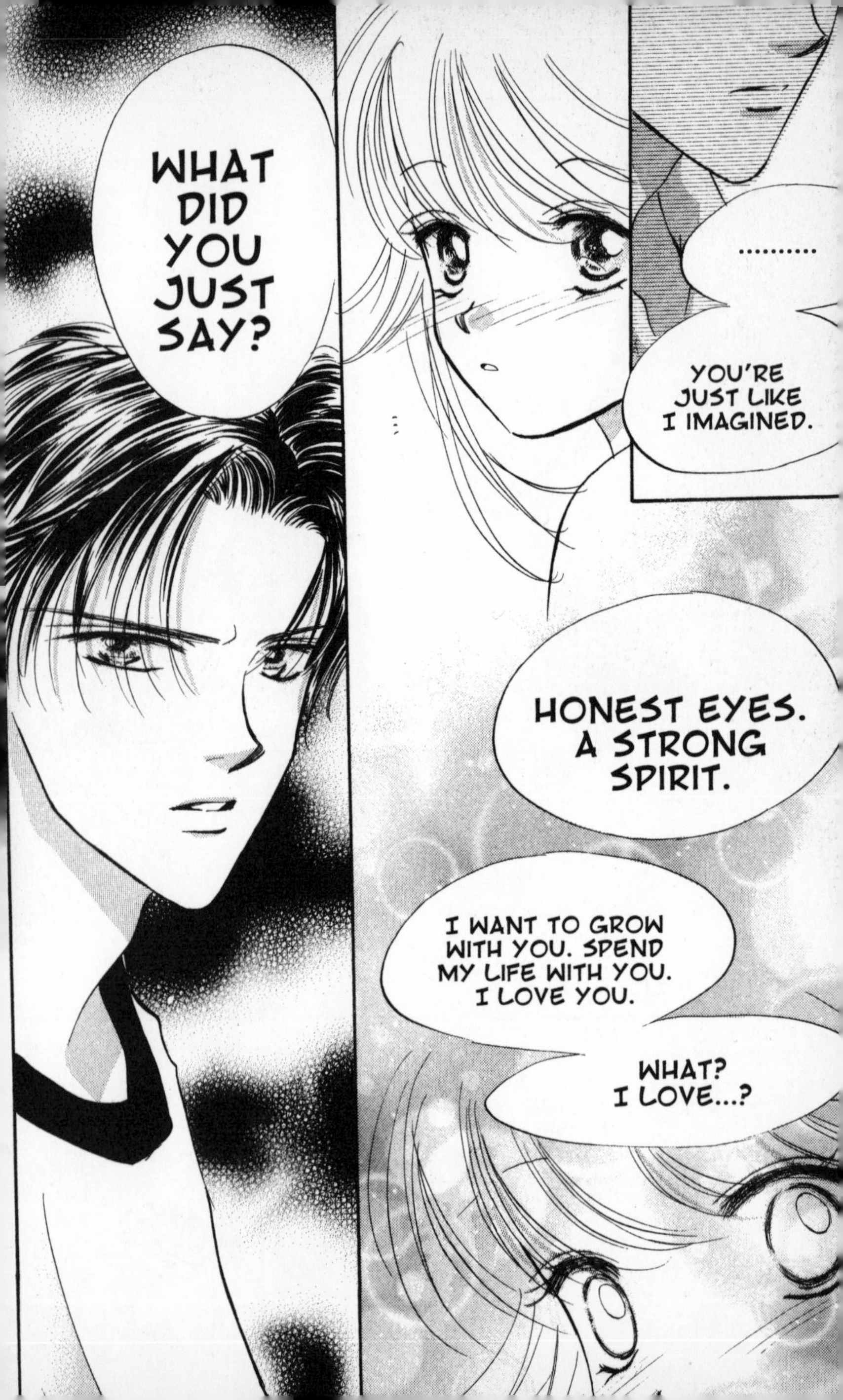

....
YOU'RE JUST LIKE I IMAGINED.
HONEST EYES. A STRONG SPIRIT.
I WANT TO GROW WITH YOU. SPEND MY LIFE WITH YOU. I LOVE YOU.
WHAT? I LOVE...?
WHAT DID YOU JUST SAY?

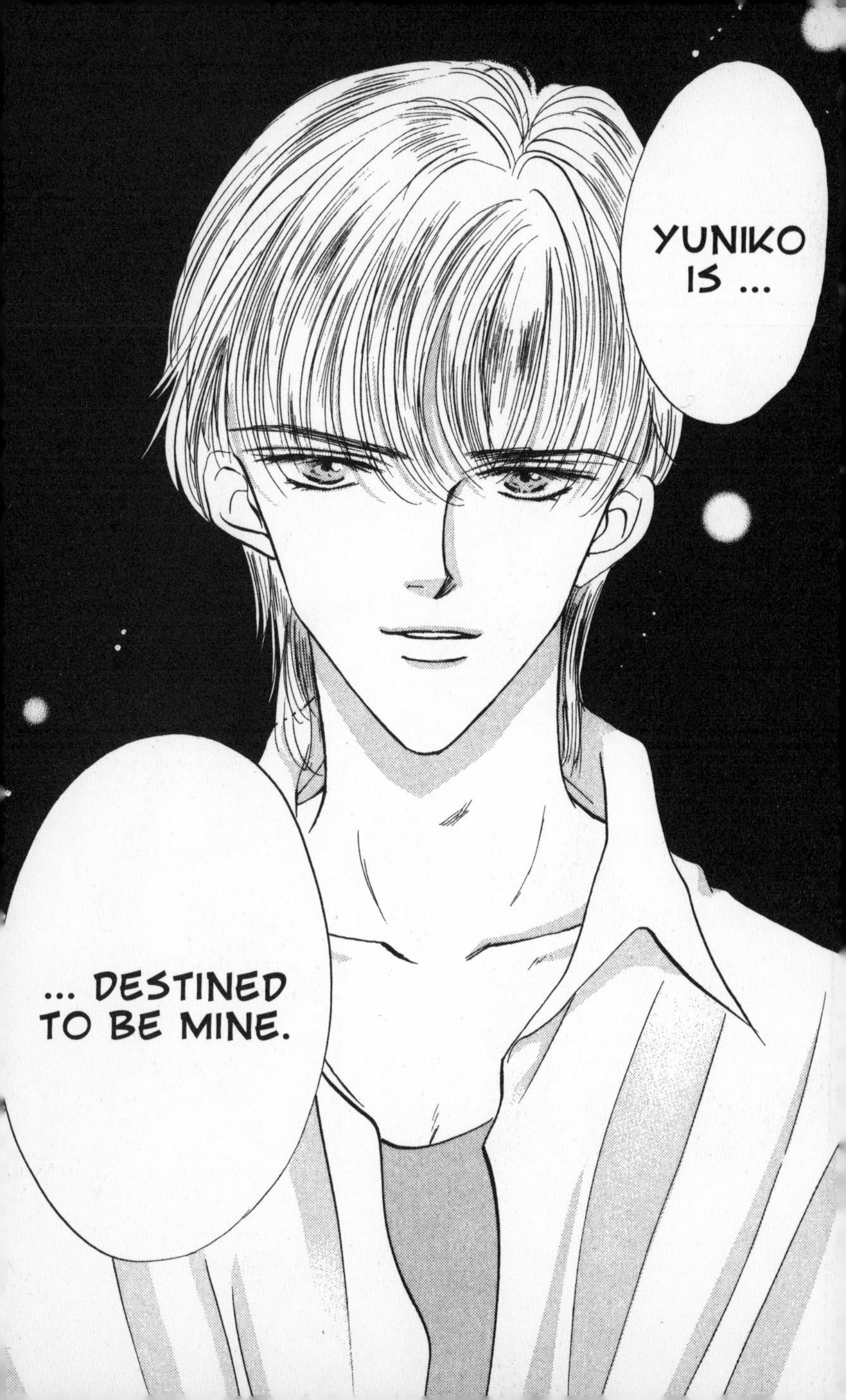
YUNIKO IS ...
... DESTINED TO BE MINE.

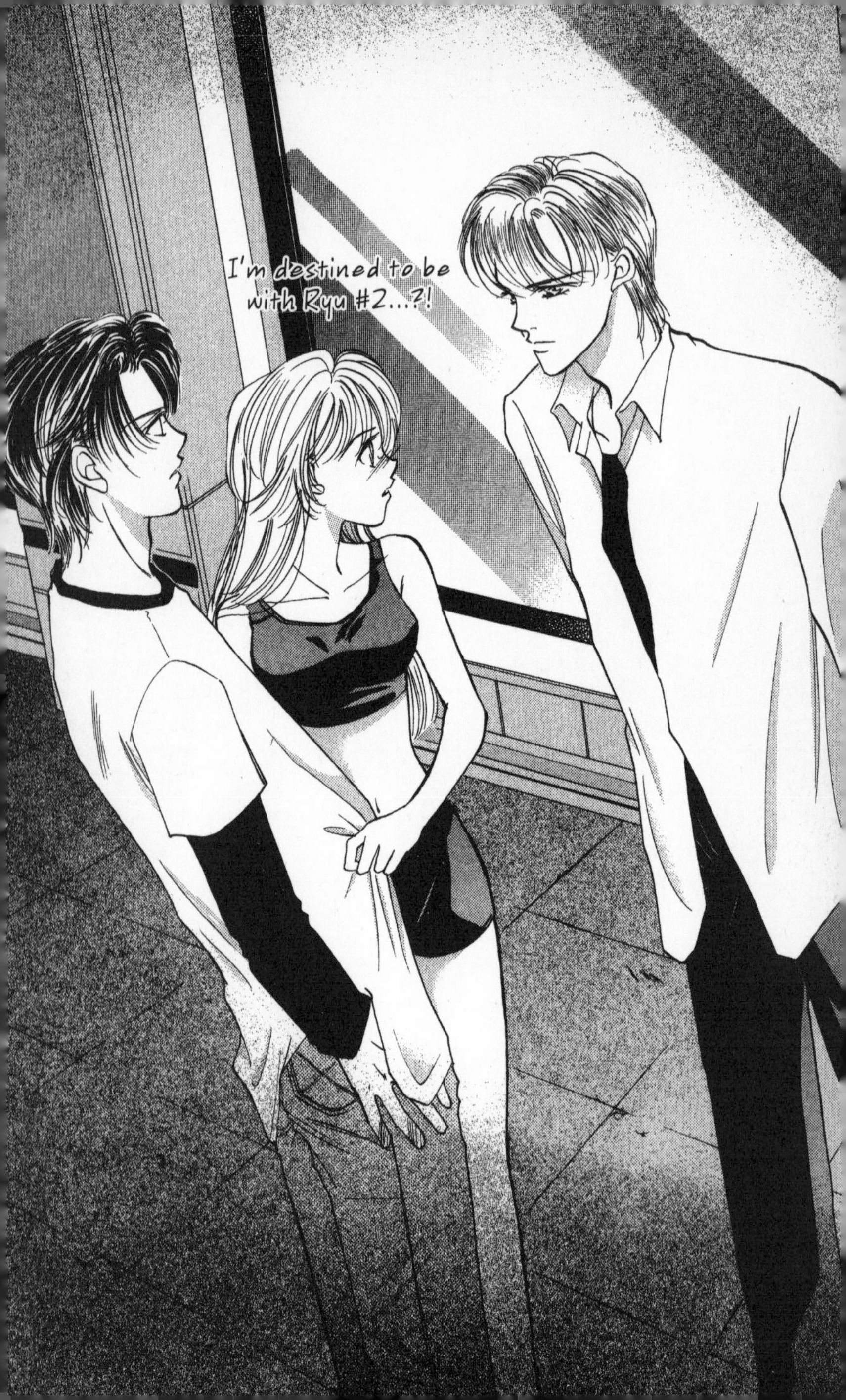
I'm destined to be with Ryu #2...?!

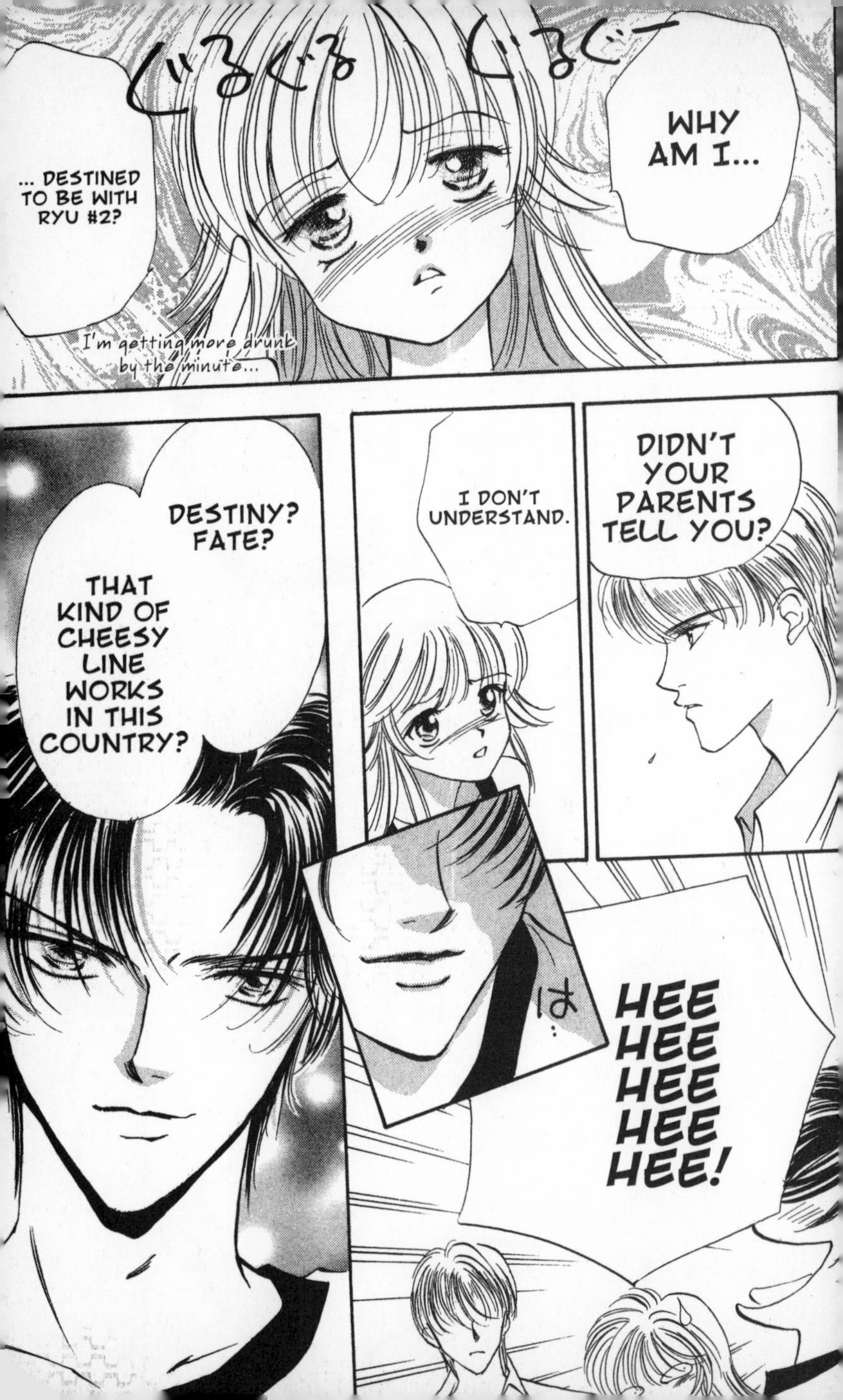
ぐるぐる ぐるぐー
WHY AM I...
... DESTINED TO BE WITH RYU #2?
I'm getting more drunk by the minute...
DIDN'T YOUR PARENTS TELL YOU?
I DON'T UNDERSTAND.
DESTINY? FATE?
THAT KIND OF CHEESY LINE WORKS IN THIS COUNTRY?
は
HEE HEE HEE HEE HEE!

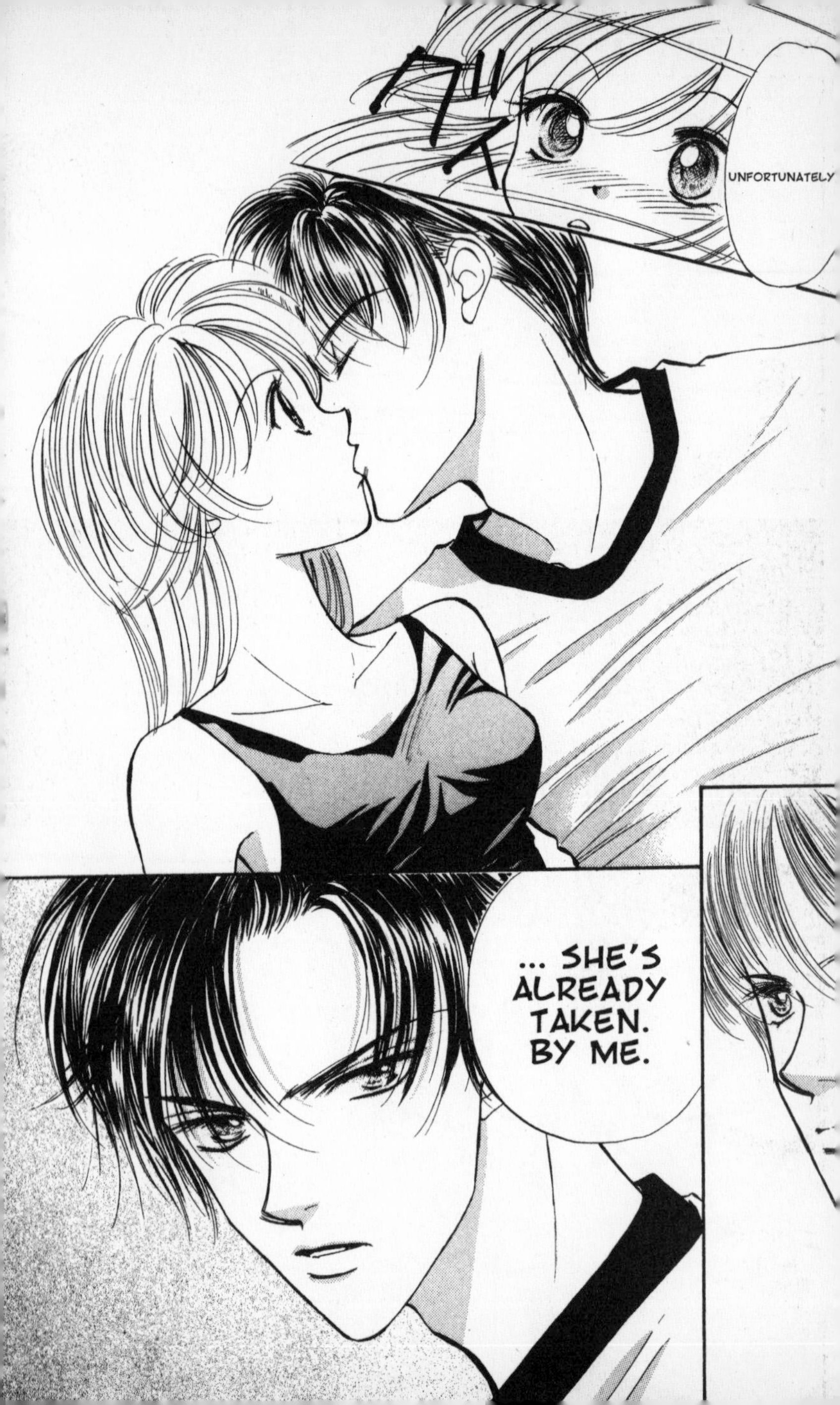
UNFORTUNATELY
... SHE'S ALREADY TAKEN. BY ME.

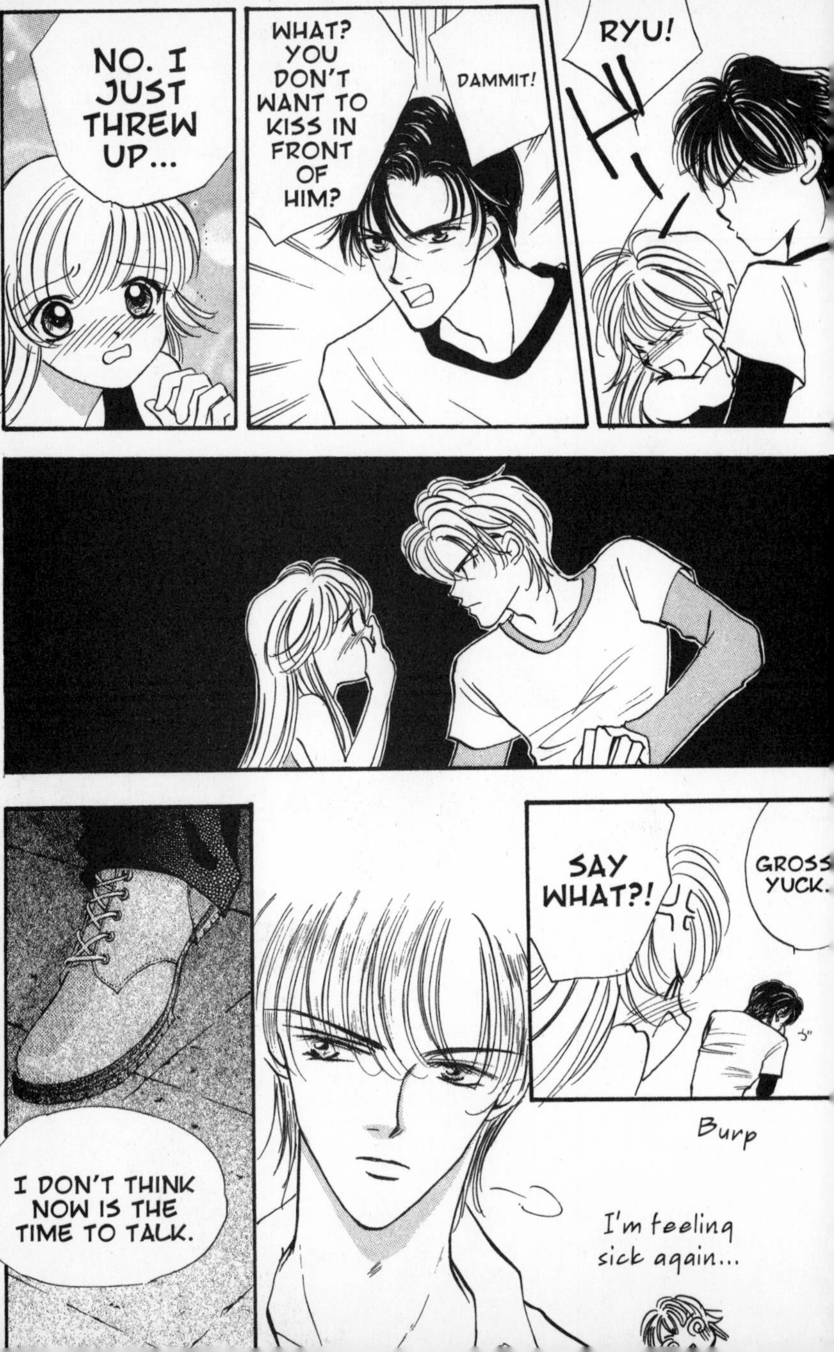
RYU!
DAMMIT!
WHAT? YOU DON'T WANT TO KISS IN FRONT OF HIM?
NO. I JUST THREW UP...
GROSS YUCK.
SAY WHAT?!
Burp
I'm feeling sick again...
I DON'T THINK NOW IS THE TIME TO TALK.

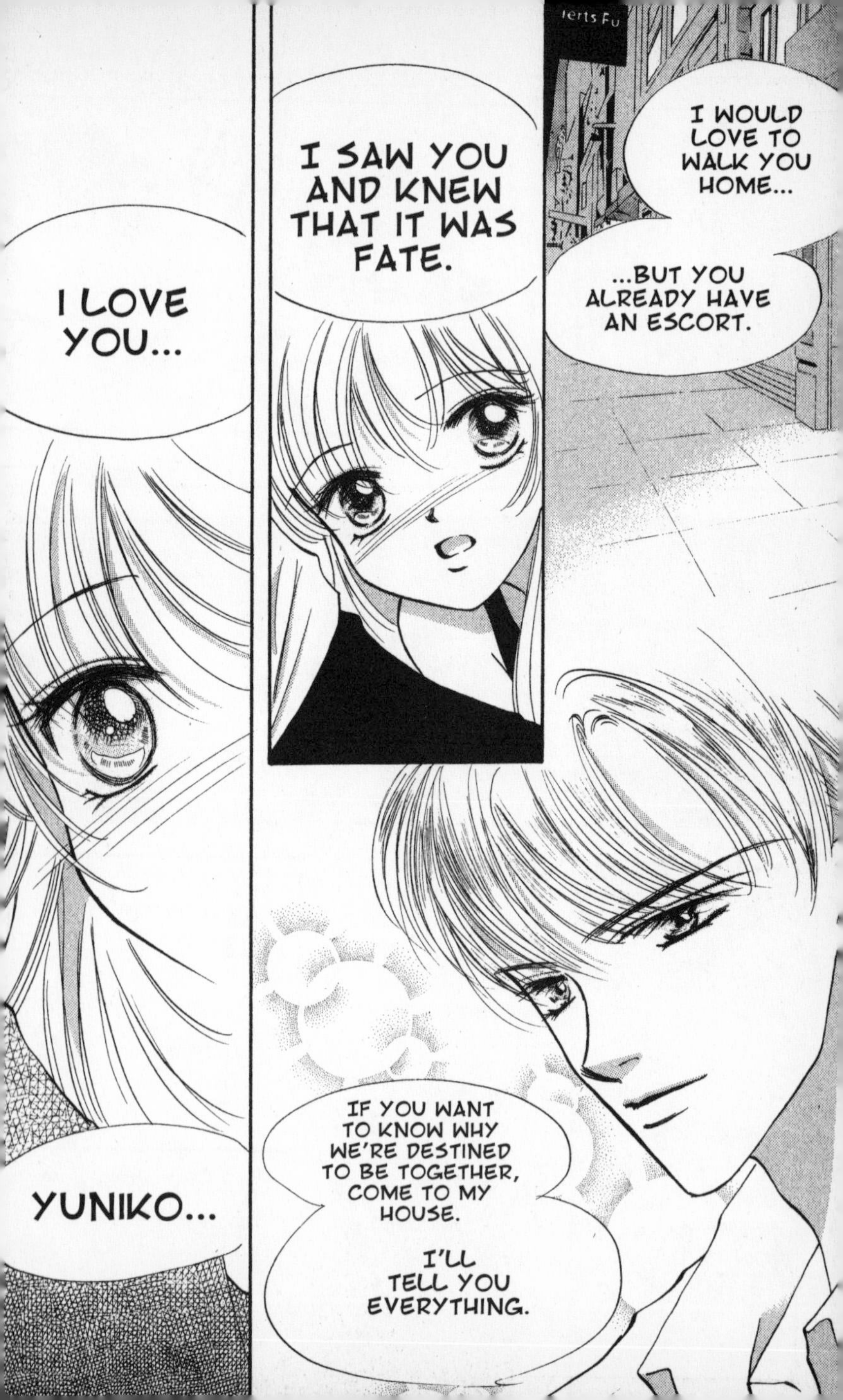

I WOULD LOVE TO WALK YOU HOME...
...BUT YOU ALREADY HAVE AN ESCORT.
I SAW YOU AND KNEW THAT IT WAS FATE.
IF YOU WANT TO KNOW WHY WE'RE DESTINED TO BE TOGETHER, COME TO MY HOUSE.
I'LL TELL YOU EVERYTHING.
I LOVE YOU...
YUNIKO...

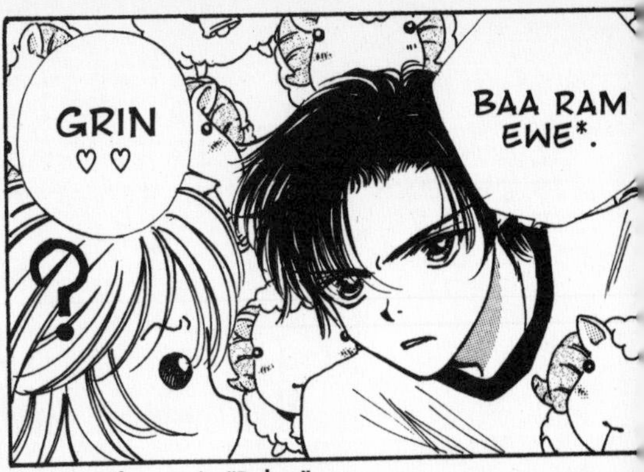
BAA RAM EWE*.
GRIN ♡ ♡
?

* From the movie "Babe."

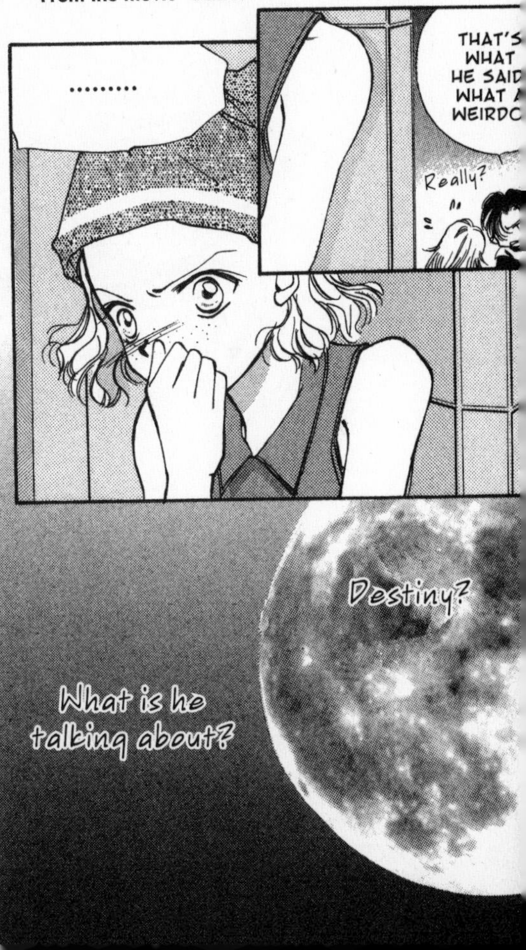
THAT'S WHAT HE SAID WHAT A WEIRDO
Really?
....
Destiny?
What is he talking about?

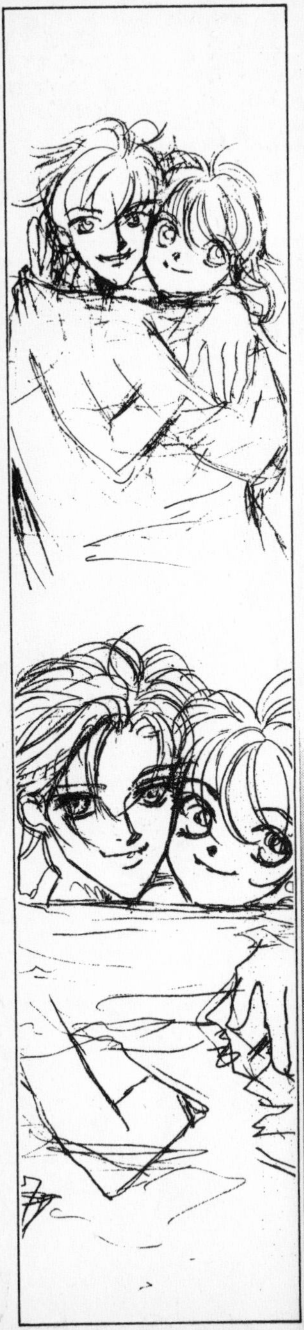

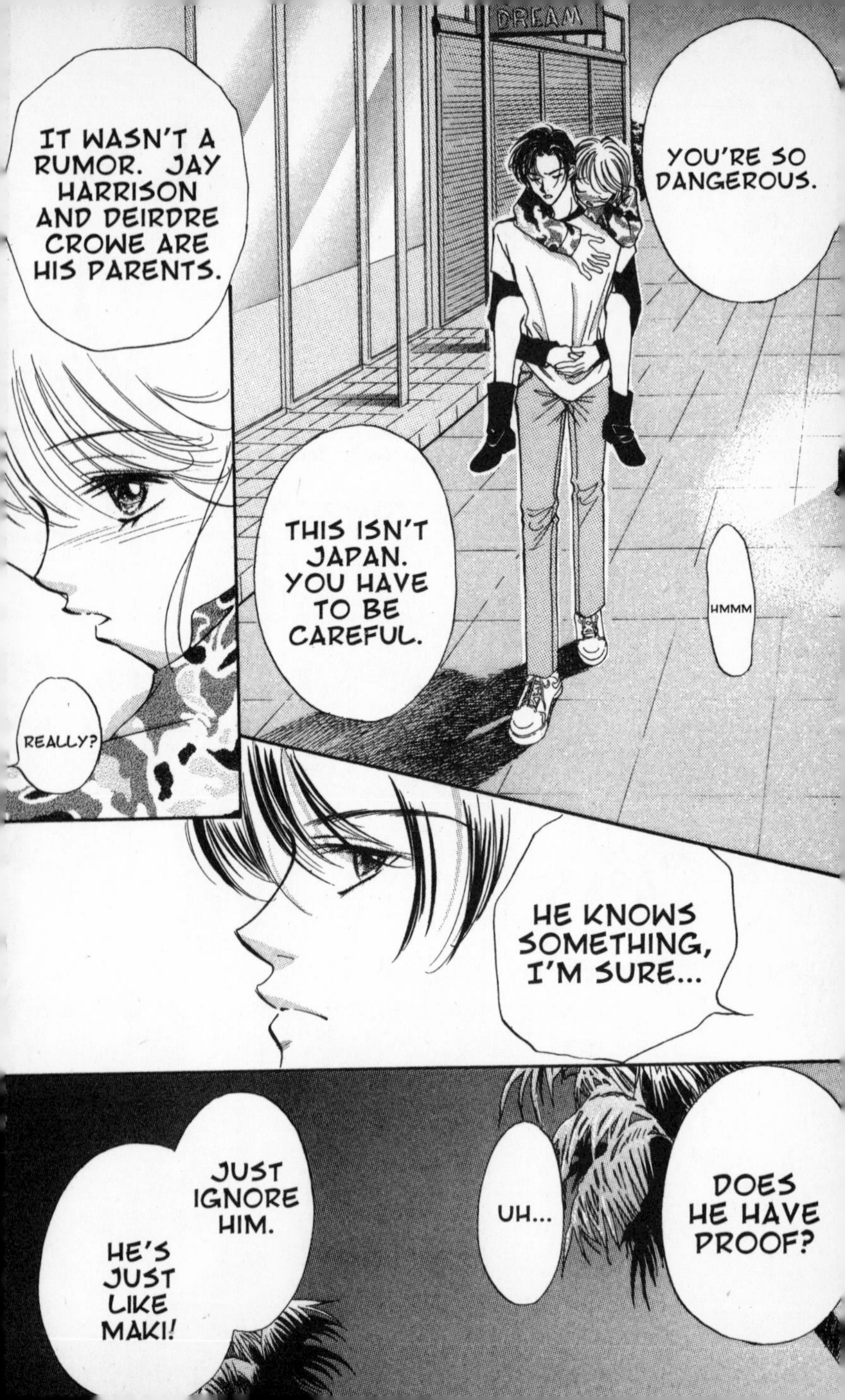
DREAM
YOU'RE SO DANGEROUS.
THIS ISN'T JAPAN. YOU HAVE TO BE CAREFUL.
HMMM
IT WASN'T A RUMOR. JAY HARRISON AND DEIRDRE CROWE ARE HIS PARENTS.
REALLY?
HE KNOWS SOMETHING, I'M SURE...
DOES HE HAVE PROOF?
UH...
JUST IGNORE HIM.
HE'S JUST LIKE MAKI!

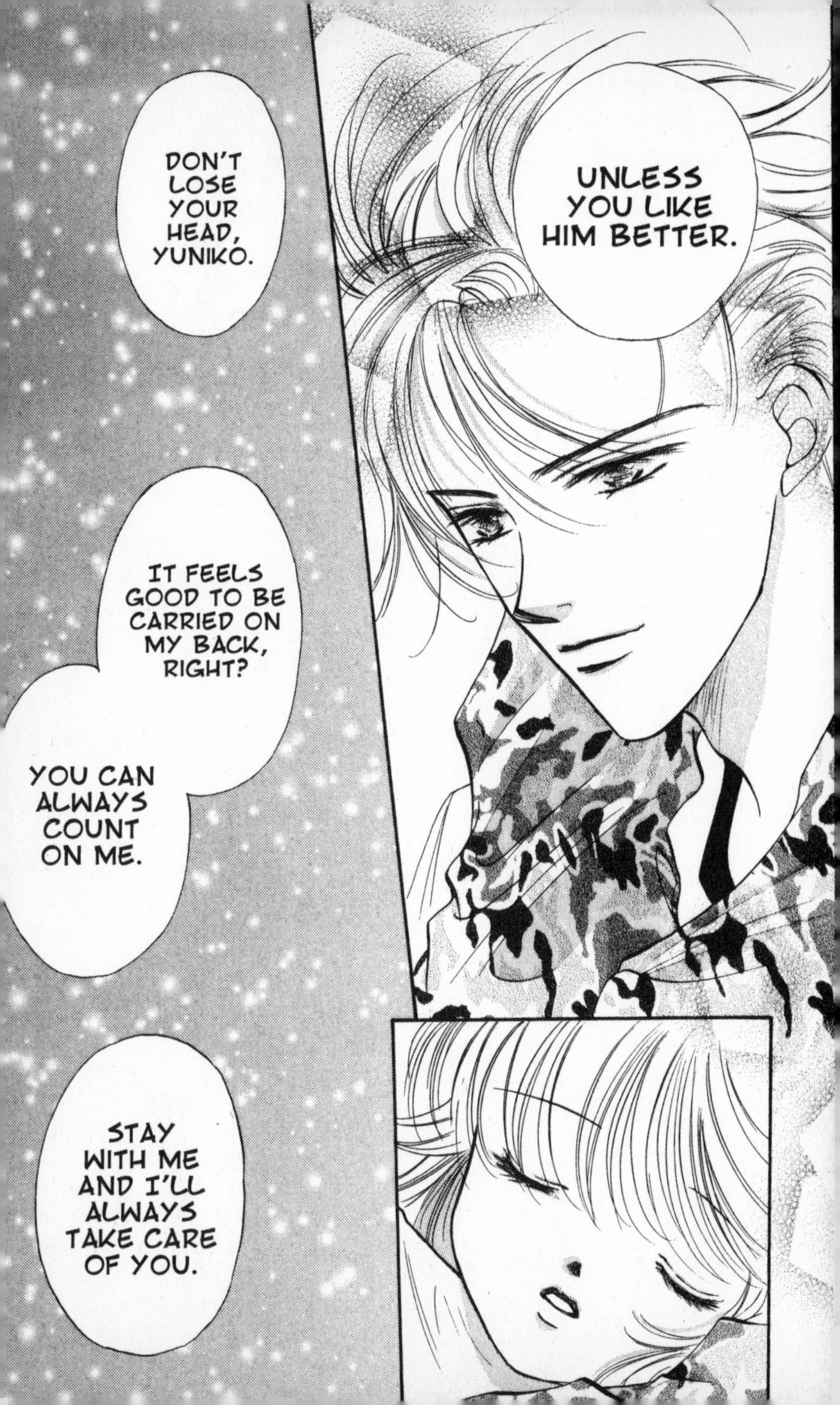
UNLESS YOU LIKE HIM BETTER.
DON'T LOSE YOUR HEAD, YUNIKO.
IT FEELS GOOD TO BE CARRIED ON MY BACK, RIGHT?
YOU CAN ALWAYS COUNT ON ME.
STAY WITH ME AND I'LL ALWAYS TAKE CARE OF YOU.

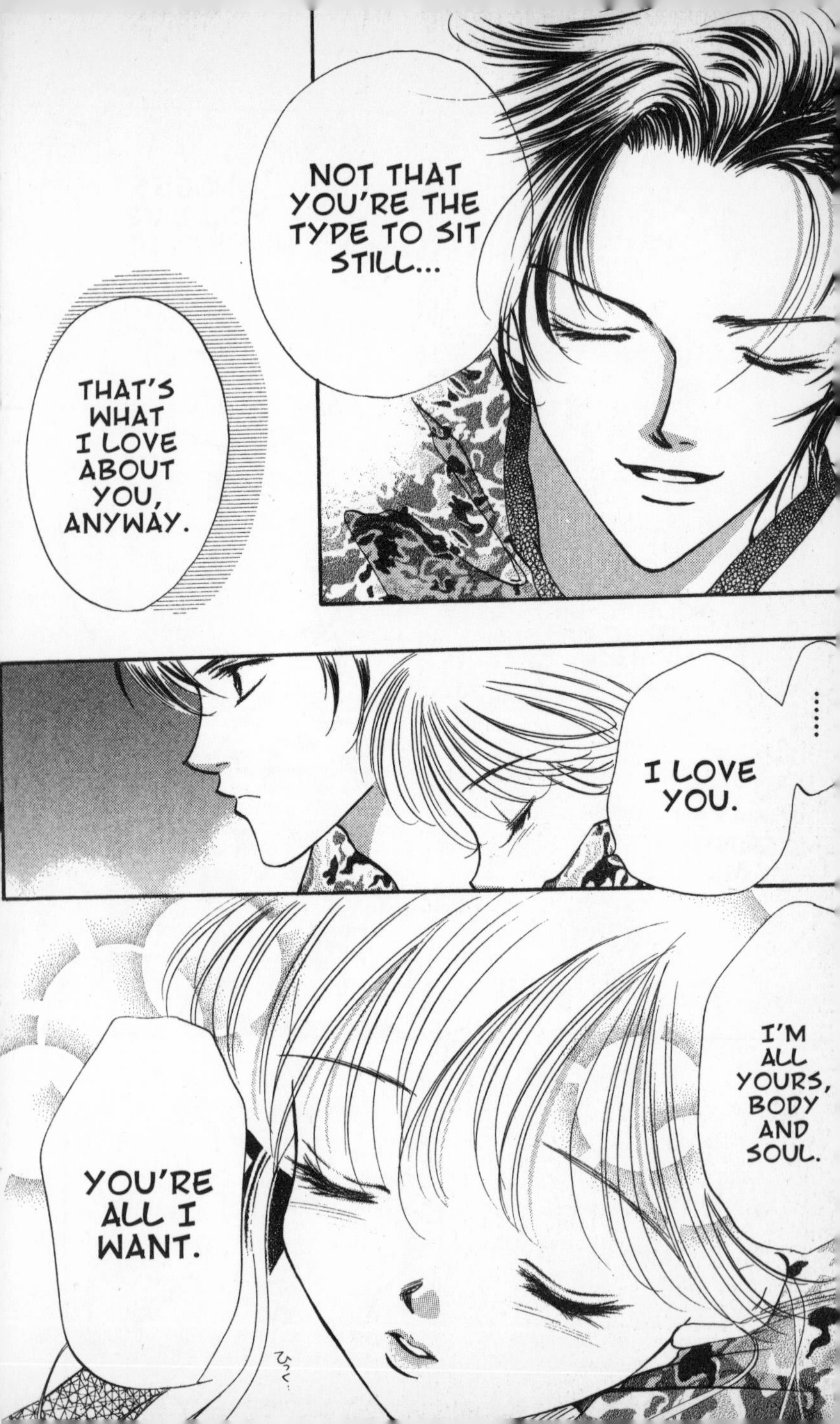
NOT THAT YOU'RE THE TYPE TO SIT STILL...
THAT'S WHAT I LOVE ABOUT YOU, ANYWAY.
......
I LOVE YOU.
I'M ALL YOURS, BODY AND SOUL.
YOU'RE ALL I WANT.

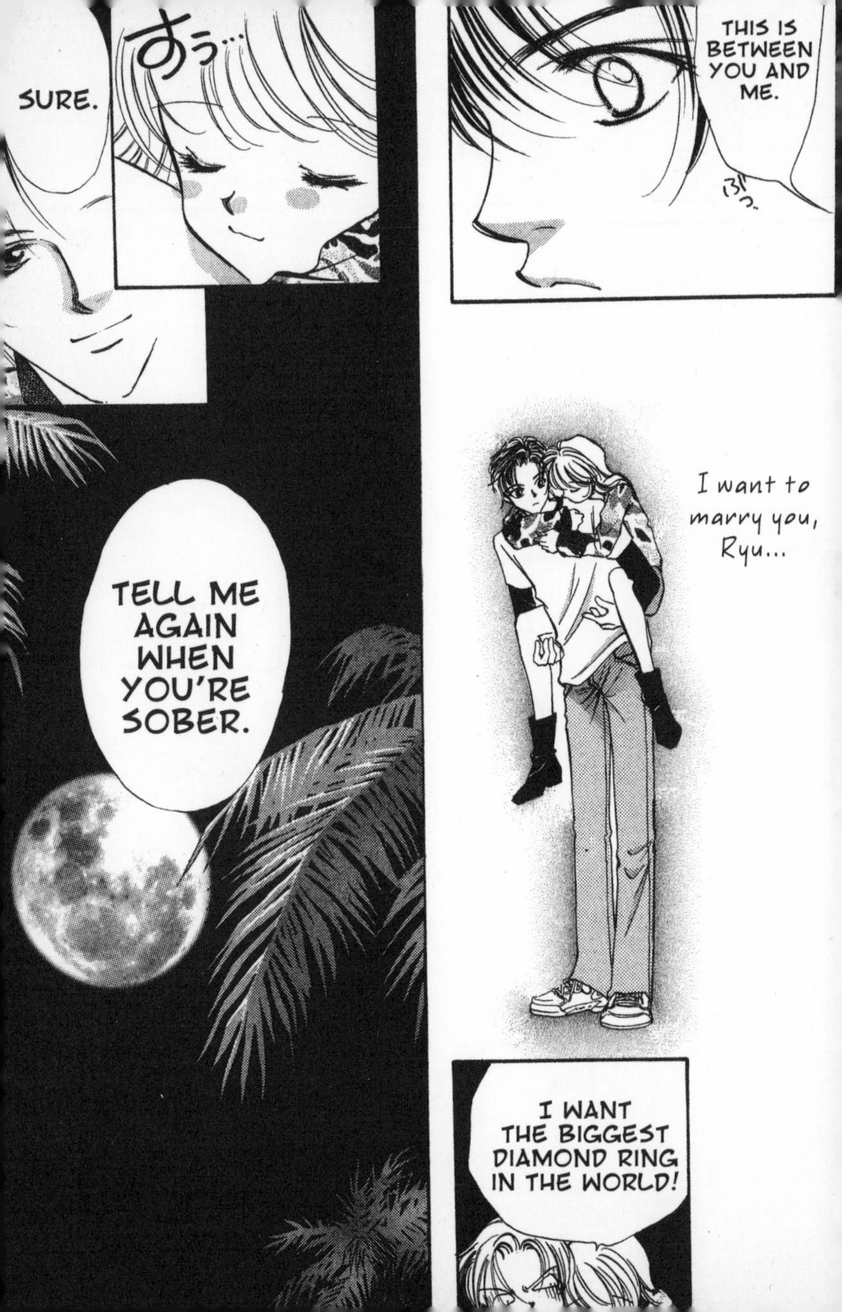
THIS IS BETWEEN YOU AND ME.
ぶっ
I want to marry you, Ryu...
I WANT THE BIGGEST DIAMOND RING IN THE WORLD!
すぅ…
SURE.
TELL ME AGAIN WHEN YOU'RE SOBER.

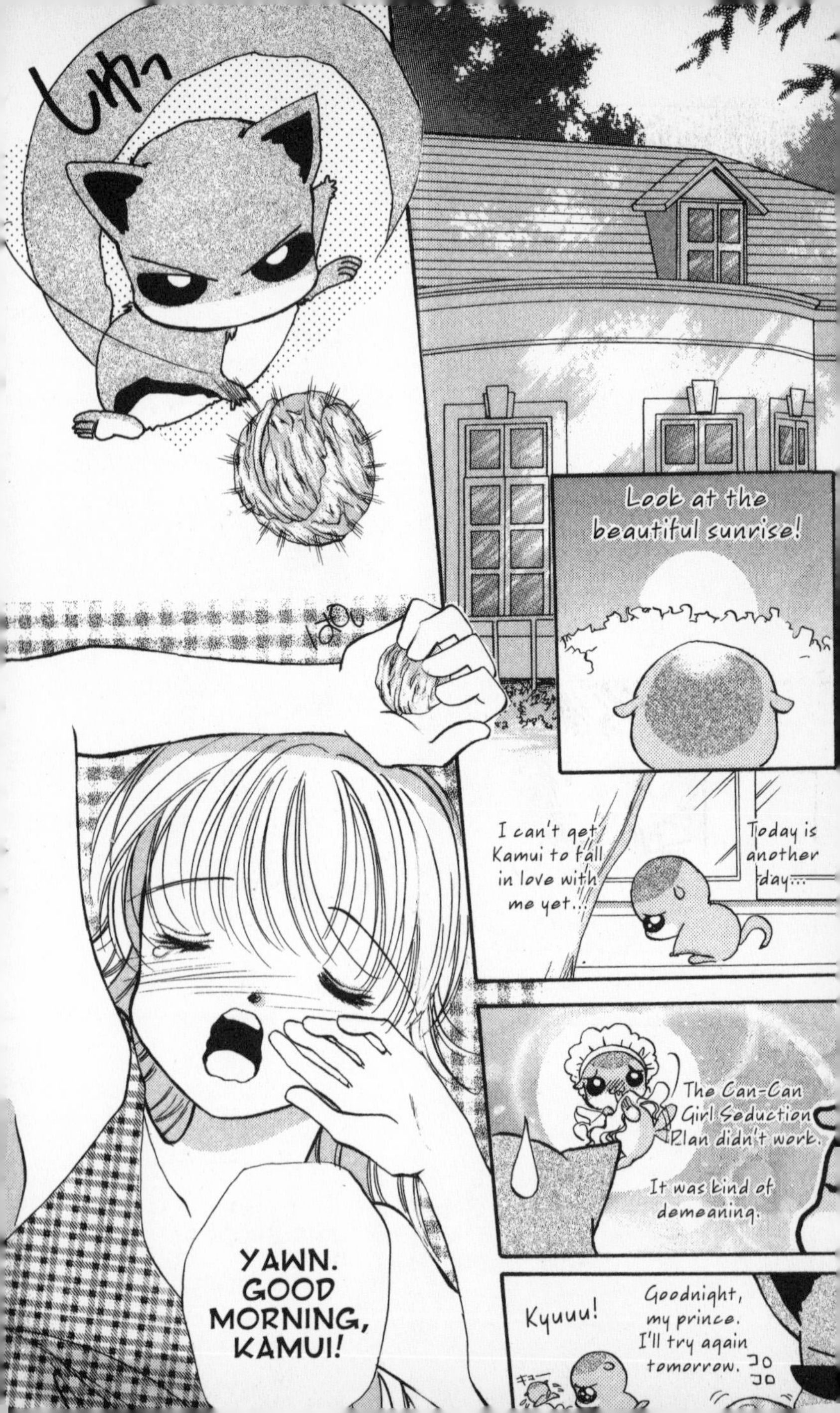
Look at the beautiful sunrise!
Today is another day...
I can't get Kamui to fall in love with me yet...
The Can-Can Girl Seduction Plan didn't work.
It was kind of demeaning.
Goodnight, my prince. I'll try again tomorrow.
Kyuuu!
YAWN. GOOD MORNING, KAMUI!

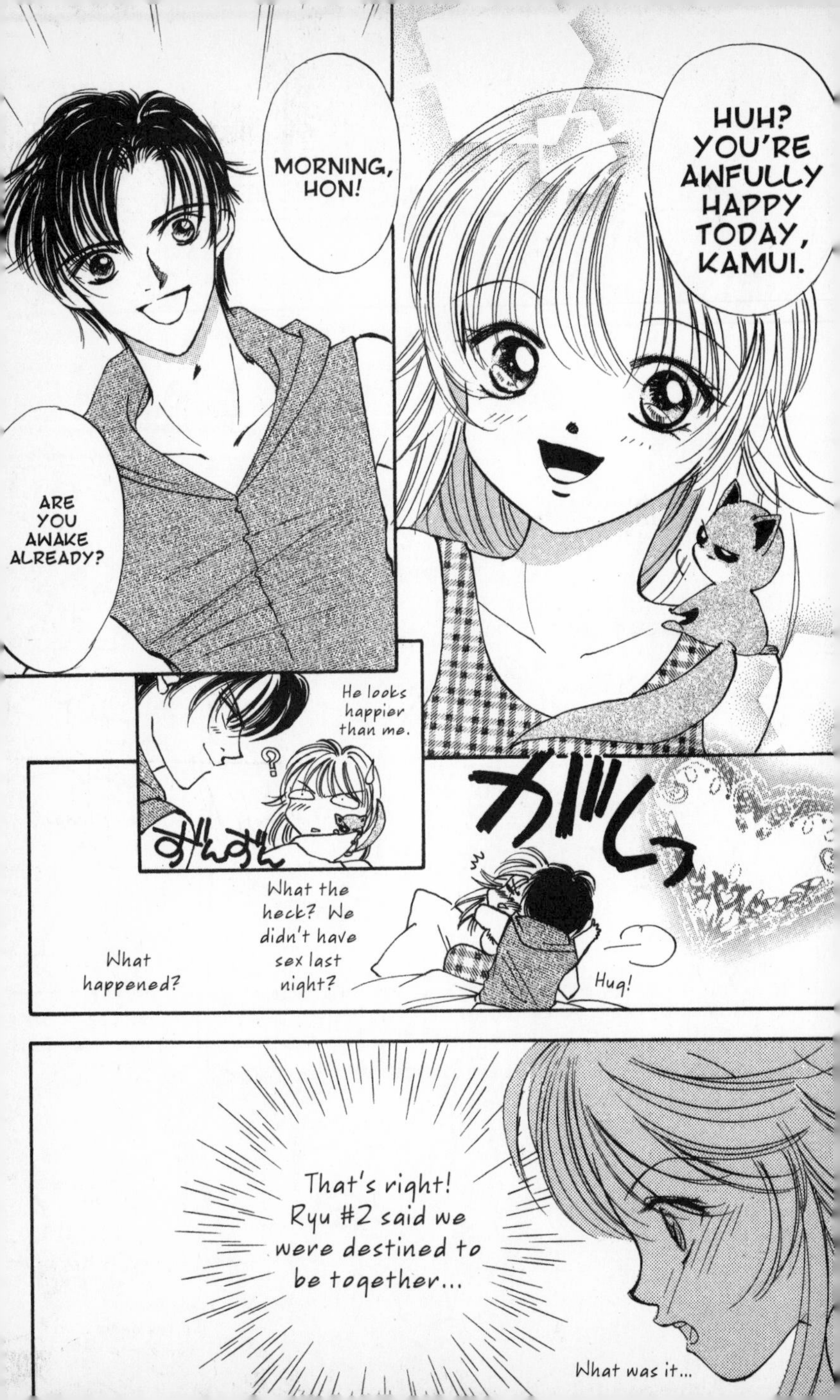
HUH? YOU'RE AWFULLY HAPPY TODAY, KAMUI.
MORNING, HON!
ARE YOU AWAKE ALREADY?
He looks happier than me.
ずんずん
がばっ
Hug!
What the heck? We didn't have sex last night?
What happened?
That's right! Ryu #2 said we were destined to be together...
What was it...

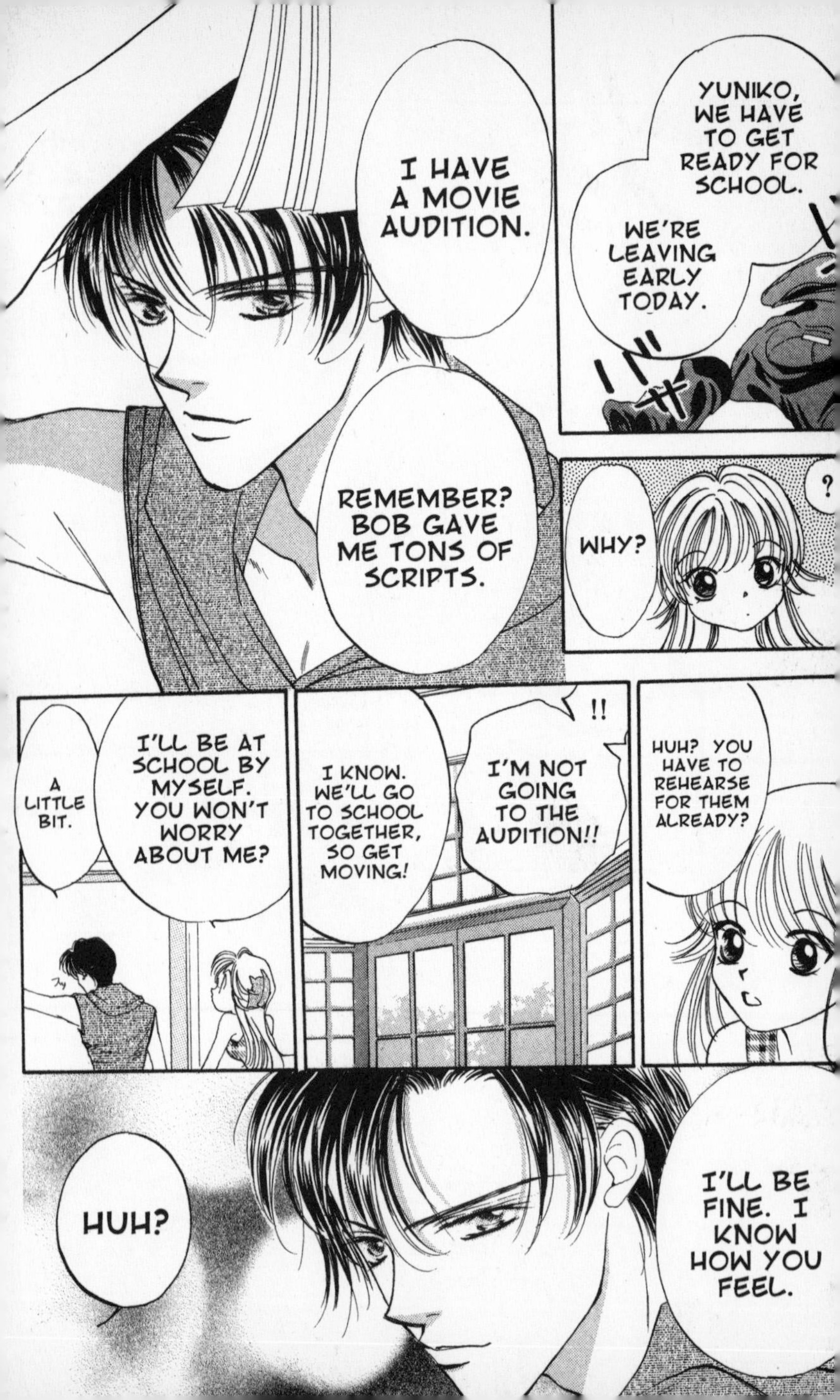
YUNIKO, WE HAVE TO GET READY FOR SCHOOL.
WE'RE LEAVING EARLY TODAY.
WHY?
?
I HAVE A MOVIE AUDITION.
REMEMBER? BOB GAVE ME TONS OF SCRIPTS.
HUH? YOU HAVE TO REHEARSE FOR THEM ALREADY?
!!
I'M NOT GOING TO THE AUDITION!!
I KNOW. WE'LL GO TO SCHOOL TOGETHER, SO GET MOVING!
I'LL BE AT SCHOOL BY MYSELF. YOU WON'T WORRY ABOUT ME?
A LITTLE BIT.
I'LL BE FINE. I KNOW HOW YOU FEEL.
HUH?

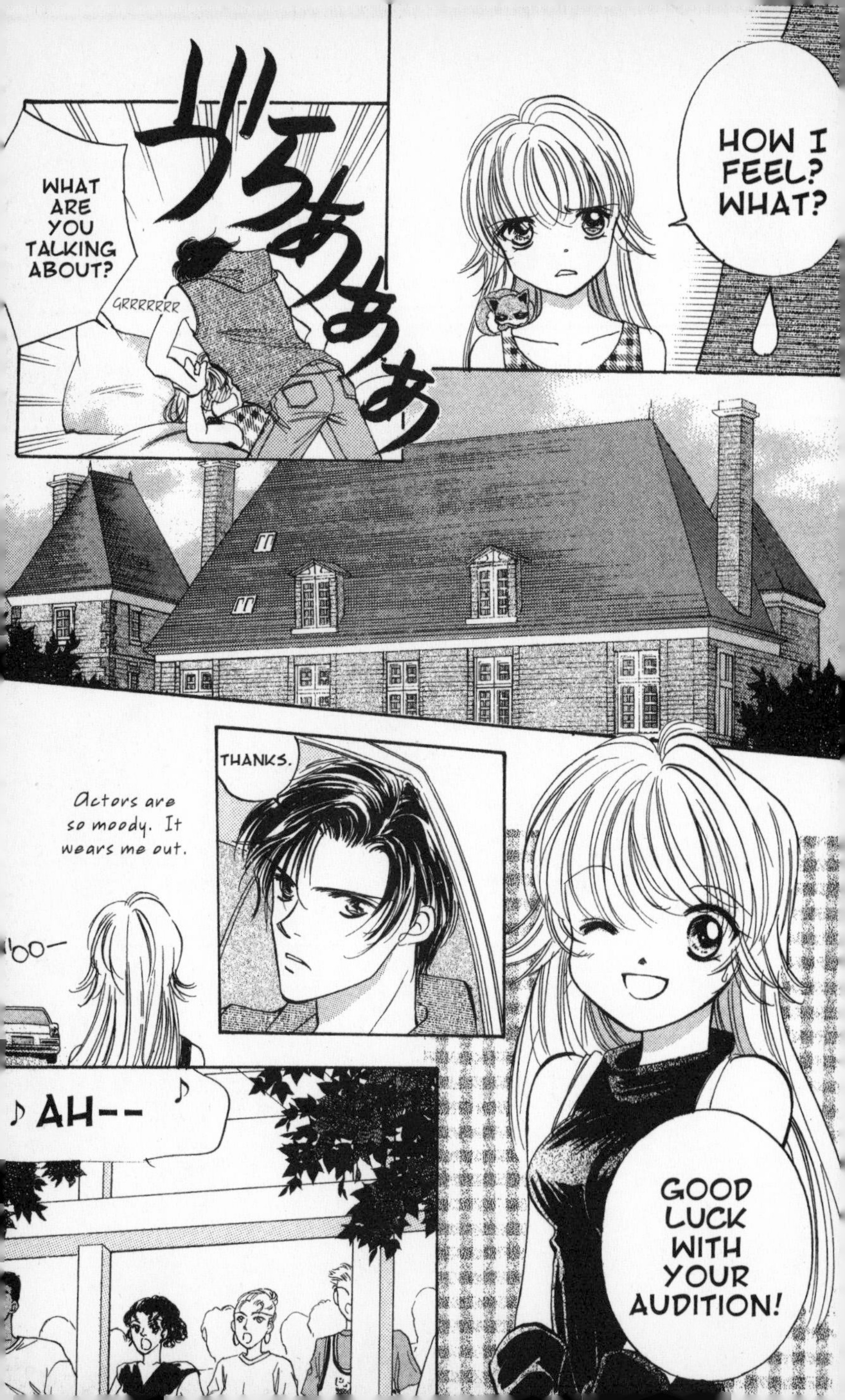
HOW I FEEL? WHAT?
WHAT ARE YOU TALKING ABOUT?
GRRRRRRR
GOOD LUCK WITH YOUR AUDITION!
THANKS.
Actors are so moody. It wears me out.
♪ AH-- ♪

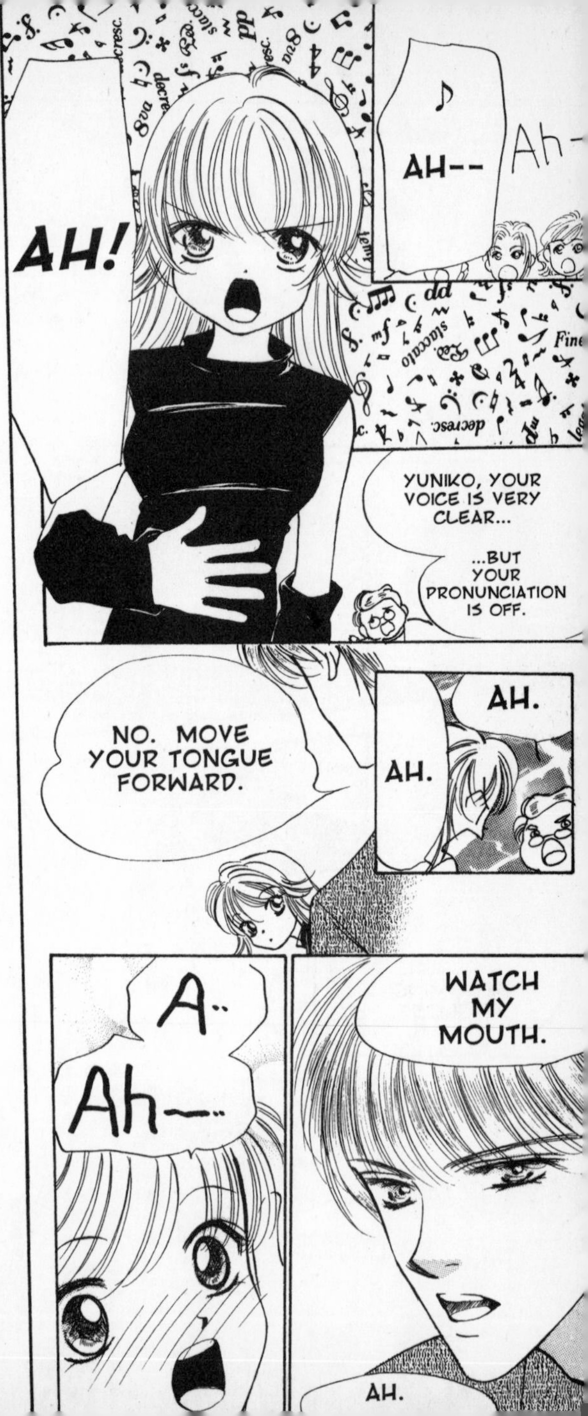
AH--
Ah-
YUNIKO, YOUR VOICE IS VERY CLEAR...
...BUT YOUR PRONUNCIATION IS OFF.
AH!
AH.
AH.
NO. MOVE YOUR TONGUE FORWARD.
WATCH MY MOUTH.
AH.
A..
Ah--..

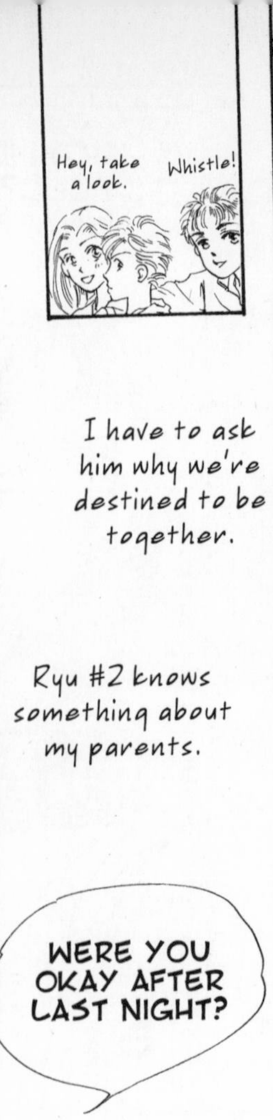
Whistle!
Hey, take a look.
I have to ask him why we're destined to be together.
Ryu #2 knows something about my parents.
WERE YOU OKAY AFTER LAST NIGHT?

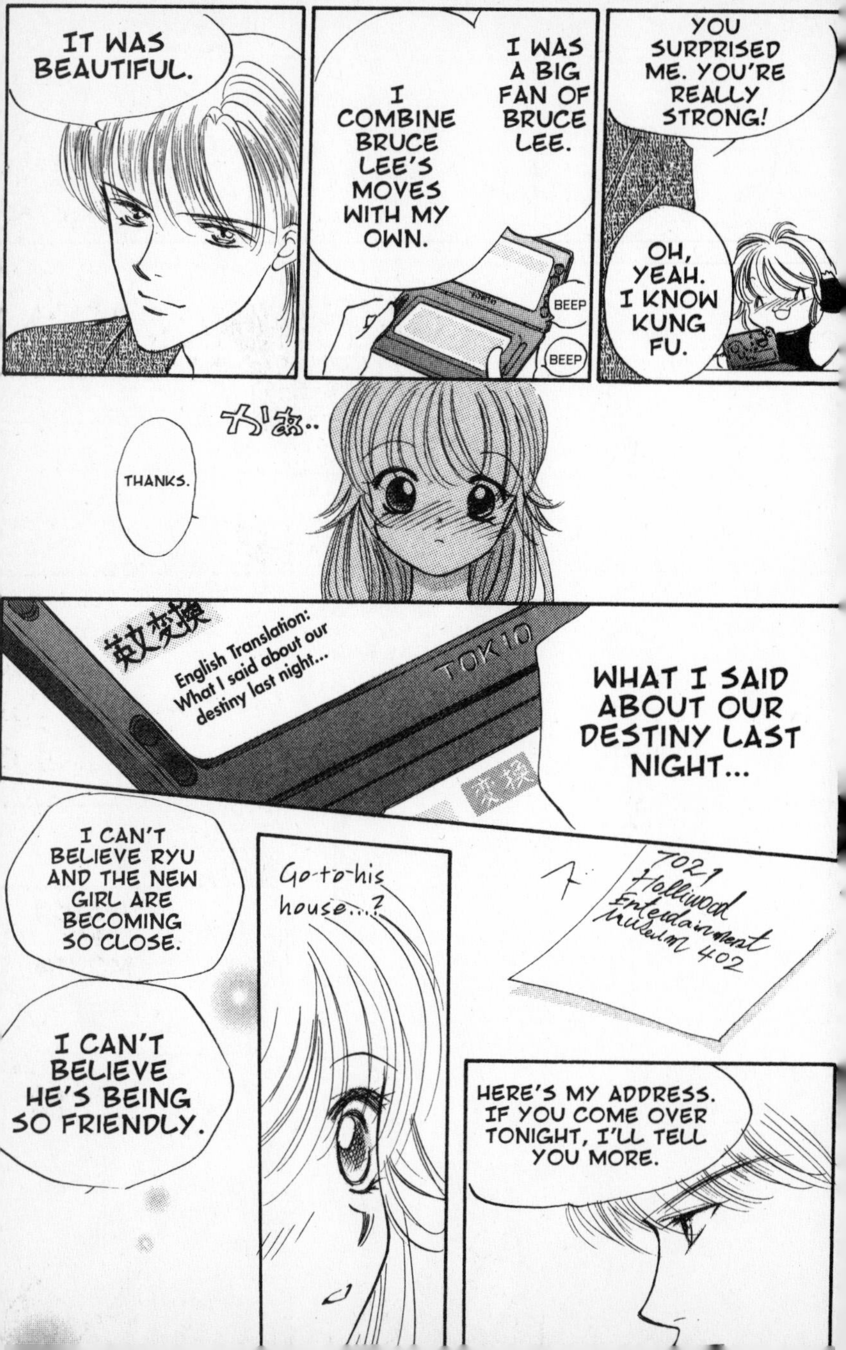
YOU SURPRISED ME. YOU'RE REALLY STRONG!
OH, YEAH. I KNOW KUNG FU.
I WAS A BIG FAN OF BRUCE LEE.
I COMBINE BRUCE LEE'S MOVES WITH MY OWN.
BEEP
BEEP
IT WAS BEAUTIFUL.
わぁ..
THANKS.
WHAT I SAID ABOUT OUR DESTINY LAST NIGHT...
TOKIO
英文変換
English Translation: What I said about our destiny last night...
変換
7021 Holliwood Entedainment Museum 402
HERE'S MY ADDRESS. IF YOU COME OVER TONIGHT, I'LL TELL YOU MORE.
Go-to-his house...?
I CAN'T BELIEVE RYU AND THE NEW GIRL ARE BECOMING SO CLOSE.
I CAN'T BELIEVE HE'S BEING SO FRIENDLY.

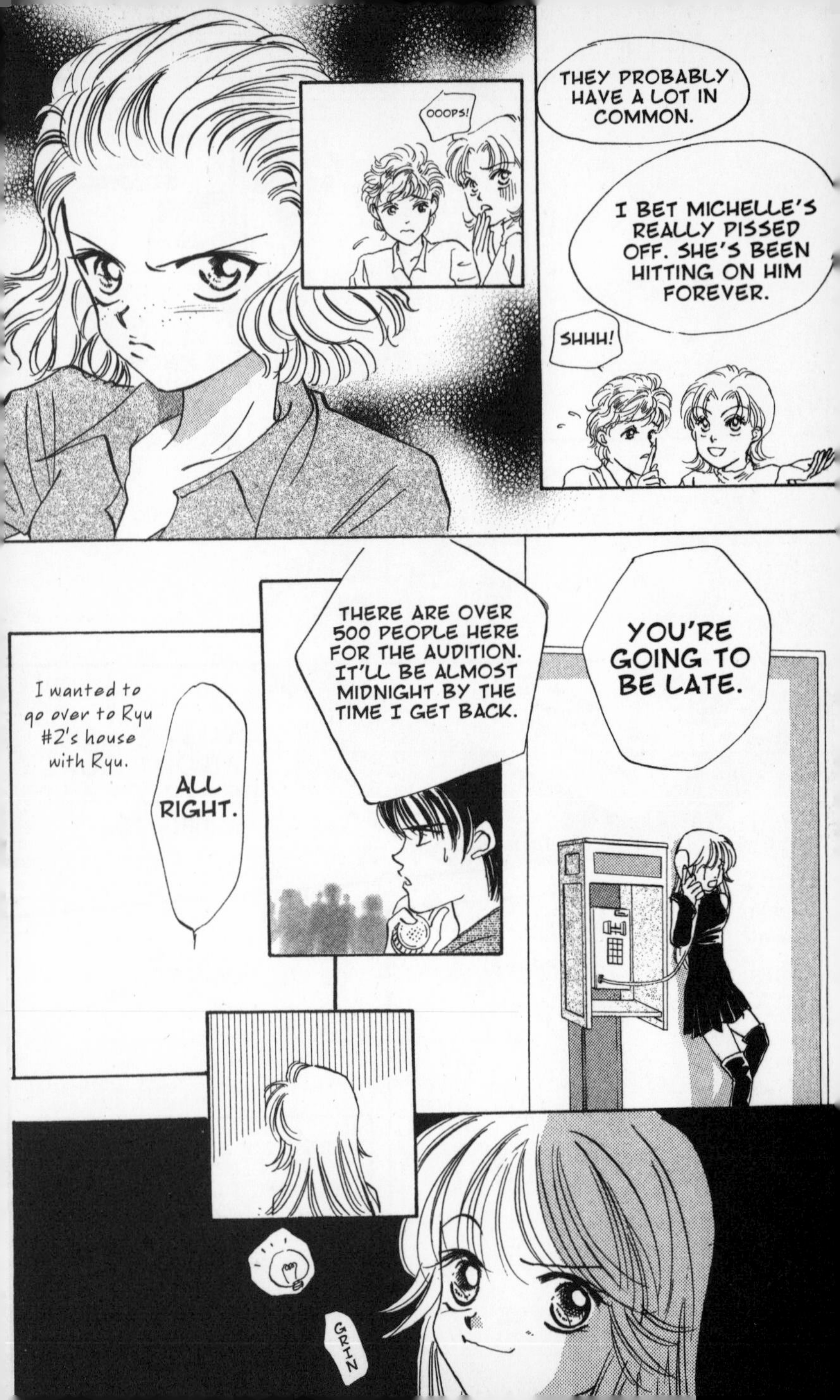
THEY PROBABLY HAVE A LOT IN COMMON.
I BET MICHELLE'S REALLY PISSED OFF. SHE'S BEEN HITTING ON HIM FOREVER.
SHHH!
OOOPS!
YOU'RE GOING TO BE LATE.
THERE ARE OVER 500 PEOPLE HERE FOR THE AUDITION. IT'LL BE ALMOST MIDNIGHT BY THE TIME I GET BACK.
ALL RIGHT.
I wanted to go over to Ryu #2's house with Ryu.
GRIN

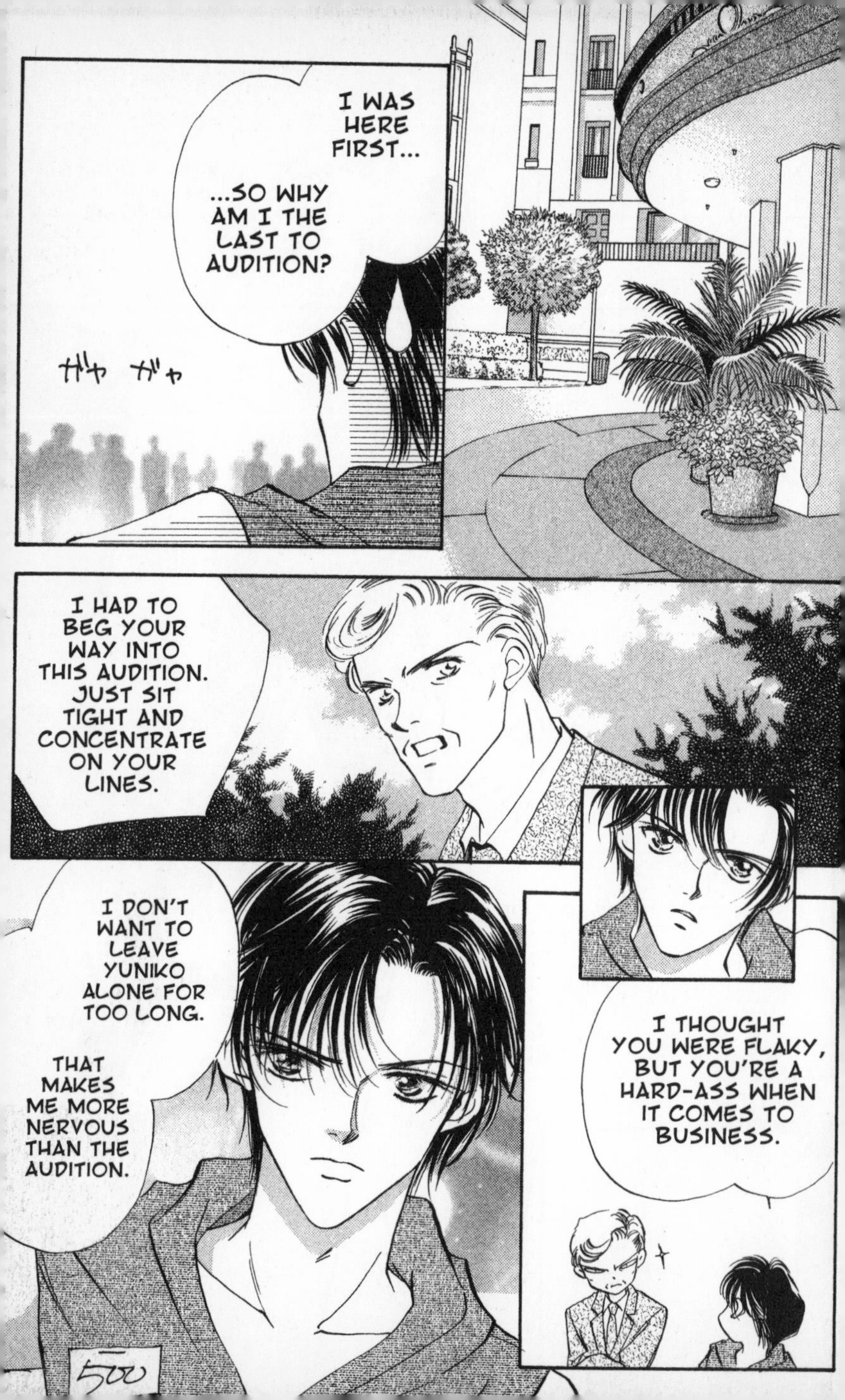
I WAS HERE FIRST...
...SO WHY AM I THE LAST TO AUDITION?
ガヤ ガヤ
I HAD TO BEG YOUR WAY INTO THIS AUDITION. JUST SIT TIGHT AND CONCENTRATE ON YOUR LINES.
I THOUGHT YOU WERE FLAKY, BUT YOU'RE A HARD-ASS WHEN IT COMES TO BUSINESS.
I DON'T WANT TO LEAVE YUNIKO ALONE FOR TOO LONG.
THAT MAKES ME MORE NERVOUS THAN THE AUDITION.
500

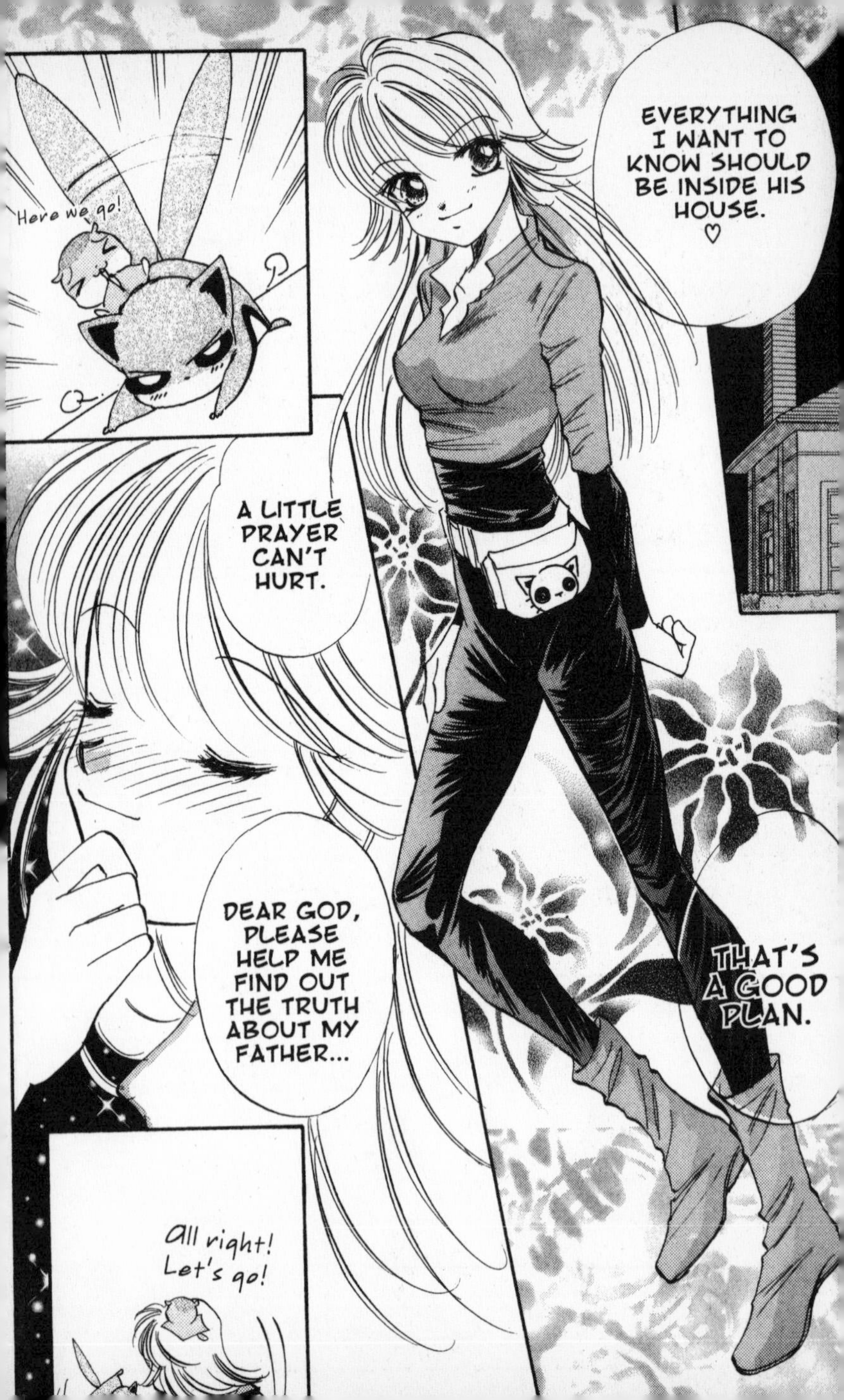
EVERYTHING I WANT TO KNOW SHOULD BE INSIDE HIS HOUSE. ♡
THAT'S A GOOD PLAN.
Here we go!
A LITTLE PRAYER CAN'T HURT.
DEAR GOD, PLEASE HELP ME FIND OUT THE TRUTH ABOUT MY FATHER...
All right! Let's go!

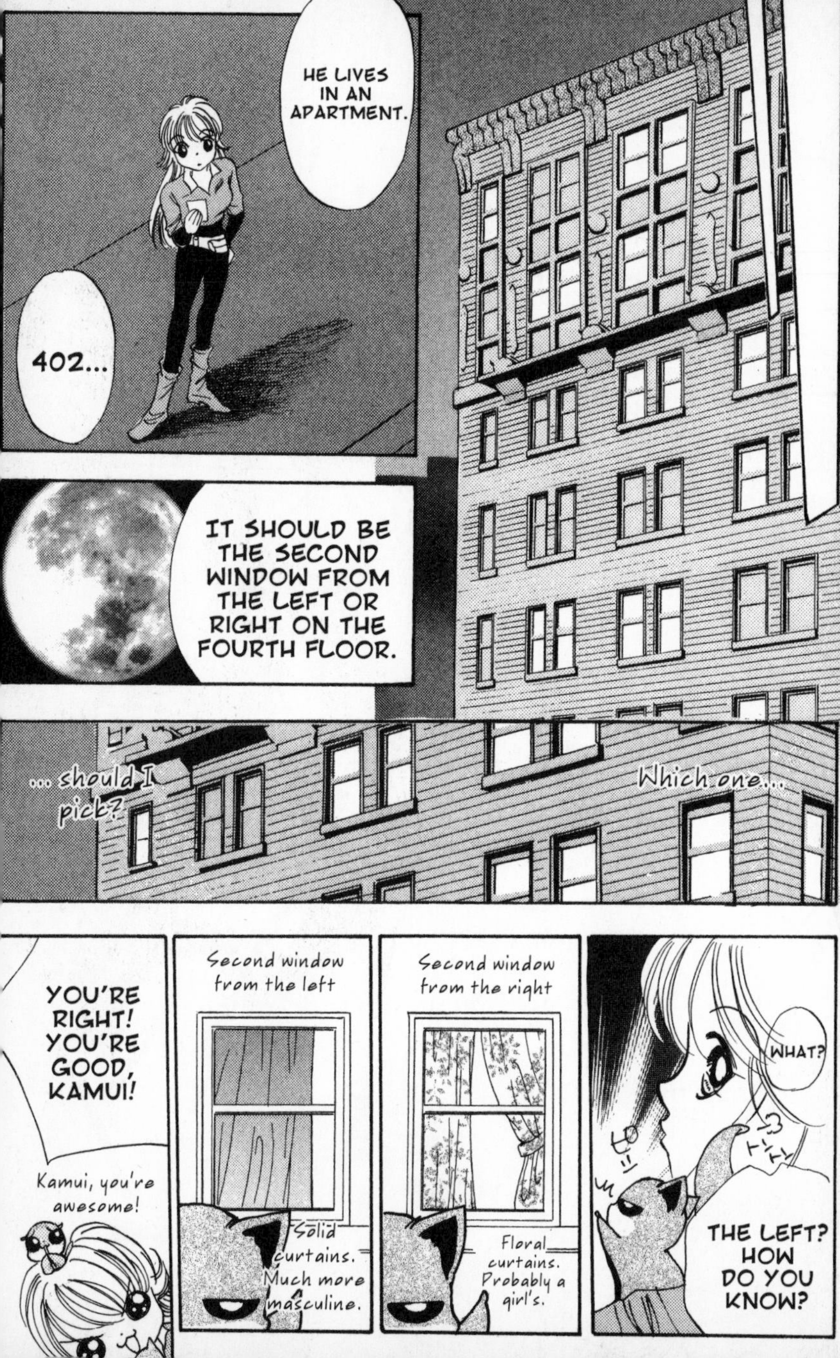
HE LIVES IN AN APARTMENT.
402...
IT SHOULD BE THE SECOND WINDOW FROM THE LEFT OR RIGHT ON THE FOURTH FLOOR.
Which one...
... should I pick?
WHAT?
THE LEFT? HOW DO YOU KNOW?
Second window from the right
Floral curtains. Probably a girl's.
Second window from the left
Solid curtains. Much more masculine.
YOU'RE RIGHT! YOU'RE GOOD, KAMUI!
Kamui, you're awesome!

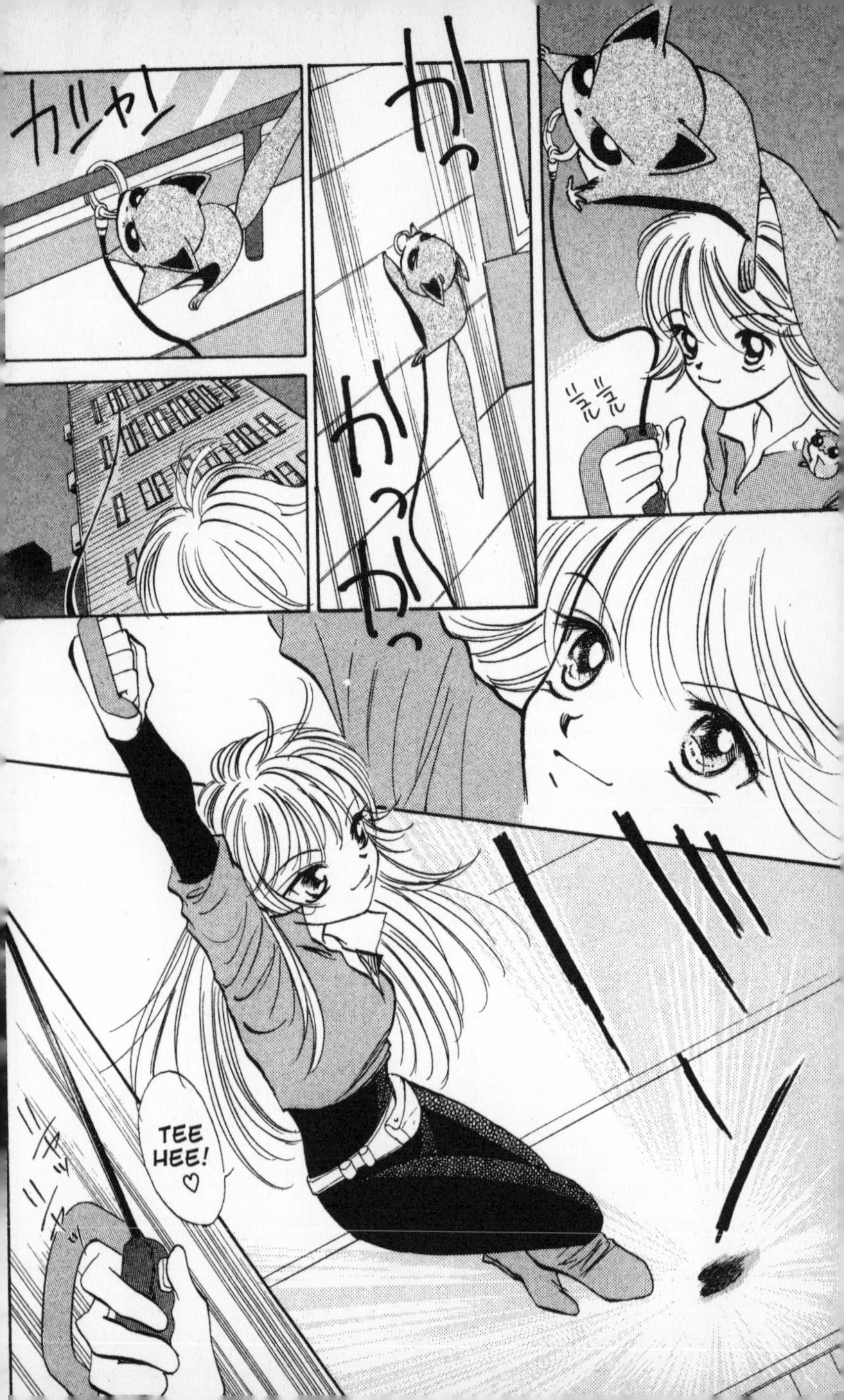
ガシャ!
わっ
わっわっ
TEE HEE! ♡

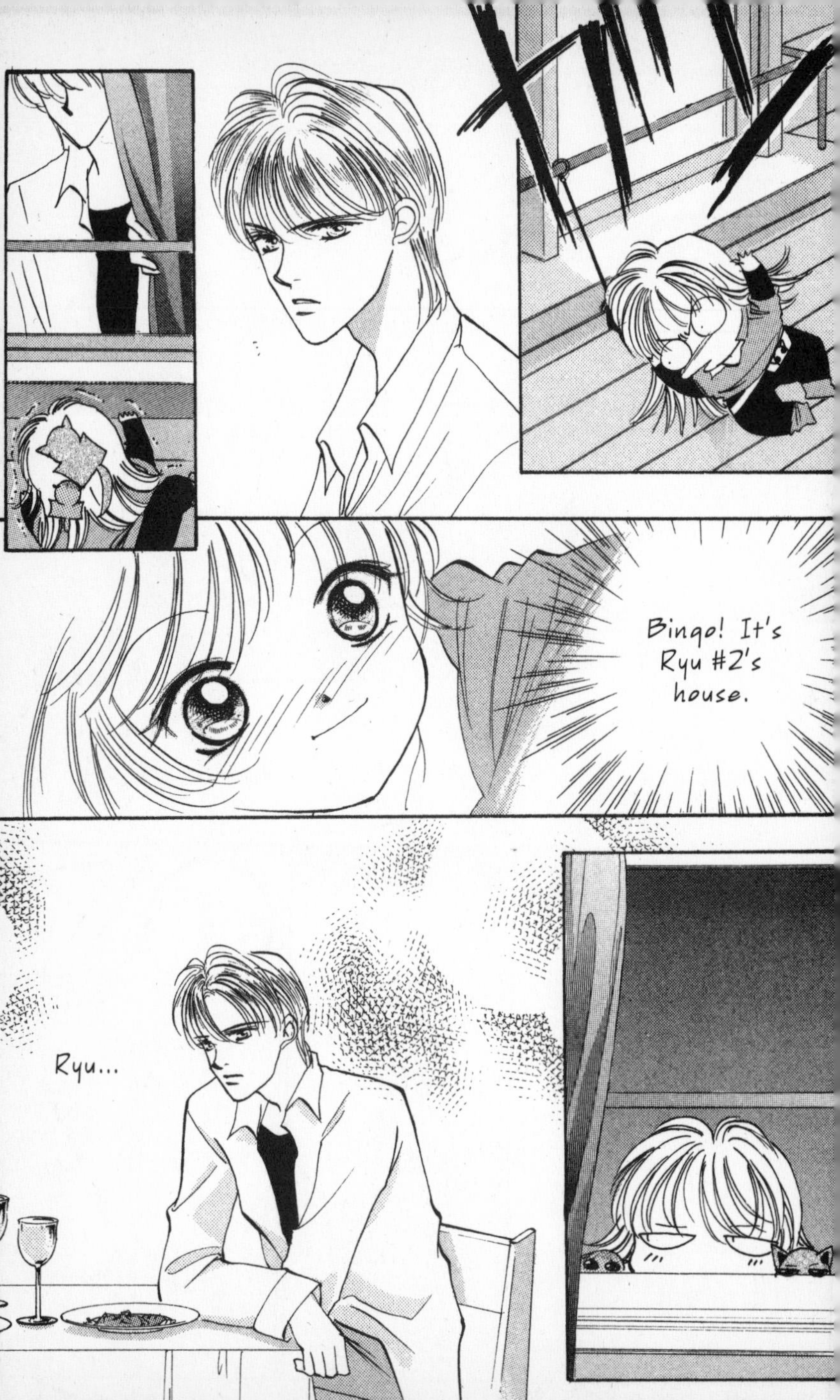
Bingo! It's Ryu #2's house.
Ryu...

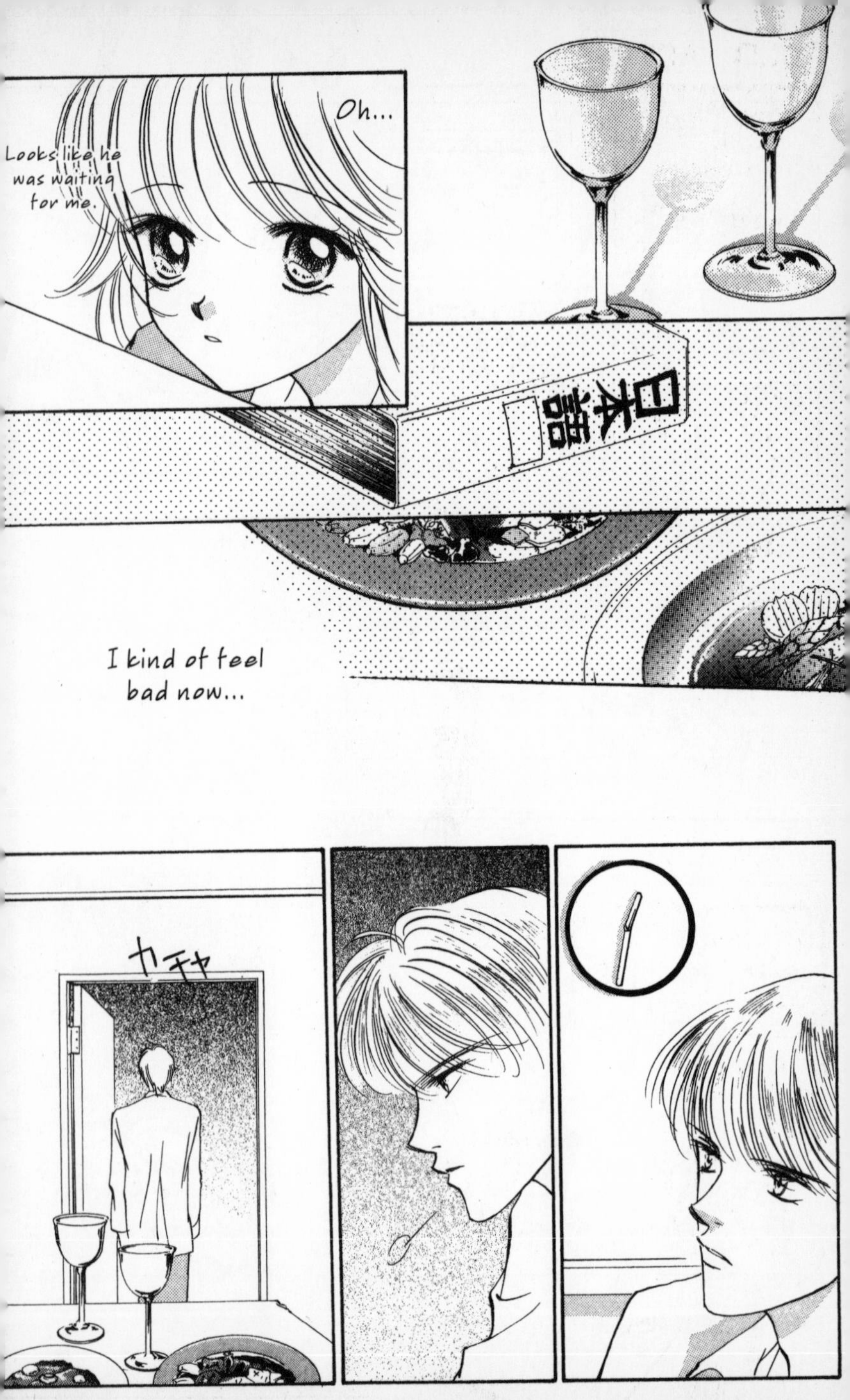
Oh...
Looks like he was waiting for me.
I kind of feel bad now...
カチャ

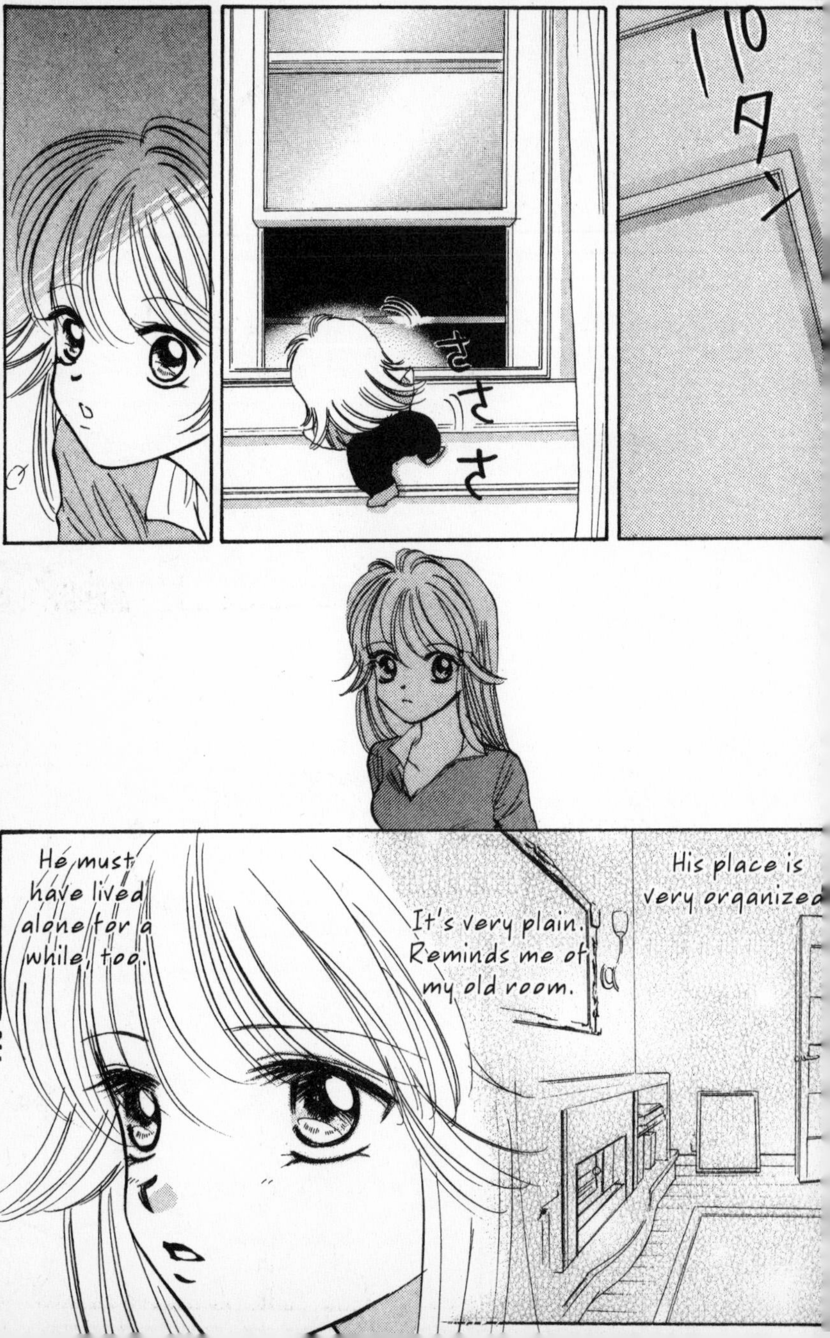
パタン
さささ
His place is very organized
It's very plain. Reminds me of my old room.
He must have lived alone for a while, too.

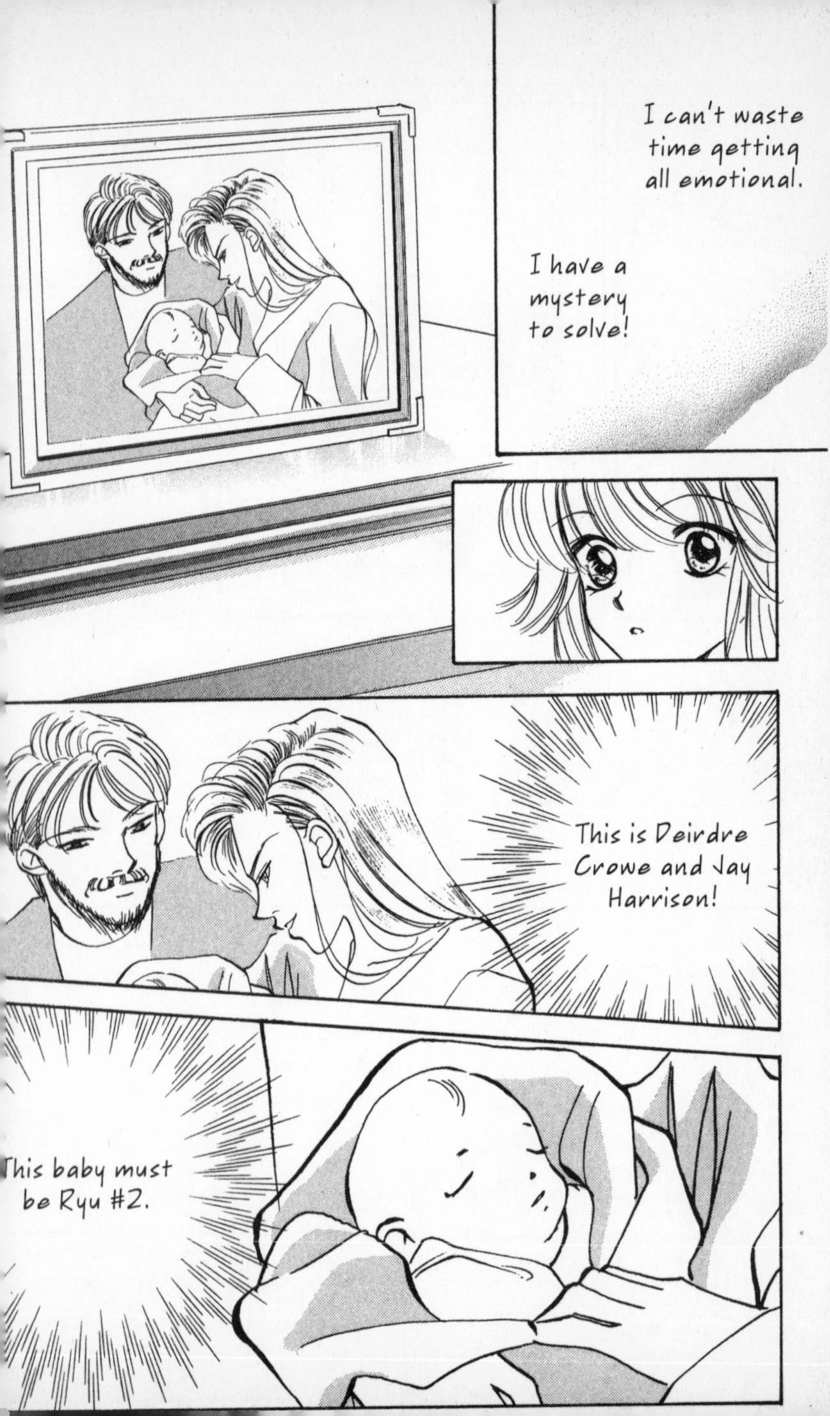
I can't waste time getting all emotional.
I have a mystery to solve!
This is Deirdre Crowe and Jay Harrison!
This baby must be Ryu #2.

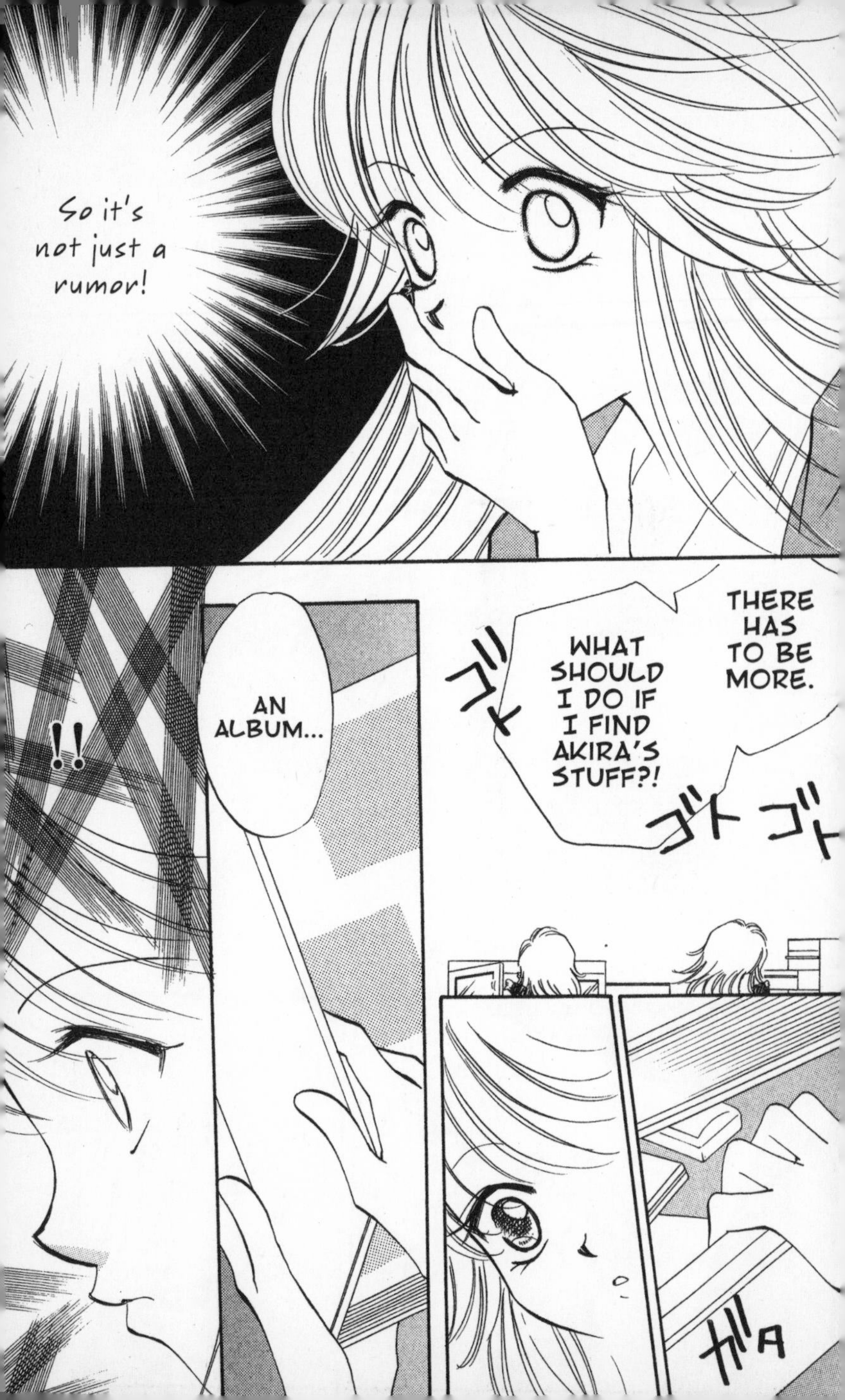
So it's not just a rumor!
THERE HAS TO BE MORE.
WHAT SHOULD I DO IF I FIND AKIRA'S STUFF?!
ゴト
ゴト ゴト
AN ALBUM...
!!

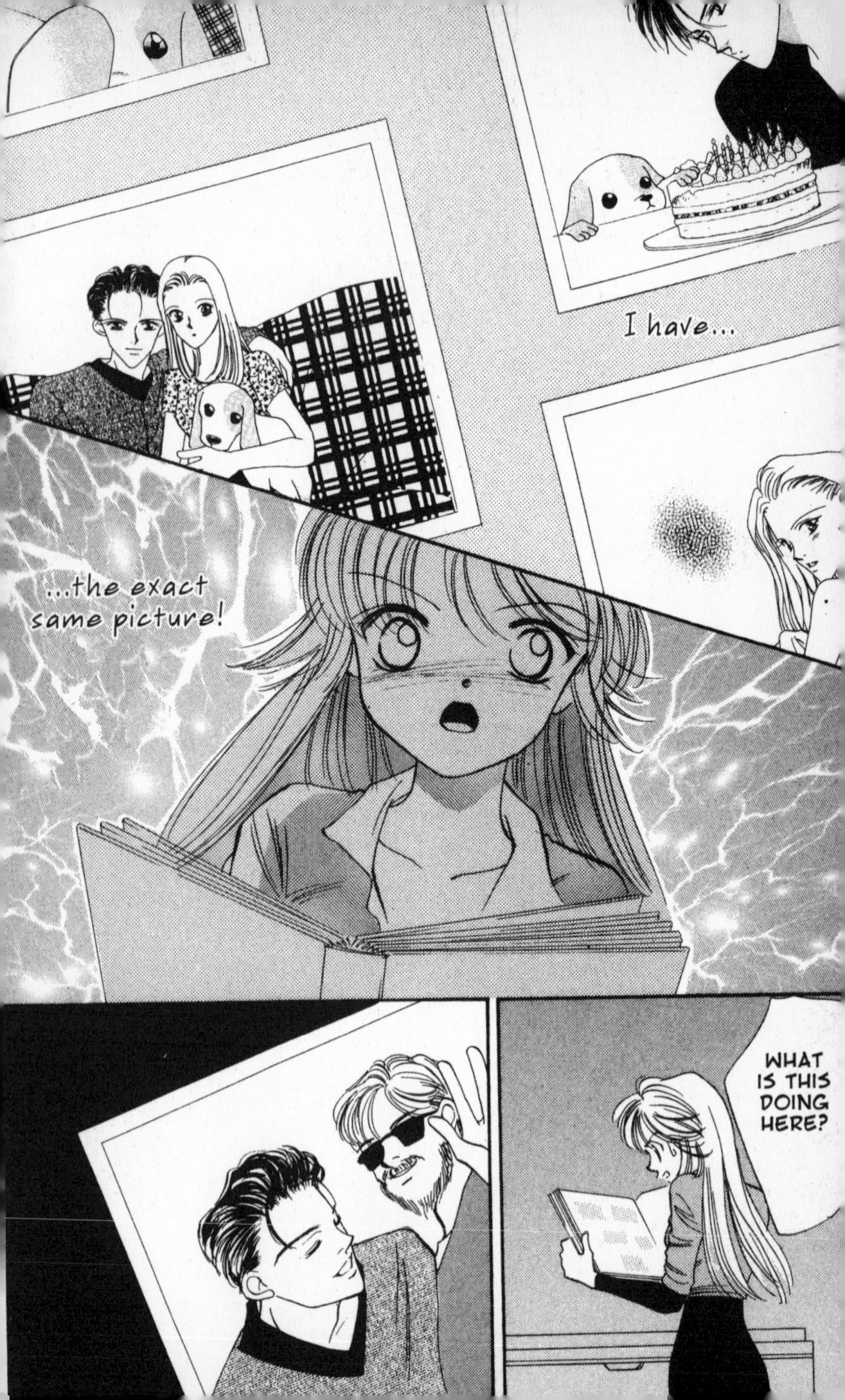
I have...
...the exact same picture!
WHAT IS THIS DOING HERE?

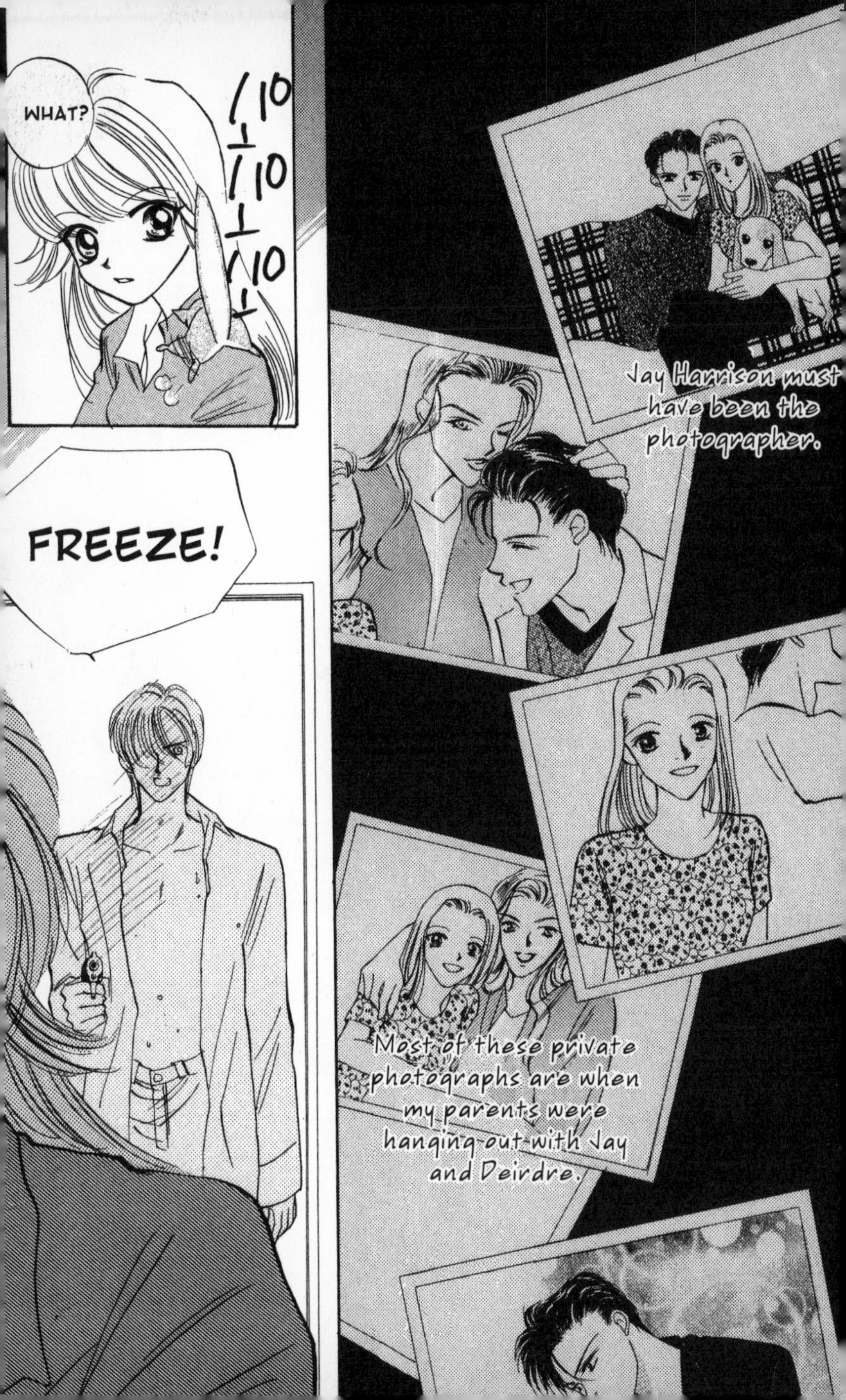
Jay Harrison must have been the photographer.
Most of these private photographs are when my parents were hanging out with Jay and Deirdre.
WHAT?
FREEZE!

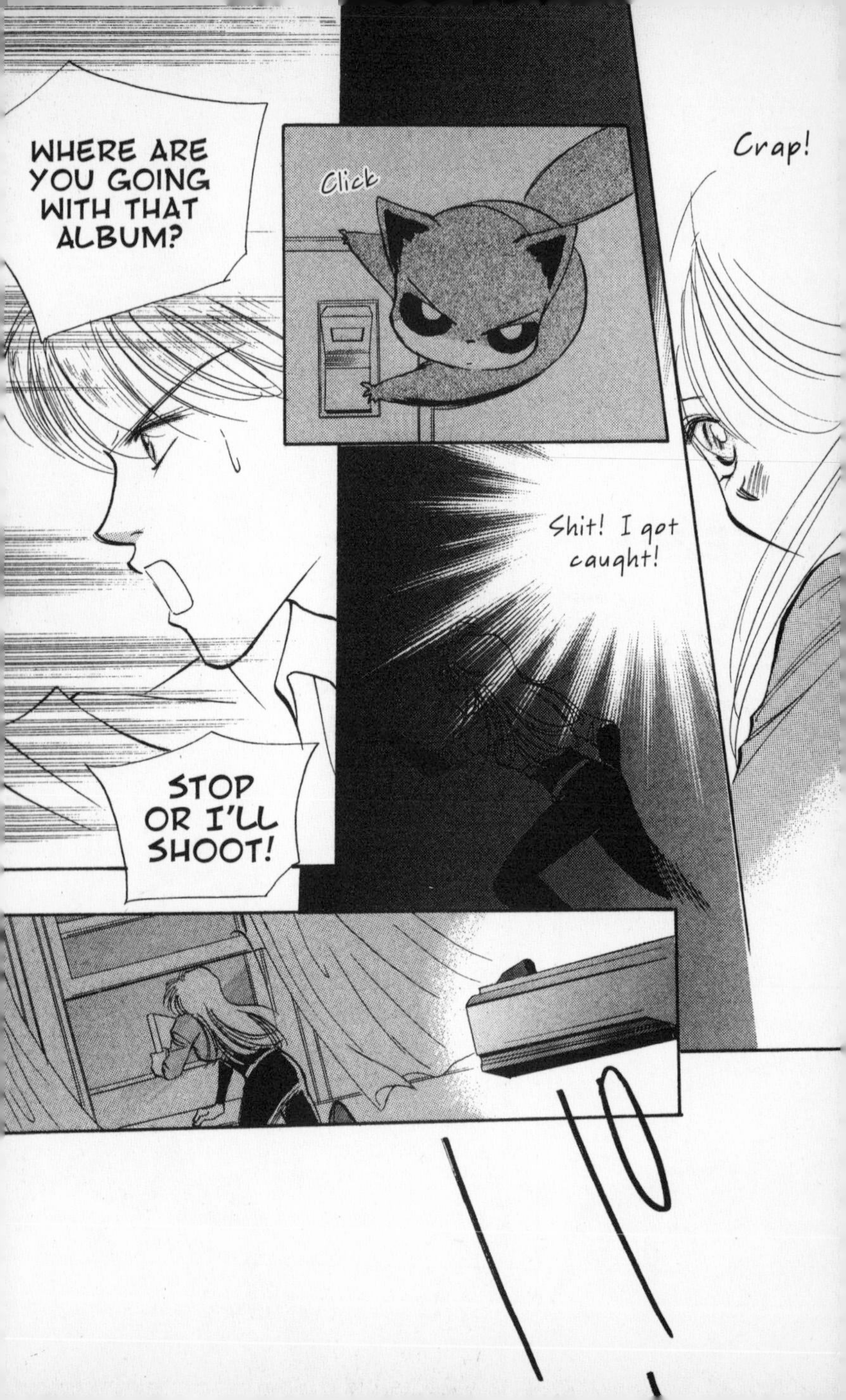
Crap!
Click
Shit! I got caught!
WHERE ARE YOU GOING WITH THAT ALBUM?
STOP OR I'LL SHOOT!

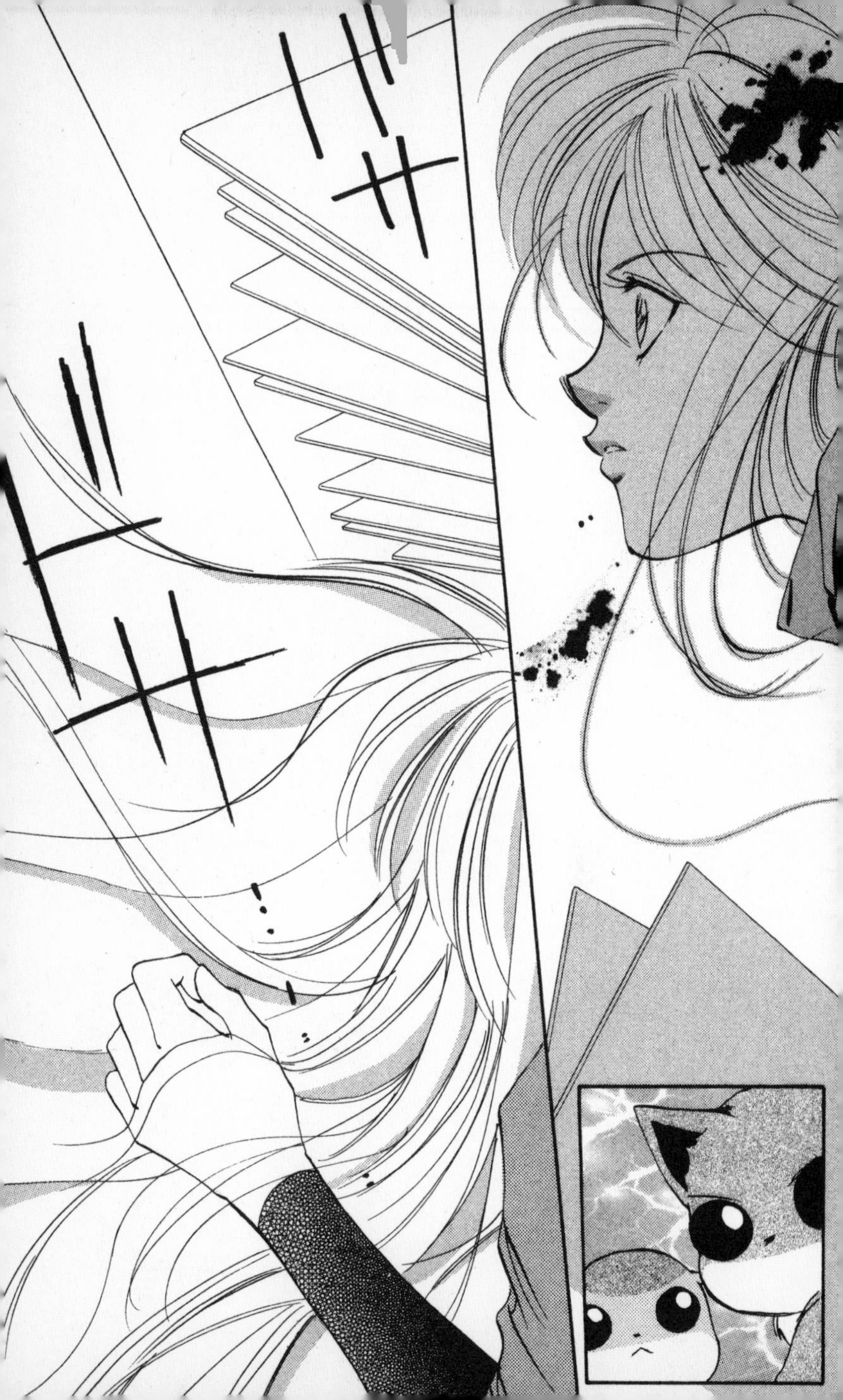

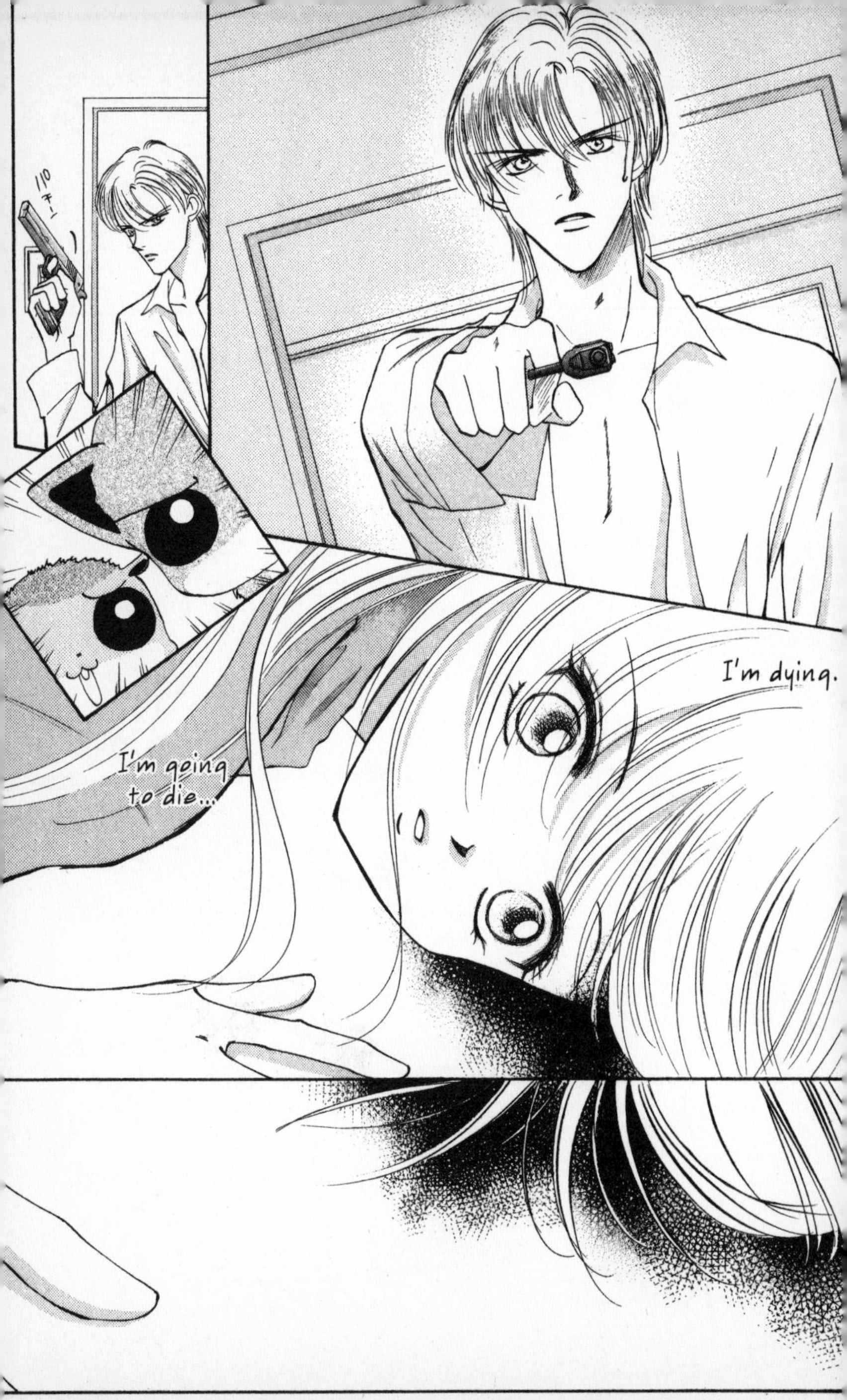

パチ！
I'm dying.
I'm going to die...

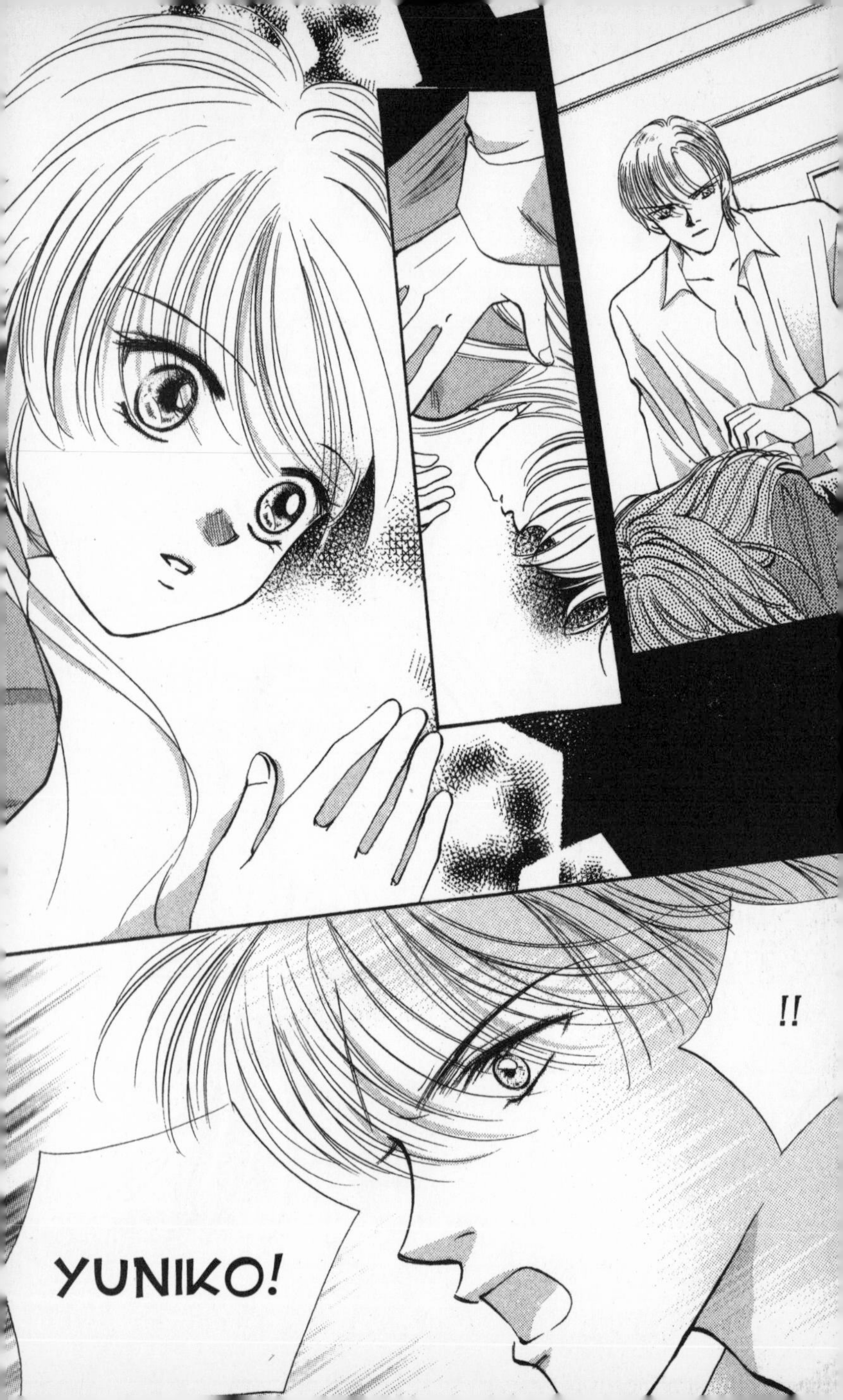
!!
YUNIKO!

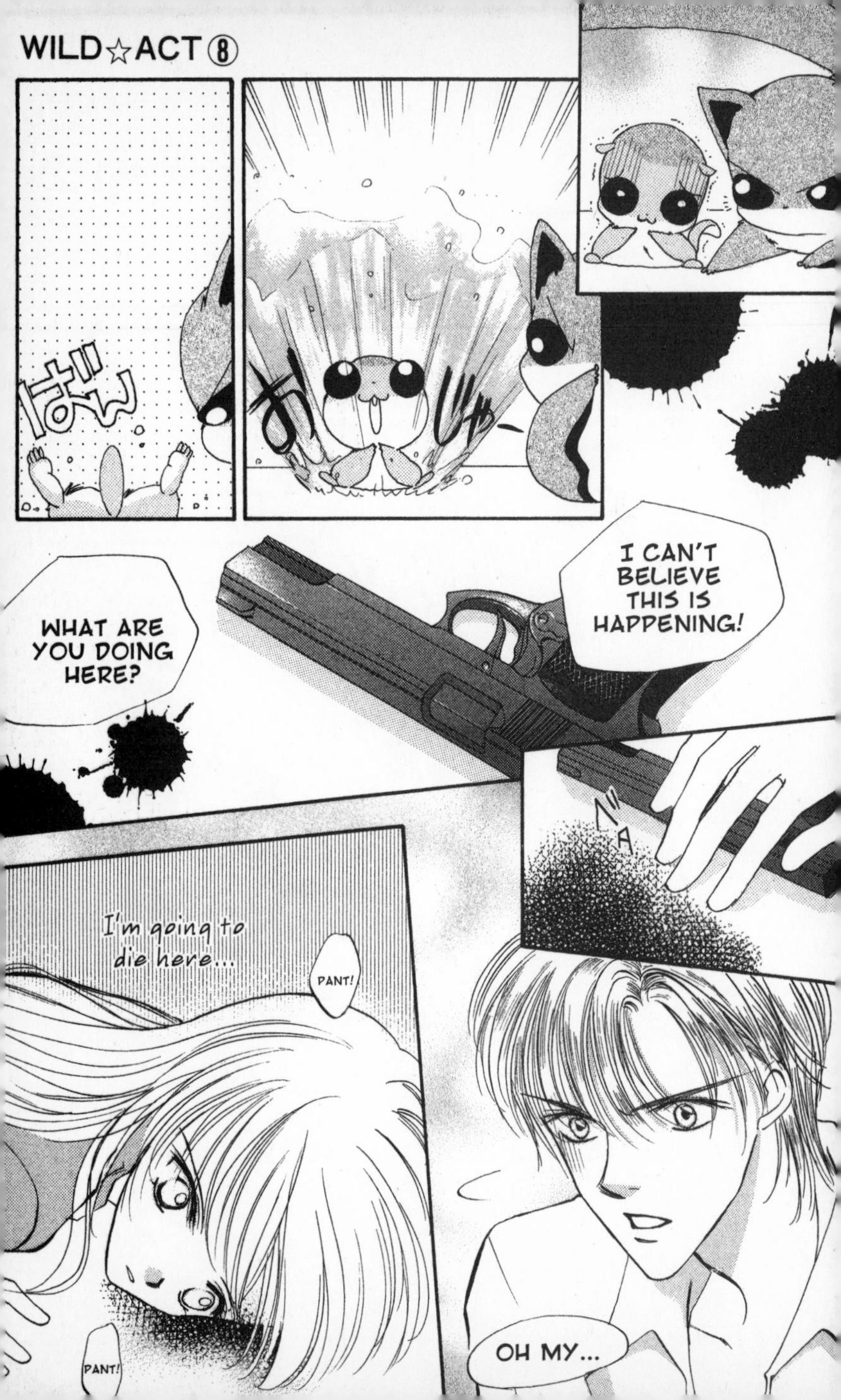
ばん
I CAN'T BELIEVE THIS IS HAPPENING!
WHAT ARE YOU DOING HERE?
OH MY...
PANT!
I'm going to die here...
PANT!

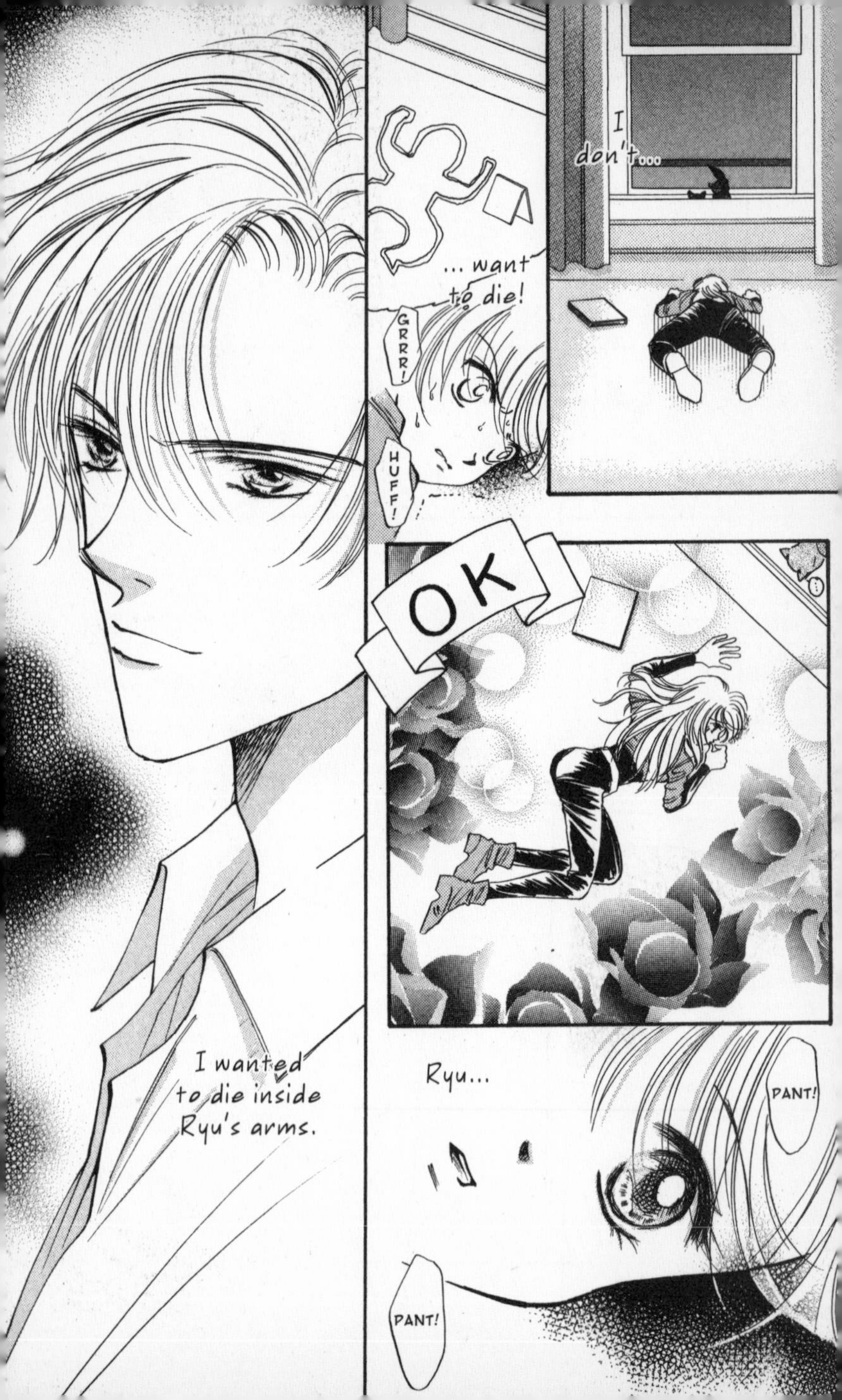
I don't...
... want to die!
GRRR!
HUFF!
OK
Ryu...
PANT!
PANT!
I wanted to die inside Ryu's arms.

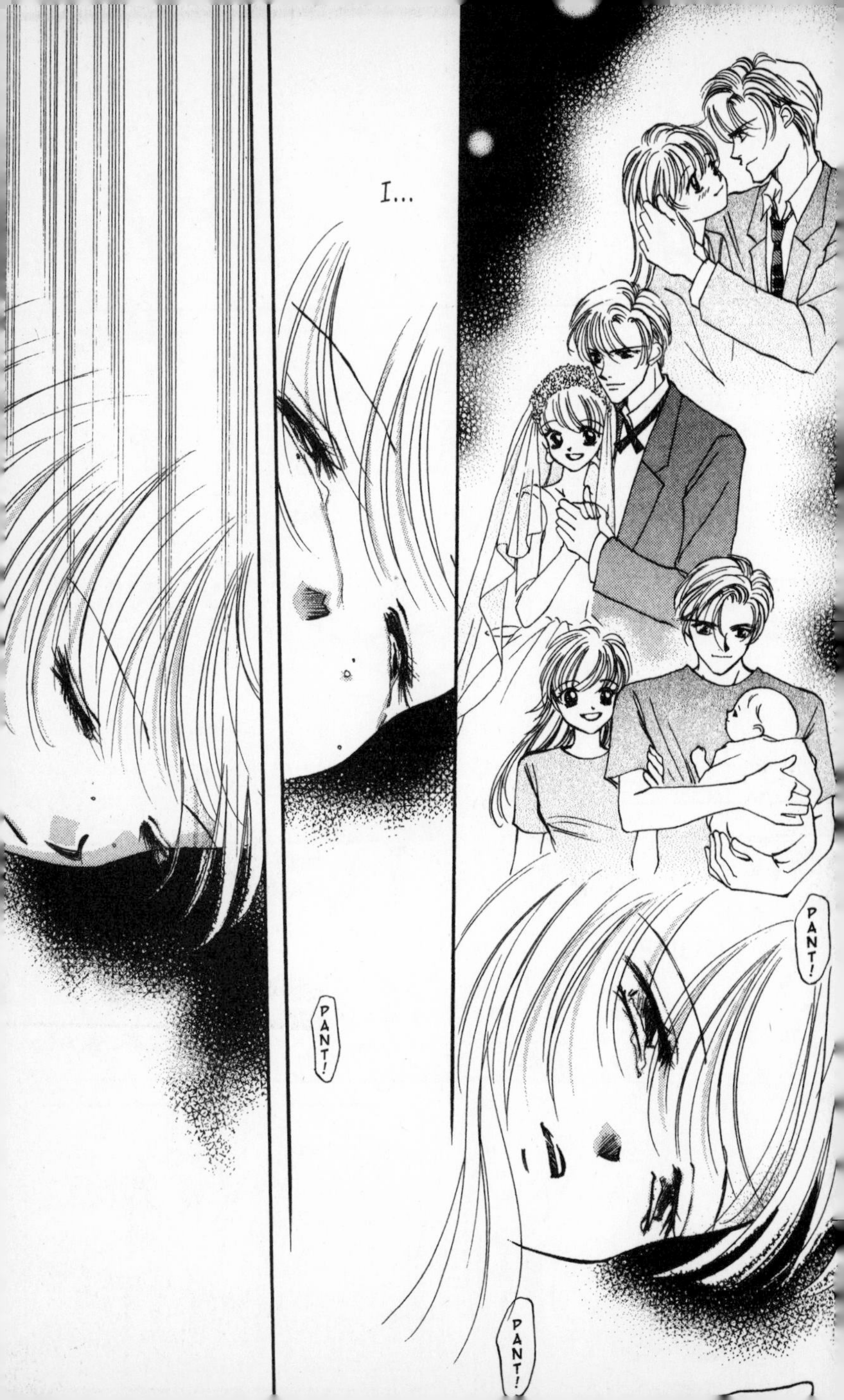
PANT!
PANT!
I...
PANT!

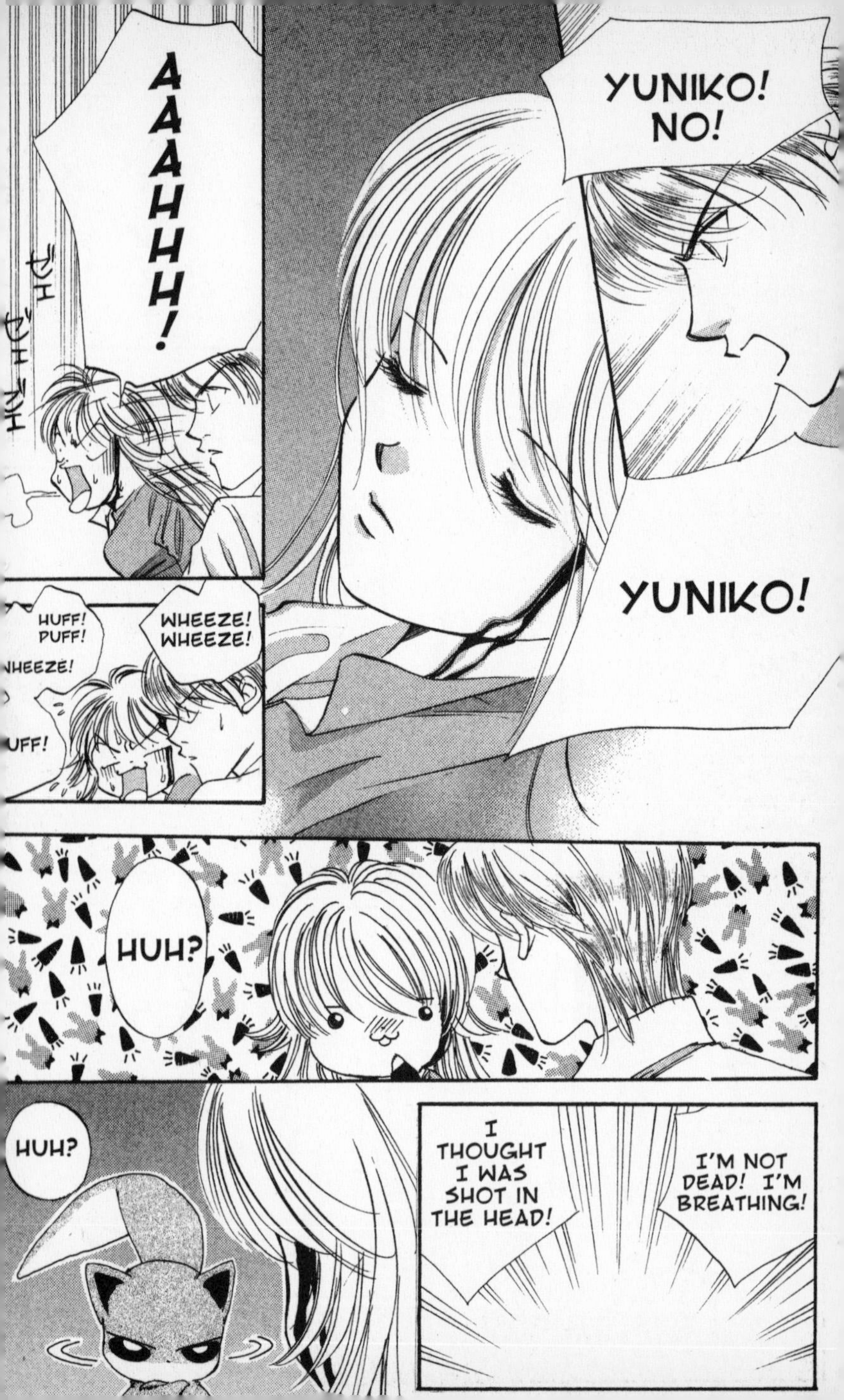
YUNIKO! NO!
YUNIKO!
AAAHHH!
WHEEZE! WHEEZE!
HUFF! PUFF!
HUH?
I'M NOT DEAD! I'M BREATHING!
I THOUGHT I WAS SHOT IN THE HEAD!
HUH?

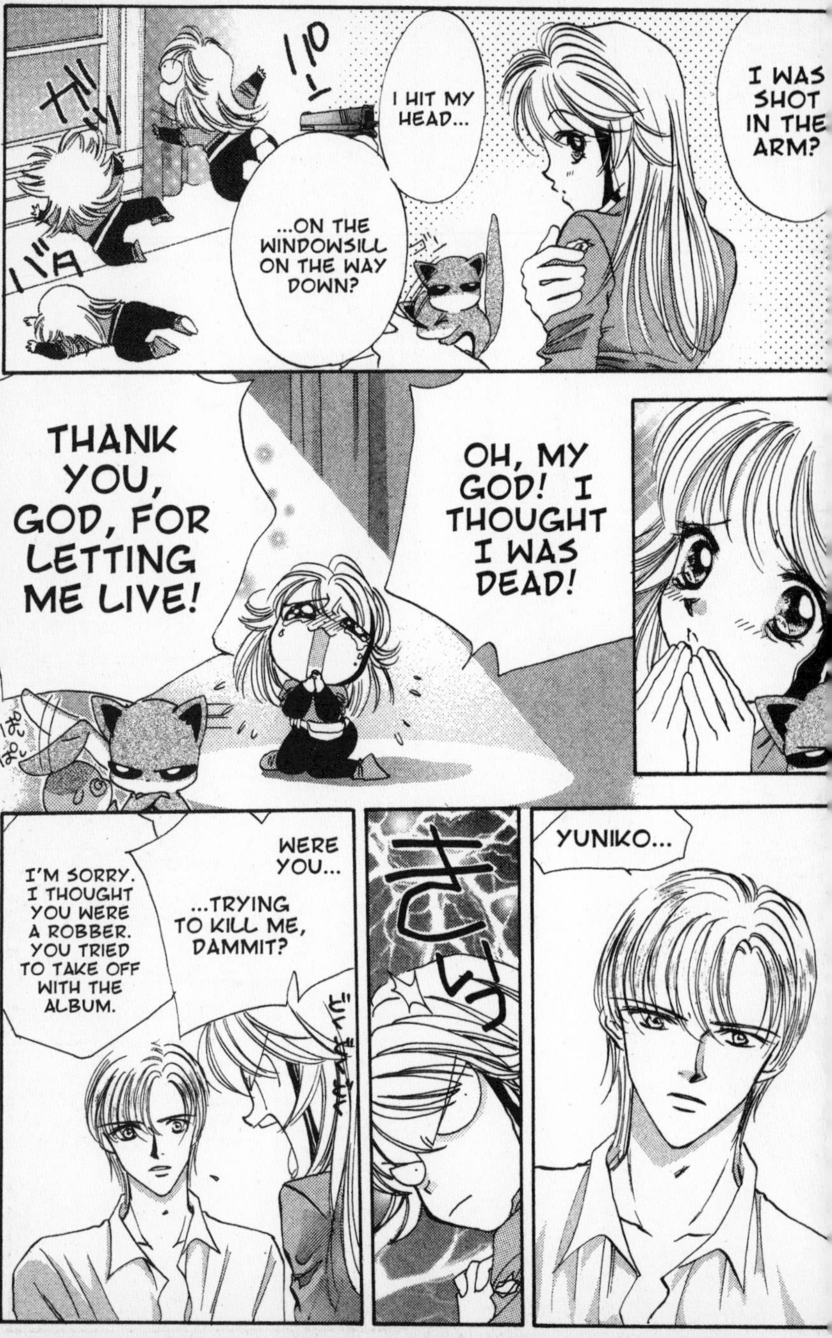
I WAS SHOT IN THE ARM?
I HIT MY HEAD...
...ON THE WINDOWSILL ON THE WAY DOWN?
OH, MY GOD! I THOUGHT I WAS DEAD!
THANK YOU, GOD, FOR LETTING ME LIVE!
YUNIKO...
WERE YOU...
...TRYING TO KILL ME, DAMMIT?
I'M SORRY. I THOUGHT YOU WERE A ROBBER. YOU TRIED TO TAKE OFF WITH THE ALBUM.

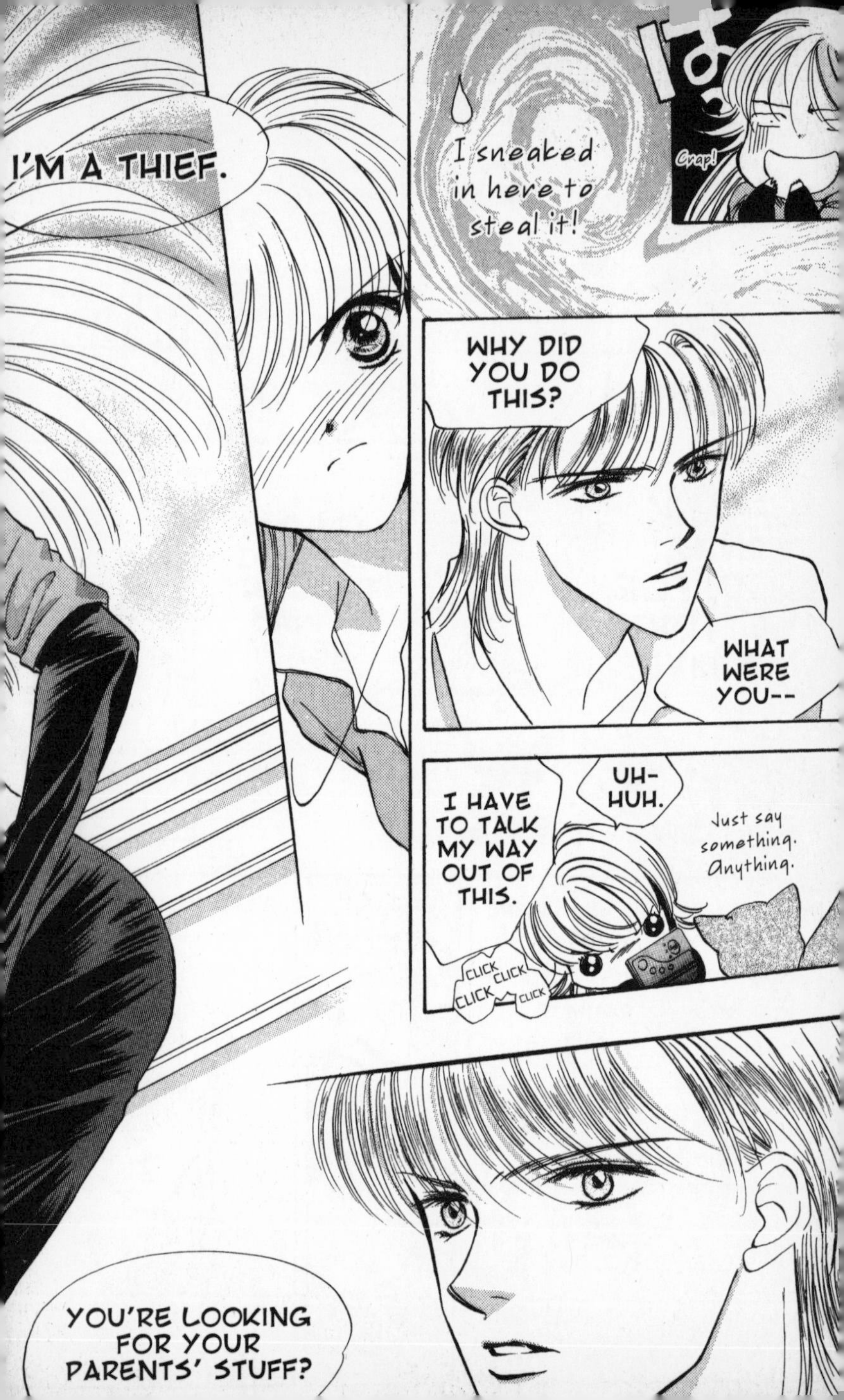
はっ
Crap!
I sneaked in here to steal it!
WHY DID YOU DO THIS?
WHAT WERE YOU--
UH-HUH.
I HAVE TO TALK MY WAY OUT OF THIS.
Just say something. Anything.
CLICK
CLICK
CLICK
CLICK
I'M A THIEF.
YOU'RE LOOKING FOR YOUR PARENTS' STUFF?

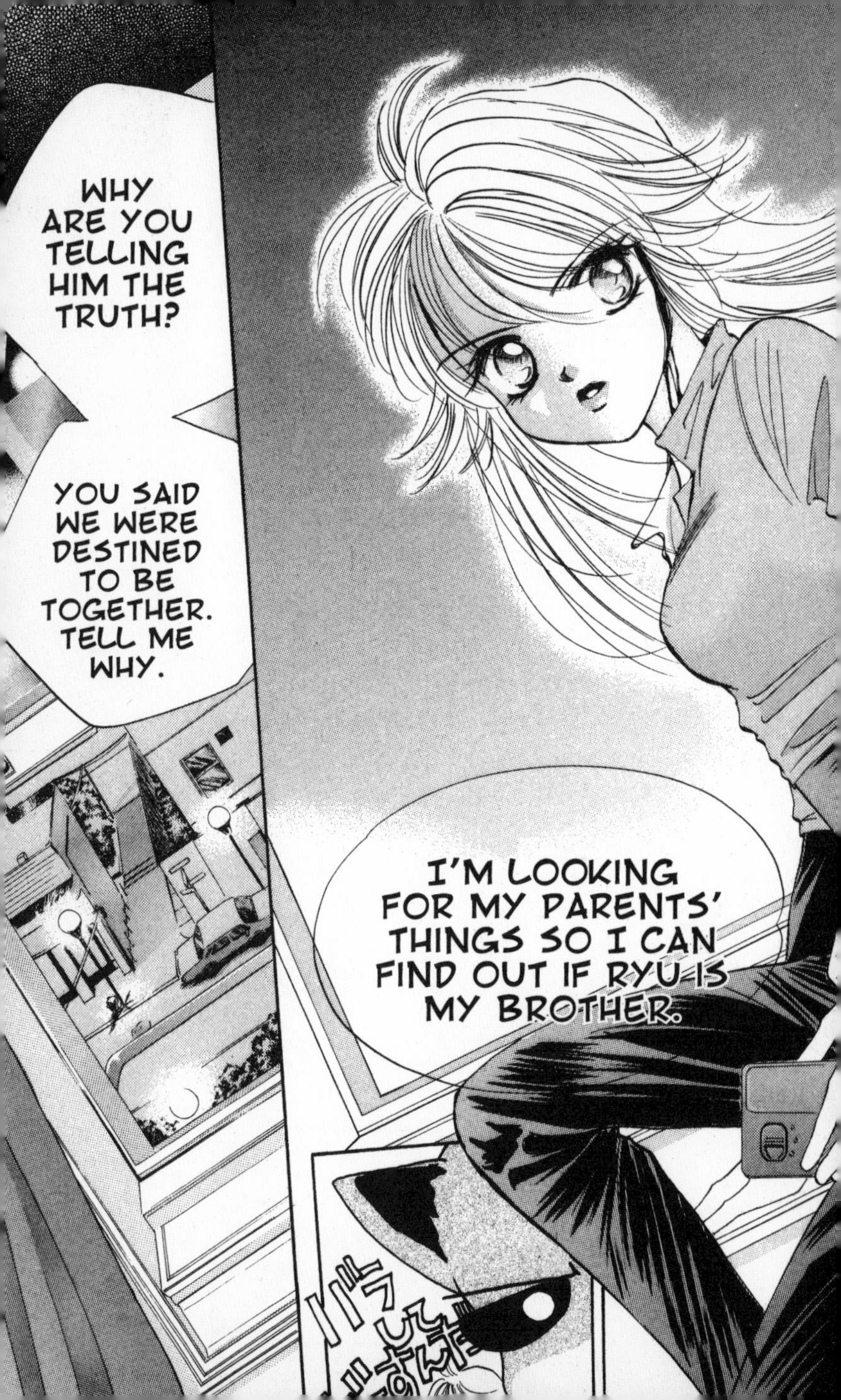
I'M LOOKING FOR MY PARENTS' THINGS SO I CAN FIND OUT IF RYU IS MY BROTHER.
WHY ARE YOU TELLING HIM THE TRUTH?
YOU SAID WE WERE DESTINED TO BE TOGETHER. TELL ME WHY.

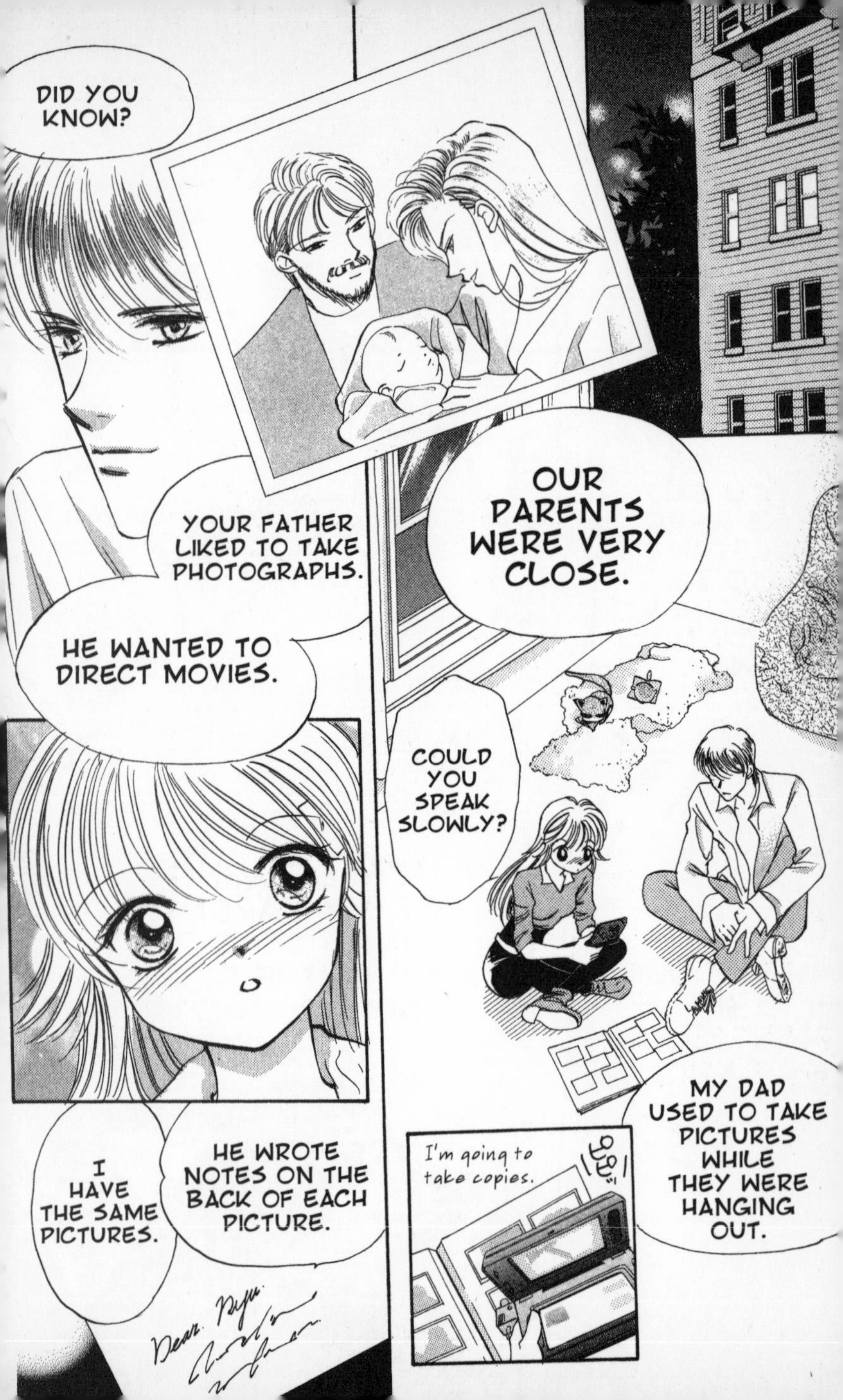
OUR PARENTS WERE VERY CLOSE.
COULD YOU SPEAK SLOWLY?
MY DAD USED TO TAKE PICTURES WHILE THEY WERE HANGING OUT.
DID YOU KNOW?
YOUR FATHER LIKED TO TAKE PHOTOGRAPHS.
HE WANTED TO DIRECT MOVIES.
I'm going to take copies.
ピピッ
HE WROTE NOTES ON THE BACK OF EACH PICTURE.
I HAVE THE SAME PICTURES.

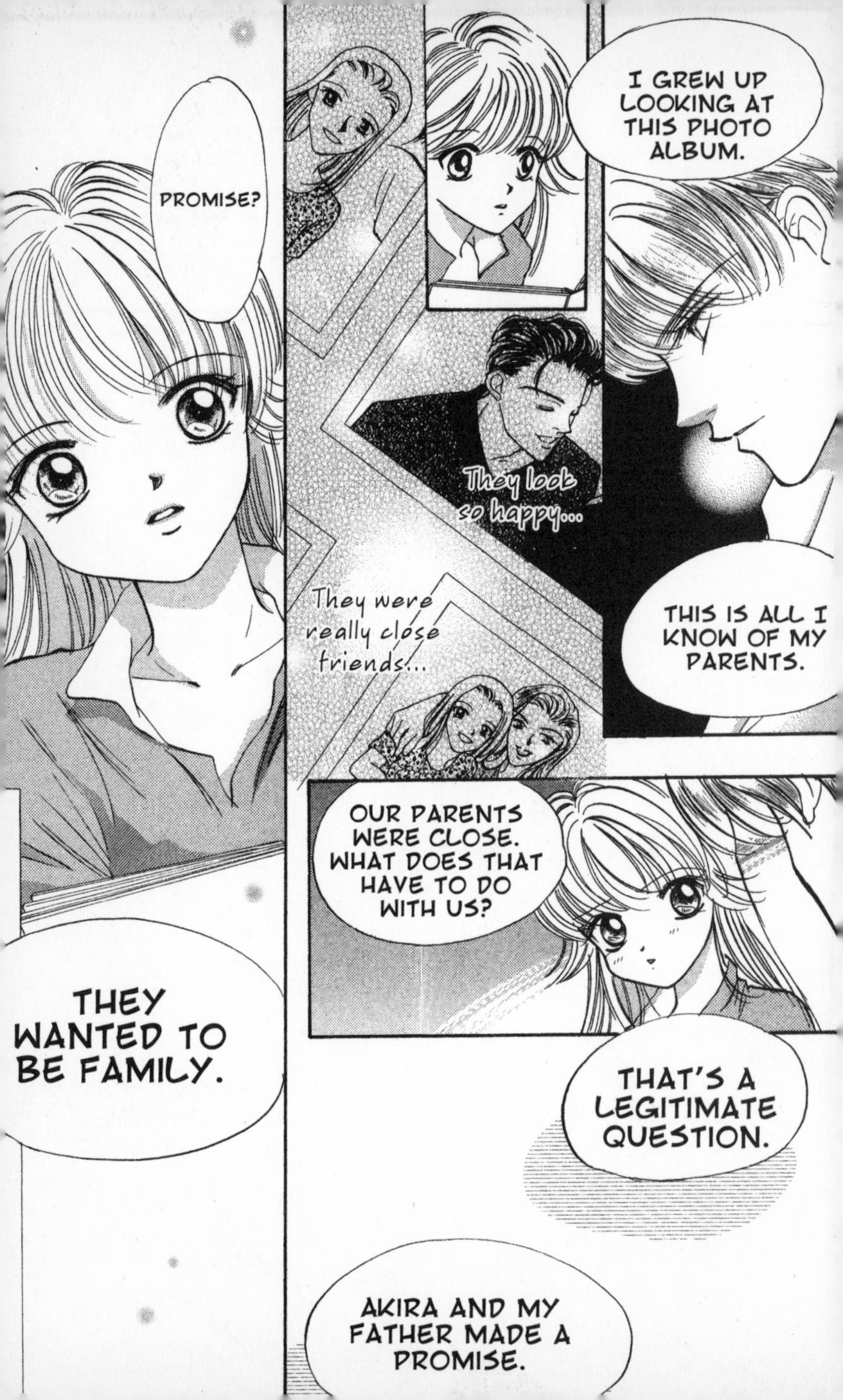
I GREW UP LOOKING AT THIS PHOTO ALBUM.
THIS IS ALL I KNOW OF MY PARENTS.
They look so happy...
They were really close friends...
OUR PARENTS WERE CLOSE. WHAT DOES THAT HAVE TO DO WITH US?
THAT'S A LEGITIMATE QUESTION.
AKIRA AND MY FATHER MADE A PROMISE.
PROMISE?
THEY WANTED TO BE FAMILY.

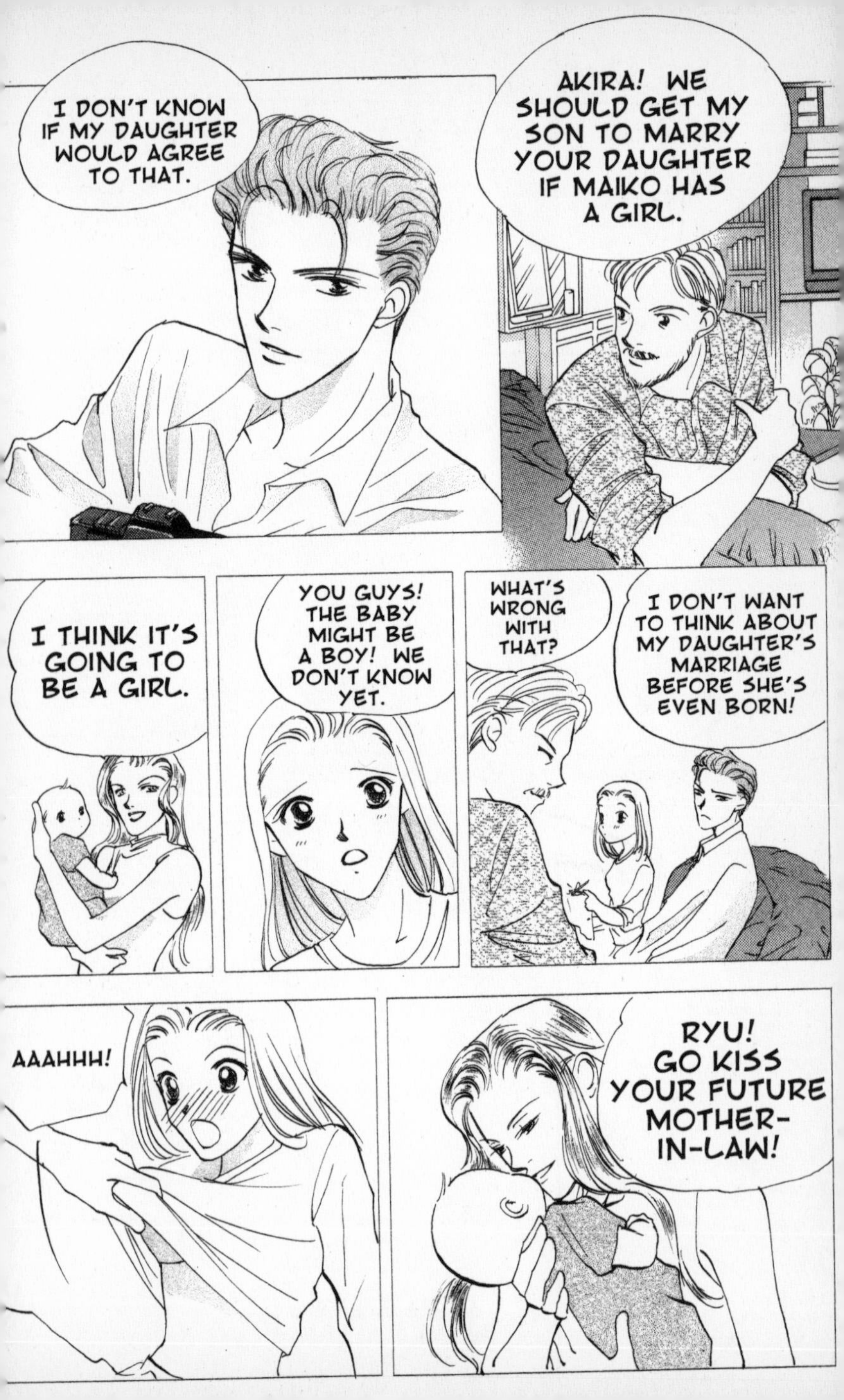
AKIRA! WE SHOULD GET MY SON TO MARRY YOUR DAUGHTER IF MAIKO HAS A GIRL.
I DON'T KNOW IF MY DAUGHTER WOULD AGREE TO THAT.
I DON'T WANT TO THINK ABOUT MY DAUGHTER'S MARRIAGE BEFORE SHE'S EVEN BORN!
WHAT'S WRONG WITH THAT?
YOU GUYS! THE BABY MIGHT BE A BOY! WE DON'T KNOW YET.
I THINK IT'S GOING TO BE A GIRL.
RYU! GO KISS YOUR FUTURE MOTHER-IN-LAW!
AAAHHH!

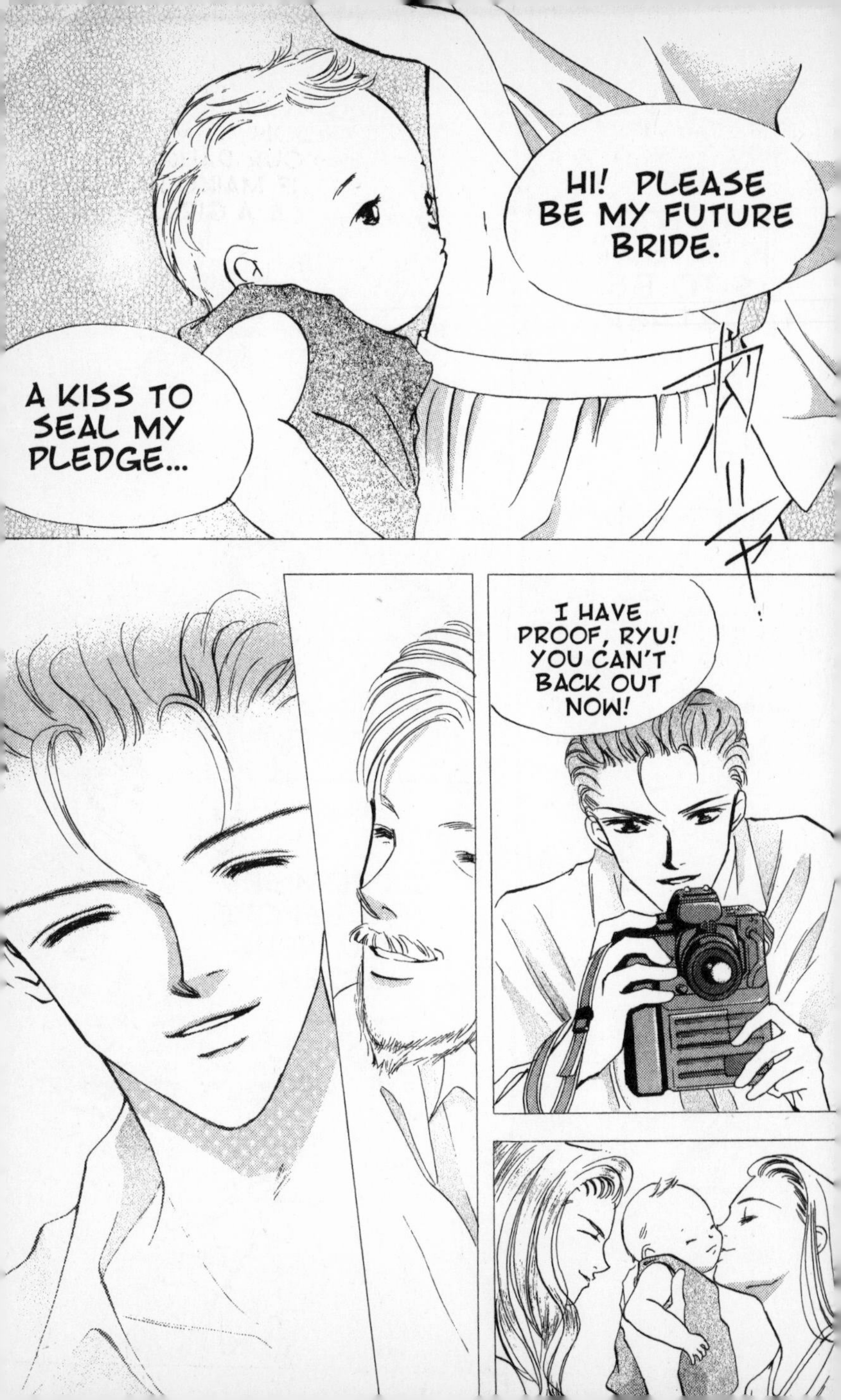
HI! PLEASE BE MY FUTURE BRIDE.
A KISS TO SEAL MY PLEDGE...
I HAVE PROOF, RYU! YOU CAN'T BACK OUT NOW!

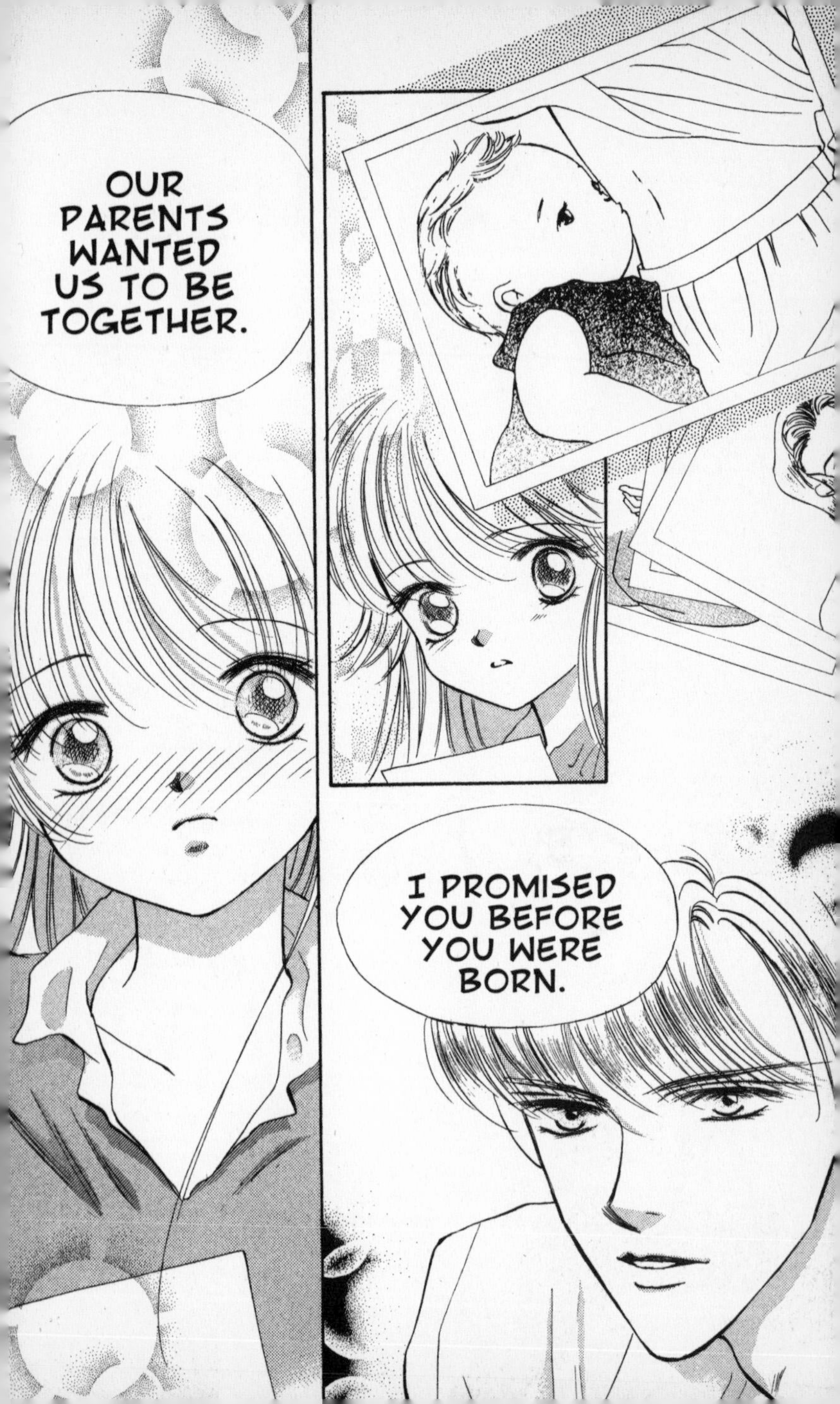
I PROMISED YOU BEFORE YOU WERE BORN.
OUR PARENTS WANTED US TO BE TOGETHER.

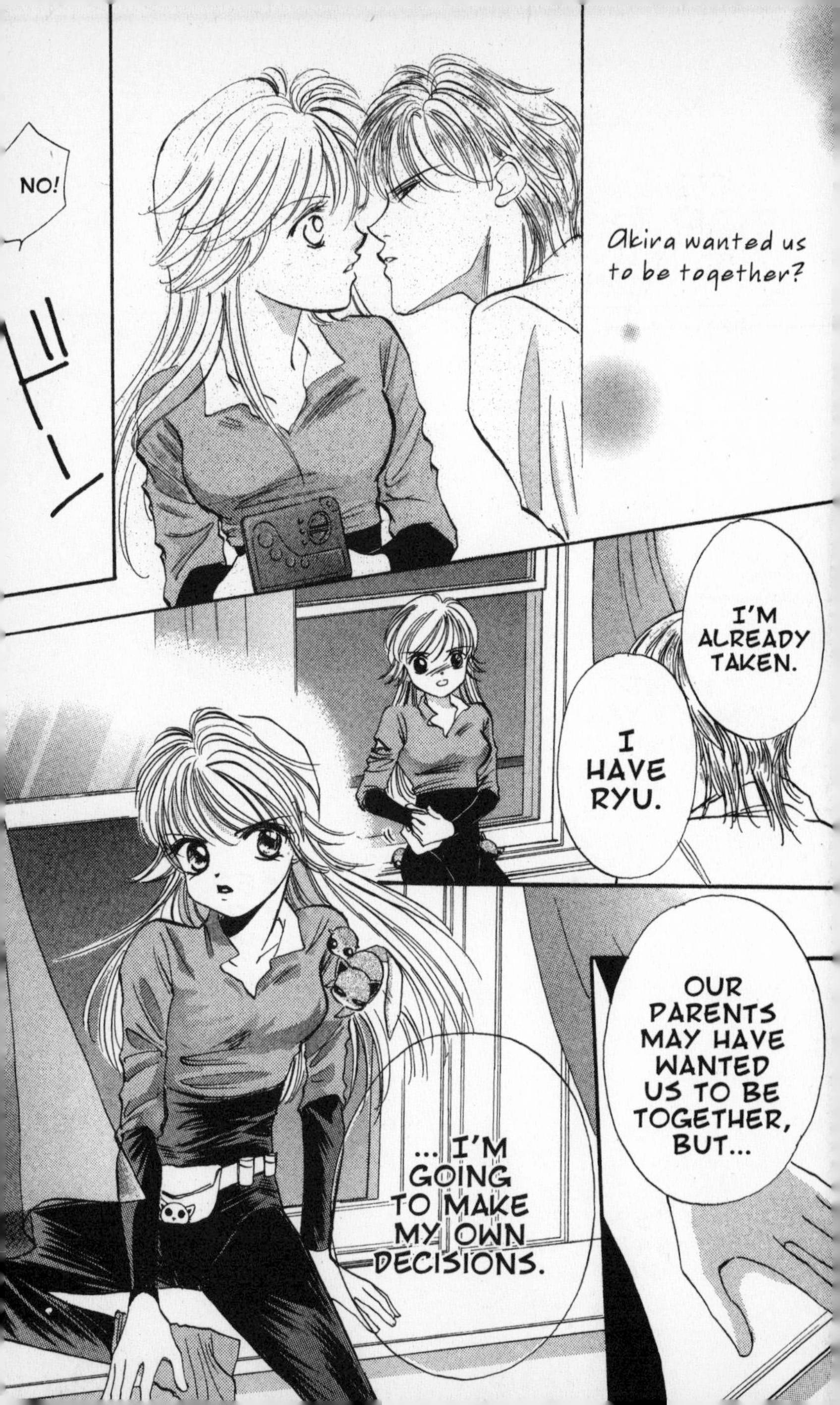
Akira wanted us to be together?
NO!
I'M ALREADY TAKEN.
I HAVE RYU.
OUR PARENTS MAY HAVE WANTED US TO BE TOGETHER, BUT...
... I'M GOING TO MAKE MY OWN DECISIONS.

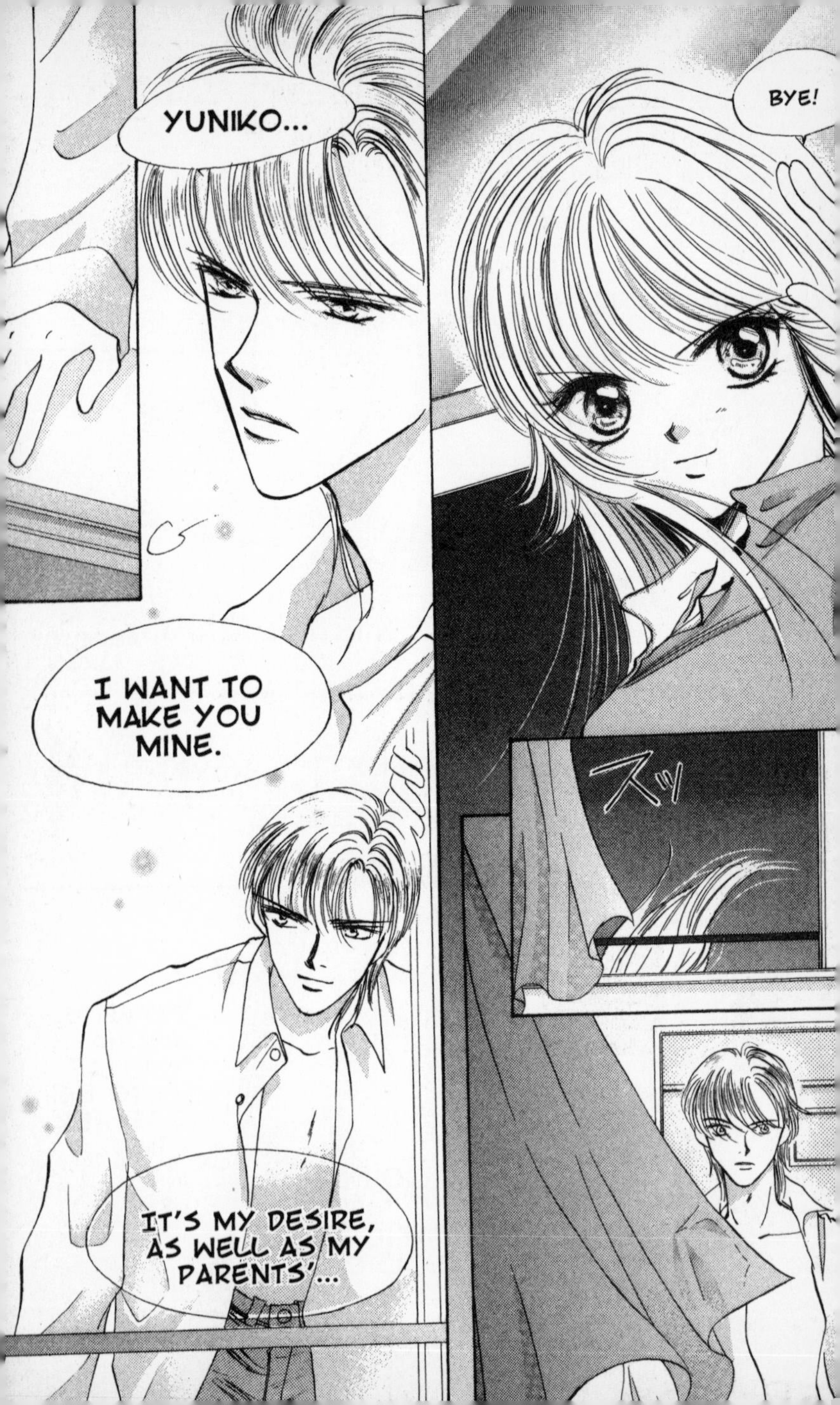
BYE!
スッ
YUNIKO...
I WANT TO MAKE YOU MINE.
IT'S MY DESIRE, AS WELL AS MY PARENTS'...

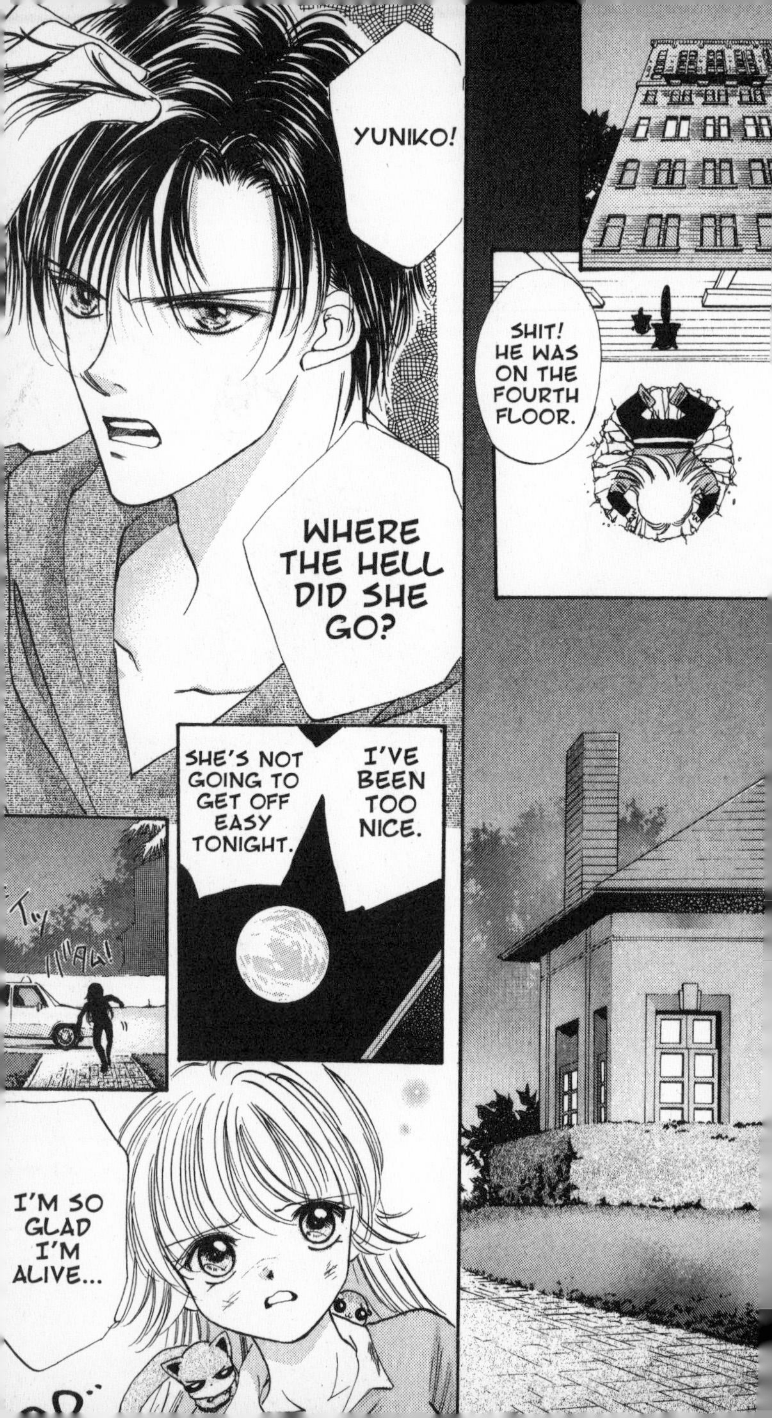
SHIT! HE WAS ON THE FOURTH FLOOR.
YUNIKO!
WHERE THE HELL DID SHE GO?
I'VE BEEN TOO NICE.
SHE'S NOT GOING TO GET OFF EASY TONIGHT.
I'M SO GLAD I'M ALIVE...

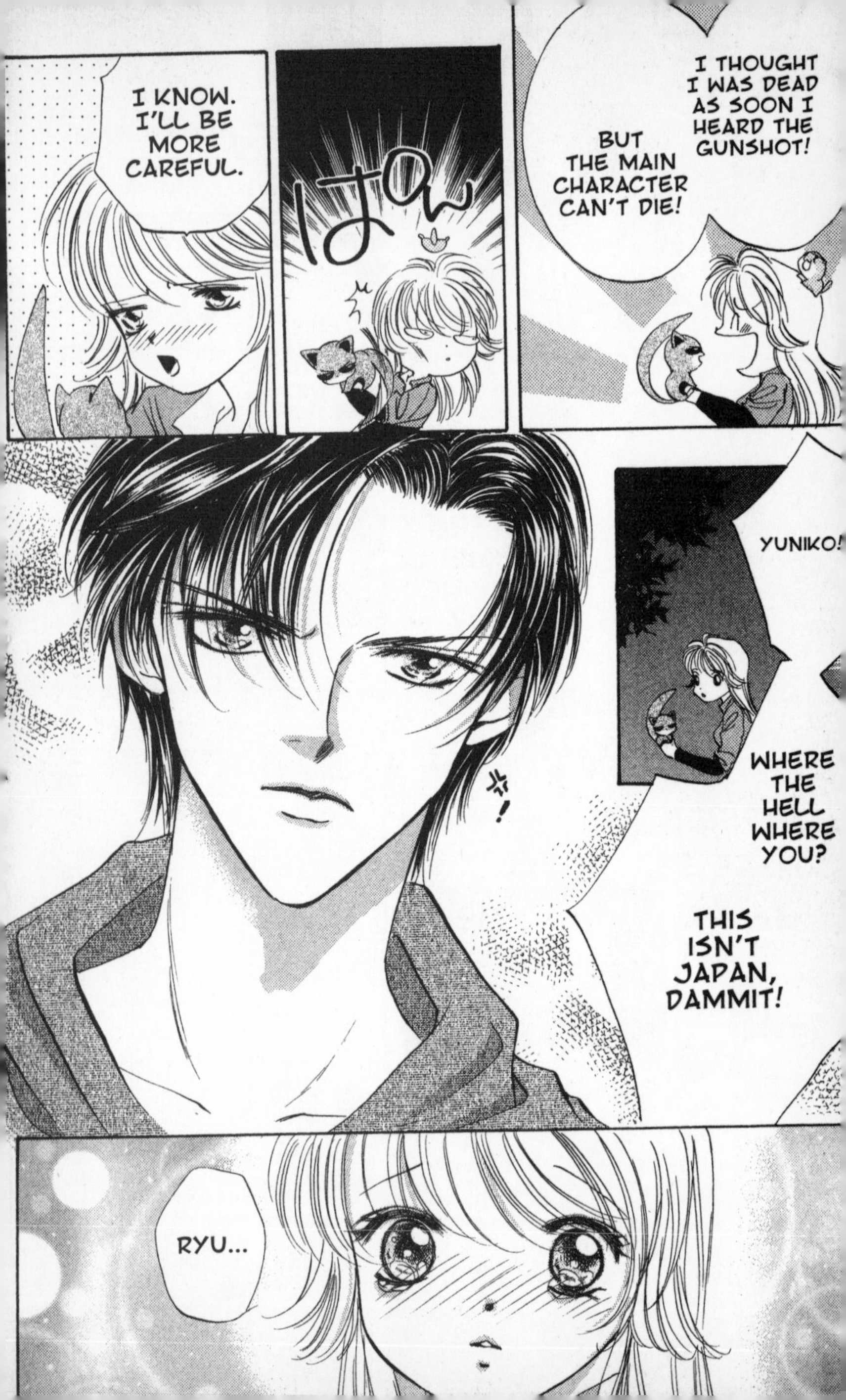
I THOUGHT I WAS DEAD AS SOON I HEARD THE GUNSHOT!
BUT THE MAIN CHARACTER CAN'T DIE!
はぁ
I KNOW. I'LL BE MORE CAREFUL.
YUNIKO!
WHERE THE HELL WHERE YOU?
THIS ISN'T JAPAN, DAMMIT!
RYU...

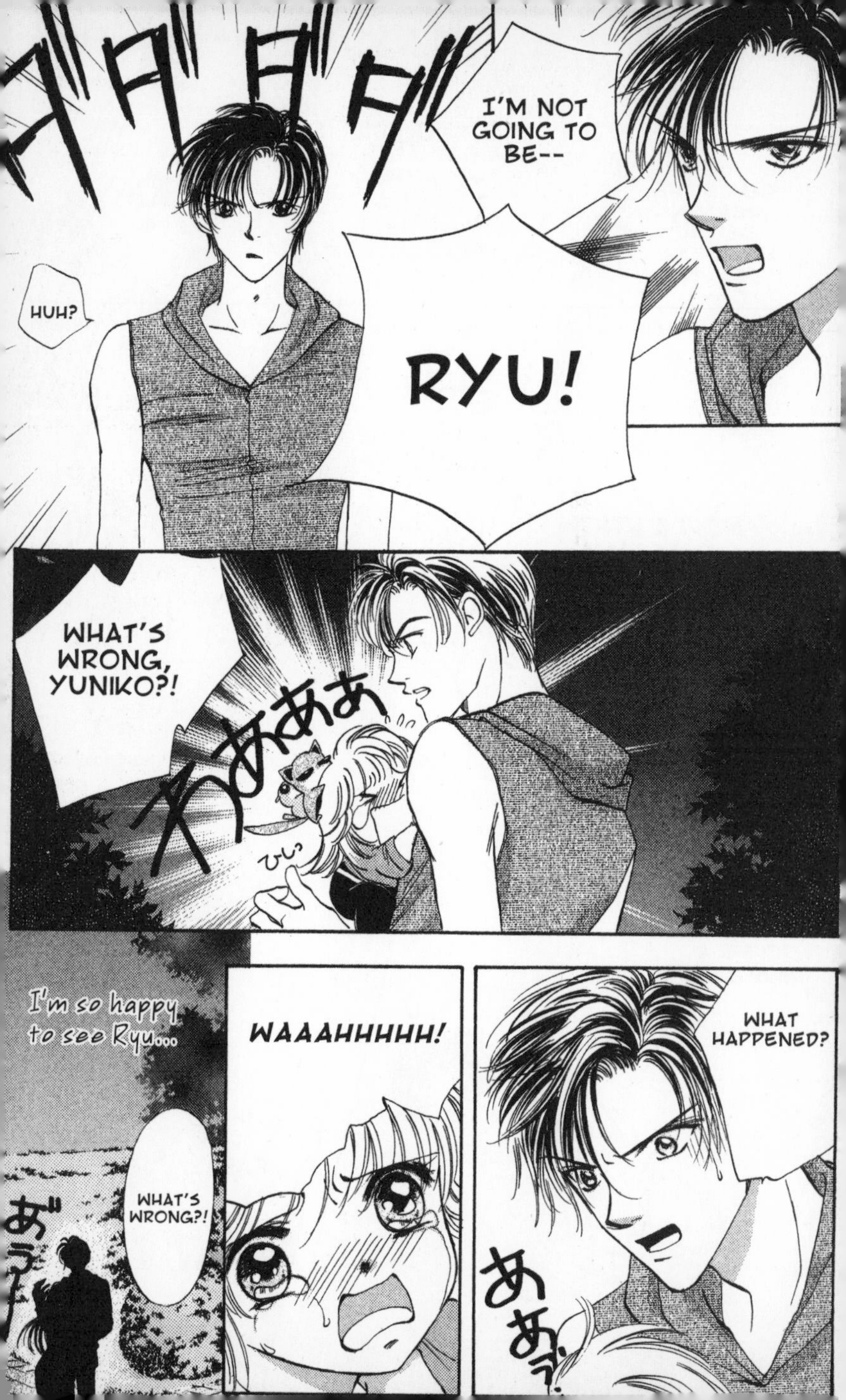
I'M NOT GOING TO BE--
RYU!
ダダダダ
HUH?
WHAT'S WRONG, YUNIKO?!
わあああ
ひしっ
WHAT HAPPENED?
WAAAHHHHH!
WHAT'S WRONG?!
I'm so happy to see Ryu...

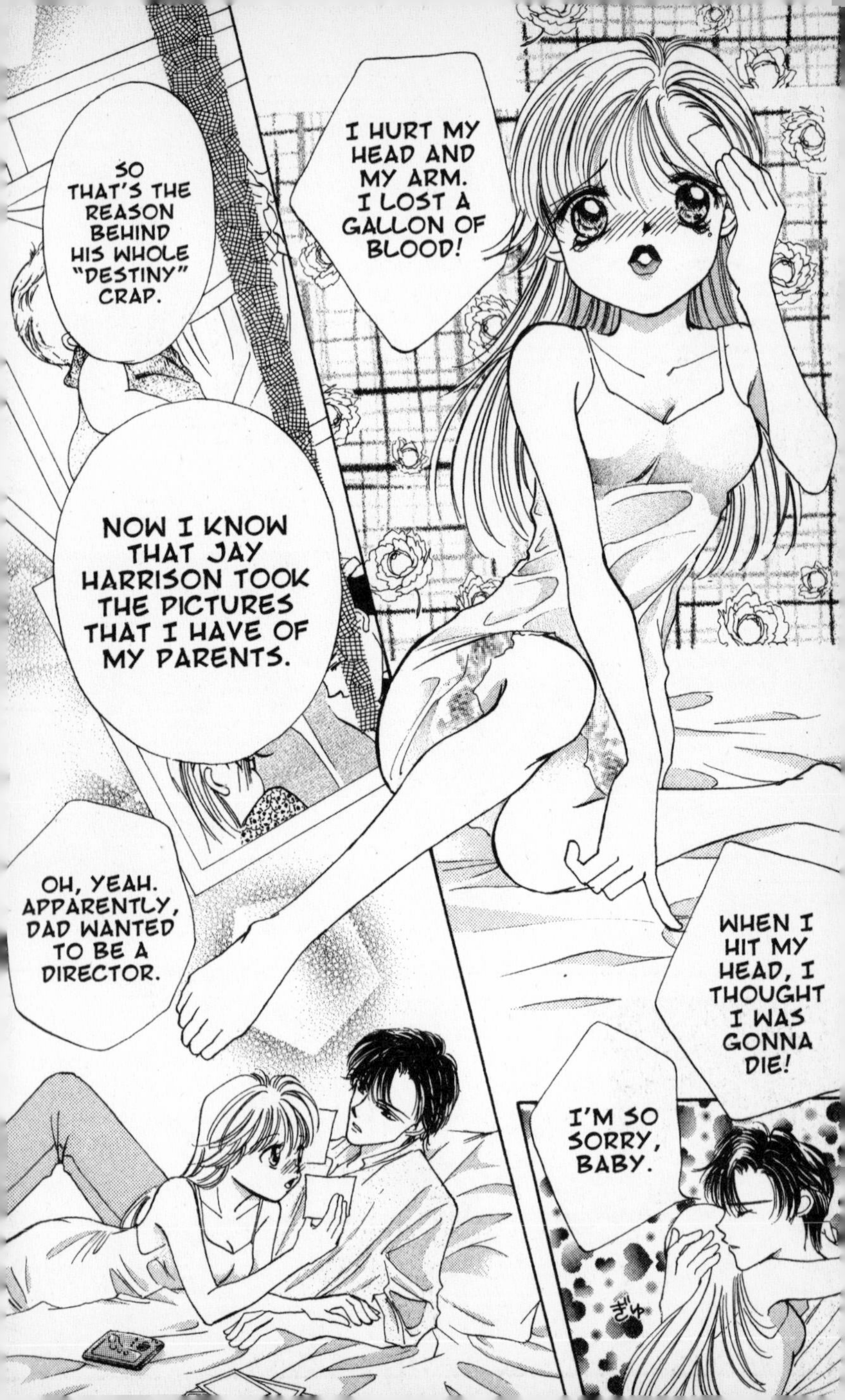

I HURT MY HEAD AND MY ARM. I LOST A GALLON OF BLOOD!
WHEN I HIT MY HEAD, I THOUGHT I WAS GONNA DIE!
I'M SO SORRY, BABY.
SO THAT'S THE REASON BEHIND HIS WHOLE "DESTINY" CRAP.
NOW I KNOW THAT JAY HARRISON TOOK THE PICTURES THAT I HAVE OF MY PARENTS.
OH, YEAH. APPARENTLY, DAD WANTED TO BE A DIRECTOR.

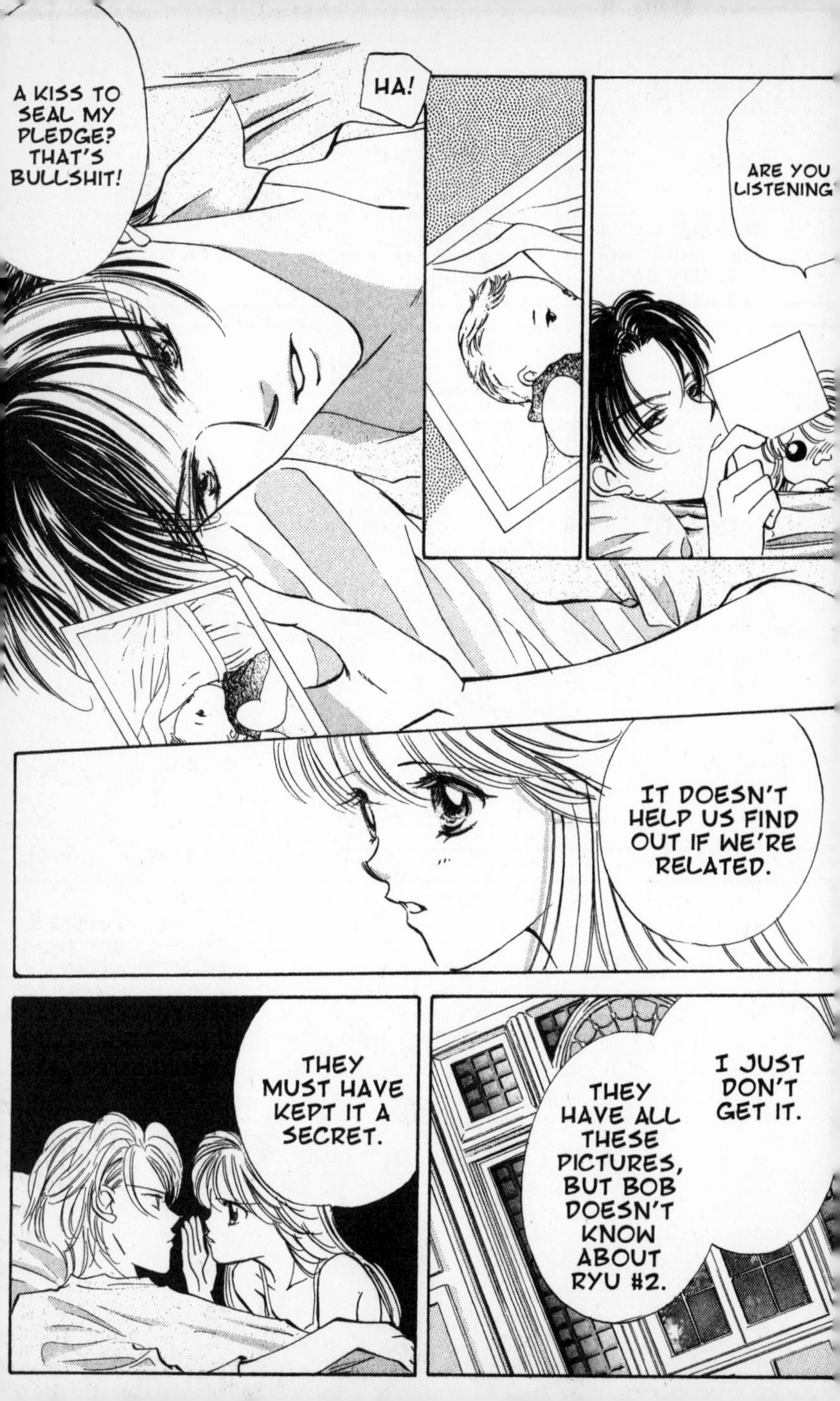
ARE YOU LISTENING
HA!
A KISS TO SEAL MY PLEDGE? THAT'S BULLSHIT!
IT DOESN'T HELP US FIND OUT IF WE'RE RELATED.
I JUST DON'T GET IT.
THEY HAVE ALL THESE PICTURES, BUT BOB DOESN'T KNOW ABOUT RYU #2.
THEY MUST HAVE KEPT IT A SECRET.

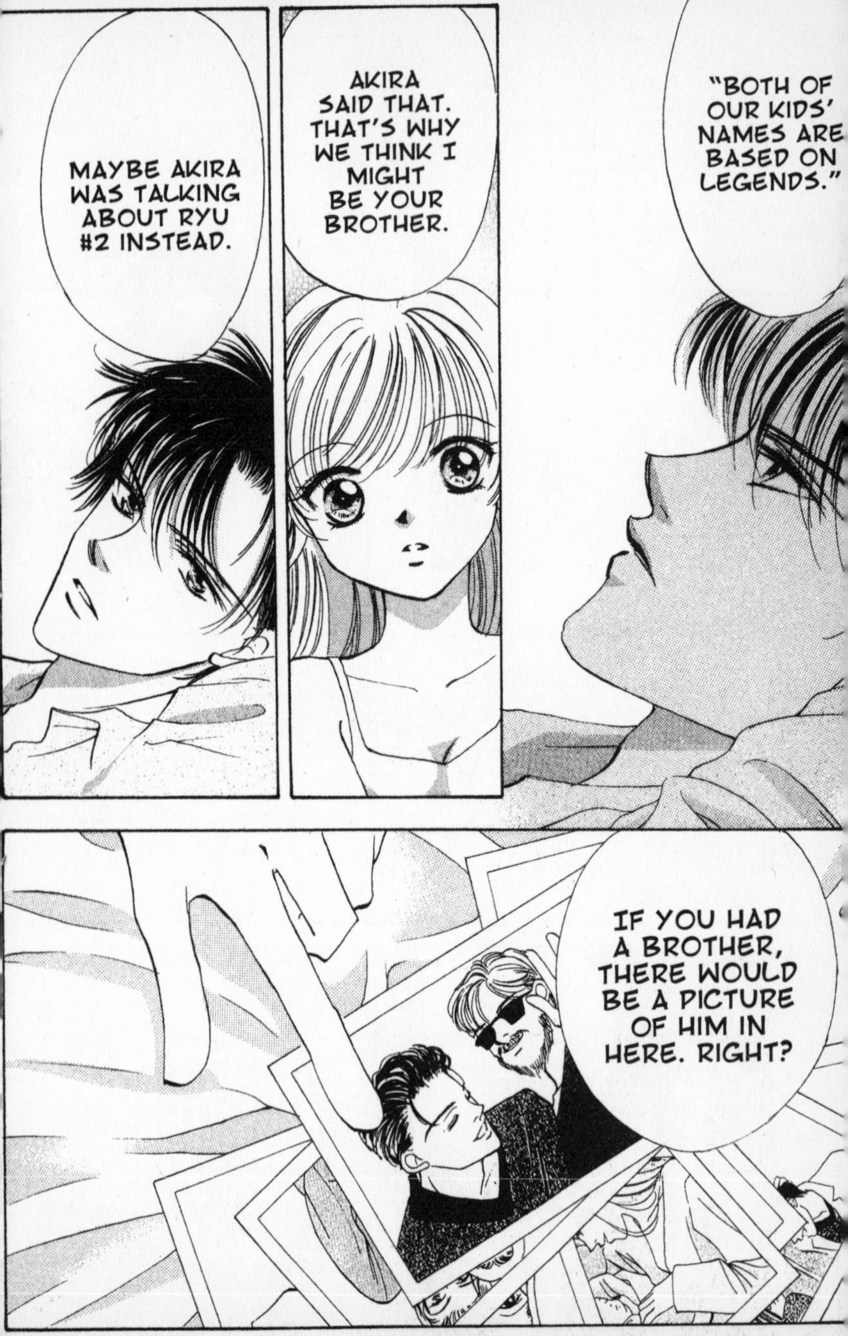
"BOTH OF OUR KIDS' NAMES ARE BASED ON LEGENDS."
AKIRA SAID THAT. THAT'S WHY WE THINK I MIGHT BE YOUR BROTHER.
MAYBE AKIRA WAS TALKING ABOUT RYU #2 INSTEAD.
IF YOU HAD A BROTHER, THERE WOULD BE A PICTURE OF HIM IN HERE. RIGHT?

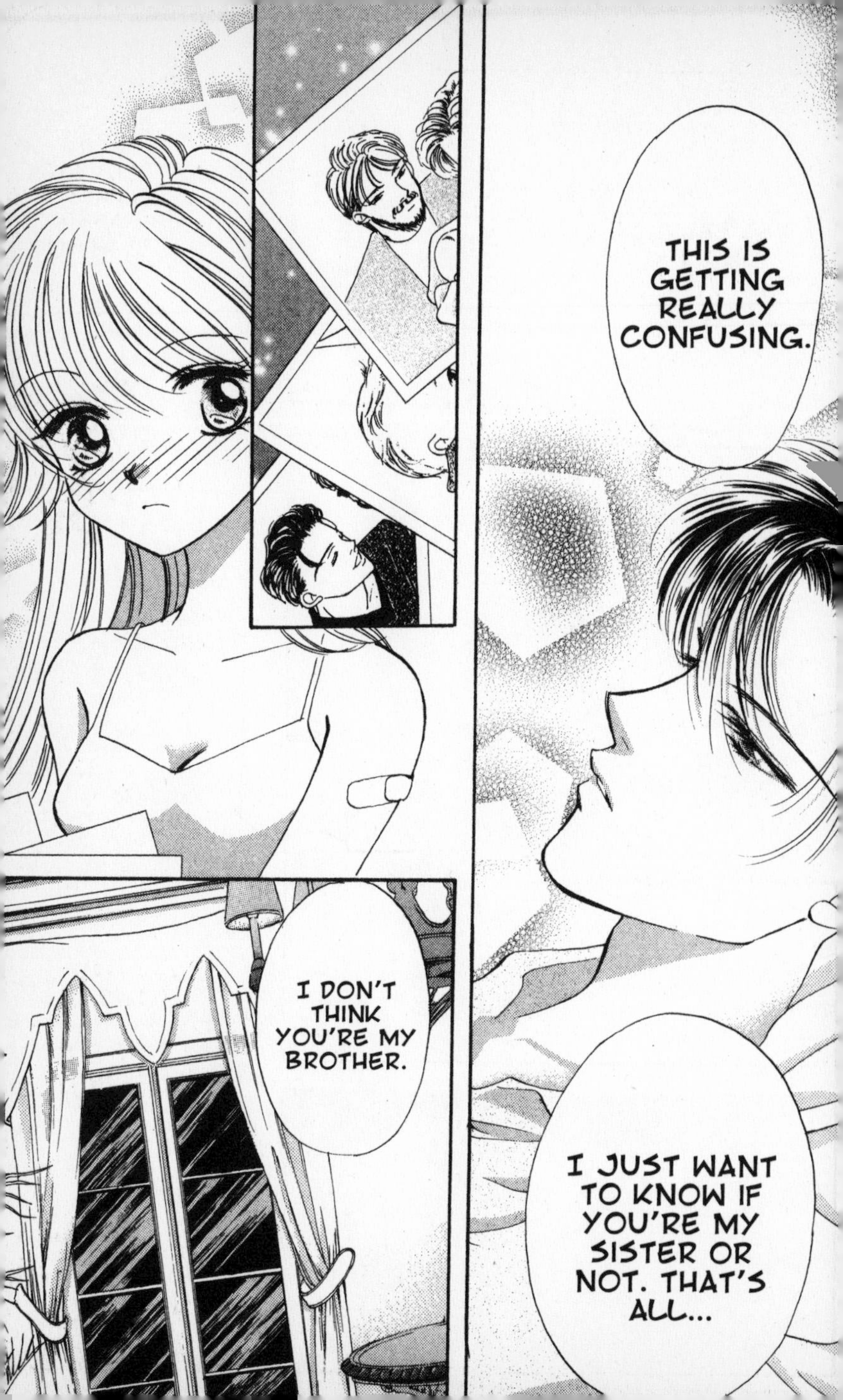
THIS IS GETTING REALLY CONFUSING.
I JUST WANT TO KNOW IF YOU'RE MY SISTER OR NOT. THAT'S ALL...
I DON'T THINK YOU'RE MY BROTHER.

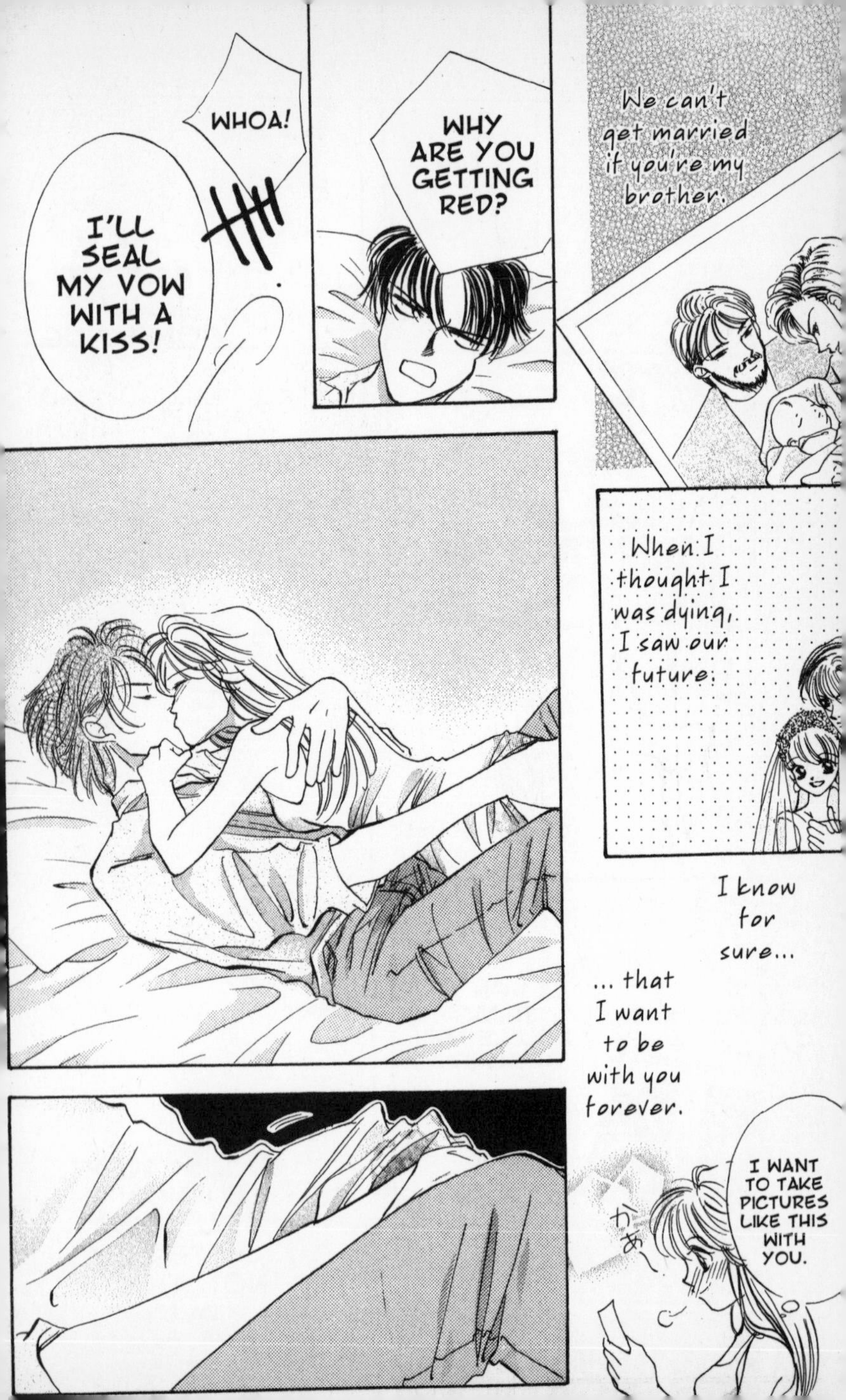

We can't get married if you're my brother.
WHY ARE YOU GETTING RED?
WHOA!
I'LL SEAL MY VOW WITH A KISS!
When I thought I was dying, I saw our future.
I know for sure...
... that I want to be with you forever.
かあ〜
I WANT TO TAKE PICTURES LIKE THIS WITH YOU.

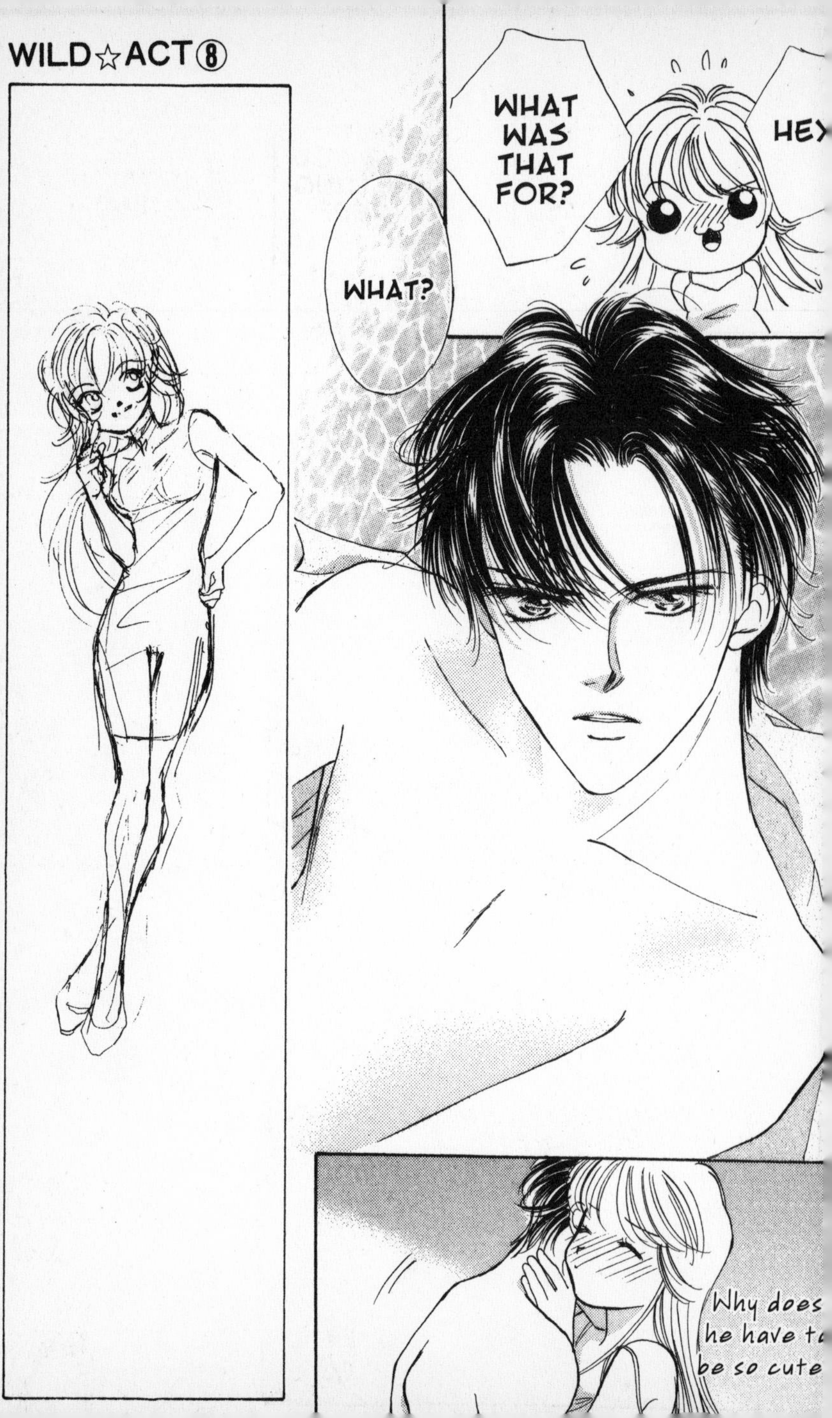
HE
WHAT WAS THAT FOR?
WHAT?
Why does
he have t
be so cute

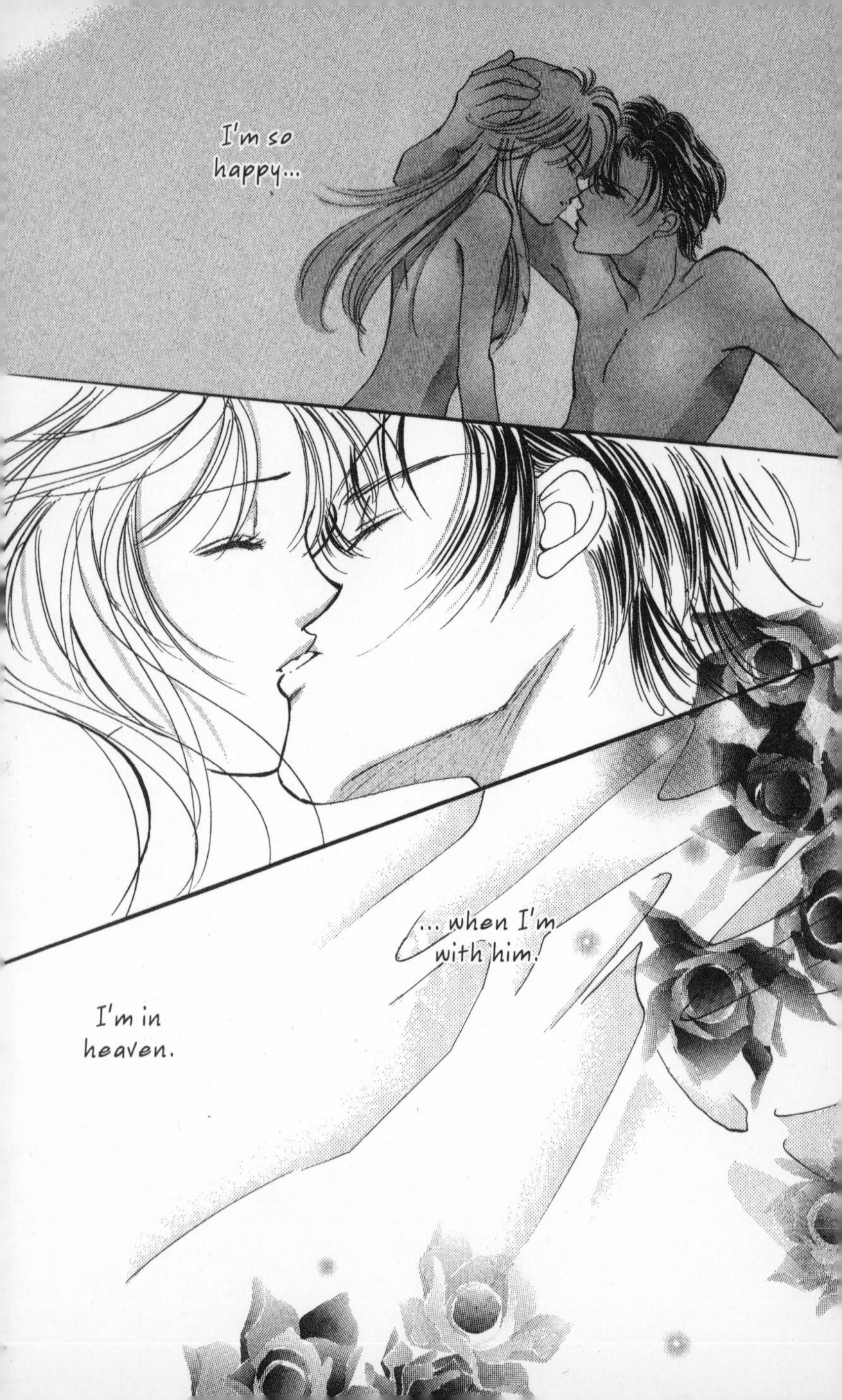
I'm so happy...
...when I'm with him.
I'm in heaven.

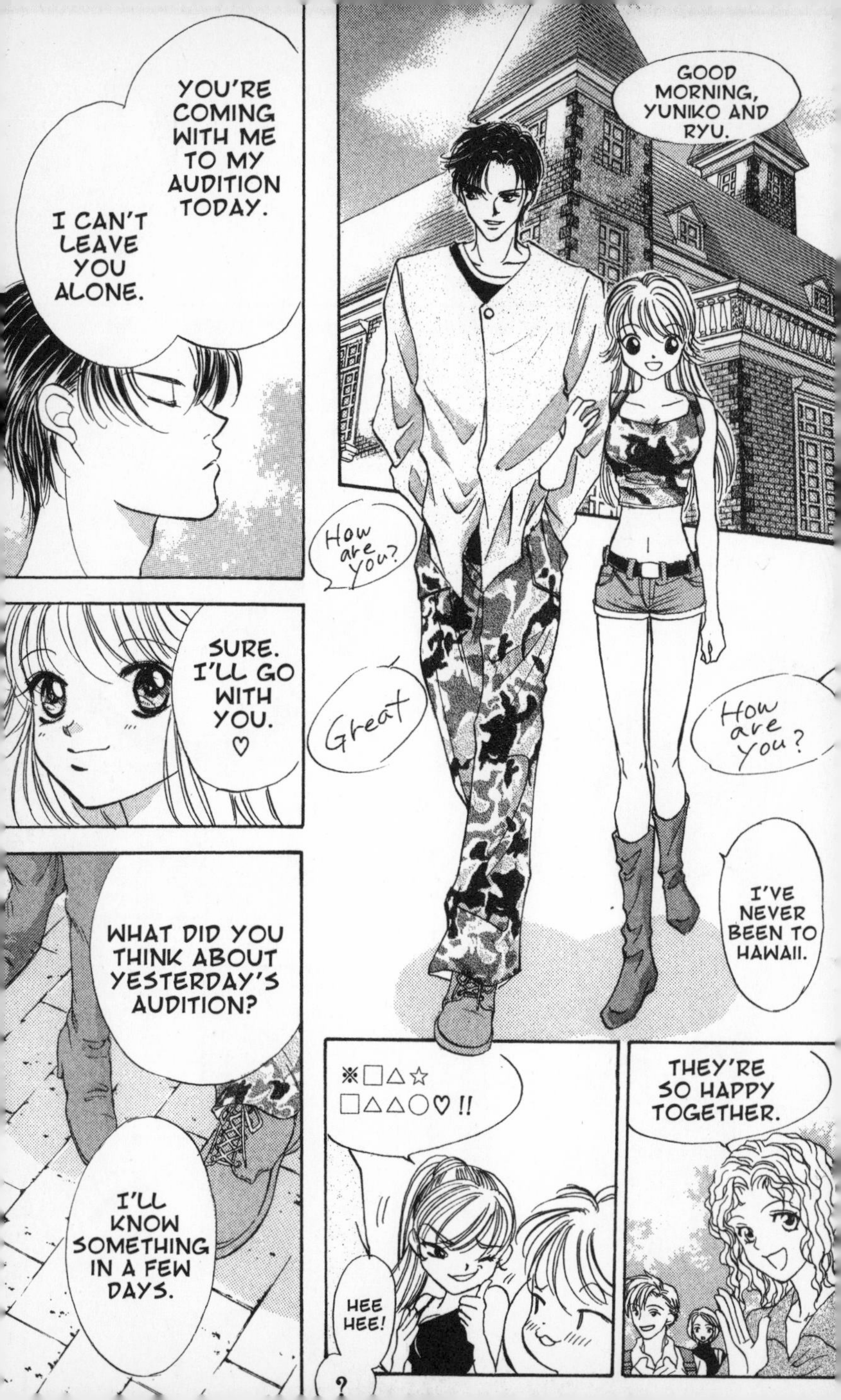
GOOD MORNING, YUNIKO AND RYU.
How are you?
Great
How are you?
I'VE NEVER BEEN TO HAWAII.
THEY'RE SO HAPPY TOGETHER.
※□△☆ □△△○♡!!
HEE HEE!
?
YOU'RE COMING WITH ME TO MY AUDITION TODAY.
I CAN'T LEAVE YOU ALONE.
SURE. I'LL GO WITH YOU. ♡
WHAT DID YOU THINK ABOUT YESTERDAY'S AUDITION?
I'LL KNOW SOMETHING IN A FEW DAYS.

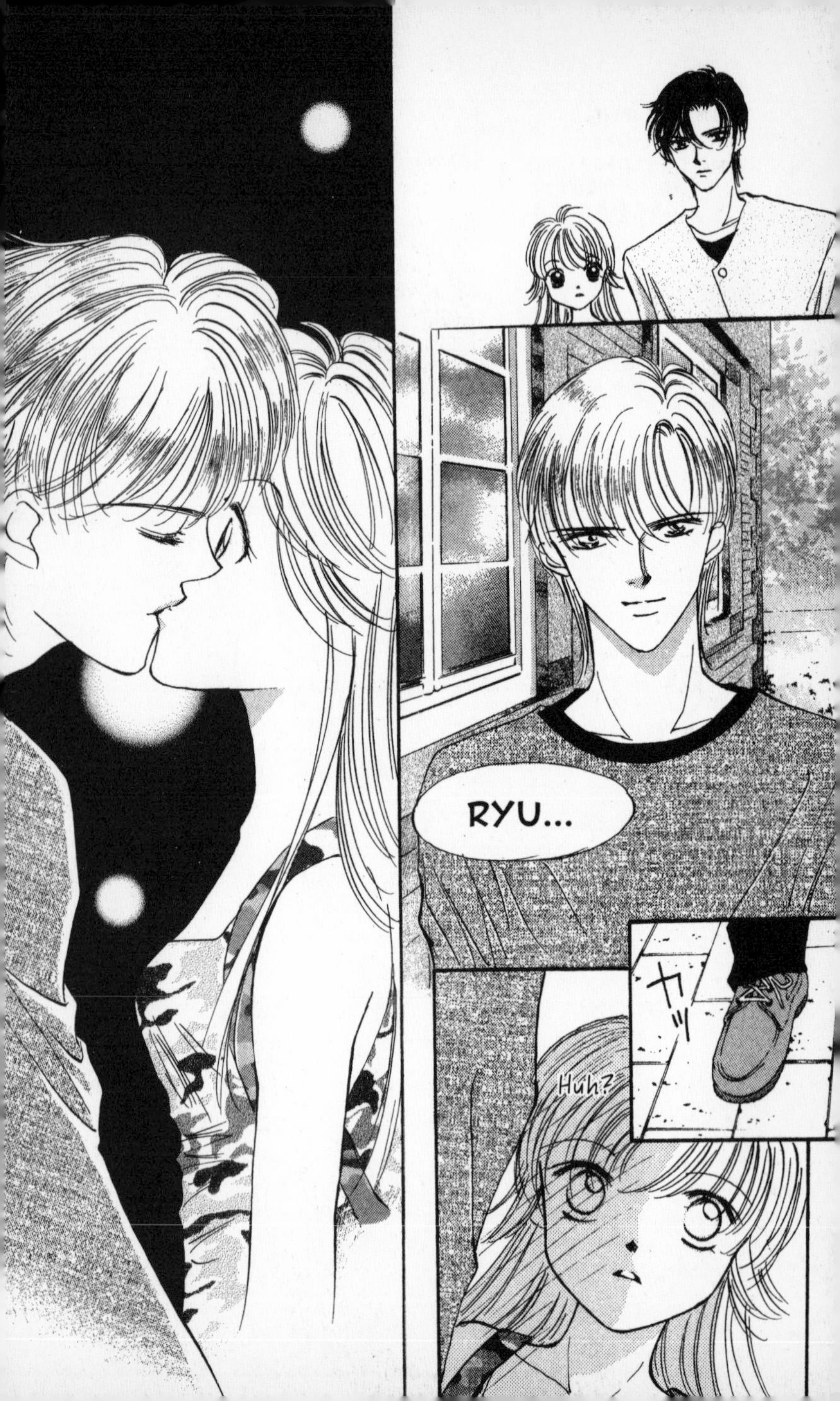
RYU...
ヤッ
Huh?

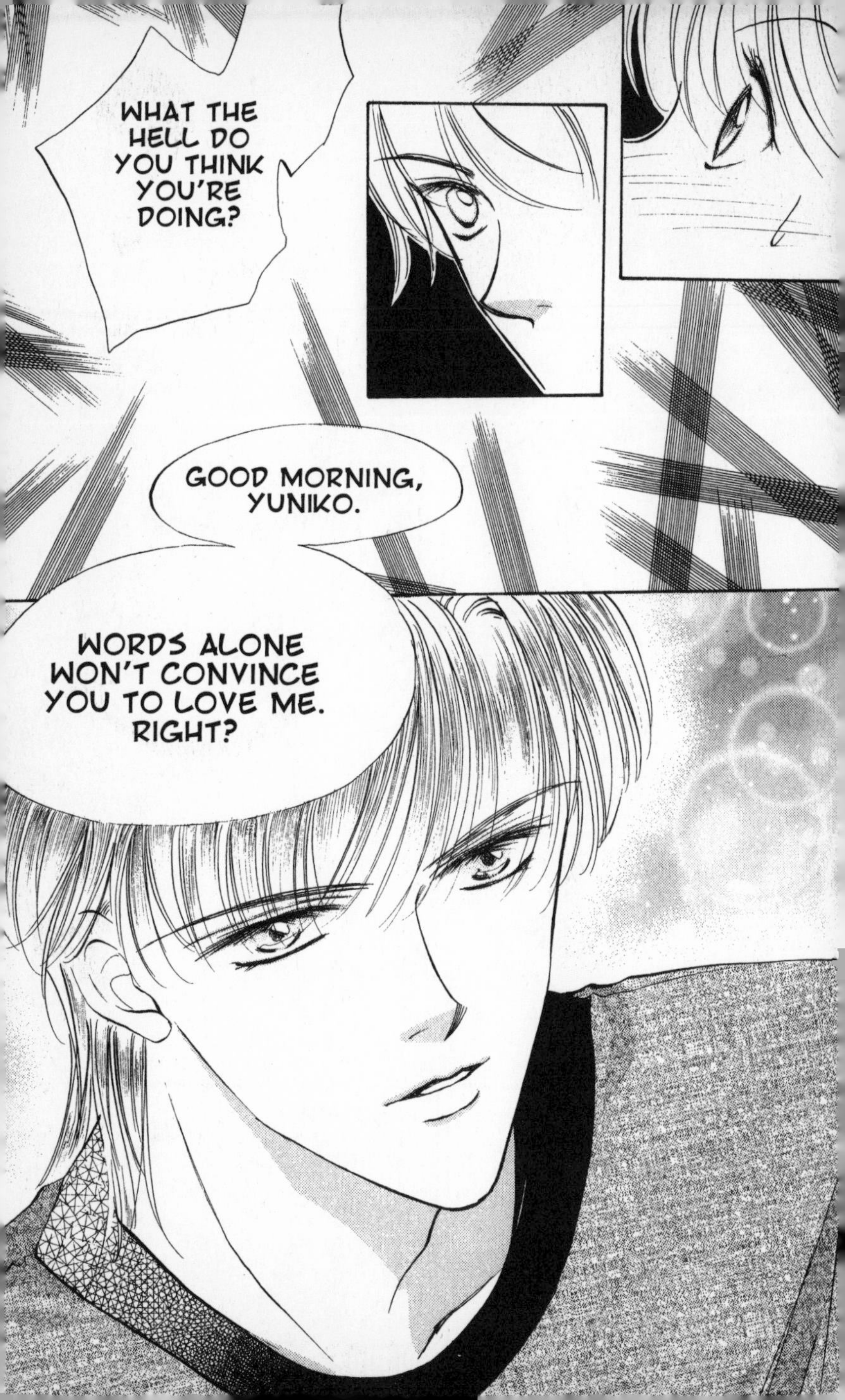
WHAT THE HELL DO YOU THINK YOU'RE DOING?
GOOD MORNING, YUNIKO.
WORDS ALONE WON'T CONVINCE YOU TO LOVE ME. RIGHT?

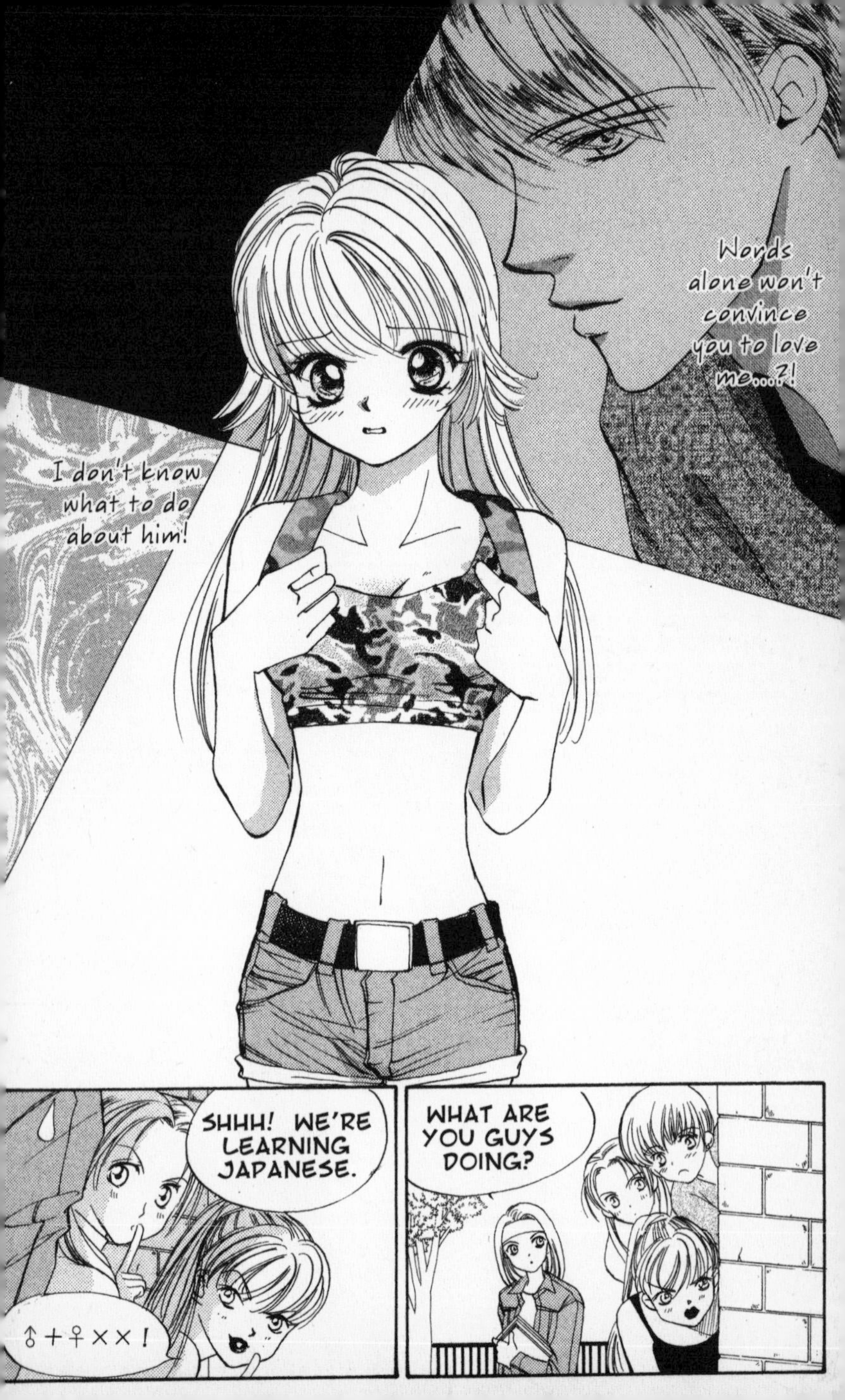
Words alone won't convince you to love me...?!
I don't know what to do about him!
WHAT ARE YOU GUYS DOING?
SHHH! WE'RE LEARNING JAPANESE.
♂+♀××!

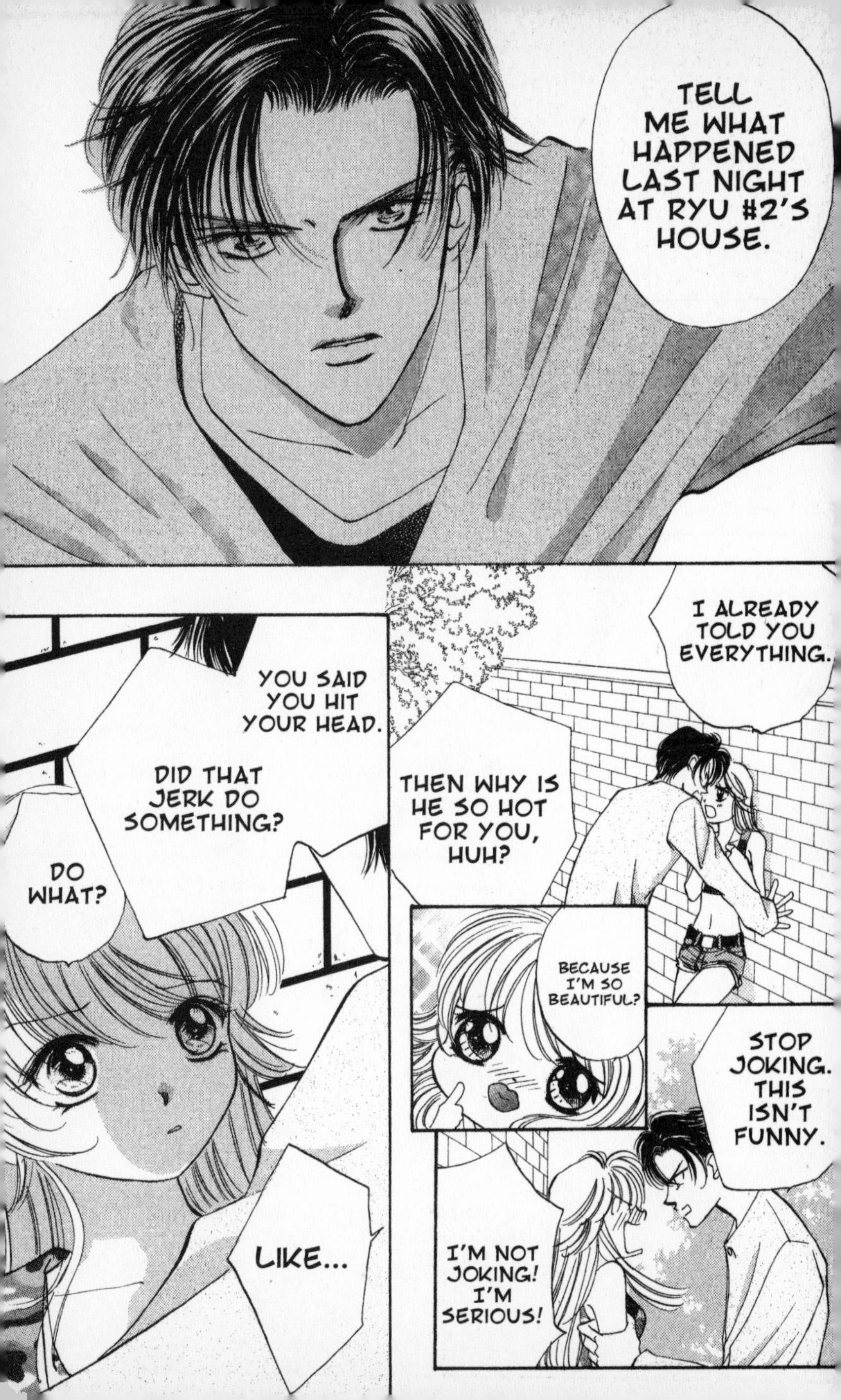
TELL ME WHAT HAPPENED LAST NIGHT AT RYU #2'S HOUSE.
I ALREADY TOLD YOU EVERYTHING.
THEN WHY IS HE SO HOT FOR YOU, HUH?
BECAUSE I'M SO BEAUTIFUL?
STOP JOKING. THIS ISN'T FUNNY.
I'M NOT JOKING! I'M SERIOUS!
YOU SAID YOU HIT YOUR HEAD.
DID THAT JERK DO SOMETHING?
DO WHAT?
LIKE...

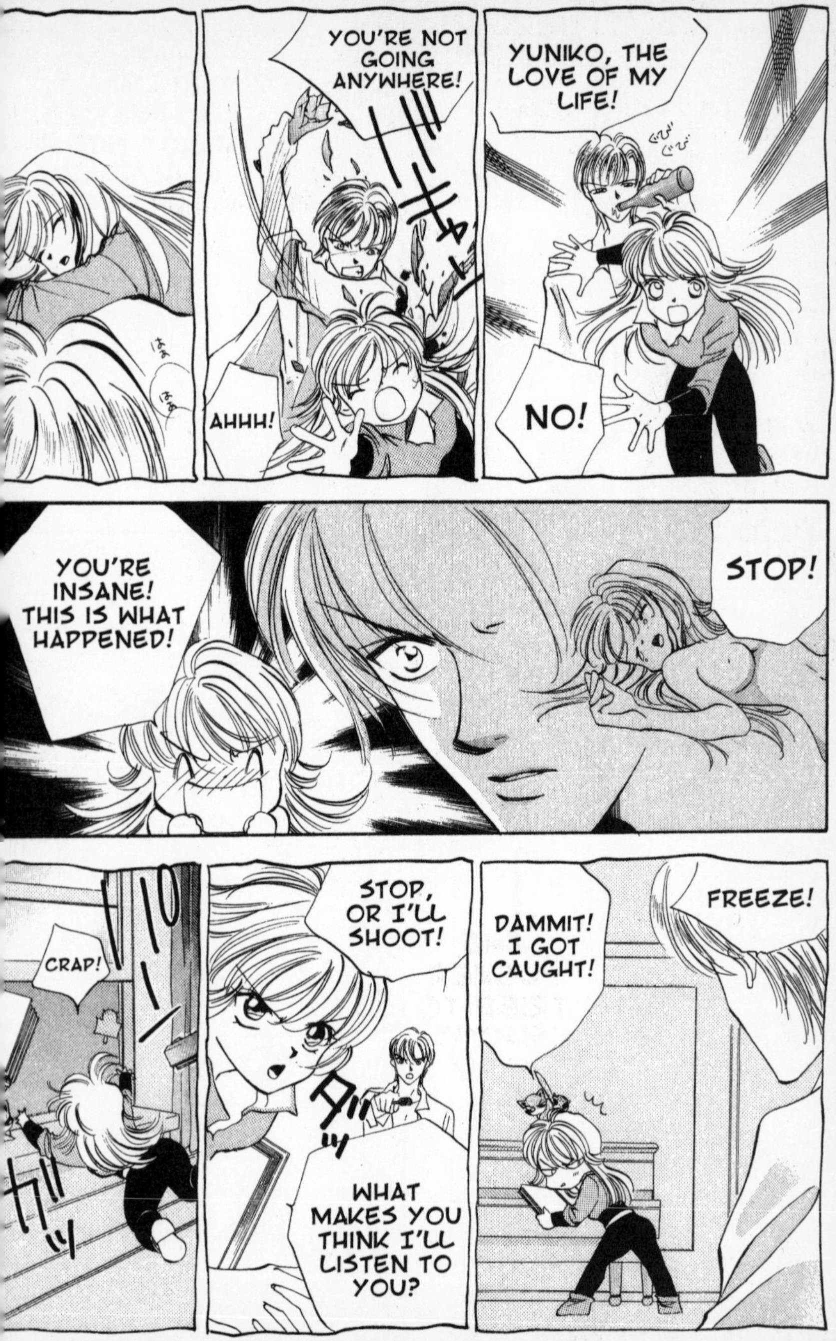
YUNIKO, THE LOVE OF MY LIFE!
ぐび ぐび
NO!
YOU'RE NOT GOING ANYWHERE!
AHHH!
はあ
はあ
STOP!
YOU'RE INSANE! THIS IS WHAT HAPPENED!
FREEZE!
DAMMIT! I GOT CAUGHT!
STOP, OR I'LL SHOOT!
WHAT MAKES YOU THINK I'LL LISTEN TO YOU?
CRAP!

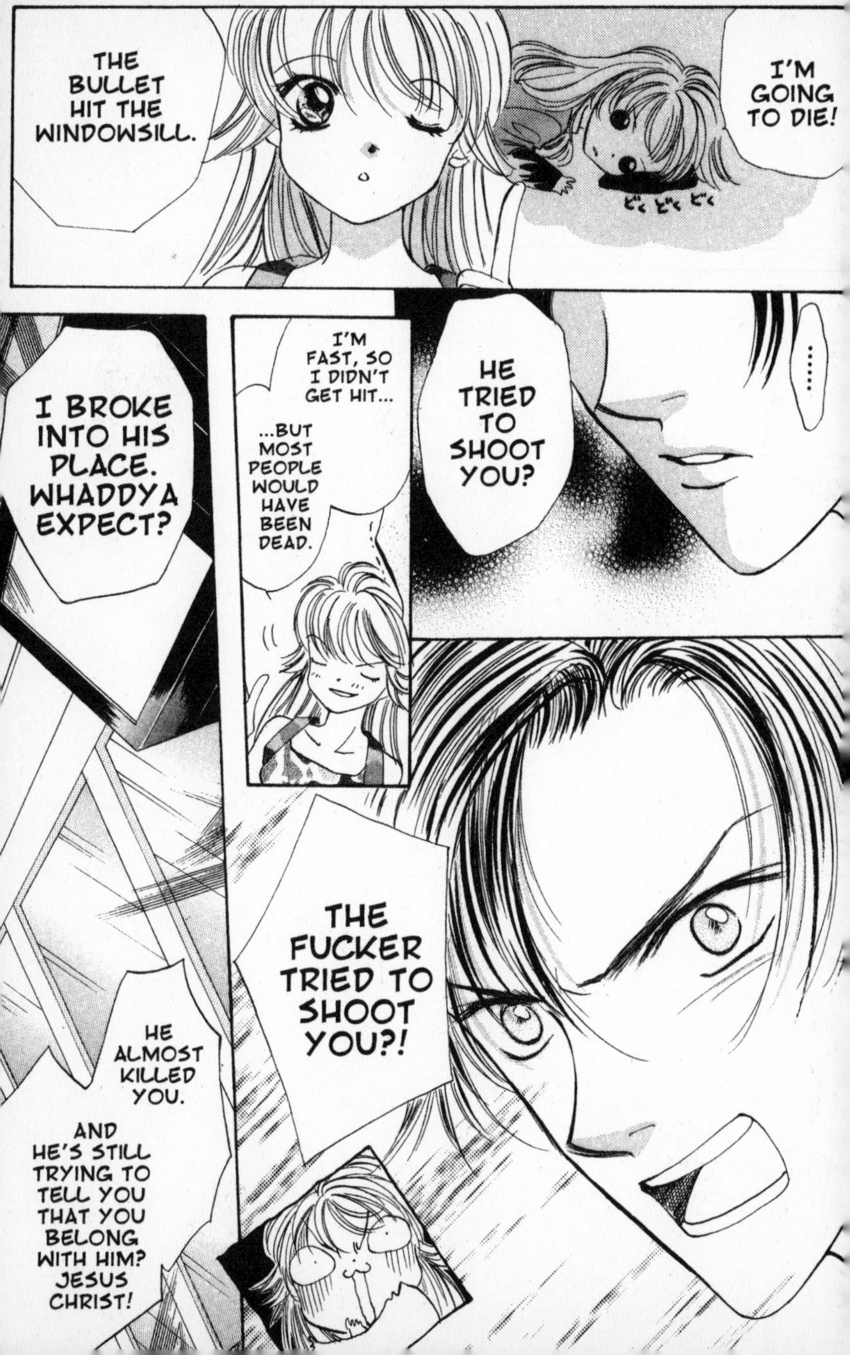
I'M GOING TO DIE!
どくどくどく
THE BULLET HIT THE WINDOWSILL.
......
HE TRIED TO SHOOT YOU?
I'M FAST, SO I DIDN'T GET HIT...
...BUT MOST PEOPLE WOULD HAVE BEEN DEAD.
I BROKE INTO HIS PLACE. WHADDYA EXPECT?
THE FUCKER TRIED TO SHOOT YOU?!
HE ALMOST KILLED YOU.
AND HE'S STILL TRYING TO TELL YOU THAT YOU BELONG WITH HIM? JESUS CHRIST!

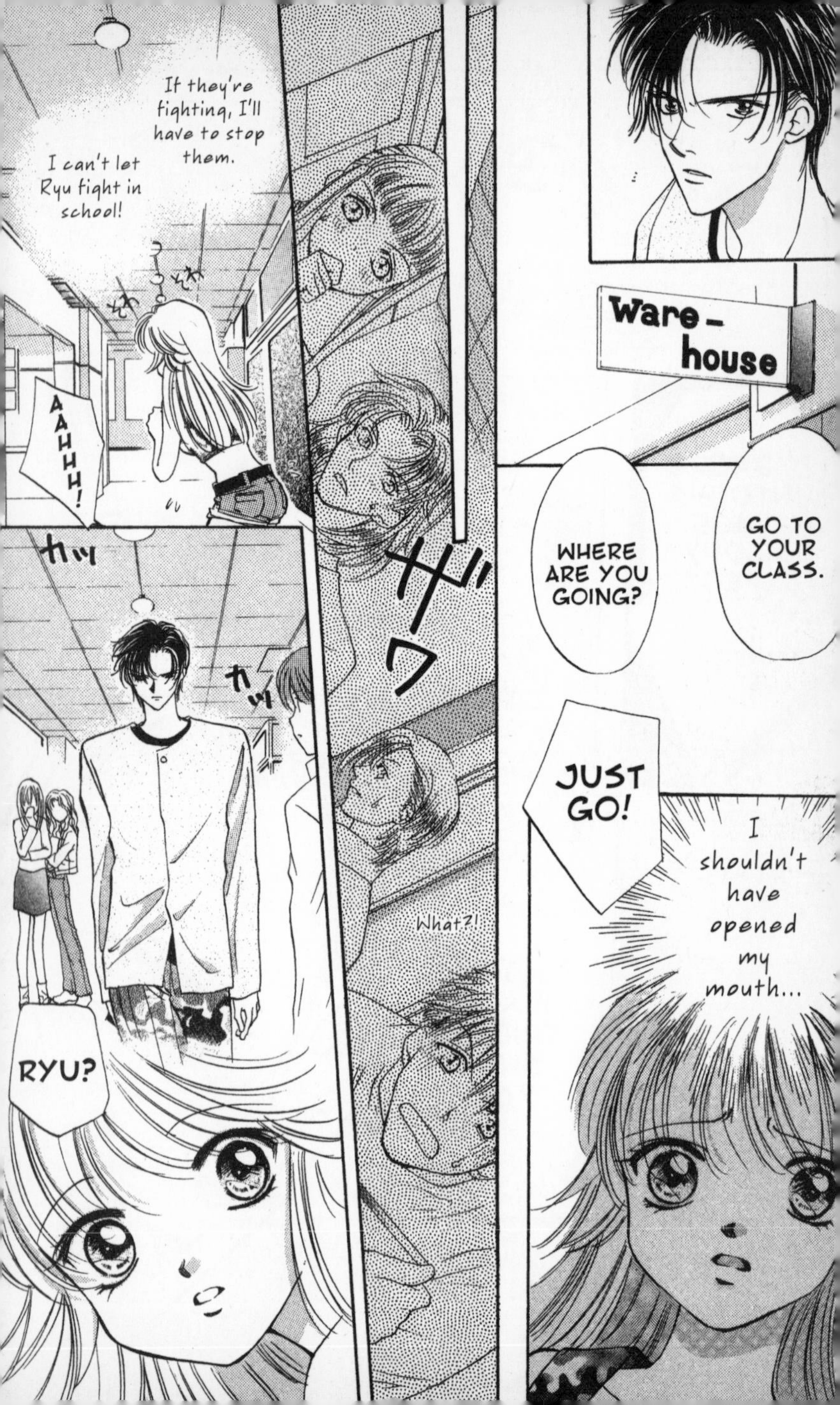
Ware-
house
GO TO YOUR CLASS.
WHERE ARE YOU GOING?
JUST GO!
I shouldn't have opened my mouth...
ザワ
What?!
If they're fighting, I'll have to stop them.
I can't let Ryu fight in school!
AAHHH!
カッ
カッ
RYU?

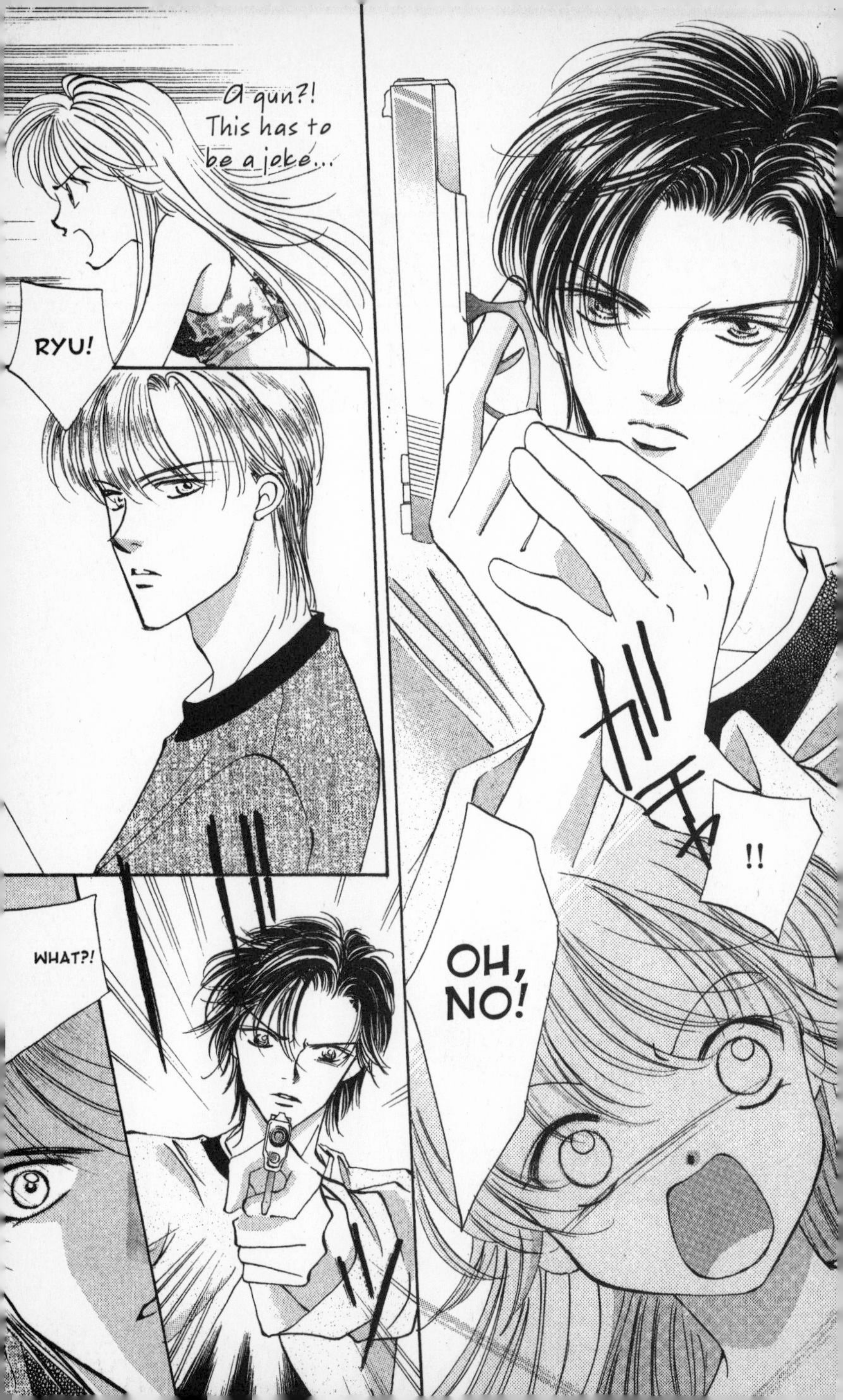
!!
OH, NO!
A gun?! This has to be a joke...
RYU!
WHAT?!

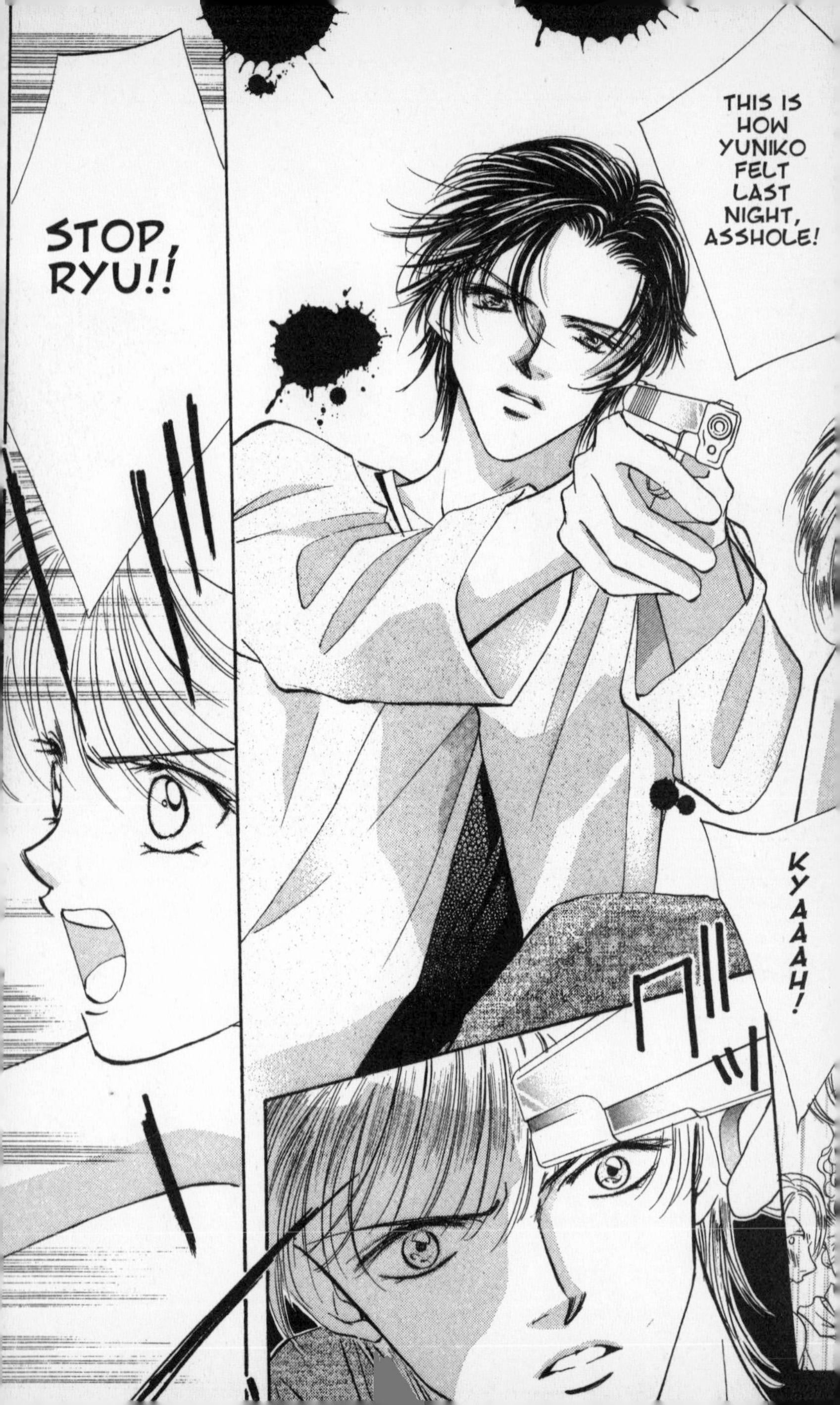
THIS IS HOW YUNIKO FELT LAST NIGHT, ASSHOLE!
KYAAAH!
STOP, RYU!!

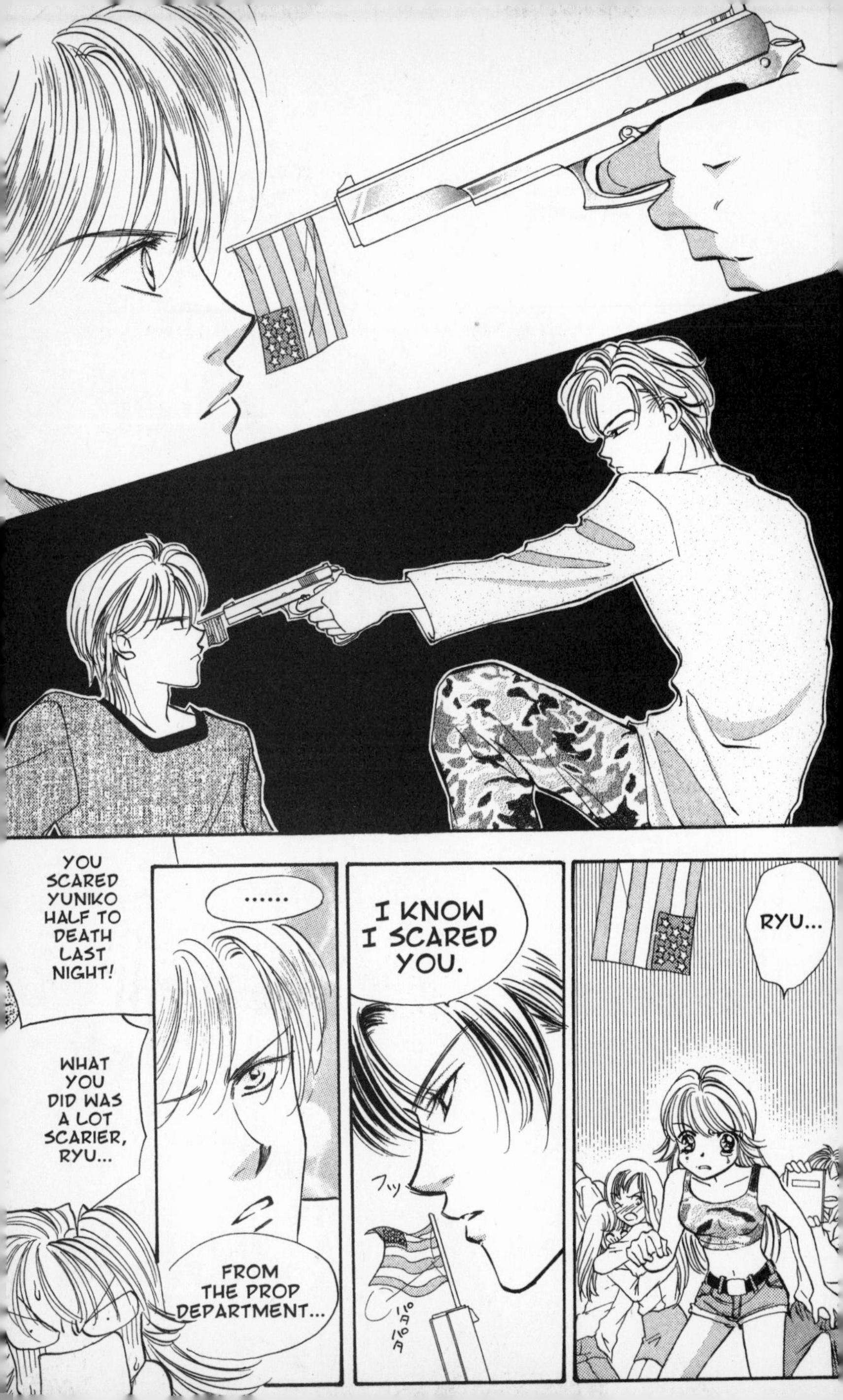
RYU...
I KNOW I SCARED YOU.
フッ
パタパタ
......
FROM THE PROP DEPARTMENT...
YOU SCARED YUNIKO HALF TO DEATH LAST NIGHT!
WHAT YOU DID WAS A LOT SCARIER, RYU...

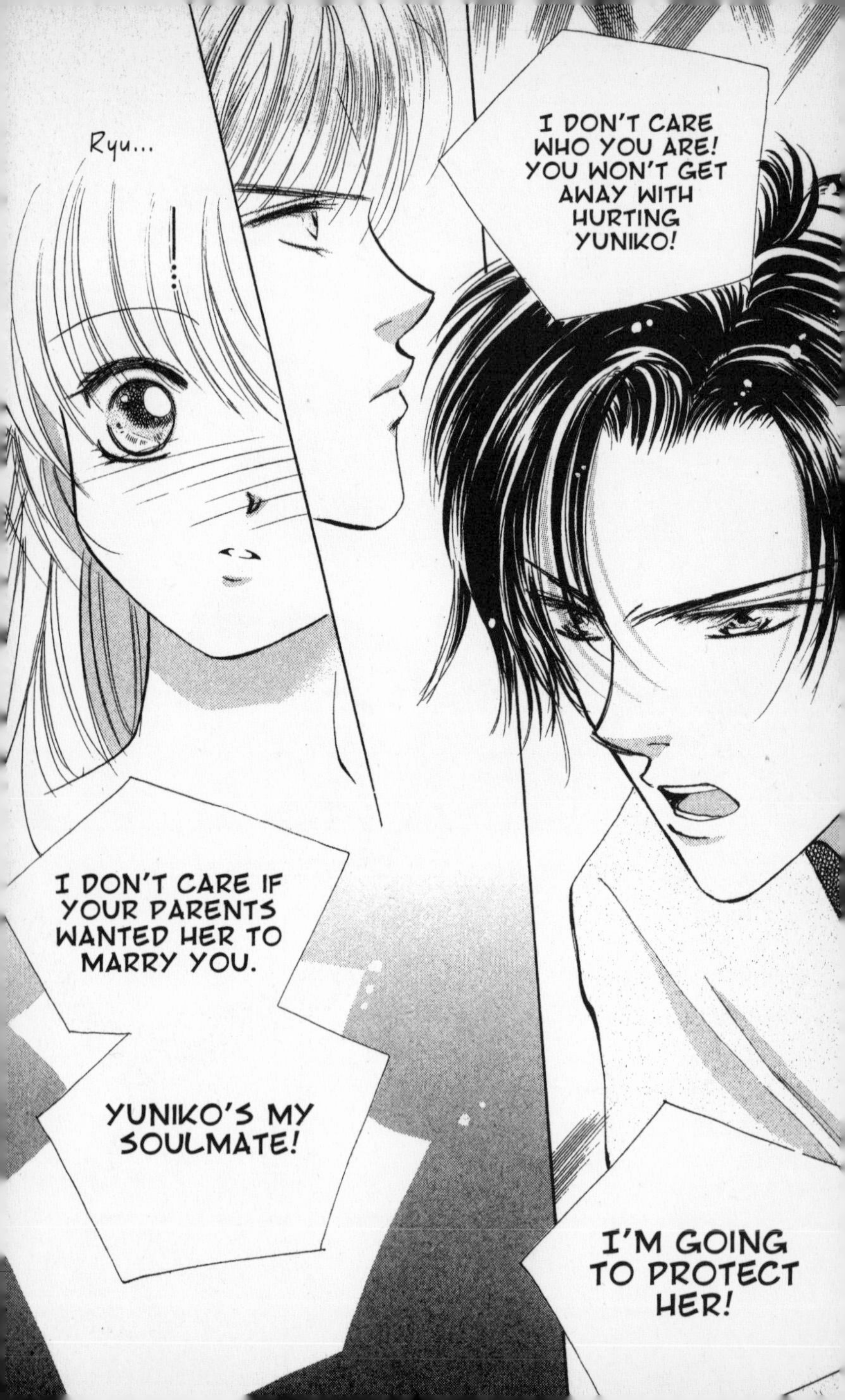
I DON'T CARE WHO YOU ARE! YOU WON'T GET AWAY WITH HURTING YUNIKO!
Ryu...
I DON'T CARE IF YOUR PARENTS WANTED HER TO MARRY YOU.
YUNIKO'S MY SOULMATE!
I'M GOING TO PROTECT HER!

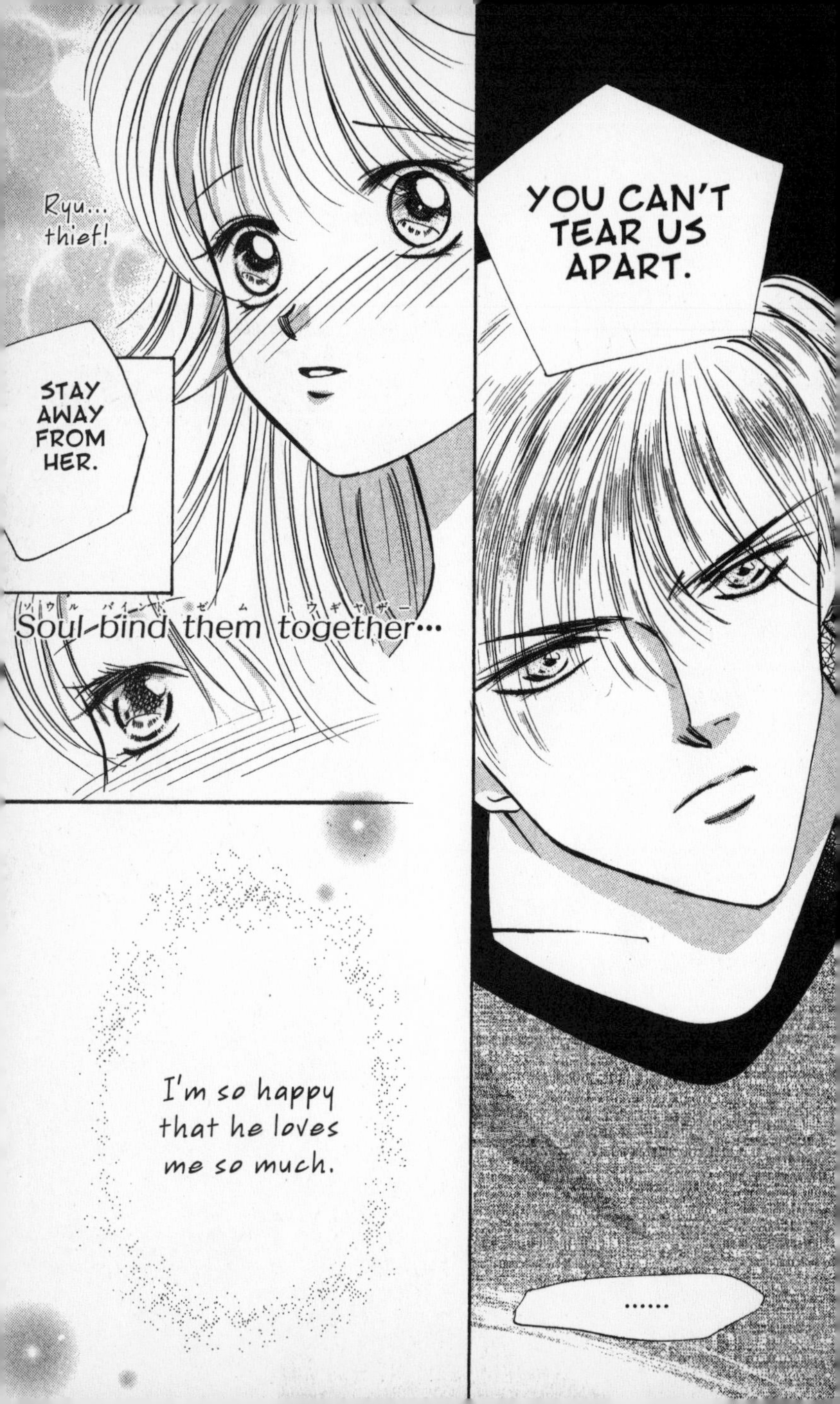
YOU CAN'T TEAR US APART.
......
Ryu... thief!
STAY AWAY FROM HER.
Soul-bind them together...
I'm so happy that he loves me so much.

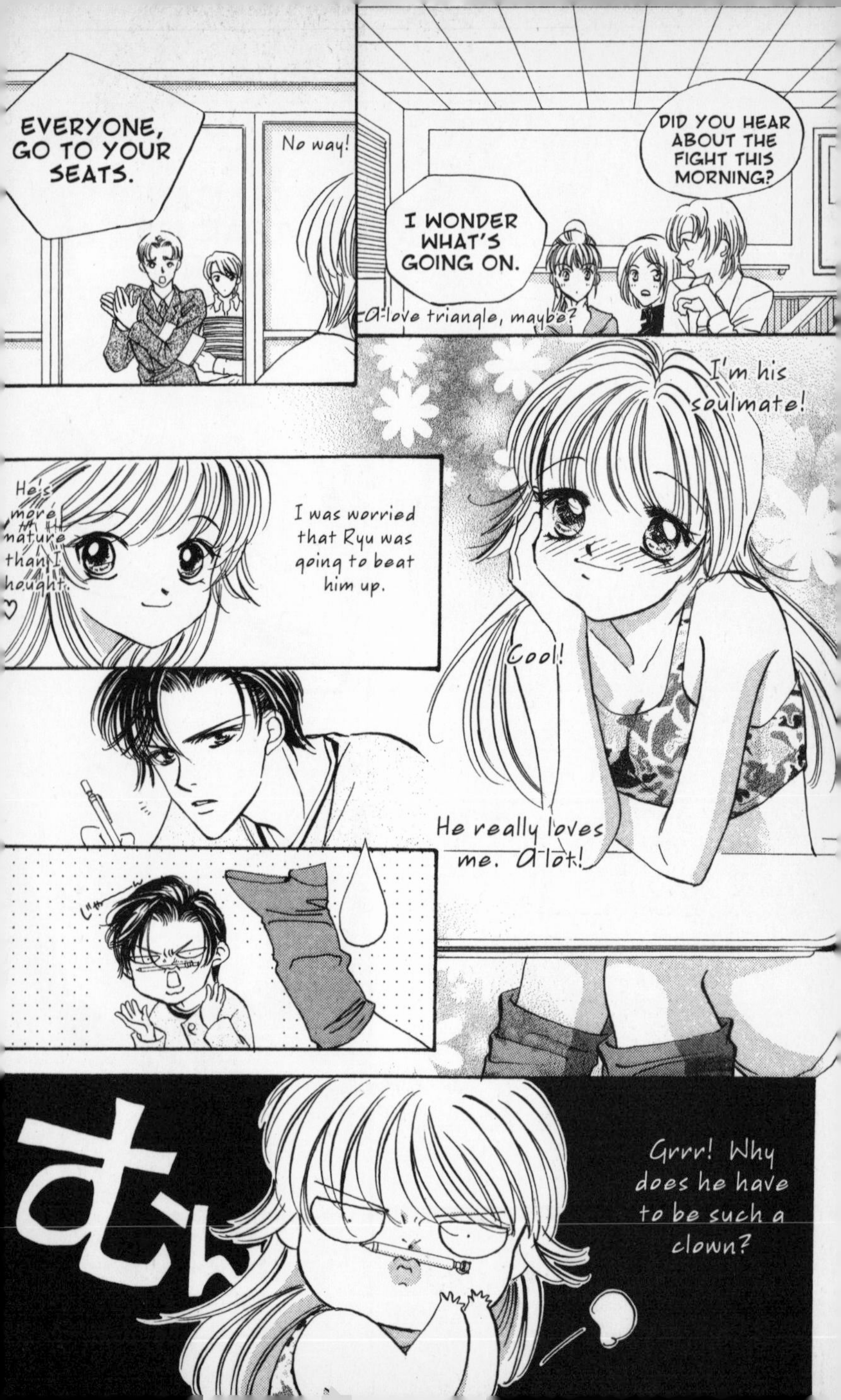
DID YOU HEAR ABOUT THE FIGHT THIS MORNING?
I WONDER WHAT'S GOING ON.
A love triangle, maybe?
No way!
EVERYONE, GO TO YOUR SEATS.
I'm his soulmate!
Cool!
He really loves me. A lot!
I was worried that Ryu was going to beat him up.
He's more mature than I thought. ♡
Grrr! Why does he have to be such a clown?
むん

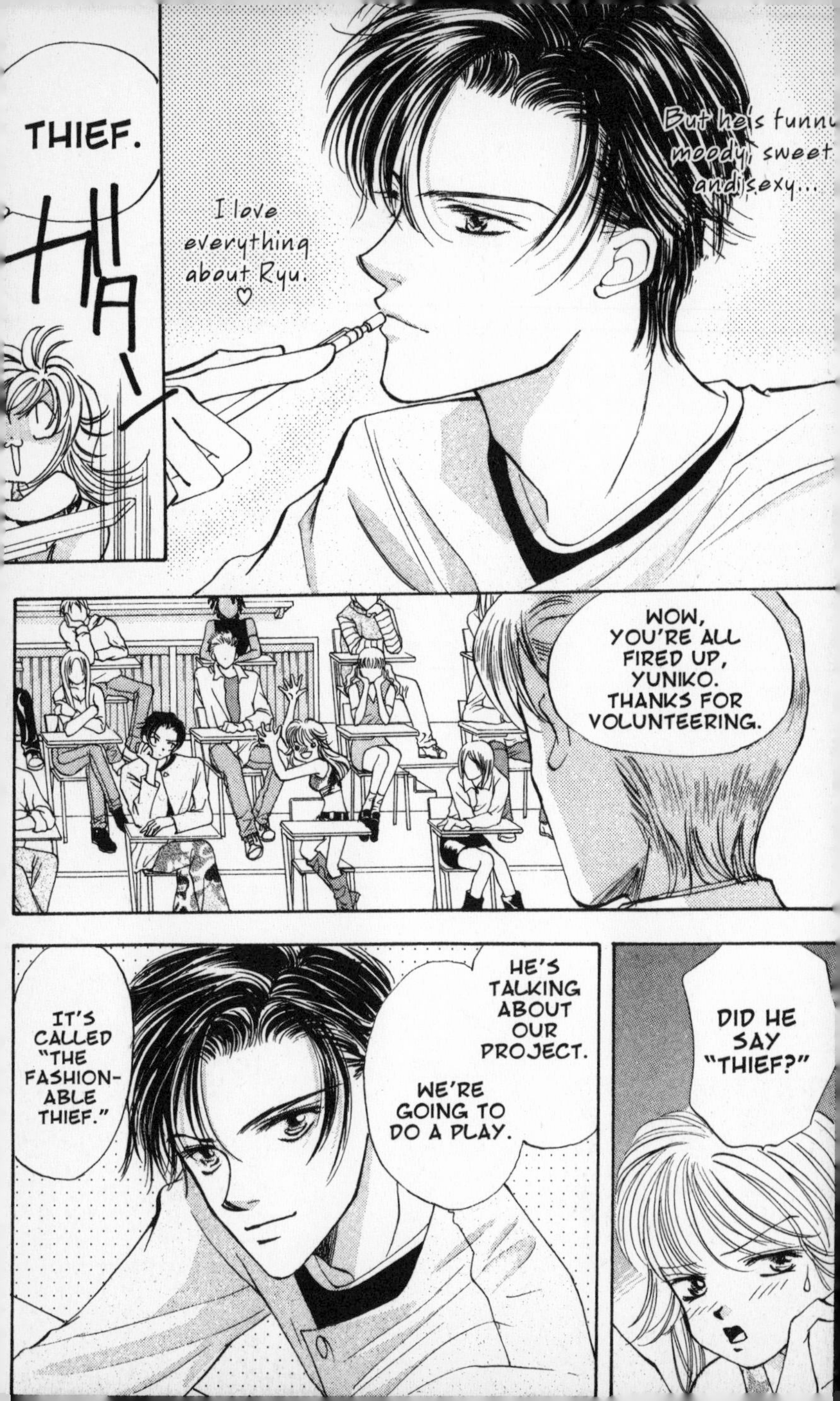
But he's funn
moody, sweet and sexy...
I love everything about Ryu. ♡
THIEF.
HA!
WOW, YOU'RE ALL FIRED UP, YUNIKO. THANKS FOR VOLUNTEERING.
DID HE SAY "THIEF?"
HE'S TALKING ABOUT OUR PROJECT.
WE'RE GOING TO DO A PLAY.
IT'S CALLED "THE FASHION-ABLE THIEF."

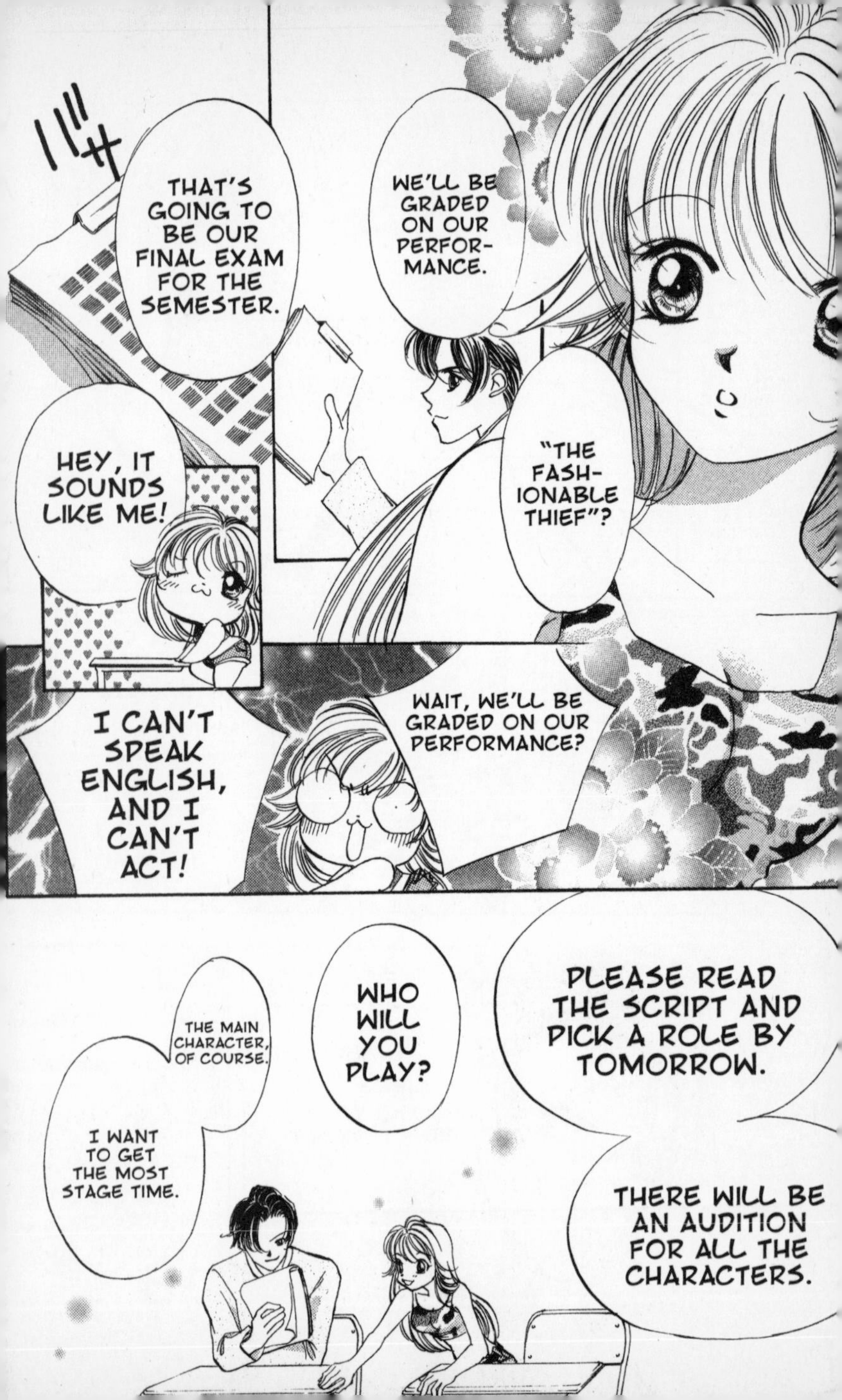
"THE FASHIONABLE THIEF"?
THAT'S GOING TO BE OUR FINAL EXAM FOR THE SEMESTER.
WE'LL BE GRADED ON OUR PERFORMANCE.
HEY, IT SOUNDS LIKE ME!
WAIT, WE'LL BE GRADED ON OUR PERFORMANCE?
I CAN'T SPEAK ENGLISH, AND I CAN'T ACT!
PLEASE READ THE SCRIPT AND PICK A ROLE BY TOMORROW.
THERE WILL BE AN AUDITION FOR ALL THE CHARACTERS.
WHO WILL YOU PLAY?
THE MAIN CHARACTER, OF COURSE.
I WANT TO GET THE MOST STAGE TIME.

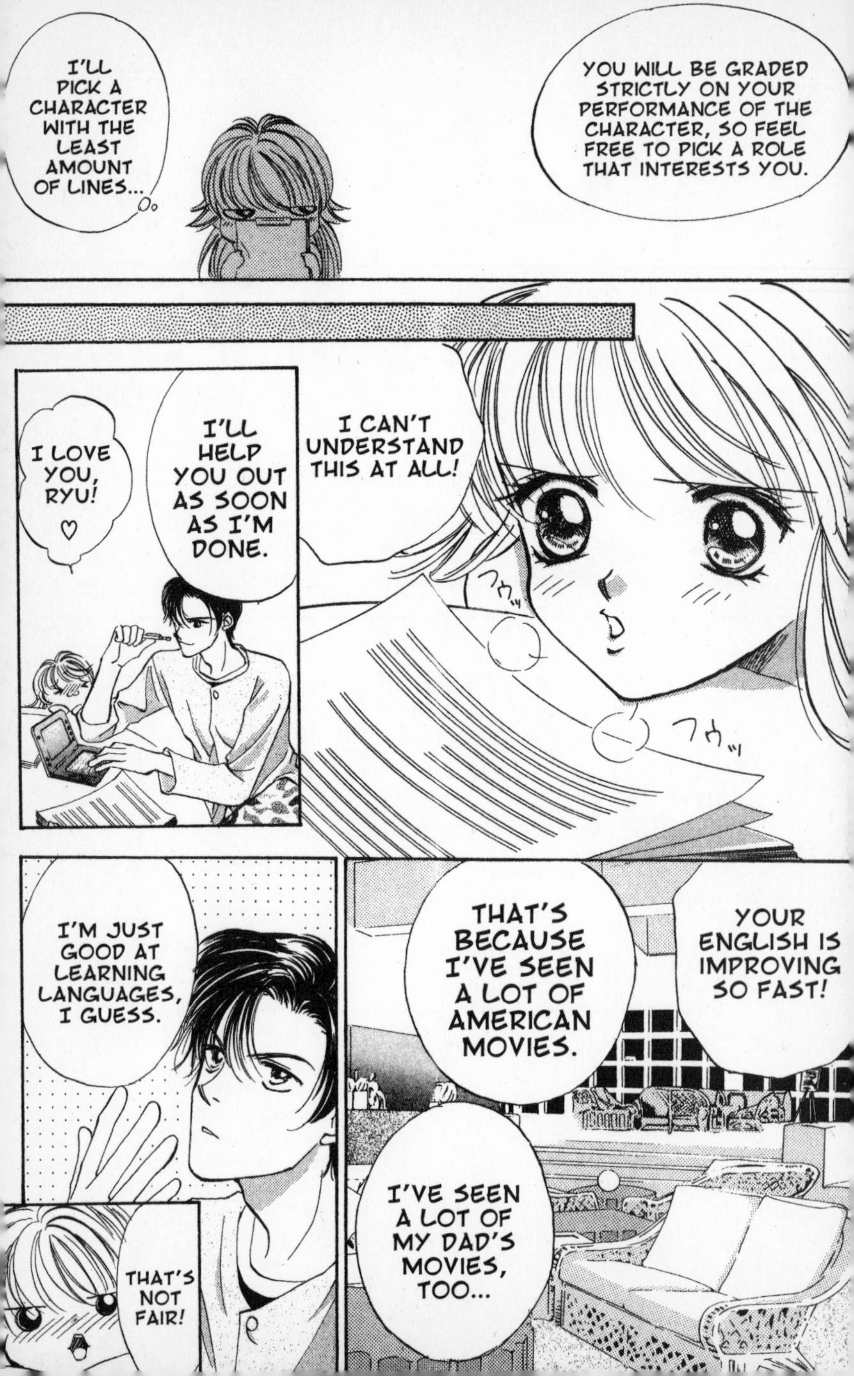
YOU WILL BE GRADED STRICTLY ON YOUR PERFORMANCE OF THE CHARACTER, SO FEEL FREE TO PICK A ROLE THAT INTERESTS YOU.
I'LL PICK A CHARACTER WITH THE LEAST AMOUNT OF LINES...
I CAN'T UNDERSTAND THIS AT ALL!
フゥッ
フゥッ
I'LL HELP YOU OUT AS SOON AS I'M DONE.
I LOVE YOU, RYU! ♡
YOUR ENGLISH IS IMPROVING SO FAST!
THAT'S BECAUSE I'VE SEEN A LOT OF AMERICAN MOVIES.
I'VE SEEN A LOT OF MY DAD'S MOVIES, TOO...
I'M JUST GOOD AT LEARNING LANGUAGES, I GUESS.
THAT'S NOT FAIR!

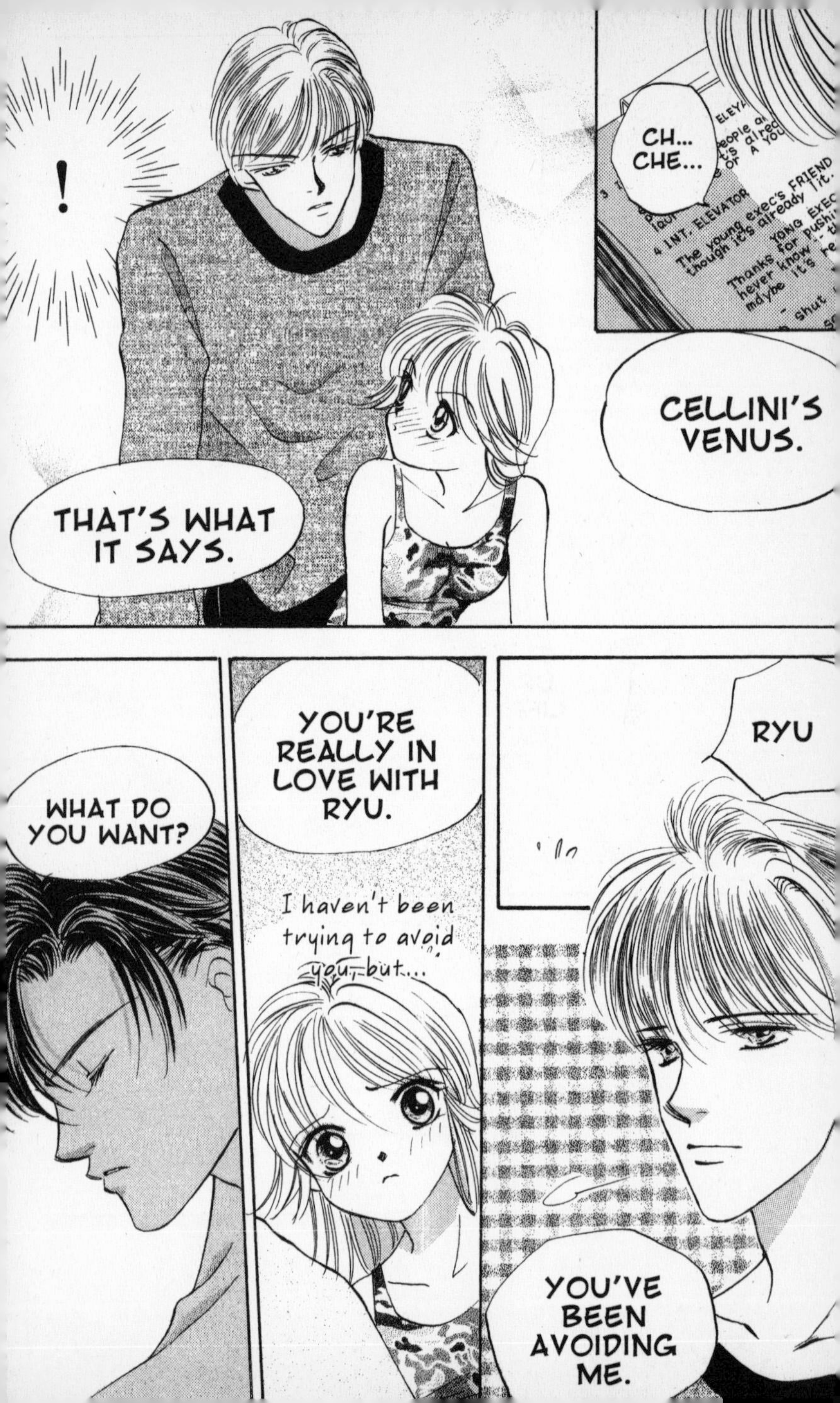
CH... CHE...
4 INT. ELEVATOR
The young exec's FRIEND
though it's already lit.
CELLINI'S VENUS.
!
THAT'S WHAT IT SAYS.
RYU
YOU'VE BEEN AVOIDING ME.
YOU'RE REALLY IN LOVE WITH RYU.
I haven't been trying to avoid you, but...
WHAT DO YOU WANT?

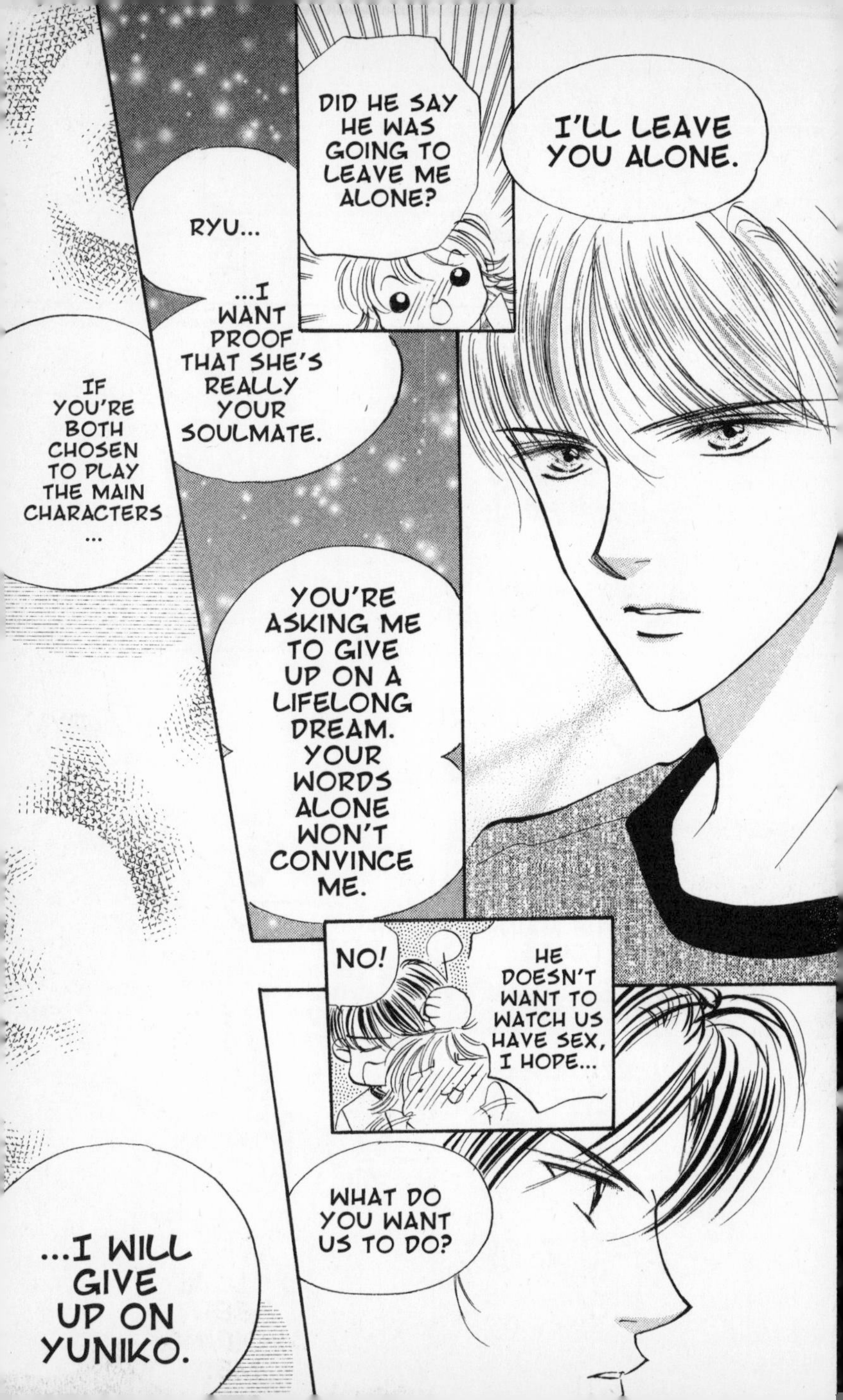
I'LL LEAVE YOU ALONE.
DID HE SAY HE WAS GOING TO LEAVE ME ALONE?
RYU...
...I WANT PROOF THAT SHE'S REALLY YOUR SOULMATE.
YOU'RE ASKING ME TO GIVE UP ON A LIFELONG DREAM. YOUR WORDS ALONE WON'T CONVINCE ME.
IF YOU'RE BOTH CHOSEN TO PLAY THE MAIN CHARACTERS ...
HE DOESN'T WANT TO WATCH US HAVE SEX, I HOPE...
NO!
WHAT DO YOU WANT US TO DO?
...I WILL GIVE UP ON YUNIKO.

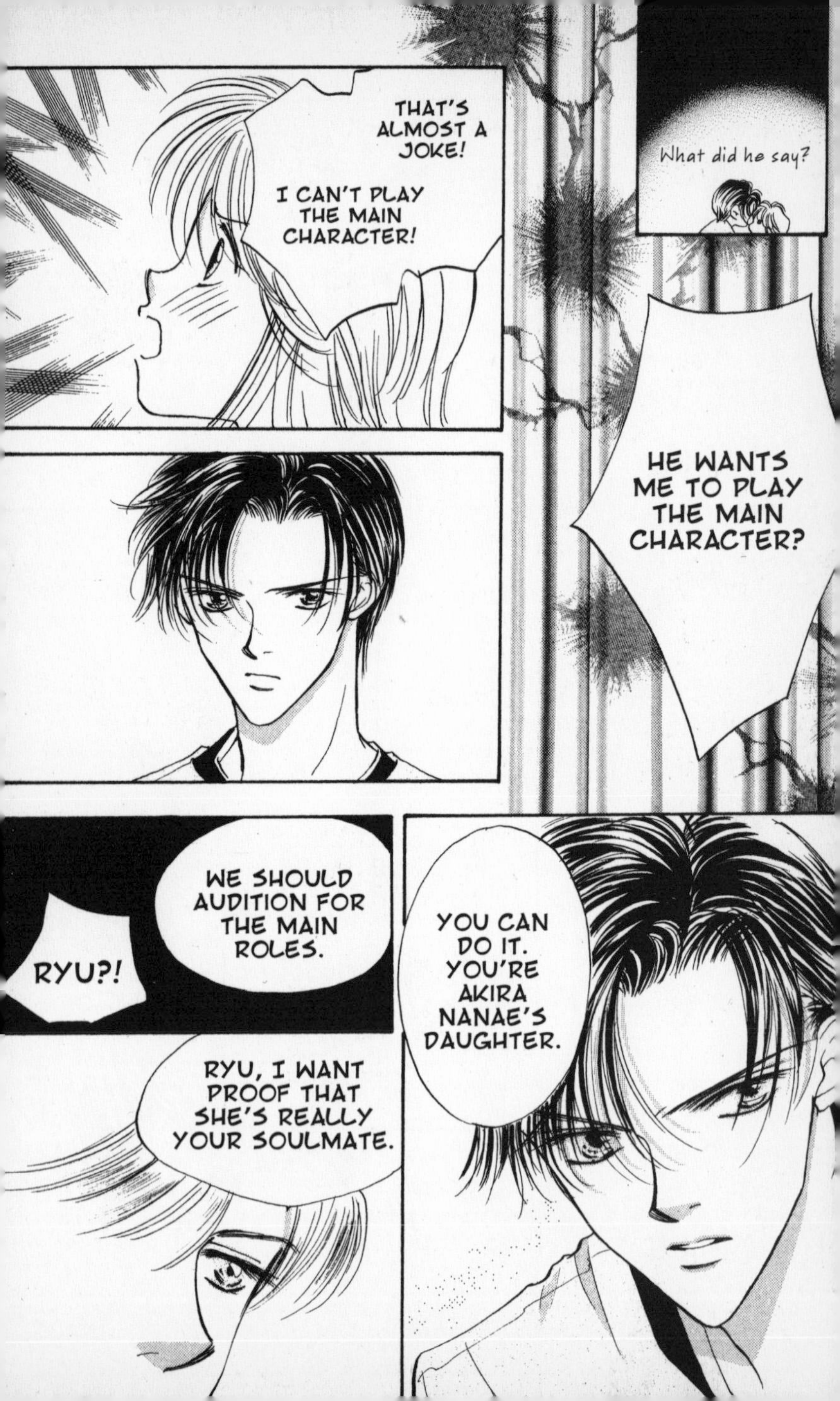
What did he say?
HE WANTS ME TO PLAY THE MAIN CHARACTER?
THAT'S ALMOST A JOKE!
I CAN'T PLAY THE MAIN CHARACTER!
YOU CAN DO IT. YOU'RE AKIRA NANAE'S DAUGHTER.
WE SHOULD AUDITION FOR THE MAIN ROLES.
RYU?!
RYU, I WANT PROOF THAT SHE'S REALLY YOUR SOULMATE.

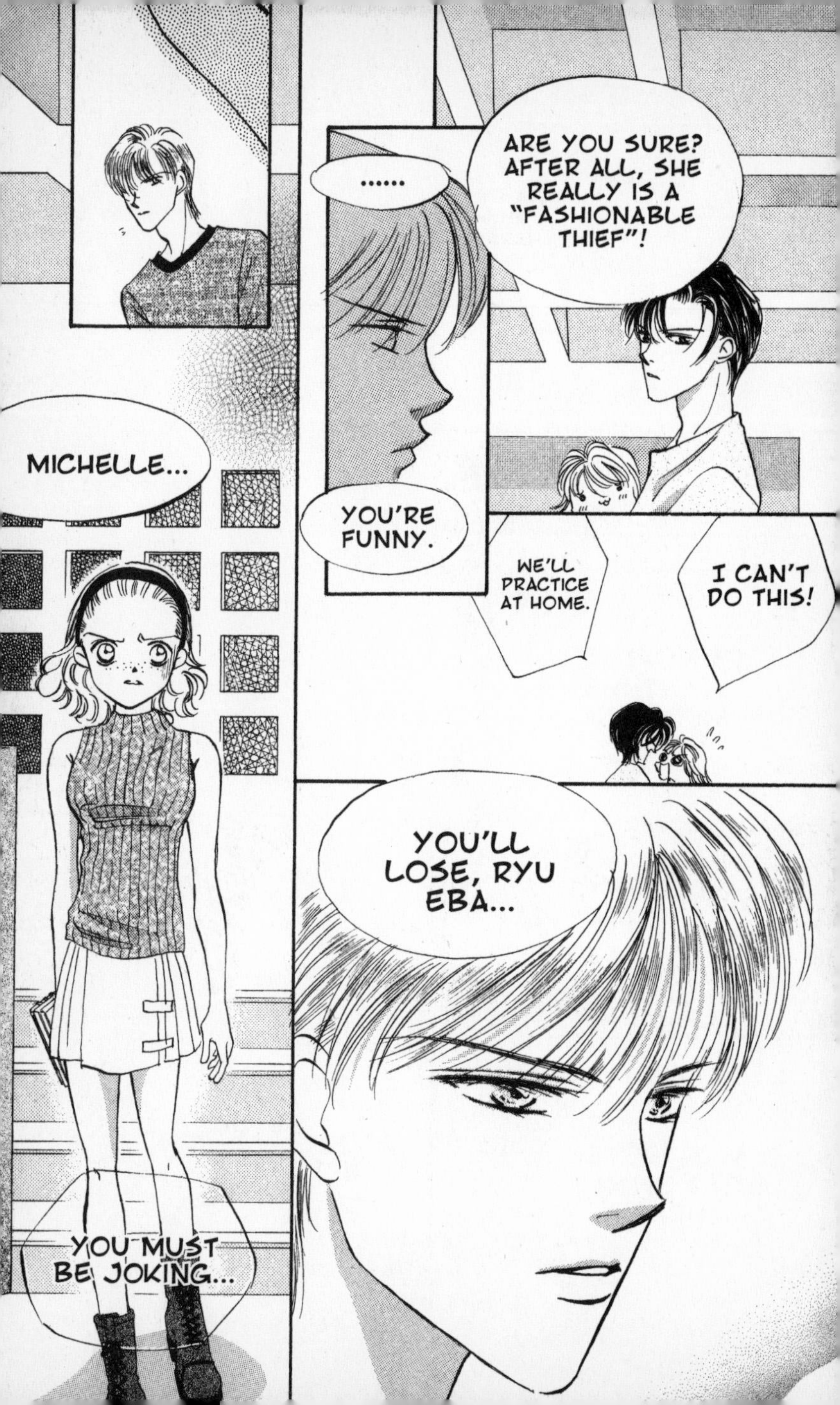
ARE YOU SURE? AFTER ALL, SHE REALLY IS A "FASHIONABLE THIEF"!
......
YOU'RE FUNNY.
I CAN'T DO THIS!
WE'LL PRACTICE AT HOME.
YOU'LL LOSE, RYU EBA...
MICHELLE...
YOU MUST BE JOKING...

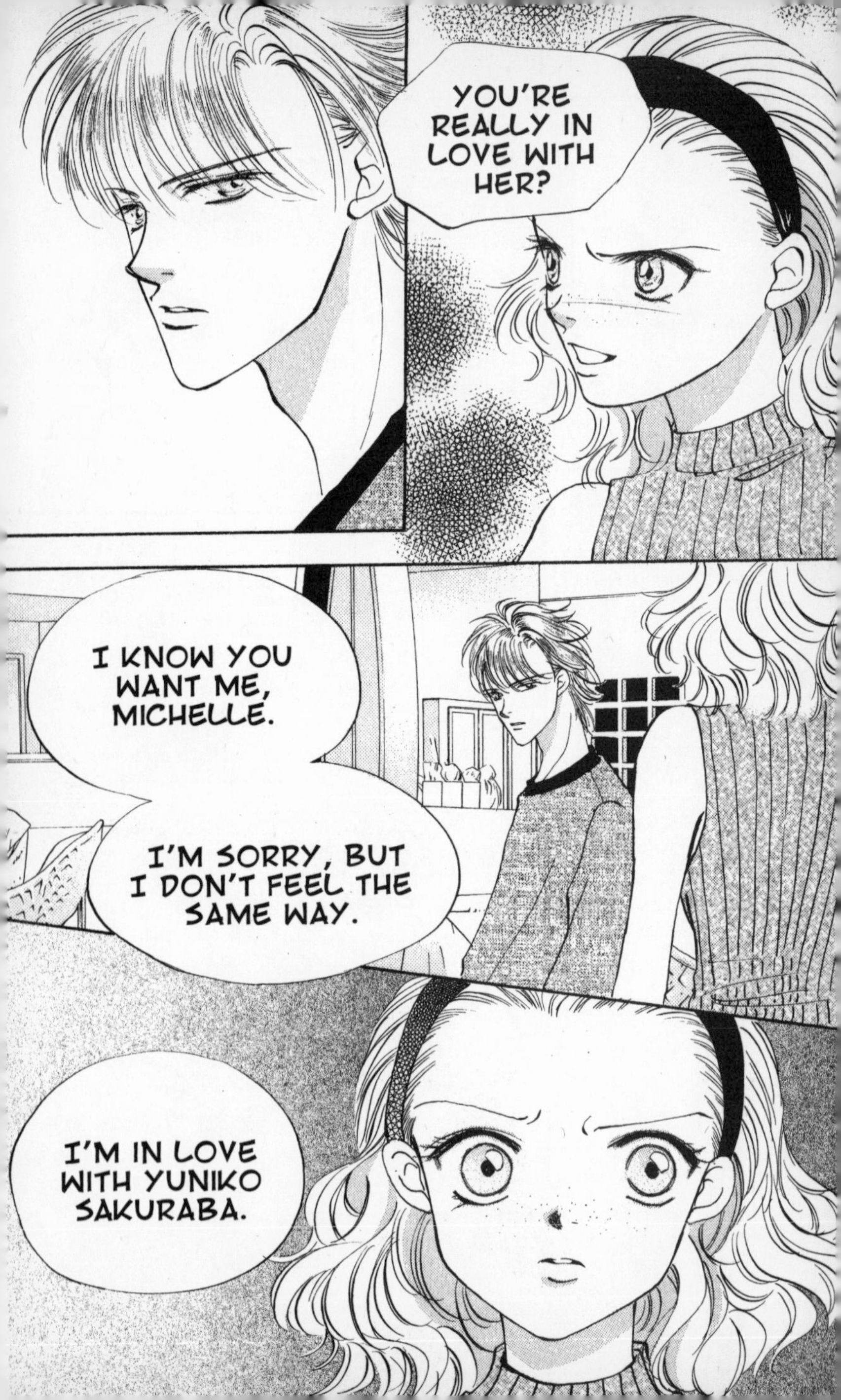
YOU'RE REALLY IN LOVE WITH HER?
I KNOW YOU WANT ME, MICHELLE.
I'M SORRY, BUT I DON'T FEEL THE SAME WAY.
I'M IN LOVE WITH YUNIKO SAKURABA.

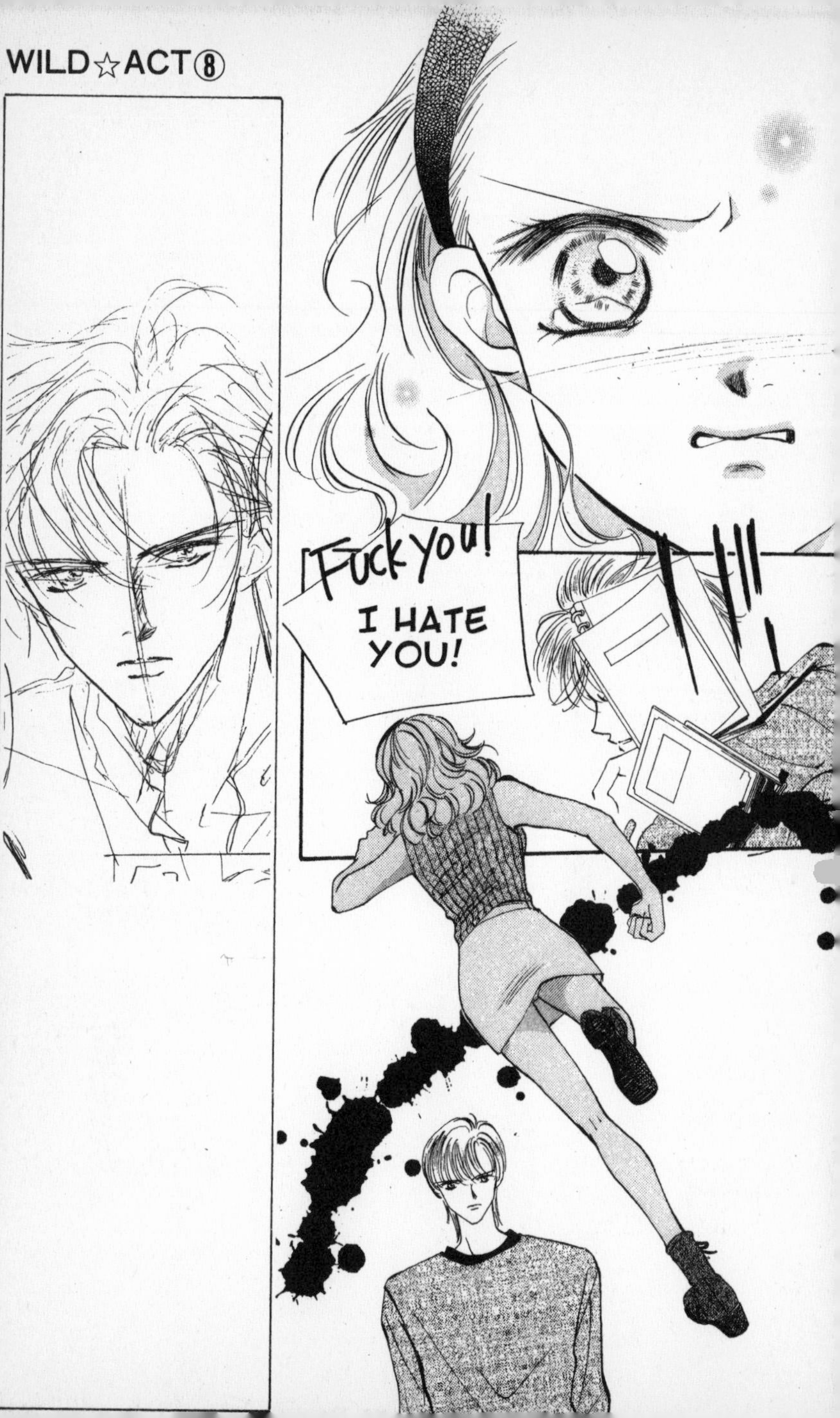
Fuck you!
I HATE YOU!

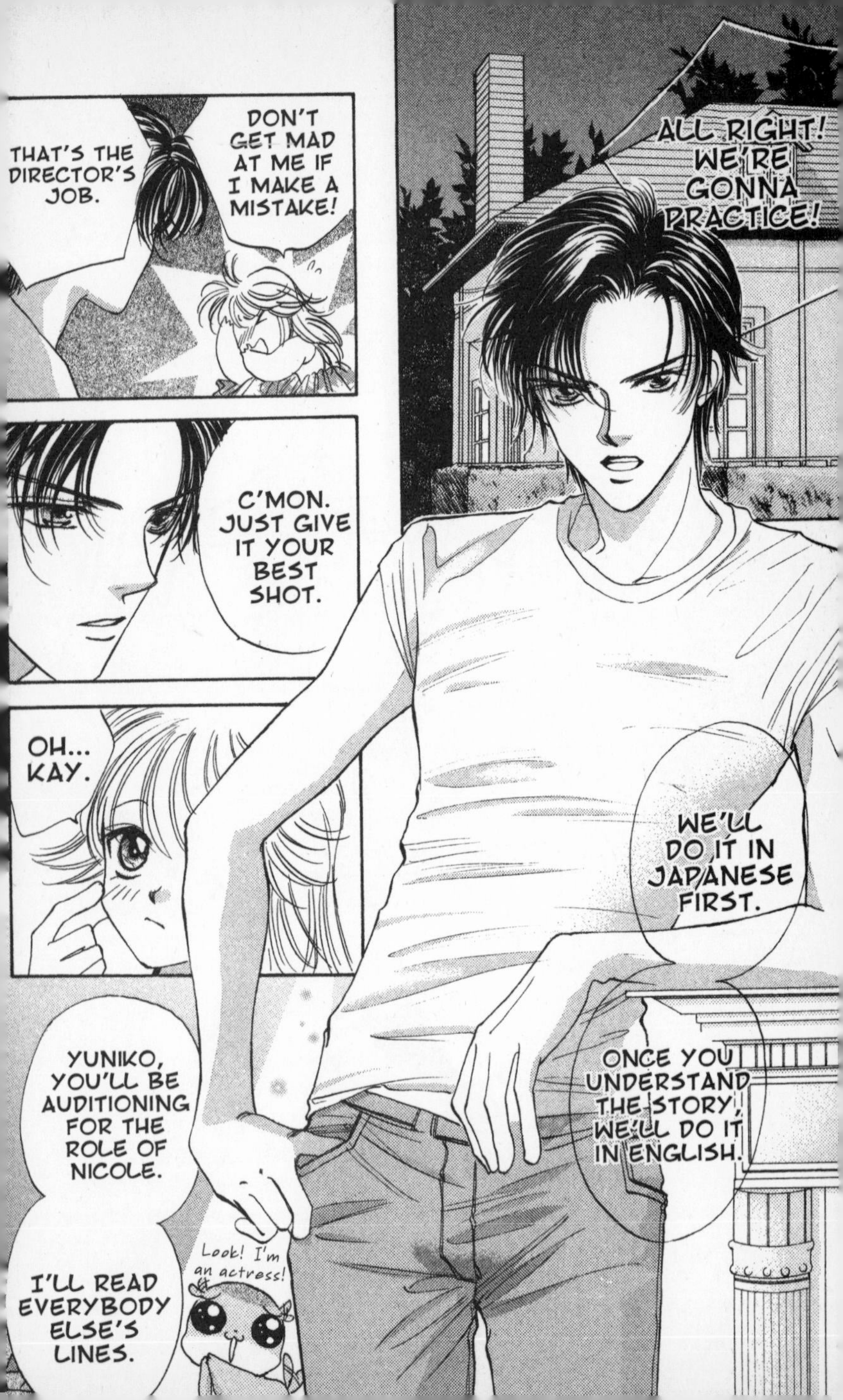
ALL RIGHT! WE'RE GONNA PRACTICE!
WE'LL DO IT IN JAPANESE FIRST.
ONCE YOU UNDERSTAND THE STORY, WE'LL DO IT IN ENGLISH.
YUNIKO, YOU'LL BE AUDITIONING FOR THE ROLE OF NICOLE.
I'LL READ EVERYBODY ELSE'S LINES.
Look! I'm an actress!
DON'T GET MAD AT ME IF I MAKE A MISTAKE!
THAT'S THE DIRECTOR'S JOB.
C'MON. JUST GIVE IT YOUR BEST SHOT.
OH... KAY.

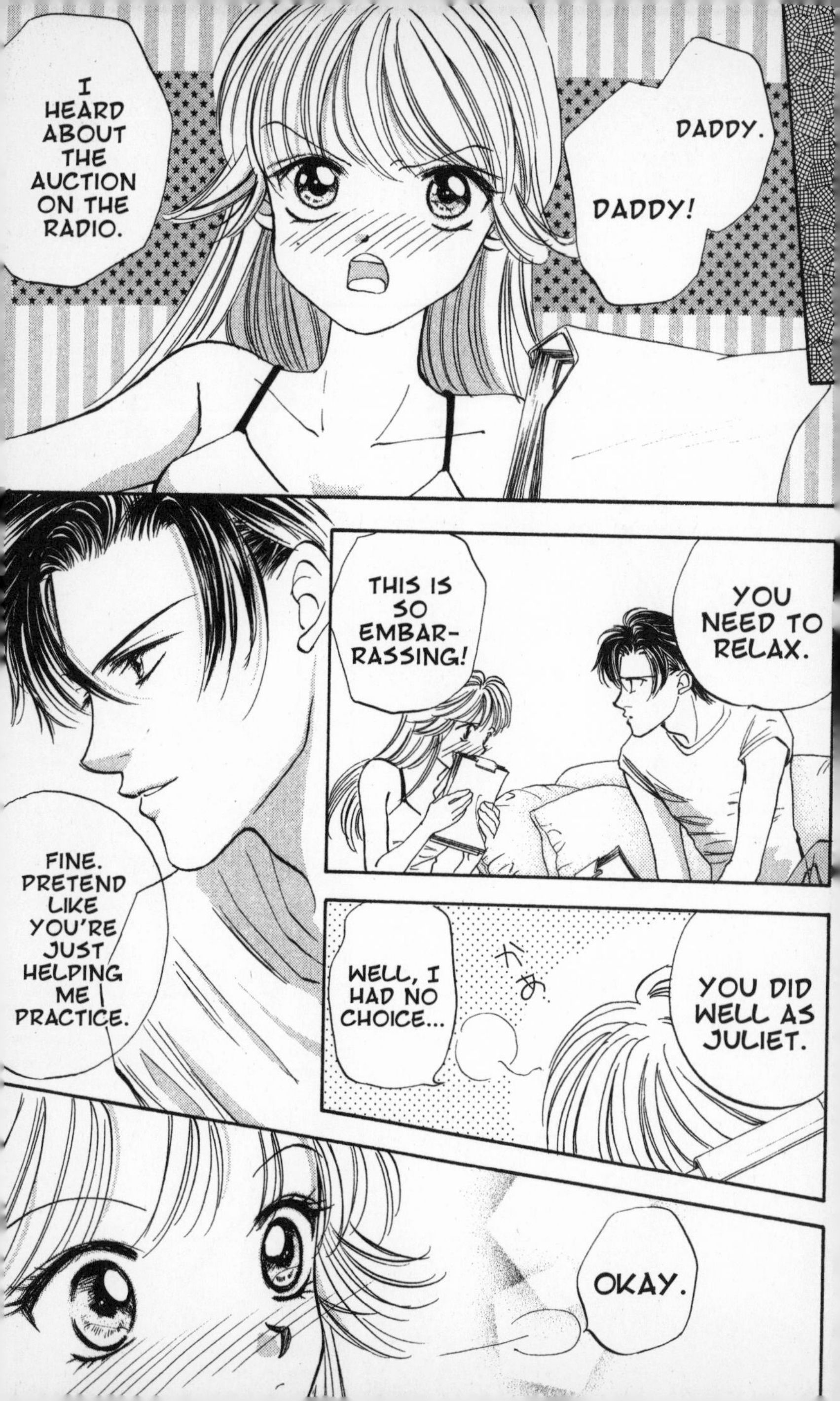
DADDY.
DADDY!
I HEARD ABOUT THE AUCTION ON THE RADIO.
YOU NEED TO RELAX.
THIS IS SO EMBARRASSING!
YOU DID WELL AS JULIET.
かぁ
WELL, I HAD NO CHOICE...
FINE. PRETEND LIKE YOU'RE JUST HELPING ME PRACTICE.
OKAY.

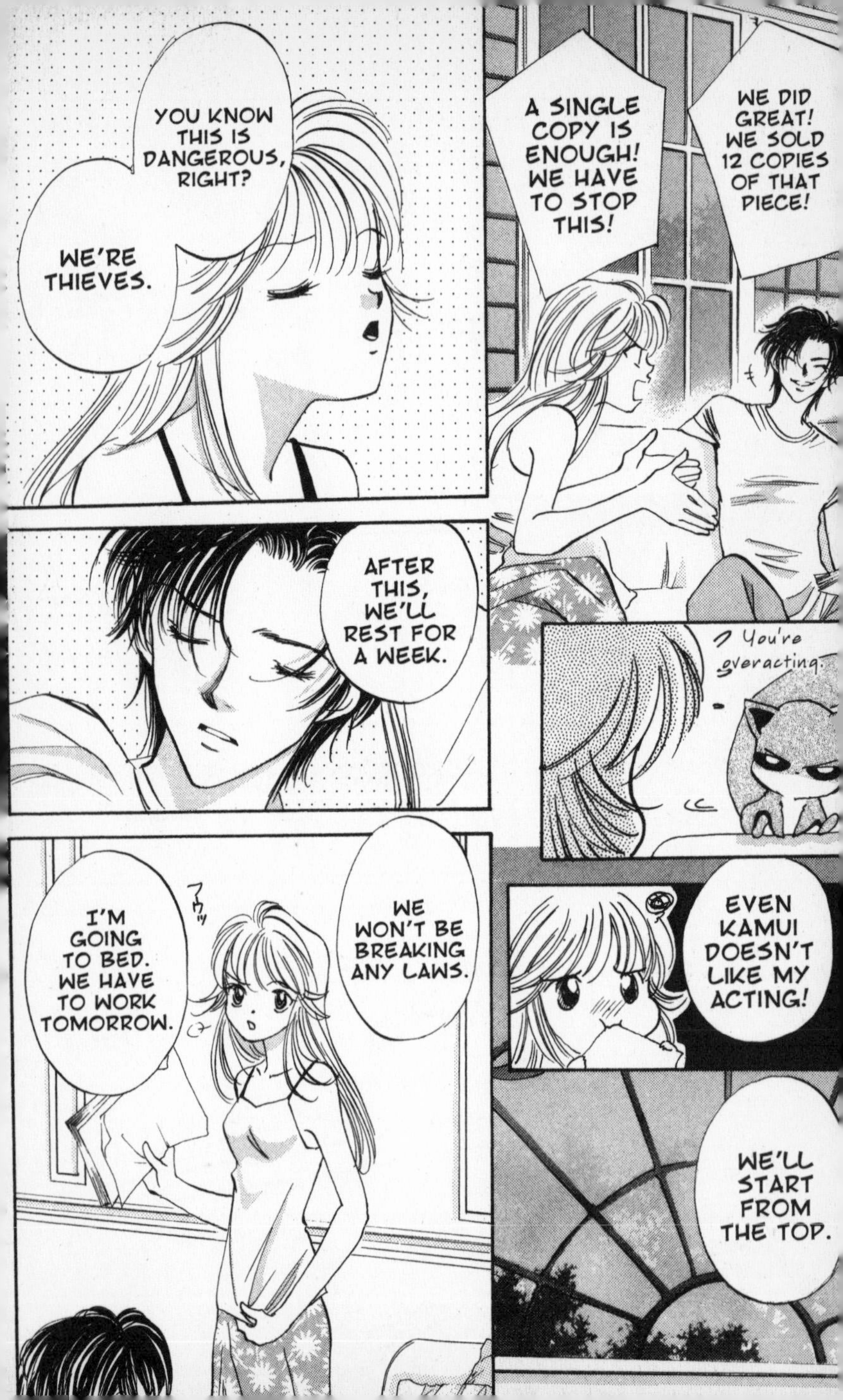
WE DID GREAT! WE SOLD 12 COPIES OF THAT PIECE!
A SINGLE COPY IS ENOUGH! WE HAVE TO STOP THIS!
You're overacting.
EVEN KAMUI DOESN'T LIKE MY ACTING!
WE'LL START FROM THE TOP.
YOU KNOW THIS IS DANGEROUS, RIGHT?
WE'RE THIEVES.
AFTER THIS, WE'LL REST FOR A WEEK.
WE WON'T BE BREAKING ANY LAWS.
I'M GOING TO BED. WE HAVE TO WORK TOMORROW.

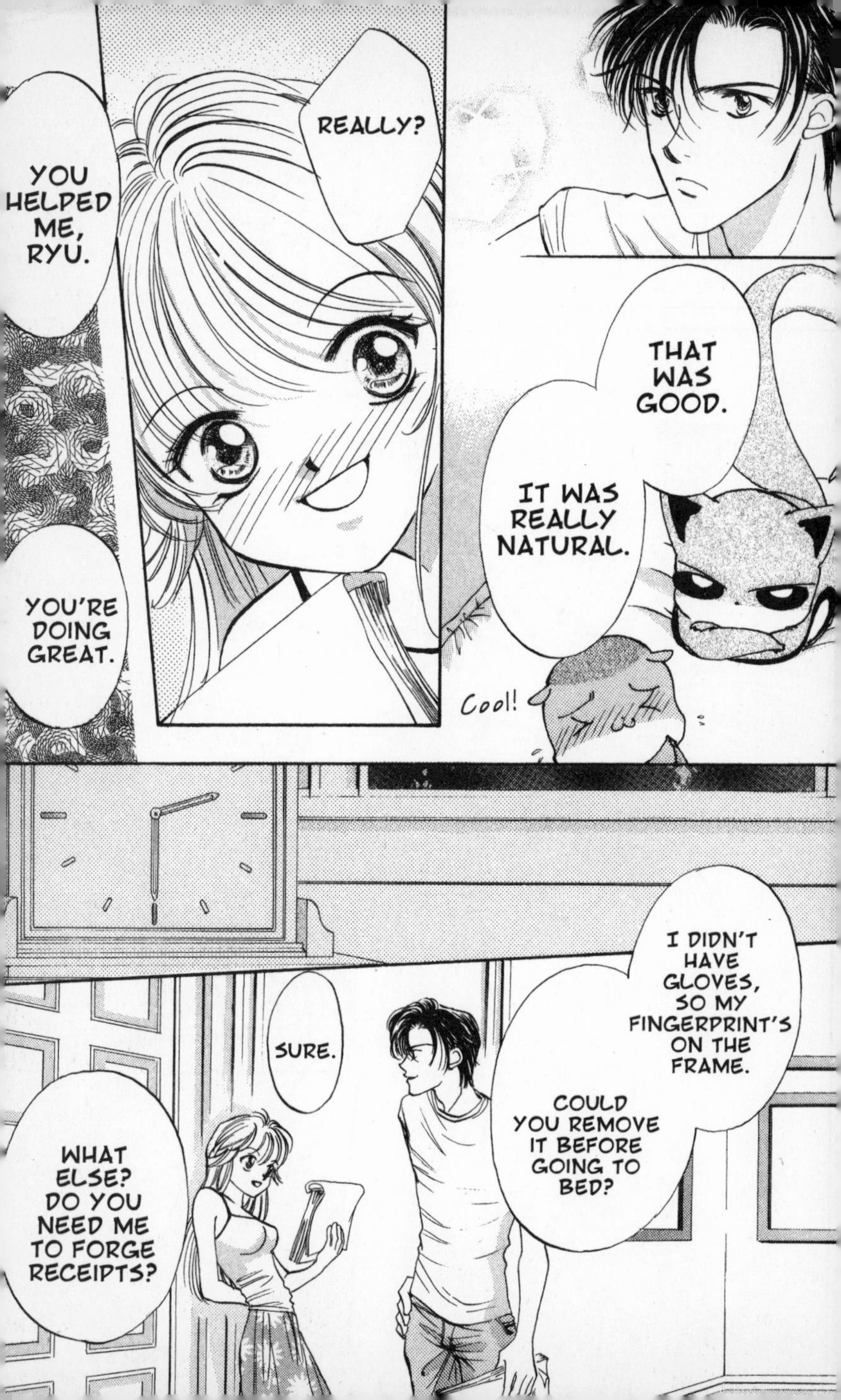
THAT WAS GOOD.
IT WAS REALLY NATURAL.
Cool!
REALLY?
YOU HELPED ME, RYU.
YOU'RE DOING GREAT.
I DIDN'T HAVE GLOVES, SO MY FINGERPRINT'S ON THE FRAME.
COULD YOU REMOVE IT BEFORE GOING TO BED?
SURE.
WHAT ELSE? DO YOU NEED ME TO FORGE RECEIPTS?

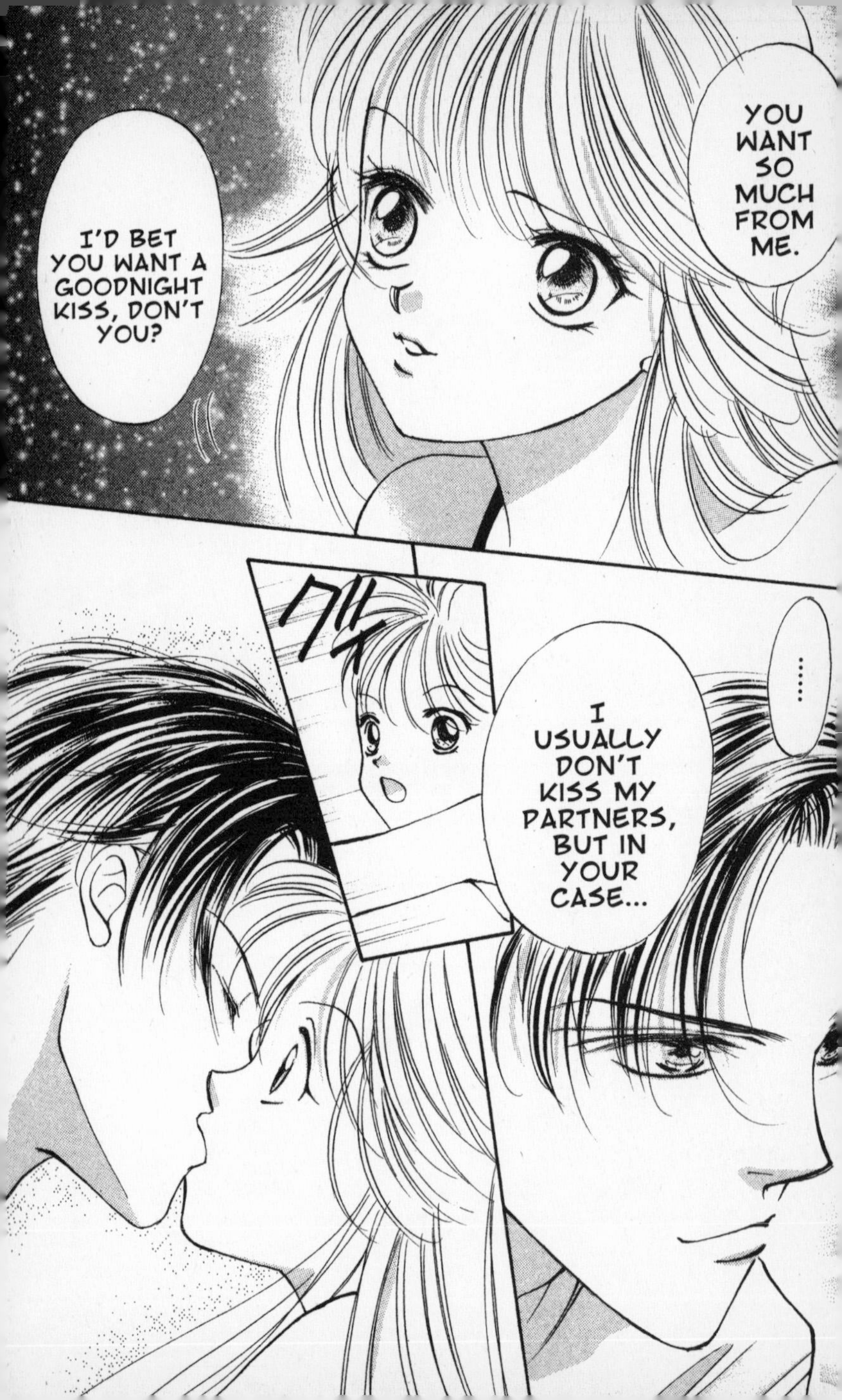
YOU WANT SO MUCH FROM ME.
I'D BET YOU WANT A GOODNIGHT KISS, DON'T YOU?
......
I USUALLY DON'T KISS MY PARTNERS, BUT IN YOUR CASE...

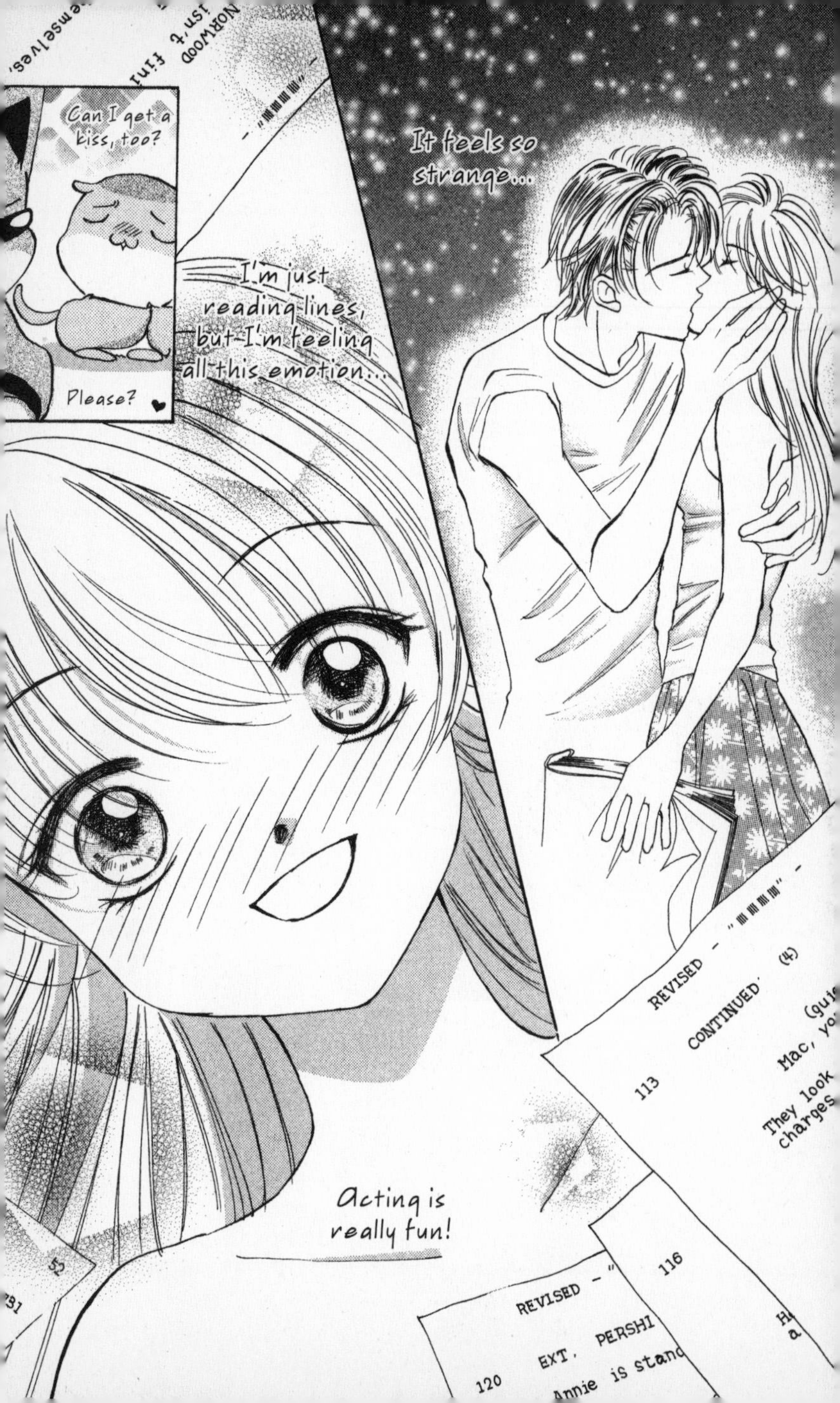

It feels so strange...
I'm just reading lines, but I'm feeling all this emotion...
Can I get a kiss, too?
Please?
Acting is really fun!
REVISED
CONTINUED (4)
113
Mac, yo
They look
charges
116
REVISED
EXT. PERSHI
120
Annie is stand

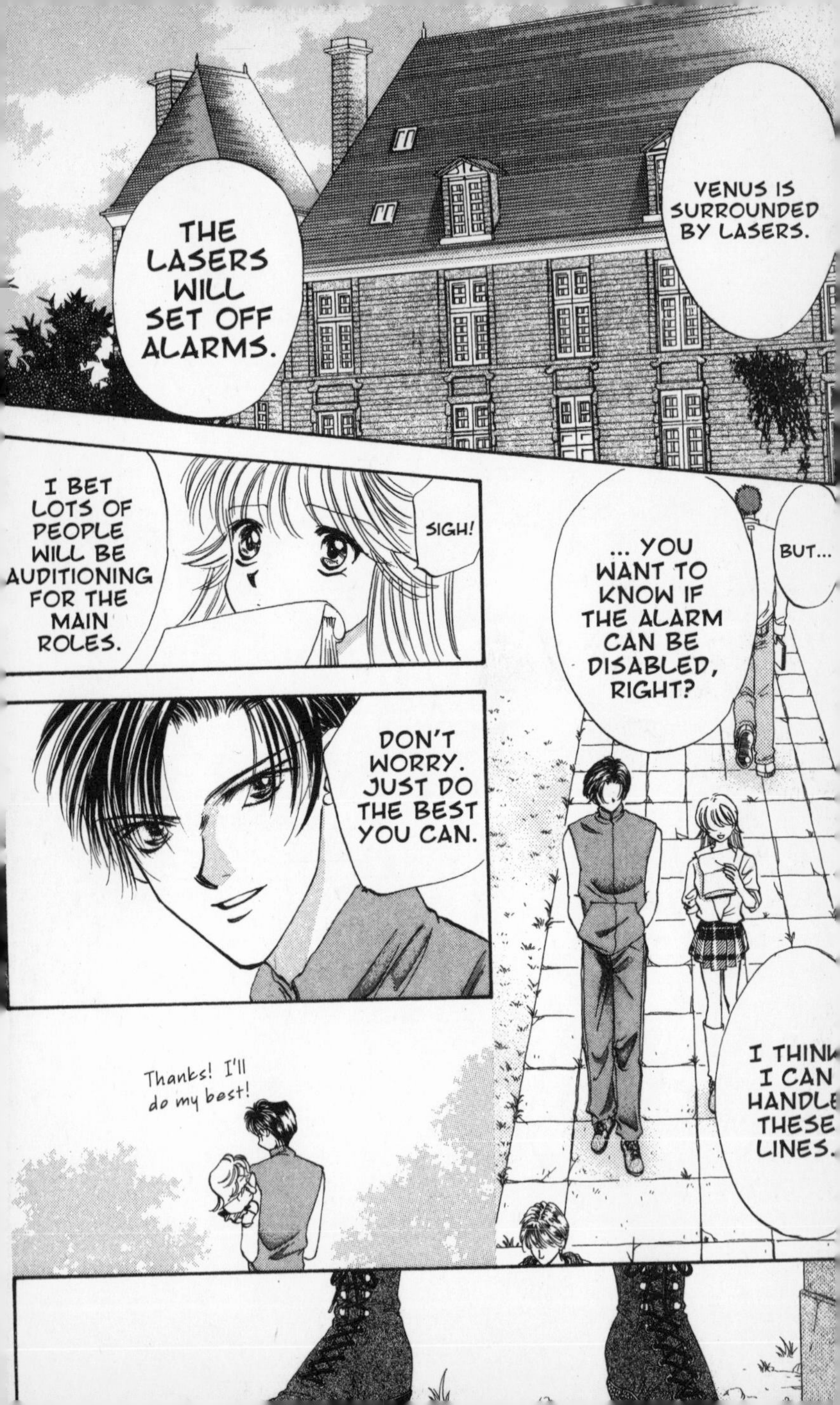
VENUS IS SURROUNDED BY LASERS.
THE LASERS WILL SET OFF ALARMS.
BUT...
... YOU WANT TO KNOW IF THE ALARM CAN BE DISABLED, RIGHT?
I THINK I CAN HANDLE THESE LINES.
SIGH!
I BET LOTS OF PEOPLE WILL BE AUDITIONING FOR THE MAIN ROLES.
DON'T WORRY. JUST DO THE BEST YOU CAN.
Thanks! I'll do my best!

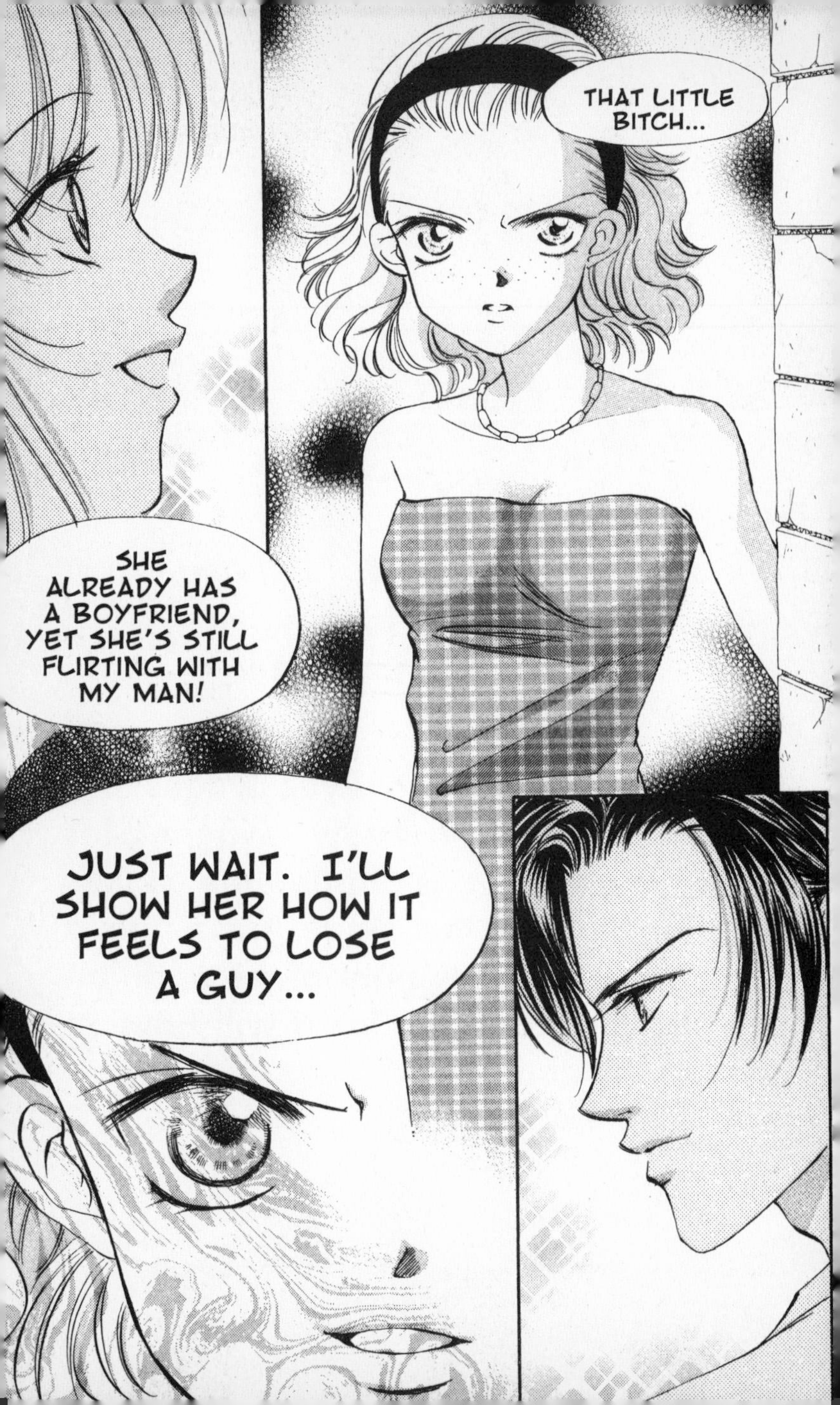
THAT LITTLE BITCH...
SHE ALREADY HAS A BOYFRIEND, YET SHE'S STILL FLIRTING WITH MY MAN!
JUST WAIT. I'LL SHOW HER HOW IT FEELS TO LOSE A GUY...

COMING SOON

WILD Act

VOLUME NINE

The battle of the two Ryus wages on! When a not-so-friendly wager for Yuniko's affection is made, the stakes become high as the stage turns into a battleground. The winner of the audition gets the girl...and the loser will have to give up the chase!

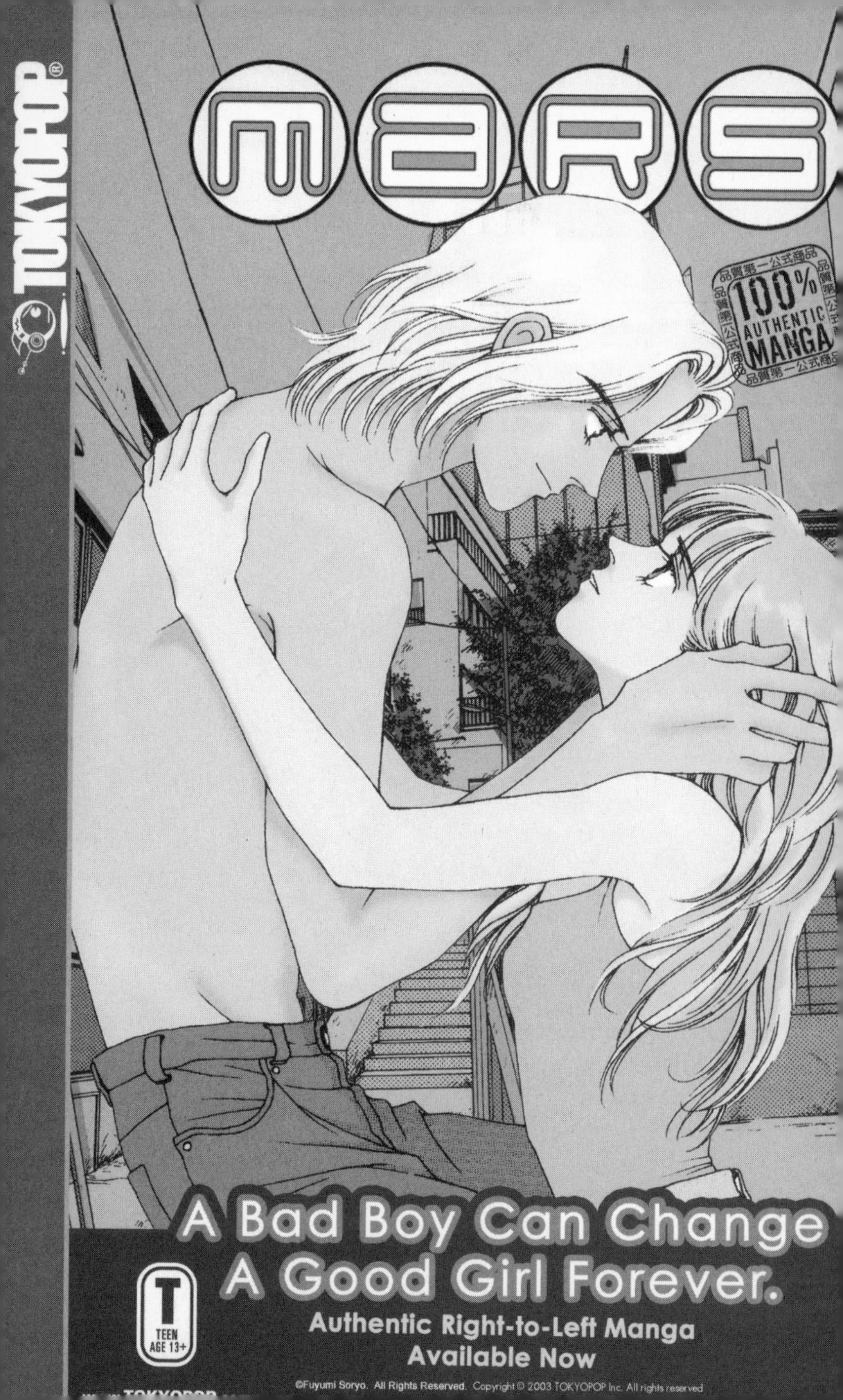
TOKYOPOP
MARS
100% AUTHENTIC MANGA
A Bad Boy Can Change
A Good Girl Forever.
T TEEN AGE 13+
Authentic Right-to-Left Manga
Available Now
©Fuyumi Soryo. All Rights Reserved. Copyright © 2003 TOKYOPOP Inc. All rights reserved

KILL ME
Kiss Me ™

TOKYOPOP®

Love Trials,
Teen Idols,
Cross-Dressing...
Just Another Typical Day At School.

www.TOKYOPOP.com

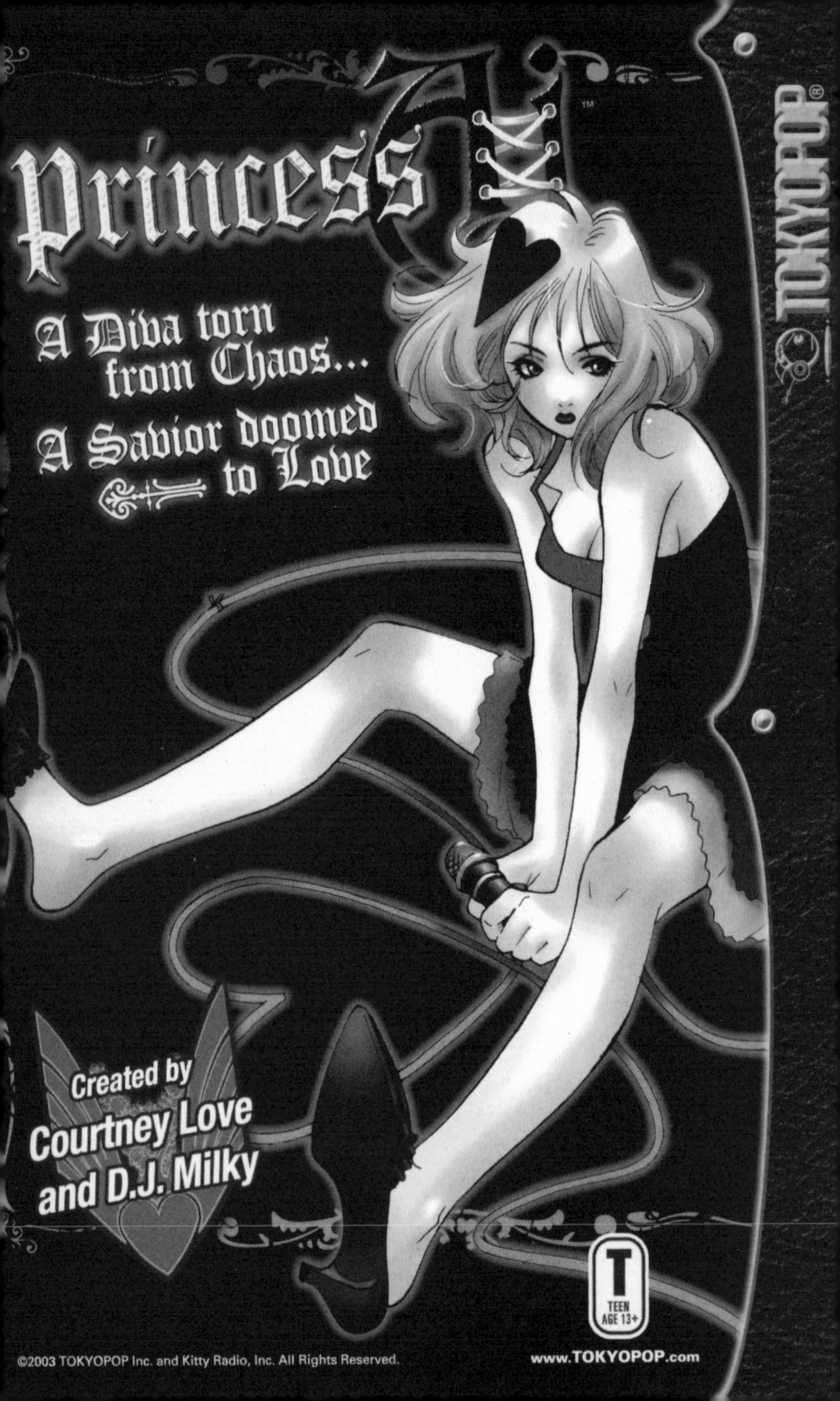

Princess Ai™
A Diva torn from Chaos...
A Savior doomed to Love
Created by
Courtney Love
and D.J. Milky
TOKYOPOP®
T
TEEN
AGE 13+
©2003 TOKYOPOP Inc. and Kitty Radio, Inc. All Rights Reserved.
www.TOKYOPOP.com

TOKYOPOP®

erica SAKURAZAWA™

Friends Lovers And Everything In Between

ANGEL · NOTHING BUT LOVING YOU · BETWEEN THE SHEETS
ANGELNEST · THE AROMATIC BITTERS · THE RULES OF LOVE

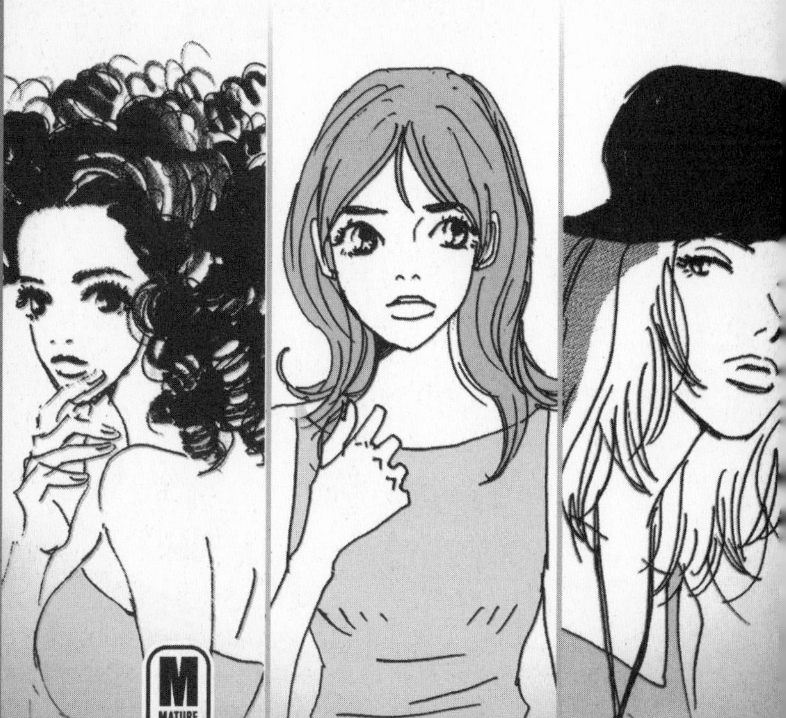

M MATURE AGES 18+

www.TOKYOPOP.com

ALSO AVAILABLE FROM TOKYOPOP

You want it? We got it!
A full range of TOKYOPOP
products are available now at:
www.TOKYOPOP.com/shop

05.26.04T

ALSO AVAILABLE FROM  TOKYOPOP

MANGA

.HACK//LEGEND OF THE TWILIGHT
@LARGE
ABENOBASHI: MAGICAL SHOPPING ARCADE
A.I. LOVE YOU
AI YORI AOSHI
ANGELIC LAYER
ARM OF KANNON
BABY BIRTH
BATTLE ROYALE
BATTLE VIXENS
BRAIN POWERED
BRIGADOON
B'TX
CANDIDATE FOR GODDESS, THE
CARDCAPTOR SAKURA
CARDCAPTOR SAKURA - MASTER OF THE CLOW
CHOBITS
CHRONICLES OF THE CURSED SWORD
CLAMP SCHOOL DETECTIVES
CLOVER
COMIC PARTY
CONFIDENTIAL CONFESSIONS
CORRECTOR YUI
COWBOY BEBOP
COWBOY BEBOP: SHOOTING STAR
CRAZY LOVE STORY
CRESCENT MOON
CROSS
CULDCEPT
CYBORG 009
D•N•ANGEL
DEMON DIARY
DEMON ORORON, THE
DEUS VITAE
DIABOLO
DIGIMON
DIGIMON TAMERS
DIGIMON ZERO TWO
DOLL
DRAGON HUNTER
DRAGON KNIGHTS
DRAGON VOICE
DREAM SAGA
DUKLYON: CLAMP SCHOOL DEFENDERS
EERIE QUEERIE!
ERICA SAKURAZAWA: COLLECTED WORKS
ET CETERA
ETERNITY
EVIL'S RETURN
FAERIES' LANDING
FAKE
FLCL
FLOWER OF THE DEEP SLEEP
FORBIDDEN DANCE
FRUITS BASKET
G GUNDAM

GATEKEEPERS
GETBACKERS
GIRL GOT GAME
GIRLS EDUCATIONAL CHARTER
GRAVITATION
GTO
GUNDAM BLUE DESTINY
GUNDAM SEED ASTRAY
GUNDAM WING
GUNDAM WING: BATTLEFIELD OF PACIFISTS
GUNDAM WING: ENDLESS WALTZ
GUNDAM WING: THE LAST OUTPOST (G-UNIT)
GUYS' GUIDE TO GIRLS
HANDS OFF!
HAPPY MANIA
HARLEM BEAT
HYPER RUNE
I.N.V.U.
IMMORTAL RAIN
INITIAL D
INSTANT TEEN: JUST ADD NUTS
ISLAND
JING: KING OF BANDITS
JING: KING OF BANDITS - TWILIGHT TALES
JULINE
KARE KANO
KILL ME, KISS ME
KINDAICHI CASE FILES, THE
KING OF HELL
KODOCHA: SANA'S STAGE
LAMENT OF THE LAMB
LEGAL DRUG
LEGEND OF CHUN HYANG, THE
LES BIJOUX
LOVE HINA
LUPIN III
LUPIN III: WORLD'S MOST WANTED
MAGIC KNIGHT RAYEARTH I
MAGIC KNIGHT RAYEARTH II
MAHOROMATIC: AUTOMATIC MAIDEN
MAN OF MANY FACES
MARMALADE BOY
MARS
MARS: HORSE WITH NO NAME
MINK
MIRACLE GIRLS
MIYUKI-CHAN IN WONDERLAND
MODEL
MOURYOU KIDEN
MY LOVE
NECK AND NECK
ONE
ONE I LOVE, THE
PARADISE KISS
PARASYTE
PASSION FRUIT
PEACH GIRL
PEACH GIRL: CHANGE OF HEART

05.26.04T

STOP!

This is the back of the book.
You wouldn't want to spoil a great ending!

This book is printed "manga-style," in the authentic Japanese right-to-left format. Since none of the artwork has been flipped or altered, readers get to experience the story just as the creator intended. You've been asking for it, so TOKYOPOP® delivered: authentic, hot-off-the-press, and far more fun!

DIRECTIONS

If this is your first time reading manga-style, here's a quick guide to help you understand how it works.

It's easy... just start in the top right panel and follow the numbers. Have fun, and look for more 100% authentic manga from TOKYOPOP®!